MW01444558

A Social History of Analytic Philosophy

A Social History of Analytic Philosophy

How Politics Has Shaped an Apolitical Philosophy

Christoph Schuringa

VERSO
London • New York

First published by Verso 2025

The manufacturer's authorized representative in the EU for product safety (GPSR) is
LOGOS EUROPE, 9 rue Nicolas Poussin, 17000, La Rochelle, France
Contact@logoseurope.eu

1 3 5 7 9 10 8 6 4 2

Verso
UK: 6 Meard Street, London W1F 0EG
US: 207 East 32nd Street, New York, NY 10016
versobooks.com

Verso is the imprint of New Left Books

ISBN-13: 978-1-80429-209-9
ISBN-13: 978-1-80429-213-6 (US EBK)
ISBN-13: 978-1-80429-212-9 (UK EBK)

British Library Cataloguing in Publication Data
A catalogue record for this book is available from the British Library

Library of Congress Cataloging-in-Publication Data

Names: Schuringa, Christoph, author.
Title: A social history of analytic philosophy : how politics has shaped an apolitical philosophy / Christoph Schuringa.
Description: London ; New York, NY : Verso, 2025. | Includes bibliographical references and index.
Identifiers: LCCN 2024054319 (print) | LCCN 2024054320 (ebook) | ISBN 9781804292099 (hardback) | ISBN 9781804292136 (US EBK)
Subjects: LCSH: Analysis (Philosophy)--History. | Social history.
Classification: LCC B808.5 .S38 2025 (print) | LCC B808.5 (ebook) | DDC 146/.4--dc23/eng/20241202
LC record available at https://lccn.loc.gov/2024054319
LC ebook record available at https://lccn.loc.gov/2024054320

Typeset in Minion by Biblichor Ltd, Scotland
Printed and bound by CPI Group (UK) Ltd, Croydon CR0 4YY

Contents

Acknowledgements

Many people have helped me in the writing of this book.

I am grateful to those who gave generously of their time to speak to me about aspects of my project: Perry Anderson, John Burgess, Michael Chanan, Martin Jay, Martin Kusch, Peter Osborne, Jonathan Rée, Cheyney Ryan, Jennifer Saul, Ellen Schrecker, Timothy Smiley, Charles Taylor and Timothy Williamson. The following kindly took the trouble to read, and comment on, draft material: Peter Dews, Alexander Douglas, Jade Fletcher, Michael Kremer, Clare Mac Cumhaill, Christopher Peacocke, Michael Potter, Eric Schliesser, Maximilian Tegtmeyer, Paolo Tripodi, Thomas Uebel, Martijn Wallage and Vanessa Wills.

For advice, responses to queries, conversations, and kindnesses of various kinds from which this project has benefited, I would like to thank Michael Brent, Étienne Brown, John Callanan, Pablo Carnino, James Connelly, Andrew Cooper, Matteo Falomi, Eleanor Fellowes, Adrian Haddock, Alec Hinshelwood, John McCumber, Martin McIvor, Philip Mirowski, Cheryl Misak, Luke Mulhall, Marco Nathan, Andrew Novak, Andreja Novakovic, David Papineau, Greg Restall, Jordan Ricker, Alessandro Rossi, Peter Salmon, Luke Seaber, Rob Simpson, Amia Srinivasan, Friedrich Stadler, Michael Thompson, Andreas Vrahimis, Joel Whitebook and Harlan Wilson. Sean Sayers kindly let me read the manuscript of his memoir. I thank Miles Leeson of the Iris Murdoch Research Centre, Frieda Midgley of the Newnham College Archives in Cambridge, Stewart Tiley of the Balliol College Archives in Oxford, and José Pérez-Benzo of the Anscombe Archive in Philadelphia, for their help with archival material. John E. Hare, Adrian Moore,

Patricia Williams and the Master and Fellows of Balliol College gave kind permission to include quotations from unpublished material in the Papers of R. M. Hare. I would not have been able to write this book without the work of the staff of the British Library, the Bodleian Library and Cambridge University Library. Thanks to my editor, Sebastian Budgen, for his encouragement at the early stages and support throughout, and to all those at Verso who have helped to see this book smoothly through the production process.

To save the best for last – to my wife Holly I owe more than I can say. She has been crucial to this creature's conception and gestation, and now its emergence into the world.

Introduction

Analytic philosophy, today the hegemonic form of academic philosophy in the English-speaking world and beyond, tends to think of itself as removed from the changing scenes of history. It acts as if it were pursuing its questions from a vantage point situated nowhere in particular, unaffected by social and political reality. It thus operates as a tradition that manages to think of itself as no tradition at all. The treatment to which it is subjected in this book directly challenges this self-image, by demonstrating how analytic philosophy is the product of, and has continued to be shaped by, the social world in which it finds itself.

It ought to be obvious that 'social history' is a pleonastic expression. History, as the attempt to understand past human action and thought, must in and of itself be social, since humans are social beings whose activities cannot be understood except as interventions in the social world within which they act. But it has not been obvious that the history of philosophy is social history, and there have been few attempts to write the history of philosophy in a social vein.

To some extent, this situation is explained by philosophy's special position as a field of enquiry, and a concomitant set of exercises of enquiry, marked out not only as intellectual, but as supposedly the most purely intellectual that there can be. It is thus imagined that philosophy can have, perhaps more than any other field, a purely 'internal' history, driven entirely by ideas, with what are then called 'external' factors acting only as interference, if they have any significance at all. The notion of the possibility of such a purely internal history is encouraged by a fantasy about the purity of philosophy that has accompanied it through its history, across times and places.[1] The potency of this fantasy can be brought out by contrasting the history of philosophy with the history of science, where social approaches have gained a much more secure foothold and have now grown to maturity, in a continuing and sometimes heated contest with more 'internalist' approaches.

There are important disanalogies with the history of science. Scientific research programmes tend to attain a level of circumscribed specificity, and of shared purpose among researchers, that is foreign to philosophy.[2] One factor in this is that philosophy tends to encourage the perpetuation of debate and contestation, rather than to seek convergence. There is something important, however, that the history of philosophy can learn from the history of science. It is instructive for philosophy that the contest between 'internalist' and 'externalist' approaches in the history of science has reached a point where it has become possible to see the deficiencies of that contrast itself. As the authors of the 1985 work *Leviathan and the Air-Pump* wrote in 2011, looking back on the intervening development of the history of science, 'What was deemed internal and external to science was, to a large extent, just our way of saying what we thought *properly belonged* to science and what we considered illegitimate, where we thought *rationality* resided, and what we deemed to be epistemically *virtuous*.'[3] This is, as I hope to show in this book, at least as true in the case of philosophy. The very idea that philosophy has an 'inside' in which it can do its work in isolation from the social and political is a substantive, contestable view – any view that claims to exempt itself from consideration as being a view at all, so that it can shrink to an ideologically extensionless point, should be met with suspicion.

Perhaps unsurprisingly, there have been few social histories of philosophy.[4] Where such an approach has been tried, the attempt has

---

1 An excellent exposé of the functioning of philosophy's purity myth in the case of inter-war Germany is given in Pierre Bourdieu, *The Political Ontology of Martin Heidegger*. A note on abbreviated references: any such abbreviated reference can be found in full in this book's bibliography.

2 To put this in terms familiar from the work of Thomas Kuhn, there is no 'normal philosophy' to counterpose to 'normal science'; there is never, in philosophy, sufficient agreement on the shape of the solution a problem demands for researchers to work with common purpose on finding it.

3 Steven Shapin and Simon Schaffer, 'Introduction to the 2011 Edition', in *Leviathan and the Air-Pump*, p. xvi.

4 A significant exception is Martin Kusch, *Psychologism: A Case Study in the Sociology of Philosophical Knowledge*. Kusch brings the sociology of knowledge to

sometimes simply caved in under the purity myth: despite the author's best intentions, what we end up with, when all is said and done, is after all an internalist narrative. One such author is Bertrand Russell, who gave his 1945 book *A History of Western Philosophy* the subtitle *And Its Connection with Political and Social Circumstances from the Earliest Times to the Present Day*. In contrast to what his subtitle promised, Russell in fact offered – with a heavy irony, given his professed animus against Hegel – a strikingly internalist narrative on a Hegelian pattern, in which the deficiencies of one set of ideas led those ideas to give birth to others in which those deficiencies were overcome, and so on, interspersed with passages on social and political developments. Russell's story is that of the self-moving development of pure philosophy, with the social dross thrown on as a kind of unappetising garnish.

This book is an essay in the social history *of philosophy*. It seeks to illuminate philosophical ideas, arguments, discussions and institutions, instead of merely regarding them as what happens to result from some activity supposedly comprehensible in isolation from what it produces. An attempt to understand what philosophers are up to without trying to understand, and to see the force of, their claims would leave their activities entirely unintelligible. The approach taken here thus distinguishes itself from that of the sociology of knowledge, if that is taken, as it often has been, to involve studying the 'production' of knowledge in 'naturalistic' terms.[5] It does not place 'knowledge' in scare quotes, as such approaches often feel themselves obliged to do, taking all claims to knowledge as merely putative.

Far from seeking to 'explain away' philosophy by means of social factors, then, what I attempt to contribute to here is the social explanation of philosophy. Much of this book is engaged in ideology critique, in line with a Marxist tradition. Ideology critique has often been thought

---

bear on the debate about psychologism around the turn of the twentieth century – an arena in which that approach is particularly illuminating given the relevance of institutional factors for explaining substantive philosophical disagreements in this case. Randall Collins, *The Sociology of Philosophies*, adopts a 'social' perspective only in the sense that it studies networks of intellectuals, and is both shaky and explanatorily weak when it comes to the philosophy itself. Ellen Meiksins Wood's admirable *Citizens to Lords* and *Liberty and Property*, published together as *A Social History of Western Political Thought*, 'starts from the premise that the great political thinkers of the past were passionately engaged in the issues of their time and place' (*Citizens to Lords*, p. 11). That is not something that can be said of philosophers *simpliciter*.

5 See, for example, David Bloor, *Knowledge and Social Imagery*.

to attribute an exaggerated status to the explanatory power of ideology, and to the material conditions that are in turn thought to be productive of that ideology. Where ideology critique takes the relatively crude form of trying to match ideas to pre-set patterns (oscillations back and forth between idealism and realism in the history of philosophy, say, to patterns in the assertion of monolithically conceived sets of class interests), this may be true.[6] But no one is a mere mouthpiece of class interests – not even philosophers. A less crude form of ideology critique recognizes that no one is exempt from having class interests speak through them in what they do and say. When this is realized, ideology critique turns out to be *more* powerful, not less so, than is often imagined. Once it is recognized that analytic philosophy, like its cousins behaviourism and neoclassical economics, serves to perpetuate a picture that is central to bourgeois liberal ideology – that of an inert realm of 'fact', simply given to the subject to be passively received, against which realm that subject stands as supposedly autonomous and spontaneous – it is seen that no passage in its history escapes ideology-critical treatment.[7]

Since this is an essay in the social history of *analytic philosophy*, my concern throughout this book is with what has sustained analytic philosophy in particular, rather than with the social reproduction of institutional academic formations in general. As an extended narrative from 1898 to the present day, it must of course also be highly selective in its treatment of this topic. To a significant degree, it focuses on the field's charismatic leading figures. This might seem surprising in a social history, but it deliberately reflects a thesis the book seeks to bear out – namely, that analytic philosophy, far more than its self-image would like us to believe, promotes a cult of the personality. Another principle of selection has been to write about those areas where an ideology-critical social treatment will yield the most interesting results. My focus is therefore on logic, metaphysics and epistemology at the expense, in particular, of political philosophy. There is a great deal to be said about the way in which liberal ideology drives the American political philosopher John Rawls's defence of liberalism, and in turn the immense influence of Rawlsianism, following the publication of his *A*

6 For an example of this approach applied to analytic philosophy, see Maurice Cornforth, *In Defence of Philosophy* and *Marxism and the Linguistic Philosophy*.

7 For a rare attempt to paint the picture in question, see the early essay by the (later conservative) Hungarian philosopher J. C. Nyíri, 'Beim Sternenlicht der Nichtexistierenden', p. 433*n*14.

Theory of Justice in 1971, on all sectors of political philosophy in elite institutions. But the mechanisms by which liberalism drives liberalism are less far to seek than, say, the mechanisms by which liberalism drives the development of modal logic.

Chapter 1 offers an outline of the elements of analytic philosophy in the present day, and links them to elements of eighteenth-century thought. The remaining chapters proceed chronologically. They can be considered as falling into two blocs. The first (Chapters 2–4) deals with three distinct formations in turn: philosophy as carried out, broadly speaking, under the banner of 'analysis' in Cambridge, Vienna and Oxford, respectively. These were distinct movements, differing fundamentally from each other. To treat them in their separateness helps to counter the myth of analytic philosophy as one continuous movement beginning in Cambridge in 1898 (or perhaps even earlier, in the Jena of Gottlob Frege in 1879). As scholars of analytic philosophy know, but analytic philosophers who do not turn scholarly attention on their own tradition tend not to, analytic philosophy, as one single, unified movement, did not exist until after the Second World War, when it emerged under specific political conditions in the United States, forged from an amalgam of the pre-war approaches, largely at the hands of European émigrés who had fled Nazism. The second bloc of chapters (Chapters 5–10) is concerned with the history of what might, by contrast with the ancestor movements covered in Chapters 2–4, be called 'analytic philosophy proper'. As the object of my treatment shifts – from a set of relatively well-defined, distinct intellectual formations to a single, large, socially homogeneous but relatively ill-defined formation – so too does the treatment. As analytic philosophy comes into its own as the monolith that we now know, it makes itself ever more readily available to ideology-critical treatment of the purest kind.

1
Elements of Analytic Philosophy

Analytic philosophy seems to be in a state of crisis. At the same time, it shows no sign of loosening its grip on academic philosophy. It will take some work to explain this state of affairs.

The apparent crisis has been going on for some time now. It was in the mid 1980s that talk of 'postanalytic philosophy' first got going, amid a growing sense that analytic philosophy could not go on forever – and a dawning awareness from within the discipline that it itself had a history that needed to be reckoned with.[1] But programmatic talk about 'postanalytic philosophy' just kept going, without a sense ever emerging that a postanalytic phase had in fact been entered. Instead, the proposals and programmes for something 'postanalytic' kept coming. In 1997, the University of Southampton opened a Centre for Post-Analytical Philosophy – though this was discreetly rebranded in 2005 the Centre for Philosophy and Value.[2] Today, the whole idea of 'postanalytic philosophy' is little more than a relic of a bygone age. It seems as if analytic philosophy will just go on dying, forever, without ever actually expiring.

The continuing sense among its practitioners that analytic philosophy is in a critical condition can in part be conceptualized in terms of an internal identity crisis. Analytic philosophers now find it difficult to

1 On the need for 'postanalytic' philosophy, see, for example, John Rajchman and Cornel West, eds, *Postanalytic Philosophy*. On the need for historical self-examination, see Peter Hylton, *Russell, Idealism and the Emergence of Analytic Philosophy*.

2 Aaron Preston, *Analytic Philosophy: The History of an Illusion*, pp. 26, 166*n*19.

say what, precisely, analytic philosophy is. Much of the time, they are moved to deny its existence altogether. This apparent diffidence resonates with a narrative according to which there was once a classical 'programme of analysis' with definable goals and methods – a programme that has since been abandoned or superseded. The programme has given way, so the story goes, to a diversity of approaches so nuanced and variegated that it no longer makes sense to bring them under a single heading.

The seeming crisis is not merely internal. It also partly takes the form of an altered relationship to rival approaches. Not only are analytic philosophers less stridently self-confident about their own approach; they are also less likely than they once were to assert their superiority over the proponents of other approaches – in particular, those it groups together under the umbrella term 'continental philosophy' (covering phenomenology, hermeneutics, existentialism, deconstruction, and so on). Analytic philosophers would seem to have learned a new modesty, through a complex negotiation with their traditional other, resulting in a state of rapprochement. This allows them to regard the dispute between analytic and continental approaches as, for all practical purposes, over. There is now – we are often told by those who hold to this line – only 'good' and 'bad' philosophy.

But the crisis, like the rapprochement, is only apparent. Anyone who encounters academic philosophy will quickly discover that analytic philosophy shows no sign of relinquishing its institutional power. Indeed, it continues to enjoy hegemonic status in the academy. The kind of philosophy practised in elite universities in the Anglophone world is instantly recognizable, in terms of the topics selected and the style in which they are discussed, as analytic. Where a department is predominantly analytic, not only analytic philosophers are subject to the characteristic demands and imperatives of analytic philosophy: everyone is. Beyond the Anglophone world, analytic philosophy is more thinly spread. It is dominant in Scandinavian countries. In Germany, where it has had substantial success for some decades, it continues to consolidate its position.[3] In those places where it comes up against major rivals, such as China and South America, it benefits from the cachet and selling power that attach to North American exports more generally.

---

3 Indicative of this is the creation of 'junior professorships' specifically devoted to analytic philosophy.

It is undeniable that analytic philosophers are now less strident about the merits of their own approach, and less dismissive of others. The outright dismissiveness about the possibility that, for instance, Heidegger or Derrida might have something even minimally intelligent to say has gone. This change in attitude does not mean, however, that these others are encountered, or engaged with, on their own terms. It is still analytic philosophers who dictate acceptable forms of discourse; Heidegger and Derrida, and others, are reconstructed and reformatted so as to appear to be answering to the kinds of demands of enquiry characteristic of analytic philosophy.[4]

While analytic philosophers go on debating whether there is any such thing as analytic philosophy, for outsiders it is very easy to recognize when they see it. Analytic philosophers, in their written work, share argument types, turns of phrase, a technical apparatus and a literature. They also interact with each other in distinctive ways in the seminar room, reflecting their particular notions of how philosophical dialogue is to be carried out. The readiness with which analytic philosophy can be isolated from other kinds of philosophy stands in stark contrast to the difficulties analytic philosophers profess to find with specifying what it is, to the point of feeling the need to deny that it even exists. Part of the professed difficulty is that analytic philosophers have tended to favour answering questions of the form 'What is *x*?' by providing lists of necessary and sufficient conditions. Such a list, if one could be found, would provide a watertight test for whether someone is an analytic philosopher, so that all and only analytic philosophers would survive the test. It seems that providing such a list is not possible; it hardly ever is, outside domains that admit of a high level of technicality, such as mathematics. At this point, analytic philosophers can often be relied upon to fall back on the Wittgensteinian idea of 'family resemblances': even though there is no set of necessary and sufficient conditions by means of which all analytic philosophers can be isolated from everyone else, there is a sufficiently overlapping set of resemblances between members of the group to hold them together, albeit loosely. It is striking that analytic philosophers tend to be so ready to make this move, since almost none of them are Wittgensteinians – and indeed, those making it tend to disavow the Wittgensteinian picture in which family resemblances have their home when discussing other topics.[5]

---

4 For more on the tendency of analytic philosophy to colonize its others, see Chapter 10.

5 For one such appeal to 'family resemblances', see Hans-Johann Glock, *What Is*

How can it be that analytic philosophers are so easily identifiable, if identity conditions seem impossible to provide? Answering the question of what constitutes the unity and coherence analytic philosophy possesses, in spite of the denials, requires us first to see that the story about a classical 'programme of analysis' giving way to a profusion of diverging approaches is precisely wrong. It takes historical work to show this, and the chapters that follow will be devoted to this task.

The crucial points are as follows. There was never any classical programme of analysis. In the period when it is supposed to have existed, prior to the Second World War, there was, instead, a variety of differing approaches, all of them intensely methodologically self-conscious and opposed to each other on fundamental points. In Cambridge, an important cradle of analysis, there was not one such approach, but two: the 'logical-analytical method' favoured by Bertrand Russell and the 'commonsense analysis' associated with G. E. Moore. In Vienna, another major birth site, there was logical positivism. All shared an enthusiasm for the 'new logic' (or 'logistic', as it was then often called) deriving from the work of mathematicians such as Gottlob Frege and Giuseppe Peano. Their conception of the use to which these logical tools were to be put in philosophy differed markedly, however.[6] Only after the Second World War were these different approaches welded together to form 'analytic philosophy'. Just as there was no classical programme of analysis before this act of fusion, neither did the fusion result in such a programme. Instead, what resulted was an unstable amalgam that began to decay almost as soon as it was formed. But analytic philosophy had asserted itself as the dominant form of philosophy in the American academy, and in the American sphere of influence beyond. The fighting-out of methodological issues receded into the background, since the analytic style had now established itself de facto as dominant. It may have been in a state of internal disintegration, but its stability as a social structure ensured its continuing survival.

Analytic Philosophy?, Chapter 8. The idea of family resemblances seems to those who invoke it to help, because it allows in instances that do not meet all the conditions – so long as there is a sufficient pattern of overlap. But this only shifts the problem to the question: What makes for a sufficient overlap?

6 A very important contribution was made by Polish logicians, whose use of the logical methods again differed from the others'. Unfortunately, Polish logic, despite its importance, exceeds the scope of the inevitably selective treatment of analytic philosophy in this book.

The Analytic Style

The chief characteristics of the analytic style, as established after the Second World War, immediately impress themselves on anyone who has encountered academic philosophy in those places where the analytic strain is dominant. This is as palpable now as it was in 1972, when Jonathan Rée, then a young graduate student at Oxford University, wrote:

> People who don't know anything about philosophy courses are likely to be astonished and dismayed by their effects. The main thing they will notice is that the philosophy student acquires a very mannered way of speaking and a knack of shrugging off serious ideas with half frivolous complaints about the words in which they are expressed.[7]

The habits of speech to which Rée adverts, along with pettifoggery about the use of words, are understood by analytic philosophers themselves to form part of a commitment to precision and plain-speaking. 'Rigour' and 'clarity' are often cited by them as hallmarks of their style. Anyone who can speak plainly and clearly may enter the discussion. At the same time, the style of debate is generally highly combative. Indicative of this is that, while the tone may be more or less overtly hostile, the presenter at a seminar is expected to stand ready to fend off even the most wrongheaded or silly objection, often taking the form of a single counterexample deployed with the intention of undermining the entire edifice the speaker has constructed. Officially, all comers are welcome to participate in discussion. In reality, a certain pushy, too-clever-by-half type predominates.

There are various oddities and inconsistencies. Officially, it is supposed to be argumentation that wins the day; often, however, objectors rest their demurral on such statements as 'That strikes me as false'. Objections the speaker feels incapable of dealing with are dismissed with the declaration, 'I don't know what you mean' – the implication (sometimes voiced) being that the objector is 'confused', not that the speaker needs to listen more attentively or learn something new. Officially, analytic philosophers favour plain language, free of jargon and technicality; in reality, presentations and discussions tend to be not only laden with technical jargon, but also attended with numerous highly

7 Jonathan Rée, 'Professional Philosophers', p. 2.

characteristic turns of phrase to which insiders have become acculturated. There is a deeper peculiarity still. Analytic philosophers like to think of themselves, on an analogy with teams of scientists, as engaged in a collective endeavour in which their individual work consists of piecemeal contributions to the overall body of knowledge. This would suggest a shared project seeking to converge on fundamental issues, of the kind found in the natural sciences. But something quite different happens in analytic philosophy. Each contributor is expected to occupy their *own* position in 'logical space' – a space in which every conceivable position, however implausible, is assigned its place. Each position must *diverge* from the positions occupied by others (if only in some minimal respect). Credibility is thus lent to a view on the basis of its incredibility. It is somehow not noticed that the need for each person to distinguish their view from *all others* must surely *reduce* the likelihood of anyone's being right.

The analytic style is highly ahistorical and acultural. This feature makes it immediately evident to 'continental' philosophers just how far they stand from their analytic counterparts, even if this is not clear to analytic philosophers themselves. It is, after all, more difficult for analytic philosophers to see what they are missing. Analytic philosophy tends to remain ignorant of large bodies of theory, particularly those concerned with culture, politics, anthropology, psychology, sexuality, religion, literature, and so on. To analytic philosophers, this is of no concern, since their assumption is that any idea can be quite readily explained without prior immersion in a wider theoretical context. They are comfortable with, for instance, theorizing about the phenomenon of 'thought insertion' in schizophrenic subjects without having any compunction about contradicting the empirical literature on the subject. After all, they will say, this is philosophy, not psychology. It can all be done 'from the armchair'. For them, since it is not apparent that there is anything that might elude the grasp of analytic philosophy, there seems little need to engage with the bodies of literature in, for instance, sociology, psychoanalysis or theology. In the analytic philosophy seminar, if an interloping interlocutor finds it relevant to bring up, for instance, Merleau-Ponty's phenomenological study of perception, she might well be called upon to convey Merleau-Ponty's contribution to a hearer entirely ignorant of the phenomenological tradition in a few sentences. After all, what could not be readily stated in a few sentences so as to be made intelligible to the analytic philosopher, the very prototype of the intellectually vigilant and maximally curious enquirer?

In the undergraduate classroom, which students are likely to enter without any prior acquaintance with academic philosophy, teachers often fail even to identify analytic philosophy as one approach among others. As a result, students can easily gain the impression that this is just philosophy as such – an impression teachers show little concern to correct. The history of philosophy before analytic philosophy is largely studied using analytic methods, and heterogeneous styles of writing are regimented into the clean types of argument form favoured by analytic philosophers. It bears noting that almost all students who have come into the orbit of analytic philosophy had originally come to philosophy with a set of expectations relative to which the habits of thought into which they thus become acculturated represent a deviation. Usually, their initial interest in philosophy was prompted by existential questioning of the kind that analytic philosophy disparages. Once they see that what is instead on offer is the regimen of analytic philosophy, they either find it uncongenial enough to leave, or quickly learn to internalize its demands.

One who left was Perry Anderson, who had 'come up' to Oxford in 1956 to study Philosophy, Politics and Economics, but subsequently switched to French and Russian, and soon after began his rise to become one of Britain's leading Marxist intellectuals. In the first term of his second year at Oxford, at the age of nineteen, Anderson published an excoriating attack on Oxford philosophy in the pages of the student magazine, *The Isis*. English philosophy was, he wrote, 'far from being a symposium of truth and independent of time and place . . . in the pristine sense of the word, a class ideology'. Indicative of this was the confinement of the curriculum to a narrow, mostly British tradition, with lecturers making cheap jokes at the expense of Hegel and Heidegger with an 'imbecile chauvinism' that was 'greeted with roars of laughter from the cavalry-twilled canaille who make up the bulk of the audience'. The then twenty-eight-year-old philosophy don Bernard Williams wrote a reply in the pages of the magazine that used a standard tactic among analytic arguers, accusing Anderson of equivocating over his precise target – was it English philosophy, or the linguistic type of philosophy more generally, or just academic philosophy as such? Anderson, replying to Williams's reply, doubled down. Williams's insinuation that Anderson was motivated by a vague 'hatred of philosophy' as such was met by Anderson's retort: 'splashing around in phrases about "hating philosophy" is not an especially educated or interesting way of conducting a discussion'. Anderson could be perfectly clear about his targets, if Williams wanted: 'linguistic philosophy' was a 'peripheral phenomenon', one manifestation among others of the ideology of a dominant class. Its attractiveness to its practitioners was to be understood in terms of its erasure of the social and political: 'silence is always the most vociferous supporter of the status quo'.[8]

Allies: Marginalism and Behaviourism

Analytic philosophy might seem unique in the academic landscape. It would appear to be concerned with a special type of abstract enquiry, unlike any other. Perhaps, as analytic philosophers often say, its relation to other fields of enquiry is that it asks the most fundamental questions it is possible to ask about those other fields. Perhaps it is related to them as a 'second-order' (or 'meta-') enquiry, relative to the 'first-order' pursuits of those other fields.

But analytic philosophy is much more intimately bound up with what we find elsewhere in the academy than such a schema recognizes. There are close affinities, in particular, with marginalism in economics, and with behaviourism in psychology. Between these two cousins of analytic philosophy, there is of course a crucial difference: marginalism continues to be the dominant paradigm in economics, whereas behaviourism is officially dead, living on only as transmogrified into successor paradigms.

Marginalism (also known as 'neoclassical economics' since Thorstein Veblen gave it this name in 1900) displaces the economic category of value with that of 'marginal utility'. Utility is conceived of in terms of the preferences of agents. That goods and services exchange at certain rates is a function of utility. The theory is clearly highly idealized: everyone knows that real people in the real world do not act as utility calculators. But it is difficult to show that the theory is wrong even as an approximation. As a result of adherence to it, economists are powerless to predict or explain events in the actually existing capitalist economy, such as the catastrophic crashes to which it has periodically been subject. The stature of neoclassical economics, however, remains more or less untainted by such failure.

Not so in the case of behaviourism. Behaviourism began in 1912 when, as the American psychologist and devotee of behaviourism John

8 Perry Anderson, 'The Minstrels of MI5'; Bernard Williams, 'The Hatred of Philosophy' (including Anderson's reply).

B. Watson put it, a group of psychologists 'decided either to give up psychology or else to make it a natural science', on the basis that 'they could no longer be content to work with intangibles and unapproachables'.[9] The 'intangibles and unapproachables' were mental phenomena, the most capacious of them being 'consciousness' ('neither a definable nor a usable concept', no better than 'the "soul" of more ancient times', Watson wrote), that could not be empirically observed.[10] The subject matter of psychology was no longer to be consciousness, but outward behaviour. Behaviourism was perhaps the most extraordinary example of the compulsion to model all forms of enquiry on the natural sciences. The programme quickly collapsed, not least because it failed on its own terms. The animals subjected to its experiments failed to behave as behaviourists predicted: they did not simply repeat the same responses to stimuli, but seemed to suffer from 'instinctual drift', a seemingly inexplicable reversion to their native tendencies. After 1959, when Noam Chomsky's damning review of B. F. Skinner's *Verbal Behavior* drove long nails into the coffin of behaviourism, its basic impulses were redirected, into a preoccupation with computers as taking the place of conscious agents. Today, this trend finds its counterpart in analytic philosophers' obsession with 'artificial intelligence' as supposedly analogous to conscious minds. The 'AIs' they obsess over, such as large language models, are nothing but very complex statistical predictors, and hence utterly different from conscious minds.[11] Analytic philosophers manage to find mysteries here, but only because they remain in thrall to the notion that even our minds might be systems to be characterized in terms of nothing but inputs ('stimuli') and outputs ('behaviour').

Marginalism and behaviourism share with analytic philosophy a central preoccupation and a mindset. Problems are regarded as decomposable: they are to be broken down into small parts. Subjectivity is not thought of as playing any role, other than as a mechanism for choosing the decomposable parts and ordering them appropriately. In the case of behaviourism, subjectivity is even expunged entirely: mechanism is all.

---

9 John B. Watson, *Behaviorism*, p. 6.

10 Ibid., p. 3.

11 Compare the perceptive comments of the Canadian philosopher Charles Taylor on the connection between behaviourism and 'theories purporting to explain intelligent performance on a model based on the digital computer' (*Human Agency and Language*, p. 1).

Liberalism, Empiricism and Eighteenth-Century Philosophy

For most of its history, analytic philosophy has been overtly ahistorical. There is a deep irony here. Far from being eternal and situated nowhere in particular, analytic philosophy is a tradition, one that has deep historical roots in eighteenth-century European philosophy. It continues and extends eighteenth-century European philosophy, reconnecting to it so as to expel the post-Kantian tradition that subsequently shaped European philosophy, and modifying it through the adoption of a set of logical techniques developed by mathematicians at the end of the nineteenth century. The post-Kantian trajectory appears, in this light, as a regrettable diversion. Compared with competitors such as phenomenology and existentialism, which were imbued with a modernist spirit seeking to break away from inherited tradition, analytic philosophy is remarkably stuck in the past. Not only this, but it will be by understanding analytic philosophy as a continuation of a basically eighteenth-century mindset marked by bourgeois ideology's twin faces – liberalism and empiricism – that we will be able to understand its twentieth-century history.

Empiricism is the view that all knowledge is derivable from sensory experience; liberalism exalts the autonomy of the subject. Together, they form the ideology of the bourgeois class that rose in the seventeenth and eighteenth centuries. The rise of the bourgeoisie was driven by capitalism, whose success in imposing itself as the global economic logic was in turn secured by the European colonial exploitation of the 'new world'.[12] The empiricist–liberal tradition, one of whose earliest and most ardent spokesmen was John Locke in the seventeenth century, reached its high point in the mid eighteenth century in the work of David Hume.

Analytic philosophy established its connection with this eighteenth-century tradition across an intervening chasm. On the European continent, philosophy after Hume was shaped by the systematic philosophy of German idealism and its aftermath. In Britain, this systematic idealist philosophy never fully took hold, although it aroused interest there in the earlier nineteenth century largely through the promotional work of literary figures such as Samuel Taylor Coleridge, Thomas De

12 'In turn', because the wealth that capitalism amassed relied on the theft of resources from the world that Europeans were learning to exploit. See Rosa Luxemburg, *The Accumulation of Capital*, especially Chapter 27.

Quincey and Thomas Carlyle. In nineteenth-century British philosophy, idealism imported from the continent jostled for attention with a native utilitarian tradition that had sprung from empiricism and liberalism. Then, for a brief period at the end of the nineteenth century – the period in which Russell and Moore emerged – idealism secured for itself a newfound kudos. In light of this brief success of the 'alien import' of absolute idealism, the Oxford philosopher G. J. Warnock could write that Russell 'symbolically joins hands with at least two centuries of British philosophy, across a gap of a few years occupied with new and strange things'.[13]

The continuity of analytic philosophy with empiricism–liberalism, across this brief 'alien' abyss, is not generally recognized by today's analytic philosophers. But it seemed obvious enough to A. J. Ayer when he wrote, in the opening words of his polemical and carefree logical-positivist manifesto *Language, Truth and Logic*, that the views set out in that book 'derive from the doctrines of Bertrand Russell and Wittgenstein, which are themselves the logical outcome of the empiricism of Berkeley and David Hume'.[14] Two decades later, another Oxford philosopher, Iris Murdoch, told listeners to the BBC's Third Programme in 1955 that by 'modern philosophy' she meant 'that present-day version of our traditional empiricism which is known as linguistic analysis'.[15]

The internal connection of empiricism with liberalism, too, was recognized by older philosophers. The Oxford philosopher H. H. Price told the audience at a public lecture at the Institute of Philosophy in London on 14 February 1939, as the threat of war loomed over Europe, that 'Empiricism is hostile to humbug and obscurity, to the dogmatic and authoritative mood, to every sort of *ipse dixit*' and that 'the same live-and-let-live principles, the same dislike of humbug and of the *ipse dixit* sort of authority, are characteristic of Liberalism too'. For empiricism, philosophy was 'a free and co-operative inquiry, where anyone may put forward any hypothesis he likes, new or old, provided it makes sense'. The threat coming from the continent was a terrible warning: its 'totalitarian political systems' were 'the long-delayed effects of the philosophies

13 G. J. Warnock, *English Philosophy Since 1900*, p. 9.

14 A. J. Ayer, *Language, Truth and Logic*, p. 9. Later in the same work, Ayer wrote: 'we may fairly claim that in holding that the activity of philosophizing is essentially analytic we are adopting a standpoint which has always been implicit in English empiricism', and that it was with 'members of this school' 'that we have the closest historical affinity' (p. 42).

15 Iris Murdoch, 'Metaphysics and Ethics', p. 99.

of Fichte, Hegel, and Marx, or at least of the psychological attitudes which underlay those philosophies'. But, Price hoped, 'if Empiricist philosophy is strong to-day', there might be 'a vigorous revival of Liberalism the day after to-morrow'.[16] In his hopes for a revival of liberalism, Price will not have been disappointed. After the war, Bertrand Russell, in a similar vein, told another London audience, gathered on 23 October 1946 for the Fourth National Book League Lecture at Friends House:

> The only philosophy that affords a theoretical justification of democracy, and that accords with democracy in its temper of mind, is empiricism. Locke, who may be regarded, so far as the modern world is concerned, as the founder of empiricism, makes it clear how closely this is connected with his views on liberty and toleration, and with his opposition to absolute monarchy.[17]

He concluded by exhorting his readers to embrace 'empiricist Liberalism'.[18]

The ideological workings of empiricism–liberalism are evident in the way analytic philosophy is carried out today. Each liberal subject plays their role in adjudicating what can be claimed on the basis of the publicly available, empirically verifiable facts. Each may enter into this joint adjudication on equal terms with the others who do so. This hides the fact that the ideological function of liberalism is the justification of a system of subjugation. Instead, and because of this, it works hard to appear as a fair, reasonable and peaceable system in which all participants are treated equitably. If any seem still subjugated, this is to be regarded as an unfortunate and temporary impediment, to be lifted at some indefinitely timed future moment: *potentially*, at least, everyone is a full participant.

Characteristic of empiricism–liberalism is an emphasis on equity, coupled with a fantasy of neutrality. In Hume's terminology, the 'impressions' of sense, the most immediate deposits of the world in our minds, record 'matters of fact'. These are received passively by the subject. The subject is, by contrast, in principle autonomous and free. But their autonomous freedom pertains only to them as a private individual, and so effectively has nowhere to go. It cannot reach back into the world; and so, after all, the self is just as inert and ineffective as what

16 H. H. Price, 'The Permanent Significance of Hume's Philosophy', p. 8.

17 Bertrand Russell, 'Philosophy and Politics', p. 14.

18 Ibid., p. 20.

comes their way through the senses. Far from being a subject, they are merely subject to the world as something they can do nothing about, just as they are simply subject to capital as it reproduces itself through them and through all the other cogs that it turns.

In eighteenth-century thought, we find three distinct kinds of philosophical response to this predicament. Each response is characterized by having already made peace with the inescapability of leaving the status quo in place. They are: deference to science, the retreat to common sense, and the impulse to therapy. As will become apparent in the chapters that follow, analytic philosophy reproduces, over and over, the adoption of these three basic stances. In the next chapter, for example, on philosophy in Cambridge, we will see the first in Bertrand Russell, the second in G. E. Moore, and the third in Ludwig Wittgenstein. One sense in which the work of David Hume marks the apogee of eighteenth-century empiricism is that it has the distinction of combining all three together in one place. It is as if Hume presents the menu of options for analytic philosophy.

Deference to Science

Hume set out to model his own new 'science of man' on the natural philosophy of Isaac Newton and Robert Boyle, and opined that his new science would do no less 'honour to our native country' than had theirs 'in natural philosophy'.[19] He argued the need for this new science in the following terms in the introduction to his early masterpiece, *A Treatise of Human Nature*:

> Here then is the only expedient, from which we can hope for success in our philosophical researches, to leave the tedious lingring method, which we have hitherto followed, and instead of taking now and then a castle or village on the frontier, to march up directly to the capital or center of these sciences, to human nature itself; which being once masters of, we may every where else hope for an easy victory. From this station we may extend our conquests over all those sciences, which more intimately concern human life, and may afterwards proceed at leisure to discover more fully those, which are the objects of pure curiosity. There is no question of importance, whose decision is not compriz'd in the science of man; and there is none, which can be decided with any

19 David Hume, *A Treatise of Human Nature*, p. xvii.

> certainty, before we become acquainted with that science. In pretending therefore to explain the principles of human nature, we in effect propose a compleat system of the sciences, built on a foundation almost entirely new, and the only one upon which they can stand with any security.[20]

The 'science of man', Hume continued, must itself be 'laid on experience and observation'. Since Hume subscribed to the empiricist view that science in general 'cannot go beyond experience', for him this science too had to be conducted through 'careful and exact experiments'. Hume's commitment to putting the 'science of man' on an equal footing with other forms of science was unequivocal. This is today often called Hume's 'naturalism'.[21]

Analytic philosophy has tended to exhibit two forms of deference to science. The first is deference in the form of emulation, in which philosophy embarks on an ambitious project of making itself scientific, as in the 'scientific philosophy' advocated by Bertrand Russell. The second is more like deference in the strict sense: here, philosophy effectively shrinks itself to an extensionless point, affecting to be nothing more than the handmaiden of the empirical sciences. Some members of the Vienna Circle saw the relationship of philosophy to science in this way.

Sometimes, deference to science by analytic philosophers has taken the form of scientism: the mistaken treatment of some discipline (here, philosophy) as if it were governed by the standards of the natural sciences. If scientism is, in Bernard Williams's formulation, 'a misunderstanding of the relations between philosophy and the natural sciences which tends to assimilate philosophy to the aims, or at least the manners, of the sciences', then analytic philosophy has in recent years frequently run the risk of scientism.[22]

The Retreat to Common Sense

Where the project of a science of man runs into its limits in Hume, the second option comes into its own. This is for philosophy to retreat to common sense. Hume's scientific project ran into difficulties at various

20 Ibid., p. xvi.

21 For a treatment of Hume's philosophy in its entirety as 'naturalism', see Don Garrett, *Hume*.

22 Bernard Williams, 'Philosophy as a Humanistic Discipline', in *Philosophy as a Humanistic Discipline*, p. 182.

points. The basic scientific principle governing his science of man, the 'copy principle', states that all mental representations, if they are not illusory, have as their source an 'impression' (a sensory input with a distinct 'force and vivacity'). In the case of the idea of 'cause', Hume notoriously thought that such an input cannot be found: observing a game of billiards, we see the movement of a white ball, its collision with a red ball, and the subsequent movement of the red ball, but we never experience the '*power, force, energy* or *necessary connexion*' by which the impact of the first ball seems to *make* the second ball move.[23] Hume, in response, falls back on customary habits of mind. We are entitled to continue using the concept 'cause', he tells us, because of a well-entrenched custom based on our expectations about the movements of billiard balls.[24]

In analytic philosophy, the appeal to common sense has, again, taken various forms. For G. E. Moore, common-sense propositions served as a bulwark against the apparent problems raised by, as he liked to say, 'other philosophers'; the true task of philosophy was to analyse those common-sense propositions. The 'ordinary language philosophy' prevalent in Oxford during the reign of J. L. Austin in the 1950s elevated common sense to the canon of philosophical truth itself. Wittgenstein, a philosopher to whom Austin owed more than he liked to admit, had a more complex stance on the role of common sense: rather than *appealing* to common sense, he sought to 'return' philosophy to common sense, leaving open the possibility that things would be different after the return. This Wittgenstein envisaged as a tortuous process, lacking the homeliness of the Moorean or Austinian approaches.[25]

There are notorious problems with common sense. One issue is that, as Antonio Gramsci noted, 'there is not just one common sense'.[26] Common sense notably varies between different social groups and

---

23 David Hume, *An Enquiry Concerning Human Understanding*, 7.1.49.

24 The story of the place of common sense in eighteenth-century Scottish philosophy can be told in various ways. One standard way would emphasize those who criticized Hume on behalf of common sense, such as Thomas Reid. However, their objections are prefigured in Hume's work itself, which already makes use of the device of common sense. See James A. Harris, 'Hume and the Common Sense Philosophers'.

25 As he spelled out in his *Blue Book*, 'There is no common sense answer to a philosophical problem. One can defend common sense against the attacks by philosophers only by solving their puzzles, i.e., by curing them of the temptation to attack common sense; not by restating the views of common sense.' Wittgenstein, *The Blue and Brown Books*, pp. 58–9.

26 Antonio Gramsci, *Selections from the Prison Notebooks*, p. 325.

economic classes. As Gramsci also wrote, 'common sense is an ambiguous, contradictory and multiform concept, and . . . to refer to common sense as a confirmation of truth is a nonsense'.[27] It is highly unsuited as a principle of philosophy not only because it is multiform, but because it is tied up in complex ways with religion and other belief systems.[28]

When Austin and his Oxford colleagues align themselves with common sense, they attribute to it some version of 'direct realism'. In other words, they take it that the common-sense view is that subjects are acquainted with ordinary objects such as pieces of furniture 'directly' – that is, not by means of sense data or some other intermediary. As a result, questions about the nature of fundamental reality – as supposedly lying 'beyond' or 'behind' appearances – are disarmed. They thus take themselves not to be intellectuals at variance with common sense, but its representatives. But this conceit is extremely dubious. For one thing, it is not at all clear that common sense does not draw precisely the distinction between reality and appearance on which they want to cast suspicion.

Bernard Williams – a philosopher who was capable of seeing the limitations of analytic philosophy but tended to fall back into line with its expectations if its integrity was too severely challenged – mounted a perceptive critique of the tendencies of the ideologues of common sense in a 1959 review of a book by Austin's acolyte G. J. Warnock. Warnock maintained that metaphysical theses, and even metaphysical perplexity itself, are always produced by theorists, whereas *ordinary* people hold the 'Common Sense view of the world', which is 'perfectly unsurprising, undistressing, quite certainly true'.[29] According to Warnock, it is philosophers who have imposed on ordinary people metaphysical notions such as belief in the soul (which Warnock mocks as the idea of 'the man inside'). This, Williams says, is like Rousseau's view 'of the natural man corrupted by the machinations of priests and kings'. But, as Williams points out, it is very implausible that ordinary people have had such beliefs imposed on them – after all, 'the belief in some sort of human soul, possibly separable from the body, seems to

27 Ibid., p. 423.

28 'The principal elements of common sense are provided by religion, and consequently the relationship between common sense and religion is much more intimate than that between common sense and the philosophical systems of the intellectuals.' Ibid., p. 420.

29 Warnock, *English Philosophy since 1900*, p. 55. Warnock is here giving a sympathetic presentation of the views of G. E. Moore.

be about as old as the human race, and so, presumably, not younger than "common sense"'.[30]

Whereas Warnock thinks it is 'priests and kings' who impose metaphysical ideas from on high, it is in fact he and other 'ordinary language philosophers' who are imposing 'common sense' from on high. This, as Williams points out, is made evident by the strangeness of Warnock apparently 'soberly recognizing obvious truths which incomprehensibly escape the notice of others'.[31] If this really was common sense, why did people seem to need Warnock to tell them this? The question is not why ordinary people have so willingly accepted the absurd theories of philosophers; it is what peace is brought to the men in an Oxford common room by convincing themselves that it is their task to return the masses to common sense.

The Impulse to Therapy

The third option prefigured by Hume is the notion that philosophy is a kind of cure for an ailment. Hume got himself into great difficulties trying to satisfy himself, on the basis of his empiricism, that he could be sure that objects remained in existence while he was not receiving any impressions of them. The resultant scepticism, he concluded, was 'a malady, which can never be radically cur'd, but must return upon us every moment, however we may chace it away, and sometimes may seem entirely free from it'. It could never be got rid of. 'Carelessness and in-attention alone can afford us any remedy.'[32]

The idea that philosophy is an ailment to be cured appears in a variety of guises in analytic philosophy. It has often bled over into the idea that what is wanted is not philosophy, but a critique of philosophy. Philosophy is, in that case, critique of philosophy, or its own liquidation. It was Wittgenstein, more than anyone, who pushed the idea of philosophy as pathological, as a set of ailments or 'cramps' from which relief was to be sought. As he put it in his late work, *Philosophical Investigations*, 'What is your aim in philosophy? – To shew the fly the way out of the fly-bottle.'[33] The fly is the philosopher, trapped in the fly-bottle

30 Williams, '*English Philosophy since 1900*, by G. J. Warnock', p. 169.
31 Ibid., p. 170.
32 Hume, *Treatise of Human Nature*, 1.4.2.
33 Ludwig Wittgenstein, *Philosophical Investigations*, §309.

and now too addled by the sweet liquid that lured him in to be capable of flying out again. It is questionable to what extent Wittgenstein's professed approach is properly described as therapy: John McDowell, perhaps more aptly, has called such a procedure 'exorcism'. It is as if Wittgenstein would expel the demons of philosophy, and be done with it. But it is not clear where this leaves those on whom the exorcism is performed – in particular, whether they are thereby healed. Again, Wittgenstein wished to draw attention to existing linguistic and other practices that are woven into 'forms of life', but it is not apparent how those forms of life could be criticized or improved if not through the constructive philosophy that he eschewed.

Logic and Language

Analytic philosophy could not be pure empiricism in the way in which prior forms of empiricism were. It is distinct from all such earlier forms thanks to its attempt to combine the empiricist mindset with the 'new logic' pioneered by Gottlob Frege, Giuseppe Peano and others. A great part of the significance of this logic lies in its anti-psychologism, rendering it directly at variance with empiricism. The new logic swept aside all attempts to provide an empiricist theory of logic, such as that of John Stuart Mill, according to which logic studies something psychological – the regularities of thought – as physics studies the physical regularities of nature. The attempt to marry the new logic, in spite of its non-empiricist tendencies, with empiricism is a common feature of analytic modes of philosophy; the Vienna Circle enshrined it in the very name of its doctrine, 'logical empiricism' (or 'logical positivism').

Analytic philosophy has often been thought to have two main currents. (This way of seeing things was particularly common in the 1950s and 1960s.) There were those for whom its linguistic dimension was marked by a concern with formal languages, and those for whom natural ('ordinary') language took the place of formal ('ideal') languages. Underlying this distinction, and thus common to both sides, is the idea that, as the Oxford philosopher P. F. Strawson put it, 'ordinary language has no exact logic'.[34] Only later, in the work of the American logician Richard Montague, was the suggestion seriously entertained that natural language might itself possess a precise logic.

---

34 P. F. Strawson, 'On Referring', p. 344.

There is little doubt that the contributions made to logic by analytic philosophers are of lasting importance. It is doubtful, however, to what extent these contributions have been fruitful in philosophy beyond the confines of logic itself. Analytic philosophers often suppose that a training in logic makes people better able to think in other domains – a plausible-sounding idea for which there nevertheless appears to be no evidence. And, again, it is often supposed that work in analytic philosophy, outside logic itself, relies in important ways on the use of logical devices. This is likely to be, at best, a gross exaggeration.[35]

The logic that resulted from the Fregean revolution (named for Gottlob Frege) largely developed under its own steam, with offshoots into computer science. It is striking that its development has not joined up seamlessly with analytic philosophy, and has in fact posed a threat to it. In Chapter 8, I concentrate on the threat posed by the work of Saul Kripke, which made it impossible for analytic philosophy to continue extruding traditionally *verboten* intensional logic, and on the remarkable way in which it nevertheless succeeded in absorbing this threat by means of the innovations of another analytic philosopher, David Lewis.

35 Grounds for scepticism are provided in Bonino, Maffezioli and Tripodi, 'Logic in Analytic Philosophy: A Quantitative Analysis'.

2

The 'Rebellion Against Idealism'

Today's students, receiving their initiation into analytic philosophy, are usually told one of two origin stories. According to the first story, it all began with the work of the German mathematician Gottlob Frege, perhaps specifically with the innovations in mathematical logic carried out in his short book *Begriffsschrift* (1879), which introduced a new 'conceptual notation' rendering the validity, or invalidity, of proofs visible at a glance. According to the second story, the founding moment of analytic philosophy is the 'rebellion' carried out jointly by two Cambridge philosophers, G. E. Moore and Bertrand Russell, in 1898.

The Frege story has its value principally as a retrospective myth. A plausible history of analytic philosophy can certainly be written that begins with Frege.[1] In a social history, however, Frege assumes his proper place at a later juncture in the story: that of the promulgation and propagation of the retrospective myth. Frege's main appearance in this book will, accordingly, be delayed until Chapter 7, which deals with the era in which analytic philosophers started to construe themselves as the inheritors of a distinctive Fregean legacy conceived in terms of the 'problem of meaning'.

The construal of Moore and Russell as the originators of a new movement in philosophy is less mythical. Although analytic philosophy, as a single, unified phenomenon, did not come into being until after 1945, Moore and Russell each originated a component of the amalgam called 'analytic philosophy' that would be forged after the Second World War.

1 For a recent such history, see Michael Potter, *The Rise of Analytic Philosophy.*

When they rebelled in 1898, they acted in concert – although what they rebelled against was only one limited and transitory phase of philosophy: a set of ideas they had recently imbibed from the Oxford philosopher F. H. Bradley, and from a young don in Cambridge, J. M. E. McTaggart. Moreover, Moore and Russell quickly diverged, in terms of both their ideas and the type of influence they exerted. Russell's writings continued to be of fundamental importance to subsequent philosophers, even if he retreated from institutional academic life, while Moore exerted powerful institutional influence as a permanent and central fixture in Cambridge.

This chapter deals with an institution of minute size – Cambridge philosophy – which consisted, at any time, of only a small group. This group was dominated by three people: Russell, Moore, and Russell's one-time student Ludwig Wittgenstein.[2] It is difficult to overemphasize just how few philosophers there were in this monastic crucible of twentieth-century philosophy. There were in Cambridge only ever two professorships in philosophy (the second of them created in 1896 as a chair in 'mental philosophy', which included psychology).[3] Most of the philosophy took place in just one of the university's constituent colleges, Trinity College, an elite within an elite.

Russell, Moore and Wittgenstein came from different backgrounds, although each arrived with social prestige and economic heft. Russell was born into the radical wing of an aristocratic political dynasty; Moore was from an *haut bourgeois* environment, and descended on his mother's side from the Sturge family, a significant Quaker dynasty; and Wittgenstein was the son of one of Austria's wealthiest industrialists. They also exercised very different forms of influence. Russell's early work in mathematical logic has been of lasting significance for logic, philosophy and computer science. His influence on Cambridge philosophy after the First World War was, however, more that of an intellectual progenitor than a direct institutional participant. Russell now built a career as a public intellectual that made him into a household name, but

2 This chapter mentions the prodigiously talented Cambridge philosopher, mathematician and economist Frank Ramsey (1903–30) only in passing, since his short life necessarily limited his influence. Had Ramsey lived beyond his tragically early death, Cambridge philosophy would likely have looked very different. In particular, he might have been able to counterbalance Wittgenstein's influence.

3 The older professorship is the Knightbridge Professorship of Philosophy. The chair founded in 1896, at first nameless, was given the name 'Bertrand Russell Professorship' in 2010, after a campaign to endow it.

he produced nothing of significant philosophical value. Wittgenstein's *Tractatus Logico-Philosophicus*, largely composed away from Cambridge during the First World War, exerted a tremendous immediate influence, in particular on the Vienna Circle (see Chapter 3). After his return to Cambridge in 1929, his influence was, in the first instance, personal: he cultivated a small group of disciples, as philosophy became in his hands a form of exorcism aimed at casting out philosophical demons. It has been said that Moore, although once supremely highly regarded as a philosopher, has 'disappeared from history'.[4] He was, however, the most influential of the three in terms of his institutional role in shaping Cambridge philosophy. Unlike Russell and Wittgenstein, who alternated between presence and absence in Cambridge, Moore remained there continuously from 1911 onwards. It was he above all who promoted a programme of philosophy as 'analysis', and it was his followers who set up the journal *Analysis* in 1933, with the intention of implementing it. Moore himself never clarified what analysis was, but his followers, among them Susan Stebbing, Max Black and John Wisdom, worked hard to do so. But his most important legacy was a certain style of philosophical discussion. It was highly conversational, and relied heavily on the iterated deployment of the question 'But what exactly do you *mean*?' The general atmosphere was one of studied ignorance and incomprehension, articulated by gasps of incredulity.

Moore has often been portrayed, from within Cambridge philosophy and the analytic philosophy into which it later flowed, as a 'philosopher's philosopher', and as a saintly figure bordering on childlike naïf. Far from being a figure of inexplicable uniqueness, however, his importance is as a conduit between the secret Cambridge society known as the Apostles and the effete Bloomsbury Group. While Russell manifests the aspiration of analytic philosophy to scientific status, and Wittgenstein its tendency to therapeutic self-dissolution, Moore gravitates towards its tendency to give way to common sense. He therefore shows just how deeply analytic philosophy could be implicated in the reproduction of the status quo: here, that of a world whose appeal has now become almost entirely unfathomable, marked by the superior aestheticism of an upper layer of Edwardian society whose thin veneer of modernism masks an insecure conformism.

4 Ray Monk, 'He Was the Most Revered Philosopher of His Era. So Why Did G. E. Moore Disappear From History?'

Cambridge Philosophy Before Russell and Moore

The University of Cambridge is composed of a set of colleges, in each of which a range of academic disciplines is studied.[5] Each has a monastic atmosphere, with its body of students and 'dons' (teachers) taking their meals in college, and often living there. By the nineteenth century – like Oxford, which had a similar structure and origin – it had lost much of its standing as a place of learning, and functioned largely as a playground for the wealthy. The average 'outlay and payments requisite for obtaining a degree, independently of the annual expenditure' for a Cambridge University student starting his studies in 1891 was calculated at £49 10s (around £5,000 in today's money).[6] Colleges were for men only, until the founding of Girton College in 1869 and Newnham College in 1871; the first men's colleges to admit women did not do so until a century later, in 1972. Girton and Newnham were not officially part of the university, but their students were allowed to attend designated lectures ('lectures for women') and sit examinations. Like men, they were given degree classifications; unlike men, they were unable to receive a degree. It was only in 1948 that Girton and Newnham became full colleges of the university, and women won the right to be awarded the degrees for which they had worked.

In Cambridge, then as now, a degree is called a 'Tripos'. In 1848 the Moral Sciences Tripos was introduced. It had very wide scope, encompassing moral philosophy, political economy, modern history, general jurisprudence and English law.[7] It was apparently very easy to pass; one of its examiners, the historian Henry Luard, expressed disgust at the candidates' ignorance and lack of intelligence.[8] The Tripos was subsequently reformed, primarily thanks to the efforts of the philosopher Henry Sidgwick, who had noted in 1870 that 'men, not of transcendent genius, obtain the highest (or all but the highest) places' in it.[9] By the

5 For a useful, much later account of college life that subjects it to ethnographic treatment, see William Dell, 'St Dominic's: An Ethnographic Note on a Cambridge College'. 'William Dell' is a pseudonym of the cultural historian Peter Burke. 'St Dominic's' is Emmanuel College.

6 T. F. C. Huddleston, *University Expenses and Non-Collegiate Students*, p. 83. I say 'his' because the women's colleges, Girton and Newnham, were not part of the University at this date.

7 D. A. Winstanley, *Later Victorian Cambridge*, p. 185.

8 Ibid., p. 186.

9 Ibid., p. 189.

time Russell and Moore were students, the Tripos had been narrowed to philosophy, psychology and political economy.

Sidgwick was a utilitarian, and shared the more general reforming tendencies of utilitarians, beyond mere academic reform. Having undergone a crisis of faith and become an agnostic, he resigned his Trinity College fellowship in 1869 in protest against the continued use of religious tests.[10] An advocate of women's education and women's suffrage, he was closely involved in the founding of Newnham College. His wife Eleanor Sidgwick (née Balfour) was the college's principal from 1892. It is difficult now to recover the depth of feeling against the education of women which campaigners were up against. When votes were held on the admission of women to degrees in 1897 and 1921, they were accompanied by large-scale public festivals of anti-woman hysteria. Students at the two women's colleges were not members of the university, which placed obstacles in their way in terms of use of the University Library, exclusion from University Prizes and Scholarships, exclusion from dissertations and advanced study, and 'precarious access' to lectures and laboratories.[11] It is surprising, given these obstacles, just how many women students appear on the lists of degree classifications for the moral sciences Tripos in the *Historical Register of the University of Cambridge*.[12]

Philosophy was taught by a very small number of dons, and studied by a very small number of students. In the 1890s, when Russell and Moore were students, there were just four dons: Sidgwick, James Ward, G. F. Stout and McTaggart. Ward and Stout were psychologists as well as philosophers. Cambridge philosophy, as well as being small, was diverse. It is often imagined – encouraged by Russell's own later characterizations of the event – that when Moore and Russell 'rebelled' in 1898, they did so against 'idealism', conceived as a large-scale intellectual tradition dominating Cambridge philosophy in the nineteenth century. Such an understanding of what occurred in 1898 is largely mythical. Russell and Moore were certainly arguing against idealism,

---

10 Christopher N. L. Brooke, *A History of the University of Cambridge*, vol. IV, p. 1.

11 Gordon Johnson, *University Politics*, p. 33, citing *Cambridge Review*, 13 May 1897.

12 During the years 1890–99, on average, the ratio of men to women taking Part I of the Moral Sciences Tripos was seven-to-four; the ratio of those taking Part II was three-to-one. In 1894 the number of women taking Part I exceeded the number of men (seven women, three men), and again in 1897 (ten women, seven men). See J. R. Tanner, ed., *The Historical Register of the University of Cambridge*, pp. 716–25.

but their target was a view they themselves had come to relatively recently (Russell in 1894, just before completing his Tripos), and was far from imposed on them by their teachers. Their principal idealist target was Bradley; another was the highly idiosyncratic McTaggart, a neo-Hegelian philosopher himself still in his twenties. There is no sense in which Cambridge was simply dominated by idealism at the time Russell and Moore were students in the 1890s: there was no monolithic 'idealist tradition' for them to react against. In fact, as we will see, the position they adopted in 1898 shared important premises with idealist critiques of empiricism, such as those advanced by Bradley, and before him by another Oxford philosopher, T. H. Green.

Young Russell and Moore

Bertrand Russell was born into one of the most illustrious political families in Victorian Britain, belonging to the radical wing of the Whig (later Liberal) Party. King Henry VIII, in dissolving the monasteries, had given Russell's ancestor John Russell lands including Tavistock Abbey, Woburn Abbey, and the kitchen garden of Westminster Abbey (now Covent Garden) in London. Edward VI then made him earl of Bedford in 1550. Russell belonged to a more specific, politically radical line deriving from William, Lord Russell, executed in 1683 for his participation in the Rye House Plot – an attempt to assassinate King Charles II and his brother, the future James II, because of their Catholic sympathies. John Locke, an actual or suspected co-conspirator, fled to the Netherlands as a result. In the wake of the coup – known by the victors who write history as the 'Glorious Revolution' – that installed the Protestants William and Mary on the throne of England, the earls of Bedford were promoted to the status of dukes.[13] Standing in this Whig–Liberal lineage had dual charms. The Russells were radicals challenging the status quo in their campaigns for social reform and women's suffrage; but, at the same time, ever greater favours were conferred on them by the monarchy, adding progressively to their fabulous wealth and entrenching their territorial possessions. Today, the Russell family

13 Russell later wrote: 'John Locke (1632–1704) is the apostle of the Revolution of 1688, the most moderate and the most successful of all revolutions. Its aims were modest, but they were exactly achieved, and no subsequent revolution has hitherto been found necessary in England. Locke faithfully embodies its spirit.' Bertrand Russell, *A History of Western Philosophy*, p. 604.

still owns much of the London district of Bloomsbury (the Bedford Estate).

Russell's grandfather was Lord John Russell, twice prime minister under Queen Victoria (1846–52 and 1865–66), and a principal architect of the Great Reform Act of 1832, which extended suffrage to large parts of the middle class. A younger son of the sixth duke of Bedford, he himself was created the first Earl Russell in 1861. On his death, this title went to his eldest grandson Frank, and on Frank's death in 1931 to Russell himself.

Soon after Russell's birth in 1872, the family was engulfed in tragedy. In 1874, Russell's parents, Viscount Amberley and his wife Kate, took their eldest son Frank on a holiday to Rome, and on returning home discovered that the boy had contracted diphtheria. Frank recovered, but his mother Kate and sister Rachel became infected; within a matter of days, they were both dead. The nervous Amberley, unable to cope, fell into a bottomless depression. Within another two years he was dead too, leaving the two boys – all that remained of the family – as orphans. His will entrusted them to the care of two young atheists, the tuberculous scientist Douglas Spalding, with whom Kate had shared her bed, and the artist T. J. Cobden-Sanderson. Lord and Lady Russell, however, had the will overturned in the courts, and took custody of the boys in Pembroke Lodge, a house in Richmond Park near London that they had been given by Queen Victoria. Here, the boys grew up attended by an army of servants, who, Russell later wrote, 'played a larger part in my life than the family did'.[14]

Just after Russell turned six, his grandfather died. As a result he and Frank were now left to grow up under the aegis of the intensely religious and repressive Lady Russell, assisted by Aunt Agatha, 'who always wore a white shawl and looked down-trodden', and Uncle Rollo, 'who never spoke at all'.[15] Growing up in Pembroke Lodge, surrounded by his grandfather's immense library, gave Russell a sense of dwelling at the heart of British political history. Frank, who had known the gentler care of the Amberleys, rebelled, and was rewarded by being sent away to a boarding school, Winchester College. Bertie, the golden child, was kept in solitude at Pembroke Lodge, and coached by a series of tutors hired by Lady Russell, making him, his brother wrote, 'an unendurable little

14 Bertrand Russell, *Autobiography*, p. 16.

15 Annabel Huth Jackson, *A Victorian Childhood*, pp. 62–3.

prig'.[16] It is not difficult to connect the regime of Pembroke Lodge with the harrowing emotional void that Russell struggled with later in life, reflected in his repeated and desperate attempts at autobiographical and semi-fictional writing. It was a house of horrors, in which all conversation was conducted in a 'sort of hushed and pained undertone', and whose occupants 'drifted in and out of the rooms like ghosts'.[17]

When Russell arrived at Trinity College, Cambridge in 1890, he found it a place of 'infinite delight' – unsurprisingly, given the relief it offered from the strictures and misery of Pembroke Lodge.[18] He arrived to study mathematics, but seemingly with a pre-formed intention to study moral sciences for Part II of his Tripos.[19]

Moore began his studies at Cambridge two years after Russell, in 1892, also at Trinity College – although he took Part I of his Tripos in classics. The two became friends, and Russell soon persuaded Moore to take Part II in moral sciences – though, for good measure, Moore also completed Part II in classics. Moore's background was, by contrast with Russell's, thoroughly bourgeois. His father Daniel had been able to give up his doctor's practice in Hastings after his wife Henrietta came into money from the wealthy Sturge family, from whom she was twice descended (her parents, who were first cousins, were both Sturges). The couple moved to the new suburb of Upper Norwood in south London, where Moore was sent to the 'public' (that is, private) school Dulwich College. Here, his studies were almost entirely in classics. There was no science, and almost no mathematics; Moore would remain ignorant of both. Although he became captain of the school, he later reflected: 'I was indeed rather lonely at school; but this never made me, to any serious degree, unhappy or discontented.'[20] The contrast with Russell is striking. Russell, in his autobiographical writings, thematized his sense of overwhelming loneliness and isolation, calling across to other

16 Frank Russell, *My Life and Adventures*, p. 38.

17 Frank Russell, quoted in Ray Monk, *Bertrand Russell: The Spirit of Solitude*, p. 16; Annabel Huth Jackson, *A Victorian Childhood*, p. 63.

18 Russell, 'My Mental Development', p. 8.

19 Nicholas Griffin, 'Joachim's Early Advice to Russell on Studying Philosophy', p. 119. This is corroborated by the fact that 'the Honble B. Russell' already appears in the minutes of the Moral Sciences Club (the university's philosophy society) as early as 28 November 1890, and appears regularly from then on (Cambridge University Library, GBR/0265/UA/Min.IX.40). Then, as now, a Cambridge Tripos consisted of two 'Parts', which can be studied consecutively, so that students can switch from Part I in one subject to Part II in another.

20 G. E. Moore, 'An Autobiography', p. 10.

similarly cut-off humans across chasms of misery. Although Moore's psyche is difficult to penetrate, it may seem as if he met the pain of his own loneliness with denial.

The Apostles

Soon after his arrival at Cambridge, Russell found that Alfred North Whitehead, the don who had examined him for admission to the Mathematical Tripos, had set up a series of contacts for him with fellow students. They turned out to be members of a secret society called the Apostles, composed of the intellectual elite of Cambridge, to which Russell was soon admitted. The Apostles (also called the Cambridge Conversazione Society, or, by its members, just 'the Society') included both 'senior members' (dons) and 'junior members' (students) of the university. It was exclusively male, and not without a slightly transgressive homoerotic ambience. Membership was by election, and for life. Those resident in Cambridge were expected to attend all meetings, which took place on Saturday evenings in term time. It was, however, in the characteristic vocabulary of the Society, possible to 'take wings' and be freed from the obligation to attend meetings. An Apostle then became an 'angel'. Angels vetted 'embryos' for membership, whose induction into the Society was called 'birth'. This knowingly grandiose vocabulary reached philosophical heights when it came to distinguishing events within the Society from those outside it: whatever took place within it was 'real', anything outside merely 'phenomenal' (non-members were called 'phenomena').

At its meetings, an Apostle would read a paper, followed by discussion and then a vote. The vote was often only tangentially related to the substance of the paper. The general atmosphere was an idiosyncratic fusion of seriousness and levity, with topics often straying into the risqué. Secrecy was taken fairly seriously, even if the Society's existence (and, presumably, much of its membership) were hardly a secret to outsiders. In particular, dinners organized in London for 'angels' were not openly referred to; references to them were camouflaged in correspondence with anyone outside the Society, even those who knew of its existence.

Although the Apostles were important to Russell, in particular as the source of the network of friends he rapidly built up at Cambridge, they were far more important to Moore, who was 'born', thanks to Russell's efforts, soon after his arrival in Cambridge. Moore was an immediate hit when he attended his very first meeting in 1894. According to Russell, everyone 'felt electrified by him, and as if we had all slumbered hitherto and never realized what fearless intellect pure and unadulterated really means'.[21] From this time on, Moore would remain closely and enthusiastically involved with the Apostles. (Not surprisingly, a later attempt to initiate Wittgenstein into the Apostles was ill-fated. Wittgenstein played along at first, but cut ties after just a few meetings, presumably unable to endure the silliness.)

Many of the papers that Moore presented to the Society are preserved in Cambridge University Library; he clearly did not consider them too slight to keep.[22] In them Moore advocates a conventional approach to morality, deviating from the incipiently homoerotic and free-thinking tendencies of most of the Apostles – although, early on, he had defended a hedonist position more in line with Apostles' expectations. Paul Levy, in his hagiographical biography of Moore, has suggested that, in turning to a defence of conventional morality, he had 'his tongue planted firmly in his cheek'.[23] That seems doubtful. More likely, this was simply the view Moore was more comfortable with, continuous with his tendency in early adolescence, as he went through an intensely religious phase, constantly to ask himself: 'What would Jesus do?'[24] In one paper, he told his fellow Apostles that he would defend 'a conventional view of sexual morality, such as in your nostrils will, I fear, savour rankly of puritanism and prudery'.[25] In another, he averred that

> unfortunately, copulation, like other low pleasures, has attractions for most people: so that they pursue it for its own sake, forgetting the highest pleasure of love, which alone & the means to it they ought to pursue. Hence comes that monstrous unnatural vice of copulating with a woman more often than is necessary for begetting children: hence also sodomy & sapphism, the indulgence of a desire for which stunts or kills the capability, inborn in every human being, of enjoying the happiness of true love.[26]

---

21 Russell to Alys Pearsall Smith, quoted in Monk, *Bertrand Russell*, p. 69.

22 Cambridge University Library, GBR/0012/MS Add. 8875 12/1.

23 Paul Levy, *Moore: G. E. Moore and the Cambridge Apostles*, p. 143.

24 Ibid., p. 40.

25 G. E. Moore, 'Shall We Take Delight in Crushing Our Roses?' (8 December 1894), Add. 8875 12/1/3, p. 1.

26 G. E. Moore, 'Achilles or Patroclus?' (November 1894), Add. 8875 12/1/2, p. 8. Compare: 'My view is that this developement [sic] of lust in the human species is a pure evil' ('Shall We Delight in Crushing Our Roses?', Add. 8875 12/1/3, p. 2).

His paper on masturbation, 'Is Self-Abuse Bad As an End?', has not survived. But Moore voted that 'masturbation was bad as an end'.[27]

Moore felt remarkably at home in this environment, despite its more permissive tendencies exceeding what he could endorse. He even cultivated within it an 'inner group', consisting of those he invited to regular reading parties.[28] Notably, Russell was not part of this inner circle, and when he took the step of inviting himself to such a reading party in 1903, Moore replied tartly: 'since you ask me to say if your coming would make any difficulty, I think I had better tell you that it would'.[29] Moore's central position in the Apostles, often one of leadership, and in turn the importance for him of its style of conversation, will be particularly important when we consider its close connections to the Bloomsbury Group, which contained many of the same members, augmented by intellectual and artistic women.

Russell and Social Democracy; Fellowship Dissertations

As Russell approached the end of his undergraduate studies and attained the age of majority (then set at twenty-one), he became financially independent, with an annual income of £600 (about £65,000 in today's money). Legally released from the guardianship of Lady Russell, he made use of his new freedom to announce his intention to marry Alys Pearsall-Smith, an American Quaker. In response Lady Russell launched a campaign to persuade her grandson to break off the engagement by conjuring up the mad ghosts of the family's past. There had always been insinuations about the spectre of insanity, but nothing had been stated directly. Russell learned for the first time that Amberley's brother, Uncle Willy, had been in a lunatic asylum since 1874, where he was given to violence and to 'shouting and singing and making strange faces'.[30] William Russell was eventually diagnosed with schizophrenia. In her campaign against Russell's proposed marriage to Alys, Lady Russell recruited the psychiatrist who had treated William, Dr Daniel Hack Tuke, to advise them not to have children, as any offspring would likely suffer from mental illness. When they therefore resigned themselves to a childless marriage, she mobilized her personal

27 Levy, *Moore*, p. 207. The paper was read on 27 May 1899.

28 Ibid., pp. 196–7.

29 Quoted in Monk, *Bertrand Russell*, p. 164.

30 Quoted in ibid., p. 13.

physician, Dr William Anderson, to warn them that contraception had caused Amberley's epilepsy.

In spite of this campaign of psychological terror, Russell and Alys married on 13 December 1894. Russell paid a terrible price for his defiance for the rest of his life. He wrote in his *Autobiography*:

> The fears generated at that time have never ceased to trouble me subconsciously. Ever since, but not before, I have been subject to violent nightmares in which I dream that I am being murdered, usually by a lunatic. I scream out loud, and on one occasion, before waking, I nearly strangled my wife, thinking that I was defending myself against a murderous assault.

Significantly, he continued: 'The same fear caused me, for many years, to avoid all deep emotion, and live, as nearly as I could, a life of intellect tempered by flippancy.'[31] Of Lady Russell herself he chillingly wrote in his *Autobiography* that, when she died in 1898, he 'did not mind at all'.[32]

Following his marriage, Russell's intellectual path was not yet clearly set out. His undergraduate studies had combined his interests in mathematics and philosophy, but he also had political aspirations – aspirations he would toy with again and again throughout his life. Following their honeymoon in Holland, the couple went to Berlin, where they got to know members of the German Social Democratic Party, at the time still a Marxist party. This engagement with Marxist politics, which caused consternation in Russell's family back home, may have been largely at the instigation of Alys, who also had a strong interest in feminism. Russell himself, however, had a sufficiently serious interest in radical politics that, when Sidney and Beatrice Webb asked him to give lectures at the newly founded London School of Economics, he chose German social democracy as his topic, and returned to Berlin to carry out further research in preparation. He now met the party's leading figures August Bebel and Wilhelm Liebknecht. The lectures were published as Russell's first book, *German Social Democracy* (1896), in which he examined Marxism in some detail – though in the end he called for it be tempered by the liberalism in which he was at home.

At the same time, Russell's interest in theoretical philosophy continued in a state of ferment. Far from having been indoctrinated into

31 Russell, *Autobiography*, p. 74.

32 Ibid., p. 12.

idealism by his Cambridge teachers, as he later liked to present things, his philosophical views had remained unsettled until he finally embraced idealism in May 1894, just as he was coming to the end of his undergraduate studies.[33] In 1895 he walked around the Tiergarten in Berlin plotting out a programme for a scientific philosophy on the Hegelian model, in which each compartment of science would turn out to be contradictory, leading into some higher synthesis by a dialectical transition (scholars now call this 'the Tiergarten programme'). For the moment, however, he concentrated on something more limited that would constitute an initial stage of this project: an examination of 'metageometry' ('meta' because it dealt with what is common to different geometries, including non-Euclidean). This formed the subject for a dissertation he submitted to obtain a prize fellowship at Trinity College. There were, at this time, no postgraduate degrees at Cambridge or anywhere else in England: the chief route to an academic career was to obtain such a prize fellowship, and from there to attempt to secure a lectureship. Russell's prize dissertation is still a basically idealist text; when he published it as his second book, *An Essay on the Foundations of Geometry* (1897), he ended it on a dialectical note, with its culminating contradictions presented as destined to lead into a dialectical treatment of the other parts of science.

Moore, like Russell, worked for a prize fellowship, producing a dissertation entitled *The Metaphysical Basis of Ethics.* His first attempt, in 1897, failed; but a new submission in 1898 won him a six-year fellowship.[34] The fellowships did not require the holder to do any teaching or to live in Cambridge. Russell mostly lived outside of Cambridge and, since he did not need it, gave his stipend away to the LSE. Moore availed himself of his stipend (about £200), accommodation in college and free dinners – as he later described it, 'a very pleasant place and a very pleasant life'.[35]

The Rebellion

In 1898, Moore and Russell jointly engaged in what Russell later liked to refer to as a 'rebellion'.[36] Today this is often characterized, in dramatic terms, as 'the revolt against idealism'. This now common phrase

33 Nicholas Griffin, *Russell's Idealist Apprenticeship*, p. 79.

34 The dissertations are reprinted in G. E. Moore, *Early Philosophical Writings.*

35 Levy, *Moore*, p. 191; Moore, 'Autobiography', p. 23.

36 Russell, 'My Mental Development', p. 12; Bertrand Russell, *My Philosophical Development*, p. 54.

is misleading in suggesting Moore and Russell staged an insurrection against another tradition – presumably the idealism that had allegedly dominated Cambridge philosophy until this time. What Moore and Russell reacted against was in fact something much more specific. They were rejecting their own, very recent embrace of a distinctive view of their own derived principally from Bradley, and to some extent from McTaggart. In doing so, they carried over elements of the idealists' critique of empiricism.

As Russell attests, it was Moore who led the rebellion. The rebellion put forth a new philosophical view – what Peter Hylton, in one of the earliest scholarly historical works from within the analytic tradition, has labelled 'platonic atomism'.[37] 'Platonic' signals that, according to this view, the world is composed neither of mental nor of material things, but something else (what Moore calls 'concepts', and Russell later calls 'terms'). 'Atomism' reflects the claim that reality consists of the configurations in which these concepts are put together. Contra Bradleyian idealism, this composite configuration is ultimate; concepts do not melt away into a greater unity, and neither do the relations obtaining between them.

Russell liked to present the rebellion as a breakthrough into a commonsensical conception, by contrast with the speculative excesses of idealism. Moore's new view, he liked to suggest, finally made it possible to say that, after all, grass was green. (The idealists, presumably, had thought that grass and its greenness were in the mind, and so not really 'in the world'.) But anyone expecting to find such a view spelled out in Moore's classic statement of the view in his 'The Nature of Judgment', published in *Mind* in 1899, will find themselves perplexed.[38] Moore's text, far from Russell's reminiscences of the rebellion as the assertion of healthy common sense, is difficult and obscure.[39]

Moore presents his view as a correction of the view of judgement set out by Bradley in *The Principles of Logic*.[40] Bradley is to be praised, according

37 Peter Hylton, *Russell, Idealism, and the Emergence of Analytic Philosophy*.

38 G. E. Moore, 'The Nature of Judgment'. This text was almost certainly excised from Moore's successful fellowship dissertation; the manuscript of the dissertation survived with a chunk cut out that likely corresponds to 'The Nature of Judgment'.

39 The best summary available is probably Gilbert Ryle, 'G. E. Moore's "The Nature of Judgment"', which attains a remarkable level of lucidity discussing this highly obscure text.

40 Maria van der Schaar mounts an interesting case, in *G. F. Stout and the Psychological Origins of Analytic Philosophy*, that matters are actually more complex,

to Moore, for the basic anti-psychologistic move of taking the 'idea' in a judgement not as a mental state, but as what Bradley calls a 'universal meaning'. But he thinks Bradley does not push his anti-psychologism far enough. In the end, a universal meaning is still an 'abstraction from ideas', where ideas are thought of as psychological entities. That is, it still has a mental basis, even if it is not itself lodged in any mind.

Bradley had inherited from idealist critics of empiricism the notion that the ideas that go to make up judgements had better not be subjective mental items. Such a conception set a sceptical trap; after all, what could assure us that such subjective mental items point beyond themselves to something in the world? But Moore wanted to push the objectivity of ideas further. He did so by insisting that a judgement was a composite of 'concepts', understanding concepts in a quasi-technical sense far removed from the use of the word in ordinary speech, so that they were the building blocks of reality. Concepts were non-mental but also non-physical. According to Moore, *all* concepts *are*. Some of them also *exist*. For a concept to exist is for it to stand in a relation to another concept – that of existence. Concepts are non-temporal. Some, however, possess temporal location, by standing in a relation to relevant time-concepts.

An upshot (but also a difficulty) of Moore's view is that judgements are composed of the very things they are about. This avoids the threat raised by empiricism that my concept of grass might fail to connect with actual grass – that I might be trapped in a world of private mental representations without any assurance that they point to anything beyond themselves. In fact, the view is close to idealism in that 'the world is not alien to the mind but is, rather, transparent to the intellect'.[41] But are not some judgements true, and others false? To answer this, Moore falls back on a claim about intuition. 'What kind of relation makes a proposition true, what false, cannot be further defined, but must be immediately recognised.'[42] Moore's view aimed for sophistication but, at the same time, for a homespun naivety.

---

in that Moore and Russell's turn to a form of realism was mediated by the influence of the psychological work of G. F. Stout and James Ward, which in turn put them in (distal) contact with continental figures such as Franz Brentano and Hermann Lotze (with whom Ward had studied in Germany). The splitting off of psychology from philosophy was not yet complete at this date; van der Schaar's revision to more standard accounts is important in bringing out the role psychology might have played in the formulation of Moore and Russell's essentially anti-psychologistic stance.

41 Hylton, *Russell, Idealism*, p. 137.

42 Moore, 'Nature of Judgment', p. 180.

It was hardly a modernist rebellion against the inherited pieties of the past. Here was an argument for the view that statements were, after all, about just what every Tom, Dick or Harry thought they were about. Statements about grass, for example, were about grass – the stuff of which lawns are made. Moore bought the desired objectivity at the price of an implausible denial of the distinction between the judger and what is judged, and of an overreliance on intuition when it came to detecting truth and falsehood. This price was one that Russell would pay as he took up Moore's view in his own work.

Russell and the Development of Mathematical Logic

Moore's view was at first congenial to Russell in the latter's efforts to free himself from idealism in his work on mathematics. It would take time for its problems to become apparent.

The path from Russell's studies in mathematics to philosophy, and from there to his important work in mathematical logic, was anything but straightforward. At Cambridge he had received no serious exposure to mathematical logic. Mathematics at Cambridge was in a decrepit state, innocent of the huge recent advances made by German mathematicians; Russell only learned about the work of Richard Dedekind, Georg Cantor and Karl Weierstrass on a trip to the United States in 1896. When his teacher James Ward gave him a copy of Frege's *Begriffsschrift* around the same time, he could as yet make no sense of it; in his own *Essay on the Foundations of Geometry*, the logicians cited were still the idealists Bradley, Sigwart and Bosanquet.[43] It was eventually the French logician Louis Couturat who got him up to speed. In response to a review Russell had published of Couturat's *De l'infini mathématique* in 1897, the Frenchman struck up a correspondence with him. Both were trying, it turned out, to develop logicism: the project of showing that mathematics could be derived from logic. A breakthrough came when Couturat invited Russell to the first ever International Congress of Philosophy, in Paris in July 1900.[44] Here Russell for the first

43 I. Grattan-Guinness, ed., *Dear Russell – Dear Jourdain*, p. 133; for the proposed date, see Potter, *Rise of Analytic Philosophy*, p. 208. Bertrand Russell, *An Essay on the Foundations of Geometry*, p. v.

44 'The most important year in my intellectual life was the year 1900, and the most important event in this year was my visit to the International Congress of Philosophy in Paris.' Russell, 'My Mental Development', p. 12.

time heard the Italian logician Giuseppe Peano speak. He was blown away by Peano's success in argument, which he put down to the rigour of his logical notation. Peano, he enthused, made possible a 'new philosophical logic' that would 'place our time, in this respect, on a level with the greatest age of Greece'.[45] Russell sat down to read all of the writings of Peano he could get his hands on, and in turn the writings of Frege to which Peano referred.

Russell's efforts resulted in a large book, *The Principles of Mathematics* (1903) – not to be confused with the mammoth three-volume *Principia Mathematica* (1910–13) that he co-authored with Whitehead. The latter work grew out of a projected second volume for *Principles* that would set out the formal proofs of the philosophical doctrines expounded in the 1903 work.[46] *Principles*, which combined Peano's methods with Russell's own insistence on the reality of relations, drew on the view taken from Moore, but already posed challenges to its coherence. In the book's preface, Russell is unequivocal about his adherence to Moore's philosophical views:

> On the fundamental questions of philosophy, my position, in all its chief features, is derived from Mr G. E. Moore. I have accepted from him the non-existential nature of propositions (except such as happen to assert existence) and their independence of any knowing mind; also the pluralism which regards the world, both that of existents and that of entities, as composed of an infinite number of mutually independent entities, with relations which are ultimate, and not reducible to adjectives of their terms or of the whole which these compose.[47]

Moore's view was helpful because it allowed in 'existents' as well as 'entities'. This meant that it could seem to encompass the whole subject matter of mathematics, most of which was non-spatial and non-temporal. As Russell also notes in *Principles*, however, mathematics is pervaded by phrases beginning with 'any', 'some' and 'the'. These break the mould of Moore's conception of judgement, because they are not about what they contain. Instead, they are about something that points beyond the judgement (or proposition) itself.

These phrases Russell called 'denoting phrases'. Consideration of denoting phrases would turn out to be sufficient to wreck the

45 Quoted in Monk, *Bertrand Russell*, pp. 131–2.

46 Bertrand Russell, *The Principles of Mathematics*, p. vi.

47 Ibid., p. viii.

short-lived euphoria of platonic atomism. Russell puzzled over them in Chapter 5 of *Principles*, entitled 'Denoting'. He took them up again, offering a different solution, in his paper 'On Denoting' (1905). 'On Denoting' has become Russell's most famous paper – a set piece in the teaching of analytic philosophy, considered a masterpiece in philosophical analysis and even a 'paradigm of philosophy'.[48] The theory it sets out, now known as 'Russell's theory of descriptions', treats of 'definite descriptions', one kind of denoting phrase – 'definite' because introduced by the definite article. Russell proposes that a statement containing a denoting phrase – for example, 'The present king of France is bald', containing the denoting phrase 'the present king of France' – should be analysed as follows: there is a thing that is at present king of France, *and* anyone who is at present king of France is that thing, *and* that thing is bald. The proposition is a conjunction: it contains three segments linked by the word 'and'. As with any other conjunction, if one of the segments is false, the whole thing is false. 'There is a thing that is at present king of France' is false, and so the whole thing is false whatever the segments that follow say. We are thus relieved of having to think of 'empty' definite descriptions such as 'the present king of France' as being about a kind of shadowy entity somewhere between existence and non-existence.

Russell's analysis of definite descriptions 'analyses away' an expression so that it ceases to be troublesome. It helped him with his real concern, which was not non-existent kings of France, but expressions fundamental for his logicist project, which sought the meeting point between mathematics and logic in the theory of classes, such as 'the class of all classes that do not contain themselves'. Why can Russell analyse away such denoting phrases? The answer is that he took himself to have discovered that there are 'denoting phrases' that are not actually 'denoting'; they have a certain linguistic form that makes them *as if* to denote, but they do not in fact *denote* anything. And so there is no need for a special set of concepts called 'denoting concepts' (as he had argued in his earlier treatment of 'denoting' in *Principles*).

But Russell had now opened up a fateful contrast: that between what is known by acquaintance and what is known 'by description'. Some of our knowledge is directly through acquaintance (where denoting is, as he put it, not merely 'linguistic through the phrase'); some of it is

48 This characterization is due to Frank Ramsey (Ramsey, 'Philosophy', in *Philosophical Papers*, p. 1*n*1).

roundabout, through description. This returns us to traditional philosophical issues that arise in the empiricist framework from which Russell and Moore, in their rebellion, had precisely sought to exempt themselves. The world is not simply transparent to us, made up of the very same things that make up our statements about it. Knowledge by acquaintance, as Russell now understood this, is, as the empiricists had held, sensory; knowledge by description is derivative from this more basic knowledge. Russell has been driven, by the failure of the platonic atomist picture under pressure from his attempt to spell out the nature of mathematics, straight back onto the rock of empiricism from which the logical considerations of Bradley and Moore alike had been a recoil. Russell, the secular godson of John Stuart Mill, was now set firmly on the path of a retreat to his ideological home ground of empiricism.[49]

Principia Ethica

While Russell was pursuing the principles of mathematics, Moore worked on the principles of ethics. A series of classes that he gave to working people at the Passmore Edwards Settlement (later the Mary Ward Centre) in London grew into his book *Principia Ethica*, published, like Russell's *Principles of Mathematics*, in 1903.

Although Russell's work had its own tone of enthusiasm, Moore adopted, by comparison, an almost bewilderingly strident tone, intoxicated by a sense of novelty and getting things right for the first time. His task, he tells his reader, is to clear up what ethics is all about. According to him, the 'question, how "good" is to be defined, is the most fundamental question in all Ethics'.[50] He draws on his notion of analysis to argue that 'good' is, in fact, 'indefinable', or, as he also puts it, 'good is good, and that is the end of the matter'.[51] This follows immediately, he thinks, from the fact that 'good' is a 'simple notion', and that only what is complex is definable (like 'horse', which is definable because horses are composed of parts). 'Good' cannot mean the same as 'pleasant' (or any other term that might be proposed to be synonymous with 'good'). This is because, if it were *really the case* that 'good' means the same as 'pleasant', the question, 'But is pleasure good?' would be

49 Compare Hylton, *Russell, Idealism*, part III.
50 G. E. Moore, *Principia Ethica*, §5.
51 Ibid., §6.

unintelligible. But, Moore points out, the question *is* intelligible. As he says, it remains an 'open question', even if we have specified that 'good' means the same as 'pleasant', whether pleasure is good. This is Moore's 'open question argument'. It is a shockingly bad argument; in spite of this it is still treated with reverence by analytic philosophers. It is as if they cannot allow themselves to see that Moore really is saying, as he seems to be, that even if it has been accepted that *x* is defined as *y*, we can still ask 'but is *x y*?'

In light of the air of novelty, it is striking that there is fundamentally nothing new in *Principia Ethica*. A very similar fusion of intuitionism (the view that 'good' is indefinable and only accessible through a special faculty of intuition) and utilitarianism is found in the work of Moore's teacher Sidgwick.[52] In the final chapter of the book, 'The Ideal', Moore seeks to show 'what is good in itself'. He tells us that, in order to determine this, 'it is necessary to consider what things are such that, if they existed *by themselves*, in absolute isolation, we should yet judge their existence to be good'.[53] This turns out to be very easy – it is 'far less difficult than the controversies of Ethics might have led us to expect'. That will be surprising to anyone who wonders what on earth could be involved in trying to assess the value of something in absolute isolation, as if nothing else existed. The ultimate goods turn out to be 'certain states of consciousness, which may be roughly described as the pleasures of human intercourse and the enjoyment of beautiful objects'.[54]

Moore's 1903 book had a far greater impact on a general intellectual audience than Russell's. The enthusiasm with which *Principia Ethica* was received reached hysterical heights within what became the Bloomsbury Group – which added two sisters, Vanessa Stephen (later Bell) and Virginia Stephen (later Woolf) to a collection of Cambridge Apostles.[55] One member of the group, Lytton Strachey, wrote to Moore:

> I think your book has not only wrecked and shattered all writers on Ethics from Aristotle and Christ to Herbert Spencer and Mr Bradley,

---

52 See Thomas Hurka, 'Moore in the Middle'.

53 Moore, *Principia Ethica*, §112.

54 Ibid., §113.

55 Ann Banfield, 'Cambridge Bloomsbury'. For a more extensive and ambitious treatment of the connections between Cambridge and Bloomsbury, making claims for the transference of Russellian epistemology to the work of Bloomsbury Group members, see Ann Banfield, *The Phantom Table: Woolf, Fry, Russell and the Epistemology of Modernism*.

> it has not only laid the true foundations of Ethics, it has not only left all modern philosophy *bafouée* – these seem to me small achievements compared to the establishment of that Method which shines like a sword between the lines . . . I date from Oct. 1903 the beginning of the Age of Reason.[56]

Another, John Maynard Keynes, described it as 'the opening of a new heaven on a new earth'.[57] Virginia Woolf asked: 'did you ever read the book that made us all so wise and good: *Principia Ethica*?'[58]

This reception is not so surprising if it is considered that Moore's work reflected back to the Bloomsbury Group its own conceits and preoccupations: its portrayal of the good life in 'The Ideal' corresponds very closely to the group's life of privileged and effete aestheticism. The 'common' and 'uneducated' were thematized and exalted, but always from a great height of condescension. One function Moore himself possessed was that of validating a certain way of talking when ethical intuitions conflicted, as they inevitably did. As Keynes wrote,

> In practice, victory was with those who could speak with the greatest appearance of clear, undoubting conviction and could best use the accents of infallibility. Moore at this time was a master of this method – greeting one's remarks with a gasp of incredulity – *Do* you *really* think *that*, an expression of face as if to hear such a thing said reduced him to a state of wonder verging on imbecility, with his mouth wide open and wagging his head in the negative so violently that his hair shook. *Oh!* He would say, goggling at you as if either you or he must be mad; and no reply was possible.[59]

Principia Ethica reflected Moore's style in conversation: the piling of question upon question, in a sort of never-ending philosophical filibuster. He was, as Leonard Woolf said, 'never easy to talk to'.[60] He would answer with further questions, or drop his jaw in incredulity, or stick his tongue out. He could also just be silent. In the Bloomsbury Group's Charleston Farmhouse, they 'discussed Moore's famous taciturnity: he

---

56 Strachey to Moore, 11 October 1903, quoted in Levy, *Moore*, p. 234.

57 John Maynard Keynes, *Two Memoirs*, p. 82.

58 Quoted in Thomas Baldwin, *Moore*, p. xiii.

59 Keynes, *Two Memoirs*, p. 85.

60 Leonard Woolf, *Beginning Again: An Autobiography of the Years 1911–1918*, p. 41.

was accused of silencing a generation. "I didn't want to be silent," he replied. "I couldn't think of anything to say."'[61]

The sense of excitement that permeated 'Bloomsbury', as if it were caught up in a modernist revolution, is now difficult to appreciate. Its legacy has been decisively marked by the negative judgements of the critic F. R. Leavis and the writer D. H. Lawrence, who found the group irredeemably conceited and (in Lawrence's words) lacking 'reverence'. Its world of conceit, taking itself to be in touch with 'common sense', is, however, Moore's world. Its form of conversation ('What exactly do you mean?') was not just exercised by Moore himself for many years as he formed philosophers in the Cambridge mould, but persists to this day in the tutorials and seminars of analytic philosophy.

Russell and Moore Return to Cambridge; Wittgenstein Arrives

Beyond his visits to Germany in 1895, and the book *German Social Democracy* which resulted, Russell continued to have various brief dalliances with politics. He stood on a women's suffrage ticket in Wimbledon in 1907. This was merely gestural, as his chances of winning the seat were virtually non-existent. However, after campaigning in the 1909 election to get Philip Morrell re-elected as an MP, Russell received more realistic offers to stand in two constituencies – Hastings and St Leonards, and St Pancras South. He was saved from needing to consider this seriously when Whitehead orchestrated a five-year lectureship at Cambridge for him. His acquaintance with Philip Morrell did, however, have another significant result: Russell now began a long-lived, on-and-off affair with Morrell's wife, Lady Ottoline.

Russell's marriage to Alys had fallen apart, leading him to pursue a policy of treating her with maximal cruelty, 'in the deliberate hope of destroying her affection'.[62] He himself retreated into an inner world resembling the condition of his childhood, while presenting an artless façade to those outside: 'I am constructing a mental cloister, in which my inner soul is to dwell in peace, while an outer simulacrum goes forth to meet the world. In this inner sanctuary I sit and think spectral thoughts.'[63] Russell's new relationship with Ottoline at last seemed to

61 Quoted from Virginia Woolf's diary in Levy, *Moore*, p. 298.

62 Quoted in Monk, *Bertrand Russell*, p. 151.

63 Russell to Lucy Donnelly, 1 September 1902, quoted in ibid., p. 158.

offer him a release for his tremendous passions, but it was always a fraught liaison. His interest was predominantly sexual, whereas Ottoline, who conducted many such affairs, was more interested in Russell's intellectual gifts. Russell, who struggled constantly to negotiate the intellectual and temperamental differences between them, was always trying to demonstrate that their views were *the same*, even though they were not. Ottoline was, for instance, religious, while Russell tended towards a strident atheism. When an acknowledgement of such differences was required, he diverted his energy into violently attacking her views. Faced with the prospect of a final separation, he told her of urges to commit suicide or else an unspecified 'sexual crime'.[64]

Russell returned to Cambridge in October 1910 to take up the lectureship Whitehead had arranged, and wrote: 'I enjoy living in College very much.'[65] A year later, in the autumn of 1911, Moore was back in Cambridge too. His fellowship had run out in 1904, and his application for a renewal had been turned down. Moore later claimed, surely disingenuously, that he did not mind, and even welcomed the break.[66] He had gone to live in Edinburgh with a fellow Apostle, A. R. Ainsworth, the model for the cynical philosopher Stewart Ansell in E. M. Forster's *The Longest Journey*, and the man who, in Russell's opinion, 'ruined' Moore.[67] When, in 1908, Ainsworth moved away from Edinburgh, where he had been teaching Greek at the university, and married Moore's youngest sister, Sarah, Moore moved in with his other sisters, Hettie and Nellie. Moore's return to Cambridge in 1911 was facilitated by the economist John Maynard Keynes, who helped him secure a lectureship left vacant by his father John Neville Keynes. The position was not ideal, since it included a requirement to teach psychology, and only paid about £40 a year (about £3,800 in today's money), supplemented by students' fees of up to £100 (£9,600), and lacking free accommodation or meals.[68] Moore did not need the money, however, thanks to the Sturge family money he had inherited, which he had also been able to live off while away from Cambridge and out of employment for seven years.

At the same time as Moore's return, a greater event happened in Cambridge: the arrival of the twenty-two year-old Ludwig Wittgenstein, who

64 Monk, *Bertrand Russell*, p. 266.

65 Quoted in ibid., p. 199.

66 Moore, 'Autobiography', p. 25.

67 Reported in Virginia Woolf's diary, 23 February 1924, quoted in Levy, *Moore*, p. 213.

68 Levy, *Moore*, p. 263.

had not matriculated as a student, but simply showed up with the specific intention of studying with Russell. Although lacking any previous formal education in philosophy, he repeatedly presented himself at Russell's rooms to engage in philosophical argument.[69] Such presumptuousness was not unusual for someone of Wittgenstein's background. He had grown up, like Russell, the 'golden child' in a family of extraordinary prestige and wealth.

Wittgenstein's father, an engineer and industrialist, was one of the richest men in Vienna and a prominent patron of the arts. Karl Wittgenstein financed the Secession Building, with its Beethoven Frieze by Gustav Klimt, and regularly hosted musical evenings at the family's city residence, the Palais Wittgenstein, attended by Johannes Brahms and Gustav Mahler. His expectations of his children were exacting, and his opposition to their deviant inclinations merciless. By the time Ludwig, the youngest of eight children, entered adolescence, two of his brothers had committed suicide; a third would do so at the end of the First World War. Karl decided to take a gentler approach with his two youngest sons, Paul and Ludwig, who were sent to school rather than being educated at home. Nevertheless, Wittgenstein later said that he had 'had an unhappy childhood and a most miserable youth'.[70] After the Realschule (technical high school) in Linz, where he performed poorly in technical subjects, excelling only in religion, he studied mechanical engineering at the Technische Hochschule in Berlin and aeronautics in Manchester. At Manchester, having produced a design for an aircraft engine flawed both in engineering and mathematical terms, he turned his attention to the philosophy of mathematics, and to the work of Russell and Frege.[71]

Wittgenstein's Takeover of Logic from Russell

Russell quickly overcame his initial irritation with Wittgenstein's campaign of intellectual harassment, and came to feel 'the most perfect intellectual sympathy' with him.[72] He wrote to Ottoline: 'I think he is passionately devoted to me. Any difference of feeling causes him great

69 He may have visited Frege first, or done so on Russell's recommendation; accounts vary. In any case, he had no hesitation in going straight to the top.

70 Quoted in G. E. M. Anscombe, *An Introduction to Wittgenstein's Tractatus*, p. 11.

71 For the point about the mathematical inadequacies underlying the design, see Michael Potter, *Wittgenstein's Notes on Logic*, p. 10.

72 Quoted in Monk, *Bertrand Russell*, p. 250.

pain' – an observation notably redolent of Russell's sentiments about his relationship with Ottoline herself.[73] It could not yet have been obvious to Russell that, on matters of logic, Wittgenstein would soon diverge sharply from him.

Wittgenstein, having zeroed in on the most fundamental question that Russell's approach prompted, 'What is logic?', before long started to take over from him when it came to serious work in logic. Next to Wittgenstein's overpowering intellectual passion, Russell felt 'a bleating lambkin'.[74] As he wrote to Ottoline, 'I saw he was right, and I saw that I could not hope ever again to do fundamental work in philosophy.'[75] When Wittgenstein's sister Hermine came to tea in Cambridge, Russell told her: 'We expect the next big step in philosophy to be taken by your brother.'[76] From this point on, Russell's efforts went in new directions. For example, he began to pursue a vociferous campaign against the French philosopher Henri Bergson, who was enviably famous, irritatingly popular with women, and Jewish.

As he squirmed in Wittgenstein's grip in 1913, Russell tried to make progress on an old paper asking straight out, 'What Is Logic?'[77] But he was stuck at an impasse. Logic studied the forms of complexes. The form of a complex is 'the way the constituents are put together'. But is this way things are put together itself an object? Here Russell faced a dilemma. If a form is an object, then it stands in some relation to the other items in the complex, prompting an infinite regress – what is the form holding together this object and the others? But if a form is *not* an object, there is nothing for logic to study. Strangely, Russell's total incapacity to make progress with this basic issue in logic did not deter him from embarking on a far more ambitious project. He now decided to write a book called *The Theory of Knowledge*, beginning from experience and moving through particulars, relations, predicates, logical forms, to arrive finally at the constituents of the physical world. Russell, who had become obsessed with 'scientific method in philosophy', felt sure this would be his best work.[78] But the project came to nothing.

Wittgenstein approached logic with the solitary hauteur of a visionary. He began by abandoning altogether the task of discerning what sort

73 Quoted in ibid., p. 265.
74 Quoted in ibid., p. 284.
75 Quoted in ibid., p. 301.
76 Quoted in ibid., p. 272.
77 This is printed in Bertrand Russell, *Collected Papers*, vol. 6.
78 Monk, *Bertrand Russell*, p. 295.

of *thing* a form is, to be replaced by that of constructing a proper symbolism revealing the logical form of a complex. Effectively, Wittgenstein ruthlessly demolished the pillars of Russell's logical edifice. There was to be no theory of types, of the kind Russell himself had devised to block Russell's Paradox – a notorious difficulty generated by statements about sets that contained themselves as a member, and which threatened the logicist project at its basis. Wittgenstein declared: 'I think that there cannot be different Types of things!'[79] Again, Russell's 'multiple relation theory' of judgement was to be junked, and Russell's problems over the unity of the proposition overcome through a radical rethinking. 'Cassio loves Desdemona' is not a mere collection of objects. Instead it was necessary, as Wittgenstein had been insisting for some time, to begin with the whole proposition.

In 1913 Wittgenstein worked at logic in Norway, where he would take himself off for extended periods and work in solitude, unattached as he was to universities or any source of waged income. Here, the ideas that would assume their final form in his *Tractatus Logico-Philosophicus* took shape. He worked frenetically, 'only *one* step away from madness'.[80] The *Tractatus*, when it was finished, consisted of a series of numbered pronouncements, rather than of a set of arguments in continuous prose. As a result, it has sometimes been called 'oracular', but this is misleading: what is stated at its periphery receives rigorous support from its core. The *Tractatus* set out a view of logic that, in its author's estimation, solved all of the problems of philosophy. The world is composed of configurations of basic elements. These basic elements might have been configured in various ways. There are thus ways the world might have been, as well as the way the world is. This makes it possible to say, as Wittgenstein does, that there is no fundamental difference between a proposition p and its negation not-p. What negation tracks is on which side of a list of possible configurations (actual or non-actual) a particular proposition ends up. The most important matters of all in philosophy (aesthetics, ethics and religion), however, were exempted from such regimentation, and relegated to a sanctum Wittgenstein called 'the mystical'; they were, quite literally, unsayable.[81]

79 Wittgenstein to Russell, January 1913, in Ludwig Wittgenstein, *Cambridge Letters*, p. 24.

80 Wittgenstein to Russell, January 1914, in Wittgenstein, *Cambridge Letters*, p. 69.

81 For an excellent summary of the book, see Brian McGuinness, *Young Ludwig*, Chapter 9.

The First World War

Much of the *Tractatus* was, remarkably, written during the First World War. The war was not a quiet time of reflection for Wittgenstein: he was on active service. He had spent the summer of 1914 in Vienna, with the intention of returning to Norway to finish building himself a house there. But on 28 June 1914, Archduke Franz Ferdinand was assassinated and, on 28 July, Austria declared war on Serbia. On 7 August, Wittgenstein enlisted as a volunteer in the Austrian army. Seeing the war as a test of courage, he asked to be posted to the front as an ordinary soldier, and once there to the most dangerous place at the front: the observation post. His bravery was rewarded by a series of promotions, culminating in the rank of *Leutnant* (second lieutenant), and by a range of medals, the highest of which was the Band of the Military Service Medal with Swords.

In Cambridge, Russell was resolutely opposed to the war, and joined the hard-line No Conscription Fellowship. This would eventually cost him his lectureship, from which he was removed in 1916 with the connivance of McTaggart. Moore, by contrast with both Russell and Wittgenstein, did not know what to think about the war. After much vacillation, he came out against it in January 1915, and became involved with the Union of Democratic Control, a moderate organization that, unlike the No Conscription Fellowship, stopped short of pacifism. After the sinking of the *Lusitania* in May 1915, Moore worried both that he would be considered a 'slacker' for not being in uniform, and that membership of the UDC was not anti-war enough.[82] In April 1916 he decided he was not a conscientious objector, and noted with relief in his diary: 'Have reconciled myself to idea of military service.'[83] As so often, Russell was strident and principled in his stance, and willing to pay the price – although, notably, when he was imprisoned for his criticism of the United States, he received the preferential treatment and accommodation accorded to upper-class prisoners. While Wittgenstein's stance was one of personal heroism, Moore was carried where the wind blew him.

82 Levy, *Moore*, p. 283.
83 Ibid., p. 289.

Wittgenstein's Second Cambridge Period

In the *Tractatus*, Wittgenstein understood himself to have solved, quite literally, all of the problems of philosophy. After his release from an Italian prison camp in 1919, in keeping with this self-assessment, he turned to other occupations. He gave all his wealth to family members, and turned to teaching in elementary schools in rural Austria. This was followed by stints as a gardener in a monastery, and helping the architect Paul Engelmann with the design of a new house in Vienna for his sister Margarete and her American husband Jerome Stonborough, in an anti-ornamental style derived from that of Engelmann's master, Adolf Loos.

In 1929 Wittgenstein, having reversed his change of heart about philosophy, returned to Cambridge.[84] Cambridge having in the meantime introduced the degree of PhD, he spent two terms registered as a PhD student with the brilliant young mathematician and philosopher Frank Ramsey officially appointed as his supervisor. There was, of course, something comical in this arrangement. Ramsey, who had visited Wittgenstein in 1923 in Puchberg, one of the Austrian villages where he taught as a schoolteacher, was well qualified in the sense that he had perhaps a better grasp of Wittgenstein's work than anyone else. Nonetheless, no one could really stand up to the grandeur of the older Austrian. While, in the preface to his *Philosophical Investigations*, Wittgenstein said Ramsey's criticism helped him 'to a degree which I myself am hardly able to estimate', privately he called his objections shallow.[85] On 18 June 1929, Wittgenstein was awarded the PhD, with the absurdly unsuitable *Tractatus* as his dissertation, and Russell and Moore as examiners.

Wittgenstein's philosophy underwent a complex and uncertain process of transformation. The Vienna Circle tended to read the distinction between sense and nonsense in the *Tractatus* in terms of the 'principle of verification', according to which the meaningfulness of a statement hinged on the availability of some distinct means of its verification through empirical testing of some kind. Although Wittgenstein was basically out of sympathy with this interpretation of his own work, in the 1930s he toyed for a while with his own versions of the principle,

84 For Wittgenstein's cautious engagement with the Vienna Circle and his route back to philosophy in the 1920s, see Chapter 3.

85 Ray Monk, *Wittgenstein: The Duty of Genius*, p. 259.

but then came to think there was, after all, no decisive way of determining, for instance, the applicability of a rule – a notion central to one of these versions. All that could be done was to give examples of its correct and incorrect use.

As Wittgenstein honed his approach in his classes in his rooms at Trinity College, where he cultivated a captive audience of devotees, it gradually turned into the 'later philosophy' sketched out in his posthumously published *Philosophical Investigations*. Here, the aim was not to *solve* any philosophical problems, but to find ways to loosen their hold. Wittgenstein built little stylized models of linguistic behaviour he called 'language games'. These were supposed to help clarify 'how we go on' – how certain 'forms of life' are sustained. Wittgenstein writes throughout in an amorphous first-person plural: this is what 'we' do, what 'we' are apt to say. 'Our' language is not to be interfered with or corrected; in this respect, philosophy 'leaves everything as it is'.[86] Just why language is not to be interfered with, Wittgenstein does not say. And there is the problem that 'our' language does after all, in some of its regions, produce metaphysical nonsense (or what he calls 'bumps that the understanding has got by running its head up against the limits of language').[87] But what would it be to establish these limits of language, beyond which it is *not* to be left as it is?

One crucial feature of the conception of language Wittgenstein was now operating with is that it makes linguistic communication inherently communal and public. But it is a mistake to suppose that this reflects a sympathy for Marxism, as some have been keen to maintain. Politically, Wittgenstein was in fact a reactionary, with a taste for Oswald Spengler (author of *The Decline of the West*) and Otto Weininger (author of the misogynistic and antisemitic *Sex and Character*). When he visited the Soviet Union in 1935 to see if he could get manual work there, what animated him was a Tolstoyan ideal of simplicity, not any attachment to communism. Since the only jobs the Russians were able to offer him were philosophy professorships, he quickly returned to England.

After he spent much of the late 1930s drifting in Norway and Ireland, Wittgenstein found himself, in the developing political situation, under increasing pressure, as an Austrian Jew, to seek out employment in the form of an academic position. He quickly obtained one at Cambridge. Then, when Moore retired as professor in 1938, he competed for the

86 Ludwig Wittgenstein, *Philosophical Investigations*, §124.

87 Ibid., §119.

vacancy against Stebbing, Wisdom and Gilbert Ryle. Wittgenstein was elected with practically no discussion among the electors. Even C. D. Broad, who did not like Wittgenstein's work, said: 'To refuse the chair to Wittgenstein would be like refusing Einstein a chair of physics.'[88] R. G. Collingwood, the only person on the list of electors who Wittgenstein felt might have tried to block his appointment, was out of reach, on a sea voyage in Southeast Asia.

Wittgenstein's influence was often detrimental. A set of devotees, usually much younger men, readily followed their master in regarding conventional approaches to philosophy, and to life, as contemptible, and aped his mannerisms. Wittgenstein tended to advise them to abandon philosophy and work in factories. He himself mostly shunned his colleagues in philosophy. His lectures were not advertised on the normal lecture list but through word of mouth, and were invariably given only the title 'Philosophy', reflecting the lecturer's distinctive, aristocratically spartan aesthetic. Only a few people were able to hold their own in his presence. One such person, Ramsey, died in 1930 at the tragically early age of twenty-six. Another, the Oxford philosopher Gilbert Ryle, later lamented the 'contempt for thoughts other than Wittgenstein's' that had prevailed in Cambridge.[89] Those of Wittgenstein's talented pupils who had the alacrity to wrest themselves free from his paralysing grip paid a significant price. The American Alice Ambrose, who had already gained a PhD from the University of Wisconsin and was studying for a second PhD at Cambridge, was one such student. Wittgenstein liked to accuse people of either misrepresenting or plagiarizing him. When Ambrose decided to publish her own work as her own thoughts, Wittgenstein became furious and told her to retract the paper. Ambrose refused, and Wittgenstein cut off all contact with her.[90]

Moore and His Legacy

Wittgenstein had a lasting influence on a small group of followers. Moore's influence on Cambridge philosophy, however, was deeper and more comprehensive. This influence was primarily a matter of philosophical method and approach.

---

88 Quoted in Monk, *Wittgenstein*, p. 415.

89 Gilbert Ryle, 'Autobiographical', p. 11.

90 Monk, *Wittgenstein*, p. 346.

Moore himself made no bones about the fact that his work was essentially anti-philosophical. He said of himself: 'I do not think that the world or the sciences would ever have suggested to me any philosophical problems. What has suggested philosophical problems to me is things which other philosophers have said about the world or the sciences.'[91] He pursued this approach, critical of traditional philosophy, throughout his career.

Moore's basic animus was against traditional philosophers' tendency to claim that things are not as common sense says they are. Traditional philosophers have held views that imply the falsity of what common sense takes to be truisms (such as the belief that there are physical things). In 'A Defence of Common Sense' (1925), Moore produces a long list of truisms that he takes himself to know. From these he derives the wrongness of what 'other philosophers' say, since their views (for example, that there are no spatiotemporal objects) imply the falsity of what he takes himself to know with certainty. The supposed truisms in which Moore believes consist of the following: 'There exists at present a living human body, which is *my* body. This body was born at a certain time in the past, and has existed continuously ever since, though not without undergoing changes; it was, for instance, much smaller when it was born, and for some time afterwards, than it is now.'[92] And so on and so forth.

In 'Proof of an External World' (1939), Moore spends a great deal of time casting doubt on Kant's claim to have produced the only possible proof of 'the existence of things outside us'. Moore now claims to be able to 'give a large number of different proofs, each of which is a perfectly rigorous proof'. The example he offers passes very quickly: 'I can prove now, for instance, that two human hands exist. How? By holding up my two hands, and saying, as I make a certain gesture with the right hand, "Here is one hand", and adding, as I make a certain gesture with the left, "and here is another".'[93] A great deal of ink has been spilled on Moore's supposed 'proof' here; what it amounts to is the dogmatic assertion of the credentials of common sense. Moore supplies no answer to the question of whether common sense may be mistaken, or what to do when claims made on behalf of common sense conflict.

Moore, throughout his output, hinted that what he was doing was 'analysis' – some kind of breaking things apart. The task of philosophers

91 Moore, 'Autobiography', p. 14.

92 G. E. Moore, *Philosophical Papers*, p. 33.

93 Ibid., pp. 145–6.

was to subject the common sense they put in place of traditional philosophy to such analysis. In 'The Nature of Judgment' he had already insisted that 'a thing becomes intelligible first when it is analysed into its constituent concepts'.[94] In *Principia Ethica*, he made much of the idea that 'horse' could be analysed, whereas 'good' could not. But what *was* analysis, according to Moore? The task of spelling this out was left to his followers, among them Stebbing, Wisdom and Black. Much of this work was carried out in the pages of the journal *Analysis*, founded in 1933, and edited by Austin Duncan-Jones 'with the cooperation of' Stebbing, Ryle and C. A. Mace. A 'Statement of Policy' printed in its first issue declared that its 'short discussions of questions of detail in philosophy' would be concerned 'with the elucidation or explanation of facts, or groups of facts, the general nature of which is, by common consent, already known; rather than with attempts to establish new kinds of fact about the world, of very wide scope, or on a very large scale'. Its aims were thus very constricted. The task was analysis. But, although many of the articles were devoted to the question of what analysis *was* precisely, none managed to answer it.

Susan Stebbing was one of the drivers of *Analysis* and one of the most ardent promoters of a Moorean project of analysis. Born in a middle-class home, and privately educated at James Allen's Girls' School in Dulwich, south London, she had studied in Cambridge as an undergraduate. She completed Parts I and II of the Historical Tripos, and then Part I of Moral Sciences, at Girton College; but, as a woman, was unable to take a degree. Instead, she went to King's College, London to study for an MA, and subsequently held a series of visiting lectureships at women's colleges in Cambridge and London. In addition to university teaching, she ran a girls' school in Belsize Park in north London with two friends and her sister Helen. When she became a professor at Bedford College, a women's college in the University of London, in 1933, the news made the headlines.[95] Lacking an appointment in Cambridge, Stebbing never had any secure foothold in the philosophical scene there. Notably, when she applied for Moore's professorship on his retirement, she was told by Ryle, another applicant: 'everyone thinks you are the right person to succeed Moore, except that you are a woman', and by the Cambridge philosopher R. B. Braithwaite: 'your being a woman

94 G. E. Moore, 'The Nature of Judgment', p. 182.

95 The news was reported in the *Morning Post*, *Manchester Guardian*, *Western Morning News*, *Belfast Telegraph*, *Nature* and the *Times Educational Supplement*.

would of course prevent you from applying'.[96] Although the official line held to by the authorities was that there were procedural obstacles to a woman ever becoming a professor at Cambridge, later the very same year Dorothy Garrod was appointed to the Disney Professorship of Archaeology, the first woman to hold any chair in the university.

On the whole, Cambridge philosophy was cut off from developments elsewhere. But Stebbing was important as a consummate professional forger of links between different parts of the philosophical world. In particular, she worked to bring Cambridge analysis into contact with the logical positivism of the Vienna Circle. Her 1933 British Academy lecture, 'Logical Positivism and Analysis', provided an important introduction to the work of the Vienna Circle in Britain, preceding Ayer's more bullish *Language, Truth and Logic* by three years. It was on Stebbing's invitation that Rudolf Carnap, a crucial figure in the Circle, gave three lectures at Bedford College in October 1934. She also used her institutional clout to support others, notably her student Margaret MacDonald, who had been raised an orphan in a National Children's Home in Hampshire, obtained her PhD under Stebbing's supervision, and eventually followed in her mentor's footsteps as lecturer, then reader, at Bedford College.[97]

Stebbing's efforts to specify what analysis was foundered.[98] Others tried, including Max Black (born in Baku, now in Azerbaijan) and John Wisdom. In a symposium entitled 'Is Analysis a Useful Method in Philosophy?' held at the Joint Session of the Aristotelian Society and the Mind Association, in Cardiff in 1934, Black and Wisdom came up against Maurice Cornforth, a former student of Wittgenstein's. Cornforth had turned against analysis, and offered 'to give the Marxist criticism of analytic philosophy'.[99] Unfortunately Cornforth was able to muster nothing better than a doctrinaire line about the conflict in the history of philosophy between idealist and realist tendencies, declaring that 'the logico-analytic method is the most highly developed form

96 Stebbing to Edna Purdie and Lillian Penson, 25 January 1939; Stebbing to Lillian Penson, 26 January 1939. Quoted in Siobhan Chapman, *Susan Stebbing and the Language of Common Sense*, pp. 126, 127.

97 For detail on MacDonald's life, see Michael Kremer, 'Margaret MacDonald and Gilbert Ryle: A Philosophical Friendship'.

98 See the discussion of R. G. Collingwood's criticisms of her in Chapter 4.

99 Maurice Cornforth, 'Is Analysis a Useful Method in Philosophy?', p. 90. This is one of the earliest uses of the phrase 'analytic philosophy' in print. As we shall see in Chapter 4, it was also used by R. G. Collingwood and by W. P. Montague in 1933.

of this philosophical speculation of the bourgeoisie'.[100] Stebbing's student Elsie Whetnall seems to have been subject to similar influences. Stebbing acidly commented in a letter: 'Elsie Whetnall – who is now a member of the Communist party, reads nothing but the "Daily Worker", Marx, Lenin, Trotsky, & books on allied topics, & is getting grumpier & grumpier, & more horrified at my selfish absorption in Logical Positivism!'[101]

If Stebbing rejected communism, she nevertheless considered herself left wing. It might be thought that her method of analysis, even if it could not be spelled out in methodologically self-conscious terms, could be vindicated by the uses to which she put it, attempting to make her brand of philosophy relevant to political discussion. In a series of books she set out to apply the tools of analysis to public discourse – in particular in *Thinking to Some Purpose*, issued as a Pelican paperback in 1939. Stebbing's efforts, which might be compared to present-day efforts to apply 'critical reasoning' to political issues, are disappointing. With little to contribute other than her toolbox of Moorean analysis – containing tools that no one had as yet managed to sharpen – and lacking much knowledge of the social world, the promise of Stebbing getting some significant purchase on the real world remained unfulfilled.

Moore's meticulousness, the lifeblood of the Cambridge style, lived on. But to quite what purpose the discussions in which Moore was so accomplished were to be carried on remained unclear.

---

100 Cornforth, 'Is Analysis a Useful Method?', p. 95.

101 Stebbing to Ursula Roberts, 1935, quoted in Chapman, *Susan Stebbing*, p. 89.

3

The Unity of Science in Red Vienna

Analytic philosophy is sometimes simply conflated with the logical positivism of the Vienna Circle.[1] That is a distortion – and so is the widespread image of logical positivism, largely due to Ayer's *Language, Truth and Logic*, according to which it does nothing more than trounce metaphysics and uncritically accept the findings of the natural sciences. Nonetheless, logical positivism – the real thing, not Ayer's caricature – was at least as important a component of the 'analytic philosophy' forged after the Second World War as were the forms of analysis advocated by Russell and Moore. Logical positivists now, as refugees from Nazism, played a leading role in the making of analytic philosophy in the United States.[2]

The Vienna Circle differed markedly both in doctrinal and institutional terms from the Cambridge philosophers. Whereas there was never any self-proclaimed 'Cambridge school', the Circle was a self-conscious formation. Furthermore its members were, in the first instance, not philosophers but scientists – physicists, mathematicians, economists, sociologists – who met to discuss philosophical questions at the foundations of their respective disciplines. The history of such

1 It is often said that the term 'logical positivism' should be eschewed, in favour of 'logical empiricism', as reflecting the preferences of the Circle. I use the term 'logical positivism', both because it has become established and because it was originally self-applied by a Circle member, Herbert Feigl (writing in collaboration with Albert Blumberg). See Albert Blumberg and Herbert Feigl, 'Logical Positivism: A New Movement in European Philosophy'.

2 See Chapter 5.

discussions begins earlier than is often thought. A 'Proto-Circle' that started to meet in a Viennese café in 1907 counted among its members the physicist Philipp Frank, the mathematician Hans Hahn and the economist and sociologist Otto Neurath. After Hahn succeeded in bringing the German physicist-philosopher Moritz Schlick to Vienna in 1922, the 'Schlick Circle' was formed in 1924. This was a somewhat more formal institution, which met in the building of the University of Vienna's Institute for Mathematics, although it was not officially affiliated to any university department. Later in the 1920s, the Circle entered a new 'public phase'. In 1928 its public organ, the Ernst Mach Society, was launched, and in 1929 the Circle published a brochure entitled *Scientific World-Conception: The Vienna Circle* – a manifesto for what now, for the first time, called itself simply 'the Vienna Circle'.

Cambridge was a tiny, monastic community. Vienna was, by contrast, one of the great metropolitan capitals of Europe. The Vienna Circle came into being in the city of Sigmund Freud, Gustav Klimt, Adolf Loos, Hugo von Hofmannsthal, Karl Kraus, Arnold Schönberg and others at the forefront of intellectual and aesthetic modernism. The Circle is readily, and appropriately, identified with a radical modernist impulse, and with the 'stripping away' of the decadent ornamentation characteristic of the old Habsburg world.[3] It was a participant in a genuine revolt, of a different order from the small-scale intellectual rebellion of Moore and Russell. The revolt is properly described as Oedipal, since it conceived of itself as not merely turning against a tradition, but seeking to obliterate the very idea of tradition, or parentage, as such.[4] As with parents, however, the obliteration was not fully successful. In important ways, in fact, logical positivism functioned to restore a set of ancestors – those of the Austrian liberal tradition.

The significance for the Circle of the modernism of 'Vienna 1900' can, in turn, only be understood in terms of the specific political

3 For a treatment in these terms, see Allan Janik and Stephen Toulmin, *Wittgenstein's Vienna*.

4 Carl E. Schorske convincingly links fin-de-siècle Vienna's ahistoricism with the ahistorical intellectual culture of the post–Second World War United States, including analytic philosophy: 'Vienna in the *fin de siècle*, with its acutely felt tremors of social and political disintegration, proved one of the most fertile breeding grounds of our century's a-historical culture'. Carl E. Schorske, *Fin-de-Siècle Vienna: Politics and Culture*, p. xviii. 'Above all in philosophy, a discipline previously marked by a high consciousness of its own historical character and continuity, the analytic school challenged the validity of the traditional questions that had concerned philosophers since antiquity' (p. xx).

context of Austria-Hungary. Liberals had risen to prominence in the 1860s and achieved an impressive, though never fully secure, hold on political power. It was partly through their energetic promotion of freedoms designed to dent the power of the aristocracy that the liberal bourgeoisie unleashed forces that then went on to help destabilize their own position. From the 1890s onwards, new mass movements gained enormous traction in Austria-Hungary: Christian reactionaries, non-German nationalists and Zionists all acquired a taste for self-assertion in the climate that liberals had unwittingly prepared for them.

Responses to the rise of these irrationalist – and, as they would now be called, 'populist' – mass movements were various. This variety of responses helps explain the variety within Viennese modernism. Some sections of the liberal bourgeoisie withdrew into an aestheticist modernism, expressive of a hypertrophied attitude of resignation. But Viennese modernism could also be technocratic and optimistic, promising a transformation of society. This divergence between manifestations of modernism, and the political diversity that underlay it, are crucial factors in understanding the Vienna Circle and its programme. The manifesto that the Circle (or certain of its members) produced in 1929 can seem perplexing, by both advocating liberal ideas (citing Hume and Mill as idols, and explicitly connecting itself to the tradition of Austrian liberalism) and favouring a radical social programme associated with the 'Austromarxism' of the Austrian Social Democratic Party.[5] This is not, however, mere confusion on the Circle's part, but reflective of an intellectual and political alliance formed in response to the concrete demands of Austrian politics. For liberals pushed onto the back foot by irrationalist populist movements, it made eminent sense to come out in favour of the programme of the Social Democrats. What it promised was a way to restore political order and divert the masses away from irrationalism, by seeking to capture them precisely not by means of an alternative irrationalism but through a programme of universal enlightenment.

In this context, the Circle's position was precarious. Far from being embedded at the heart of Austrian society, it was always an avant-garde movement. The First World War had reduced Austria-Hungary from a vast multicultural empire to a small, German-speaking country. At the same time, the state of Vienna within this new, reduced Austria gained

5 Otto Neurath et al., 'Wissenschaftliche Weltauffassung: Der Wiener Kreis [The Scientific Conception of the World: The Vienna Circle]'.

a social-democratic government. 'Red Vienna' remained, however, in a constant state of contestation with what Janek Wasserman has thematized as 'Black Vienna', representing the forces of fascism and irrationalism.[6] In the end, Black Vienna won out and the Circle was crushed, its surviving fragments only to be reconstituted in the United States.

The Circle's manifesto, written by Neurath with the assistance of Hahn and Rudolf Carnap, embodies the standpoint of what has become known as the 'Left Vienna Circle', according to which the theoretical project of 'unity of science' was entirely at one with a radical social programme encompassing universal housing and universal education. Not everyone in the Circle shared this position; in particular, Schlick found himself somewhat embarrassed by the manifesto that his confrères had written while he was away on a visiting lectureship in California. Nevertheless, the manifesto shows the far-reaching possibilities of the Circle's programme. It is not merely that members of the Circle could feel at home lecturing at the Bauhaus Dessau in that institution's overtly socialist phase (1928–30) and could contemplate collaboration with the Frankfurt School from considerations of expediency or indeed out of intellectual curiosity. Such activities and attempted collaborations were, for the Circle, an integral part of the ongoing articulation of its own 'world conception'. The Vienna Circle wore its ideology on its sleeve, unlike anything that subsequently emerged as analytic philosophy solidified.

The Coming of Ernst Mach

Liberals were comprehensively routed across Europe in the revolutions of 1848–49. When they finally came to power in the 1860s in Austria, it was 'almost by default'.[7] They achieved ascendancy not by their own efforts, but thanks to a complex sequence of events in Austria-Hungary's relationships with foreign powers, with the result that their hold on power was never ultimately secure. They nevertheless succeeded in instituting constitutional structures and installing the tremendous circular boulevard known as the Ringstrasse, the artery connecting Vienna's great cultural and political institutions such as the Opera

6 Janek Wasserman, *Black Vienna: The Radical Right in the Red City, 1918–1938*.

7 Schorske, *Fin-de-Siècle Vienna*, p. 5.

House, Academy of Fine Arts, Palace of Justice and Parliament. This was the *Gründerzeit* ('time of the founders'), a period of liberal efflorescence in which various families – Wittgenstein, von Lieben, Gutmann, Ephrussi – rose to prominence and tremendous wealth.

The liberals' programme transformed the institutions of the state in the image of the middle class. Directed against the upper class, the programme occasioned explosions of self-assertion from across the lower classes as well as the bourgeoisie. Georg von Schönerer in 1882 organized radical German nationalists to mobilize them for an extreme antisemitic politics. Karl Lueger, leader of the Christian Social Party, mobilized the forces of Christian reaction. Lueger was eventually elected mayor of Vienna, in 1895; although the emperor, who had a personal antipathy to Lueger and concerns about his antisemitism, blocked the election, it was finally ratified in 1897. Theodor Herzl worked in the opposite direction to the antisemites, mobilizing Jewish sentiment in favour of the Zionist cause.[8]

In 1895, the year Lueger was elected mayor, the physicist Ernst Mach was appointed to a chair in philosophy at the University of Vienna. The chair was a reinvention of one of three philosophy chairs that had been vacant for some time; it was rebaptized, specifically for Mach, as a professorship 'for the history and theory of the inductive sciences'.[9] The chair repurposed for Mach had been last held by an obscurity, Georg Schenach, author of a 'system of concrete monism', who had vacated it in 1859. For much of the nineteenth century, Austrian philosophy had been in a peculiarly regressive state, entirely distinct from philosophy in other German-speaking lands. The dominance of the Catholic Church tended to prioritize Aristotelian modes of thought; the placement of Kant's *Critique of Pure Reason* on the Index Librorum Prohibitorum was taken seriously enough there that Kantianism never flourished. Against this background, Austria's greatest philosophical

---

8 For an account of this 'trio' and the interplay between them, see ibid., Chapter 3.

9 The year 1895 was an important date in another respect. As Z. A. Jordan writes in his important survey of Polish philosophy, 'The beginning of modern philosophy in Poland can be given a precise date. It was in 1895 that Kazimierz Twardowski . . . was appointed to the chair of philosophy at Lwów University and became the founder of modern Polish philosophy.' Z. A. Jordan, *Philosophy and Ideology: The Development of Philosophy and Marxism–Leninism in Poland Since the Second World War*, p. 5. I will not, in this book, attempt to treat the development of Polish philosophy and its distinctive contribution to the development of analytic philosophy. For an initial overview, see Jordan's book.

hope in the nineteenth century was Franz Brentano, but this hope was soon dimmed. Another of the vacant chairs at the time of Mach's appointment was one from which Brentano had been forcibly removed.

Brentano, born into an illustrious literary family in the Rhineland, had entered the priesthood but withdrawn from it following a crisis of faith. Having renounced the priesthood was no obstacle to his being appointed to a professorship in Vienna in 1874. His decision made trouble for him, however, when in 1880 he decided to marry Ida von Lieben, a member of one of Vienna's great wealthy families. In order to do so, he renounced his Austrian citizenship; in Austria, since the Catholic priesthood was a *character indelebilis* (something that does not admit of being erased), he was still effectively a priest, and so barred from marriage. But, since it turned out that Austrian citizenship was a precondition of his professorship, he was now stripped of his position. As a result, Brentano, although the star philosopher in Vienna – who counted among his students the future president of Czechoslovakia Tomáš Garrigue Masaryk, the founder of psychoanalysis Sigmund Freud, and the philosophers Edmund Husserl and Alexius Meinong – taught as an unsalaried *Privatdozent*. Brentano's philosophy was a complex synthesis of Aristotelianism and empiricism which held the promise of an entirely new scientific philosophy. Mach's appointment would inaugurate a completely different kind of 'scientific philosophy'.[10]

Mach's installation in his chair was facilitated by Theodor Gomperz, a historian of Greek philosophy who was friendly to the positivism of John Stuart Mill, as well as being a member of one of Vienna's richest families. Mach had built a career at the University of Prague, where he was appointed to a chair in physics in 1867. There, he discovered Mach bands and first brought attention to Gestalt qualities. He also, in opposing the use of the Czech language in the university, adopted the standard position of the liberal bourgeoisie vis-à-vis calls for Czech cultural self-determination. As rector of the university, he proposed that Czech speakers found their own university to exist alongside the Charles University, which had been founded in 1348. But the proposal was overruled by Count Eduard von Taaffe, who supported Czech demands for full language parity in the university.[11]

---

10 For an interesting account of Brentano's 'stance *vis à vis* Mach and . . . the reception of Mach by Brentano's students', see Denis Fisette, 'The Reception of Ernst Mach in the School of Brentano'.

11 John T. Blackmore, *Ernst Mach*, p. 73.

Mach subscribed to a thoroughgoing phenomenalism.[12] That is, he denied the existence of anything other than observable sensations. It has sometimes, in later literature subsequent to Mach's work, been suggested that phenomenalism could be merely a methodological, rather than a substantive doctrine – it could amount, the thought went, to an insistence that one might as well speak as if there were nothing beyond sensations, without committing oneself to the view that there really *is* nothing else. In his book *Contributions to the Analysis of Sensations*, however, Mach made it clear that he was committed to phenomenalism of the substantive variety. He here rejected 'the monstrous notion of a *thing in itself*, unknowable and different from its "phenomenal" existence'. He went on: 'Thing, body, matter, are nothing apart from their complexes of colors, sounds, and so forth – nothing apart from their so-called attributes.'[13] Things-in-themselves – material particles, forces and the self – were to be banished from science. Thermodynamics, for instance, could be developed without any reference at all to material particles or mechanistic force.[14]

Allied to his phenomenalism was Mach's principle of economy. Science was a matter of inputs (observed sensations) making their way into a theory that would generate the right outputs (predicted sensations). The 'sole office' of concepts such as mass, force and atom was 'to revive economically arranged experiences'; physicists were mistaken if they ascribed to them 'a reality beyond and independent of thought'.[15]

The physicist Ludwig Boltzmann pointed out, against Mach's phenomenalism, that more or less all physics goes beyond experience: 'No equation ever represents any phenomenon with absolute precision. Each equation is an idealization, stressing commonalities and neglecting differences, and therefore going beyond experience.'[16] Against Mach's 'economical' approach, Boltzmann wrote: 'We would not willingly designate as mere thriftiness the establishment of the distances and

12 The view that Mach was a phenomenalist is no longer academically respectable; it is now de rigueur to insist that Mach was not a phenomenalist, but a neutral monist. For a classic recent exposition, see John Preston, 'Phenomenalism, or Neutral Monism, in Mach's *Analysis of Sensations*?' It is understandable that defenders of Mach should want to save him from phenomenalism, since it is a deeply incoherent position.

13 Ernst Mach, *Contributions to the Analysis of Sensations*, p. 6.

14 Blackmore, *Ernst Mach*, p. 88.

15 Ernst Mach, *The Science of Mechanics*, p. 505.

16 Quoted in Karl Sigmund, *Exact Thinking in Demented Times: The Vienna Circle and the Epic Quest for the Foundations of Science*, pp. 33–4.

movements, the size, physical and chemical properties of the celestial bodies, the invention of the microscope and the resultant discovery of the origins of the diseases we suffer from.'[17]

Beyond the academy, Mach was perhaps most widely known for his insistence on the elimination of the ego, summed up in his mantra, 'The ego is unsavable.'[18] The ego was, according to him, 'an ideal mental-economical unity, not a real unity'.[19] Mach has sometimes been linked with Buddhism because of his denial of a substantive self; but this denial is a set piece of empiricism. Hume, in his *Treatise of Human Nature*, was driven to the same view.[20] The mantra, and its seemingly radical implications, found favour with an impressive array of literary figures who attended his lectures, such as the *Jung Wien* authors Hermann Bahr, Schnitzler and von Hofmannsthal. According to Bahr,

> Mach's effect, especially on the youth, was at that time very great. And really this was due to a single sentence. Mach had pronounced: 'The I cannot be saved'. With that even the ego was overthrown and the last of the idols seemed to be smashed, the last boundary fallen, the highest freedom won, the work of annihilation completed. There really remained nothing left.[21]

The imprint of Mach's unsavable ego was left on Schnitzler's *La Ronde* (1900) and von Hofmannsthal's *Letter of Lord Chandos* (1902). Another writer, Robert Musil, who turned the scientific spirit of Vienna to literary purpose in his vast unfinished satire, *The Man Without Qualities* (1930–43), had initially pursued a philosophical career, and wrote his dissertation on Mach.

Mach's biographer John T. Blackmore may well be right that he 'was the philosopher of what remained of civilized, humanitarian, non-Catholic, Austrian "liberalism"'.[22] Beyond liberal circles, however, Mach is significant for occasioning a fault-line inside the Marxist tradition. To many Marxists, his phenomenalism, and the closely related 'empiriocriticism' developed by Richard Avenarius in Zurich, seemed at first

17 Engelbert Broda, *Ludwig Boltzmann: Mensch, Physiker, Philosoph*, pp. 137–8.

18 Mach, *Contributions to the Analysis of Sensations*, p. 20*n*1.

19 Ibid., p. 20.

20 Hume has likewise, very implausibly, been linked with Buddhism. See Alison Gopnik, 'Could David Hume Have Known About Buddhism?'

21 Hermann Bahr, *Bilderbuch*, p. 37.

22 Blackmore, *Ernst Mach*, p. 182.

conducive as instruments in the debunking of mystificatory ideology, and thus usable as weapons against the bourgeoisie. Peter Klimentjevich Engelmeyer, an engineer, translated Mach's work into Russian, and founded the Society for Positivism in Moscow. Many Russian socialists studied at Zurich, then a centre for politically radical thought, where they were exposed to Avenarius's teachings. Alexander Bogdanov wrote a preface to the Russian edition of Mach's *Analysis of Sensations* entitled 'What Should the Russian Reader Look for in Mach?'[23] But others – notably Lenin – denounced 'Machists' such as Bogdanov as 'would-be Marxists'. In his 1909 book *Materialism and Empirio-Criticism*, Lenin, with some plausibility, likened the philosophy of Mach and Avenarius to that of the eighteenth-century Anglo-Irish immaterialist philosopher and Protestant bishop George Berkeley.[24] For Lenin, it was a 'clear and indisputable fact that Ernst Mach's doctrine that things are complexes of sensations is subjective idealism and a simple rehash of Berkeleianism'.[25] Marx and Engels, Lenin reminds his readers, were patently materialists who fought such idealism tooth and nail.

Moritz Schlick's Circle

In 1907, a group that has since been designated the 'First Vienna Circle' (or 'Proto-Circle') began to meet every Thursday in a Viennese café. Little is known of its activities, except for the account given by one its most active members, the physicist Philipp Frank.[26] Frank, one of Lenin's targets in *Materialism and Empirio-Criticism*, had been supervised by Ludwig Boltzmann and was, in 1912, to succeed Einstein in his chair at Prague, on Einstein's personal recommendation. The membership of the Proto-Circle included, in addition to the mathematician Hans Hahn and the economist and sociologist Otto Neurath, Catholic philosophers and romantic mystics. It was one of many such discussion groups in Vienna. Groups of this kind often involved a crossover between different disciplines or métiers, and generally met in cafés,

23 Ibid., p. 239.

24 In *The Science of Mechanics*, Mach repeated many of Berkeley's criticisms of Newton. See Blackmore, *Ernst Mach*, pp. 95–6; Karl R. Popper, 'A Note on Berkeley as Precursor of Mach'; John Myhill, 'Berkeley's "De Motu": An Anticipation of Mach'.

25 V. I. Lenin, *Materialism and Empirio-Criticism: Critical Notes Concerning a Reactionary Philosophy*, p. 34.

26 Philipp Frank, *Modern Science and Its Philosophy*.

carrying on their discussions there for many hours at a time, not least thanks to the cramped nature of Viennese apartments and the difficulty of heating them. As Frank recalled their discussions, they centred on the 'crisis of science' engendered by challenges to Euclidean geometry and Newtonian mechanics, and sought to find a way to marry Mach's phenomenalism with the conventionalism that the French mathematician and physicist Henri Poincaré proposed in response to the crisis.

In 1921, Hahn, the mathematician of the Proto-Circle, worked actively to bring Moritz Schlick to Vienna, and the following year Schlick was appointed to the chair formerly held by Mach. Schlick had, in his *Space and Time in Contemporary Physics* (1917), sought to integrate the new positivism with Einstein's new science, and could be seen as the most important philosophical expositor of Einstein. In 1924 he began to organize a series of regular Thursday evening meetings at the suggestion of his students Herbert Feigl and Friedrich Waismann. Participation was at Schlick's invitation. (The reason for Karl Popper's non-participation in the Vienna Circle is that Schlick never saw fit to extend an invitation to him.) The 'Schlick Circle' (*Schlick-Zirkel*) would eventually become known as the 'Vienna Circle' (*Wiener Kreis*), when Neurath proposed the latter name as part of the title for the manifesto he and others composed in 1929. First meeting privately, it then found a home in the rear building of the Institute of Mathematics at Boltzmanngasse 5.

Schlick was born in Berlin into a well-off Protestant family, the son of a factory owner descended from Bohemian nobility. He was a physicist by training; his PhD, awarded in 1904 for a dissertation entitled *On the Reflection of Light in an Inhomogeneous Layer*, had been supervised by Max Planck. In philosophical terms, Schlick saw himself as overcoming age-old disputes such as that between idealism and materialism. To decide between the use of mental concepts and physical concepts was simply to decide which of these were better suited to forming a system of symbols that could get at the world of facts 'uniquely' – that is, decisively. If there were alternative such ways of settling how the world was, so much the better; what mattered was hitting the target. Schlick was thereby able to be much more lithe than his positivist predecessors, overturning their insistence on differentiating between directly observational concepts ('red', 'warm') and 'auxiliary' ones ('force', 'charge'), and thus making it possible, furthermore, to integrate the new physics of Einstein (with its 'four-dimensional space', 'curved space', and other non-observational concepts). Schlick's strident and confident attitude was to be well summed up in his 1930 paper 'The Turning Point in Philosophy':

> I am convinced that we are in the middle of an altogether final turn in philosophy. I am justified, on good grounds, in regarding the sterile conflict of systems as settled. Our time, so I claim, possesses already the methods by which any conflict of this kind is rendered superfluous; what matters is only to apply these methods resolutely.[27]

Somewhat bizarrely, the early meetings of the Schlick Circle were focused on reading Wittgenstein's *Tractatus* as a textbook of empiricism, operating with a sharp dividing line between verifiable and unverifiable statements so as to excise metaphysics from philosophy. This was far from what Wittgenstein understood himself to have meant by his demarcation of the sayable, and efforts to involve him in the Circle's activities during his time in Austria in the 1920s met severe resistance from the master himself. Schlick could manage to get Wittgenstein to meet him privately together with select students, but he never attended a meeting of the Circle. One such student, Friedrich Waismann, laboured for many years to produce an accurate presentation of Wittgenstein's new ideas in written form, chalked up as No. 1 in the Circle's book series, *Schriften zur wissenschaftlichen Weltauffassung*. Wittgenstein, finding all of Waismann's efforts unsatisfactory, eventually pulled the plug, and No. 1 never appeared. In any case, the Circle had produced its own Wittgenstein, with a life independent of whatever the author of the *Tractatus* might have been getting at.

Rudolf Carnap

If Schlick formed and sustained the Circle, and provided it with leadership, its intellectually most important figure was Rudolf Carnap, another German, who came to Vienna and joined the Circle in 1926. Carnap taught in Vienna until 1931, when he took up a post in Prague.

Like Schlick, Carnap was born into a Protestant family, but a more modest one, in Ronsdorf, near Wuppertal in western Germany. His father had begun as a poor ribbon weaver, but had built his own ribbon

27 Schlick, 'Die Wende der Philosophie', quoted in ibid., p. 41.

business, and married the daughter of the educational reformer Friedrich Wilhelm Dörpfeld. The Carnap residence was a home in which bourgeois convention came in for questioning, although within the bounds of decency. As a student at the University of Jena, the young Carnap took Frege's course on *Begriffsschrift* ('conceptual notation') 'out of curiosity'. He found Frege to be 'extremely introverted'; 'the possibility of a discussion seemed to be out of the question'.[28] Alongside further courses with Frege, he began to do experimental research in physics, abruptly brought to an end by the outbreak of war in 1914, in whose 'very first days' the professor with whom he was working was killed.[29]

Before the war, Carnap had been active in the German Youth Movement, which combined anti-authoritarianism with a romantic preoccupation with nature and a Nietzschean educational philosophy. Other participants in the movement, which was extremely popular, included Hans Reichenbach, later a leading Berlin positivist, and Walter Benjamin, who would become the most talented member of the Frankfurt School.[30] Carnap reluctantly but dutifully volunteered for the war, and was involved in heavy fighting on the Western Front, receiving the Iron Cross on 24 September 1916.[31] The war caused the left of the Social Democratic Party (SPD) to split off and found a new anti-war party, the Independent Social Democratic Party (USPD), in 1917. Carnap joined the USPD on 1 August 1918. He became increasingly politically active, although his understanding of political activism involved committing himself to circulating 'facts' while abstaining from 'revolutionary propaganda'.[32] He contributed writings to a newsletter, *Politische Rundbriefe*, started by his confrère in the German Youth Movement, Karl Bittel.

28 Rudolf Carnap, 'Intellectual Autobiography', p. 4.

29 Ibid., p. 6.

30 For the relationship of the German Youth Movement to logical positivism, see Christian Damböck, Günther Sandner and Meike G. Werner, eds, *Logischer Empirismus, Lebensreform und die deutsche Jugendbewegung*. Reichenbach and Benjamin were acquainted at the time. Whereas Benjamin later repressed the memory, Reichenbach wrote appreciatively of Benjamin's genius after learning of his suicide in the Pyrenees in 1940. See Hans-Joachim Dahms, *Positivismusstreit*, p. 63.

31 A. W. Carus, *Carnap and Twentieth-Century Thought: Explication as Enlightenment*, p. 56. With a characteristically bloodless modesty, Carnap in his 'Intellectual Autobiography' simply states: 'During the first years of the war I was at the front most of the time' (p. 8).

32 Unpublished parts of Carnap's 'Intellectual Autobiography', as quoted in Carus, *Carnap*, p. 58.

Carnap followed Bittel in his admiration of the anarchist Gustav Landauer. In Bittel's words, with which Carnap enthusiastically agreed, Landauer advocated '*freideutscher* socialism: *against* Marxism, materialism, centralisation, state socialism and *for* communal cooperative socialism in the spirit of brotherhood'.[33] He later recalled that he and his friends in Berlin 'welcomed the German revolution at least for its negative effect, the liberation from the old powers'.[34]

Around 1919 Carnap studied Russell and Whitehead's *Principia Mathematica*, which Frege had mentioned in his lectures, and in 1921 Russell's *Our Knowledge of the External World*, which impressed him with its statement of a 'logical-analytic method of philosophy'. In particular, Carnap was stirred by Russell's words:

> The one and only condition, I believe, which is necessary in order to secure for philosophy in the near future an achievement surpassing all that has hitherto been accomplished by philosophers, is the creation of a school of men with scientific training and philosophical interests, unhampered by the traditions of the past, and not misled by the literary methods of those who copy the ancients in all except their merits.[35]

Inspired by Russell, Carnap 'made numerous attempts at analyzing concepts of ordinary language relating to things in our environment and their observable properties and relations, and at constructing definitions of these concepts with the help of symbolic logic'.[36] He endeavoured to build up his pristine 'construction of the world' from the most basic elements, which he took to be (following Mach and Avenarius) 'experiences', or sensations. The magnum opus in which this project was laid out was *Der logische Aufbau der Welt* ('The Logical Construction of the World', 1928). Its 'main problem', Carnap wrote in 1961, 'concerns the possibility of the rational reconstruction of the concepts of all fields of knowledge on the basis of concepts that refer to the immediately given' – that is, what is immediately given in sense experience.[37] Carnap proposed

---

33 As quoted in Carus, *Carnap*, p. 59. Carus notes that Carnap heavily underlined the quoted passage.

34 Carnap, 'Intellectual Autobiography', p. 9.

35 Quoted in ibid., p. 12.

36 Ibid., p. 15.

37 Rudolf Carnap, 'Preface to the Second Edition', in *The Logical Structure of the World, and Pseudoproblems in Philosophy*, p. v.

to do so by having all knowledge rest on 'protocol sentences' – statements referring only to a subject's sensations.

Protocol Sentences and the 'Public Phase' of the Circle

Members of the Circle were united in their insistence on the 'elimination of metaphysics'. This was thought not only to produce intellectual hygiene, but to form a bulwark against regressive social forces that sought to clothe their programmes in metaphysical notions such as that of the *Volk*. But how was the elimination of metaphysics best achieved? Neurath was unhappy with Carnap's 'logical construction of the world', with sensation reports as its basis. Instead of framing the basic 'protocol sentences' as phenomenalistic sensation reports, Neurath proposed they should be stated in 'physicalist' terms. Neurath did not mean by 'physicalism' what it has come to mean in more recent analytic philosophy – a crude materialism according to which reality is exhausted by material things. Instead, physicalism presupposed a world of intersubjectively available objects, by contrast with the egocentric presuppositions of phenomenalism. When children learn to speak, it is in physicalist language, that of a world of objects inhabited by a nexus of interrelated subjects; to abstract away from this to produce the world of private sensations favoured by phenomenalism was to do violence to our basic experience.

Carnap and Neurath were the principal players in the so-called protocol sentence debate carried out in the 1930s over the nature and status of protocol sentences. This debate was complex; but there was agreement on the need for science to be orientated by some set of basic statements. In a discussion of such statements, Carnap offered various kinds of examples of observation reports, ranging from 'joy now' and 'there, now, blue; there, red' to 'A red cube is on the table'.[38] For Neurath, they were more elaborate. For instance: 'Otto's protocol at 3:17: [Otto's speech-thinking at 3:16 was: (at 3:15 there was a table in the room perceived by Otto)].'[39]

Note Neurath's multiple mentions of himself ('Otto') in the third person in his example, reflecting his rejection of the phenomenalist strategy of building out from what is purportedly given in first-personal

38 Rudolf Carnap, *The Unity of Science*, pp. 46–7.

39 Otto Neurath, 'Protocol Statements', in *Philosophical Papers 1913–1946*, p. 93.

experience. For Neurath, this was of a piece with the project of the unity of science. The unity of science – which literally meant turning all of the natural and social sciences into one unified, empirical discipline – could not be achieved so long as there was a bridge to be crossed from the first-personal into the intersubjective.

Prior to the protocol sentence debate, and Neurath's development of an intersubjective physicalism, the Circle had itself entered a 'public phase' with the foundation of the Ernst Mach Society in 1928. Its project of the unity of science could thereby begin to reach out into society. Neurath gave the Society's inaugural lecture to a packed Ceremonial Hall in the Old Town Hall, under the title 'Ernst Mach and the Exact Worldview'. A year later, the Society published a pamphlet entitled *Scientific World-Conception: The Vienna Circle*, which had been authored by Neurath, Hahn and Carnap. The term 'philosophy' was deliberately avoided, as was 'positivism'. 'Scientific world-conception' (*wissenschaftliche Weltauffassung*) was settled on; the word *Weltanschauung* ('worldview'), which Neurath had still used in his inaugural lecture, was eschewed given its metaphysical connotations. Now, at Neurath's urging, the group for the first time boldly called itself '*the* Vienna Circle'.

The manifesto bears out how the Left Vienna Circle, at least, was able to think of itself as unifying liberalism with social radicalism.[40] There was, to be sure, an exemption from political activity for those who wished to stay 'on the icy slopes of logic' and 'may even disdain mingling with the masses'; but, for the fundamental programme set out in the manifesto, the unity of science and the social projects of universal education and universal housing were of a piece. The achievement of universal enlightenment required not only a consistently rational conception of enquiry, but the rational transformation of society as a precondition for the enquiry to succeed. In practice, Neurath made concerted contributions to housing projects. All of the most significant Circle members took part in adult education, across an extremely wide range of topics, extending from physics to 'morality and culture'.[41]

40 For an excellent account, see Donata Romizi, 'The Vienna Circle's "Scientific World-Conception": Philosophy of Science in a Political Arena'. See also Malachi Haim Hacohen, 'The Culture of Viennese Science and the Riddle of Austrian Liberalism'.

41 Those who taught at Viennese adult education institutes were Frank (1907–13, 1915/16, 1919/20, 1931/32), Neurath (1907–10, 1919–24, 1926–34), Hahn (1908, 1909, 1923/24), Zilsel (1916–36), Schlick (1921/22, 1933/34, 1936), Waismann (1921–35),

In addition to the founding of the Society as a public forum, a journal, a series of monographs, and a series of international conferences were launched. Carnap and Reichenbach took charge of the journal, *Erkenntnis*, which replaced an existing journal, *Annalen der Philosophie und philosophischen Kritik*. Schlick and Frank edited the monograph series, *Schriften zur wissenschaftlichen Weltauffassung* (Writings for a Scientific World Conception). Conferences for the unity of science were held in Prague (1934), Paris (1935), Copenhagen (1936), Prague (1937), Cambridge, England (1938) and Cambridge, Massachusetts (1939) – the range of locations indicating the diaspora into which the Circle had been driven by the events of 1933–34, in which fascists tightened their grip on Austria.

As the Ernst Mach Society came under pressure from fascism, Schlick strenuously argued that it was politically neutral. He could, to some extent, argue this in good faith, since his own position was more centrist than that set out in the manifesto. The Society as a whole, however, was overt about its interest in Marxism. In 1930, Otto Bauer, the prominent Austromarxist and deputy leader of the Social Democratic Workers' Party (SDAPÖ), lectured to the Society on 'Industrial Rationalization and Science'.[42] Philipp Frank, who had given lecture tours in the Soviet Union, spoke in 1932 on 'Philosophical Trends in the Soviet Union'.[43] Marxism was a live topic of discussion, even if few of the Society's members espoused it.

Modernism and Bauhaus Dessau

In the 1920s the Circle developed a significant connection with the Bauhaus Dessau, the visionary school of art and architecture characterized by a drive to integrate the arts and by ambitious social imperatives; for a time, a group of Circle members became closely involved with the institution. The connection has been discussed by the historian of science Peter Galison, in an essay entitled 'Aufbau/Bauhaus', exploiting the proliferation of the language of *Aufbau* across Carnap's best-known philosophical

---

Feigl (1927–30), and Carnap (1934). Further details are in Friedrich Stadler, *The Vienna Circle: Studies in the Origins, Development, and Influence of Logical Empiricism*, pp. 308–33.

42 Ibid., p. 156.

43 Ibid., pp. 147, 157.

work and a range of Marxist publications.[44] Two themes operative in Galison's essay are, on the one hand, the 'transparent' constructions signalled by the very idea of *Aufbau*, and reflected in Carnap's work, and on the other, an ideal of technocratic social transformation. The philosophers Angela Potochnik and Audrey Yap have, in turn, emphasized the distinctness of these tendencies.[45] This distinctness, detectable both in the Bauhaus and in the Circle (Carnap being a better fit for the former, Neurath for the latter) leads back to the basic bifurcation in Viennese modernism, into aestheticism on the one hand and technocracy on the other.

The Bauhaus, having originally been founded in Weimar in 1919 and expelled by a new right-wing government in 1925, reopened its doors in 1926 in Dessau. Neurath was present at the opening. In a short article in the Viennese journal *Der Aufbau*, he enthusiastically evoked the strident modernist aesthetic of its buildings and the 'powerful achievement of lively people who have succeeded in seeing through an unpopular cause'.[46] Two years later, in 1928, the Bauhaus entered a new phase, as its first director, Walter Gropius, retired and handed over the directorship to the Swiss socialist architect Hannes Meyer, who had designed the social housing project Freidorf in Basel. During Meyer's two-year tenure, which shifted the Bauhaus to the left and towards technocracy, it engaged in a significant collaboration with the Vienna Circle.

Meyer's strident functionalist approach to architecture was not admired by all; Philipp Frank's architect brother Josef was one of his detractors.[47] Meyer called his approach *Die neue Baulehre* ('the new doctrine of building') and declared in his 1928 manifesto, entitled 'bauen' and published in the journal *bauhaus*:

1. sex life	5. personal hygiene	9. cooking
2. sleeping habits	6. weather protection	10. heating
3. pets	7. hygiene in the home	11. exposure to the sun
4. gardening	8. car maintenance	12. service

these are the only motives when building a house.

---

44 Peter Galison, 'Aufbau/Bauhaus: Logical Positivism and Architectural Modernism'.

45 Angela Potochnik and Audrey Yap, 'Revisiting Galison's "Aufbau/Bauhaus" in Light of Neurath's Philosophical Projects'.

46 Otto Neurath, 'Das Neue Bauhaus in Dessau', p. 217. I thank Thomas Uebel for help obtaining this text.

47 Peter Bernhard, 'Carnap und das Bauhaus'.

Meyer's text culminated in the proclamation:

> building is nothing but organization:
> social, technical, economic, psychical organization.[48]

Meyer's 'unaesthetic aesthetics', and his insistence that buildings should be low-cost and directed towards the fulfilment of social needs, could not last long. His leftism became increasingly unpalatable to the authorities, and in 1930 he was dismissed, to be replaced by Ludwig Mies van der Rohe, who took the Bauhaus in the more aestheticist direction associated with De Stijl. Meyer emigrated to the Soviet Union, participating in the redevelopment of Moscow as part of the first Five-Year Plan, before escaping Stalin's purges and settling in Geneva in 1936.

During Meyer's tenure, Neurath was twice invited back to the Bauhaus to lecture ('Pictorial Statistics and the Present', 27 May 1929; 'History and Economy', 29 June 1930).[49] In July 1929, Meyer invited Herbert Feigl to spend a week there, during which he gave lectures and got to know Wassily Kandinsky, Paul Klee and others.[50] Rudolf Carnap came to Dessau on 15 October 1929, and 'was plunged immediately into a discussion about whether one should pursue only the aesthetic properties of materials'.[51] He lectured on 'Science and Life' and, the following day, on 'The Logical Construction of the World'. As Galison suggests with some plausibility, whereas for Meyer, architecture was to be rendered 'in the neutral and universal idiom of engineering', Carnap 'pursued the analogous goal for philosophy'.[52]

The days of this community of artists and architects seeking to reshape society were numbered, however – even under the directorship of Mies van der Rohe, who moved the Bauhaus to Berlin in October 1932. On 11 April 1933, police trucks arrived to close the Berlin Bauhaus. On 10 August, it was formally dissolved.[53]

48 Hannes Meyer, 'Building', pp. 119–20.

49 Werner Kleinerüschkamp, ed., *hannes meyer 1889–1954: architekt urbanist lehrer*, pp. 177–8.

50 Galison, 'Aufbau/Bauhaus', p. 718.

51 Ibid., p. 734.

52 Ibid., p. 740.

53 Ibid., p. 746.

Otto Neurath and Full Socialization

Undoubtedly the most left-wing member of the Circle was Otto Neurath. Neurath was remarkable in not only working out a unified programme in which science and socialist politics were regarded as one, but for his active involvement in leftist politics early on in his career, when he had been a driving force in the Bavarian Soviet Republic.

Neurath, unlike many others in the Circle, had been born in Vienna itself, to a Jewish father and a Protestant mother. His father, Wilhelm Neurath, was from a poor family in Svätý Jur, near Bratislava, but rose to become professor of economics at an institute for agriculture, the Hochschule für Bodenkultur in Vienna. Neurath *père*'s non-Marxist radicalism with respect to economic and social problems would continue to exert an important influence, often showing up in the son's writings. Neurath *fils* studied economics, history and philosophy at the University of Vienna, where he met Frank and Hahn. Having written his doctoral dissertation at the University of Berlin on ancient economic history, he returned to Vienna to teach at the Neue Wiener Handelsakademie (New Business School). After serving in the First World War, a study of war economy, suggesting parallels between a war economy and a socialized economy, led to a post in the War Ministry, and to the directorship of the Museum of War Economy in Leipzig. Although he had completed his *Habilitation* in 1917, and was now qualified to teach at the University of Heidelberg, he resolved to 'conclude my life of contemplation and to begin one of action to help to introduce an administrative economy that will bring happiness'.[54] He had been gradually working out the idea of the administration of an 'economy in kind', or 'full socialization'.

An extraordinary opportunity for Neurath to try his hand at implementing full socialization was provided by the Bavarian Revolution of 1918–19. His position now resembled Marxism, but prioritized the reorganization of social production over the expropriation of the means of production – a revision that was scandalous to orthodox Marxists. While he came under fire for his conception of socialization by means of the creation of an 'economy in kind', it should not be assumed that Neurath was naive when it came to economics; the 'socialization debate'

54 Neurath, quoted in Nancy Cartwright, Jordi Cat, Lola Fleck and Thomas E. Uebel, *Otto Neurath: Philosophy between Science and Politics*, p. 21.

he helped to spark operated at a sophisticated level, offering a serious treatment of questions concerning the problems and possibilities of a planned economy that remain live to this day.[55]

Events in Bavaria moved at a frenetic pace.[56] On 8 November 1918, the day after King Ludwig III of Bavaria fled, a People's State of Bavaria (Volksstaat Bayern) was declared. Its leader was Kurt Eisner, who, from the first, had difficulties retaining control, thanks to his anti-war and thus allegedly unpatriotic record as a member of the Independent Social Democratic Party, which the media weaponized in a vociferous campaign against him. When, on 21 February 1919, Eisner was assassinated by the aristocrat and far-right activist Anton Graf Arco-Valley, chaos ensued. Some calm was imposed on the mayhem when Johannes Hoffmann, a former schoolteacher and SPD politician, formed a new Volksstaat government on 17 March. But, very soon, massive unrest was unleashed among the working class by the news that Béla Kun had declared a Hungarian Soviet Republic on 21 March, fuelling demands for such a soviet republic in Bavaria. On 7 April, the writer and USPD politician Ernst Toller declared the first Bavarian Soviet Republic, so that two governments now effectively claimed to rule Bavaria. The Hoffmann government retreated to Bamberg (in the north of Bavaria). Only five days later, on 12 April, Toller's regime was replaced by a second soviet regime, under the leadership of the Russian Bolshevik Eugen Leviné. Violent struggles ensued between the Hoffmann government and Leviné's second soviet government. Hoffmann was aided by the use of 20,000 men of the right-wing paramilitary Freikorps, under Lieutenant General Burghard von Oven, while soviet forces executed hostages. On 6 May, Oven declared control of the city of Munich, ending the revolution and all prospects of a soviet government. Leviné was condemned to death and executed by firing squad; others, including Toller, were given prison sentences.

Neurath's involvement had begun when he travelled to Munich on 23 January 1919 to discuss his economic programme with Eisner and

55 For an illuminating discussion, see Thomas E. Uebel, 'Introduction' to Otto Neurath, *Economic Writings*.

56 For a succinct overview of the Bavarian Revolution, see Ulrich Kluge, *Die deutsche Revolution 1918–1919: Staat, Politik und Gesellschaft zwischen Weltkrieg und Kapp-Putsch*, pp. 129–35. Diverging partisan accounts are given by the American historian Allan Mitchell, *Revolution in Bavaria, 1918–1919: The Eisner Regime and the Soviet Republic*, and by the GDR historian Hans Beyer's *Die Revolution in Bayern 1918–19*.

his minister of finance, Edgar Jaffé, and gave a talk entitled 'The Character and Course of Socialization' to the Workers' and Soldiers' Council, headed by Eisner. Once demands for a soviet republic flared up in response to the news of Kun's achievements in Hungary, Jaffé invited Neurath back for further talks. Neurath, known for his boisterous energy and powers of persuasion, immediately organized a leafleting campaign to inform the population about full socialization. On 25 March he was appointed president of the Central Economic Administration (Zentralwirtschaftsamt); he calculated that full socialization could be implemented within 'five to ten years'.[57] The Administration began by socializing the newspapers. Once the first Soviet Republic was declared, on 7 April, Neurath supported a decision to close all the banks in order to counteract the capital flight that had been precipitated by the revolution. Expert councils were announced, and the socialization of the mines was begun.

On 13 April, Neurath was arrested, along with other members of the first soviet government, but then released. Although he disapproved of the methods of the second soviet government that now took power, he remained head of the Central Economic Administration. On 16 May, following the defeat of the revolution, he was again arrested, and this time accused of high treason. At his trial, Neurath claimed his role had been purely administrative, not political – not an entirely implausible claim, given his bureaucratic conception of socialization, which (controversially, from a Marxist viewpoint) meant he was ready to work with anyone, regardless of political persuasion, if they were deemed to advance the goals of socialization. He was convicted of assisting high treason, and sentenced to eighteen months' imprisonment. Luckily, thanks to the intervention of the Austromarxist Otto Bauer, then Austria's foreign minister, the sentence was commuted to deportation to Austria.

Neurath was, as Otto Bauer testified in evidence at his trial, remarkably indifferent to how, and by whom, power was wielded in order to enforce socialization. Bauer called his socialism 'authoritarian', specifying that Neurath 'recommends enforcing from the top down a planned order and a transformation of economic life by a government over and above society', and 'does not care whether this is the Austro-Hungarian army command, a democratic parliamentary government or a council dictatorship'.[58] Neurath's career in the Bavarian Revolution could thus

57 Cartwright, Cat, Fleck and Uebel, *Otto Neurath*, p. 47.

58 Quoted in ibid., p. 55.

be regarded as embodying an uncompromising and activist leftism, but also as falling short of even the most minimal precepts of socialism. Judgements of Neurath's involvement have accordingly varied widely. The anarchist writer Erich Mühsam, who had been a key member of the first Soviet Republic, criticized the indiscriminateness with which Neurath presented his ideas to the bourgeoisie, as well as to the working class.[59] It was 'dilettantish', Mühsam maintained, to think his socializing measures could be carried out without changing the constitution of the state.[60] In the debate between revolutionary and evolutionary forms of socialism, however, Neurath was unequivocally on the side of those who favoured abrupt, non-continuous transformation.

Neurath made no bones about his deviations from some of the cherished tenets of orthodox Marxists. There was no need for a labour theory of value, a theory of exploitation, or a deterministic theory of class revolution. Instead, he was guided by a 'felicitology', or calculus of happiness, in the service of 'social Epicureanism'.[61] Whereas a capitalist society aimed at maximum profit for each individual business, a happy society aimed at 'a maximum of happiness, of the enjoyment of life in a community and of utility'.[62] In a happy society, production was to be allocated for the sake of the production of happiness, not profit:

> The theory of the socialist economy acknowledges only one manager or producer – the society – who organises the production and shapes the standard of living on the basis of an economic plan, without calculations of losses or profits and without taking the circulation of money as a basis, be it in the form of coins or labour. This is an opinion that corresponds with the basic ideas of Marx and Engels.[63]

Whether or not Neurath is right that his opinion 'corresponds with' the ideas of Marx and Engels, there is no doubt that Neurathian socialism

59 Erich Mühsam, *Von Eisner bis Leviné: Die Entstehung und Niederlage der Bayerischen Räterepublik*, p. 46.

60 Ibid., p. 47.

61 It is unclear what distinguishes social Epicureanism from utilitarianism. Cartwright et al., *Otto Neurath*, p. 30, seek to distinguish the two sharply on the basis that utilitarianism is concerned 'with the individual's desire for happiness'. This does not appear to be true of most forms of utilitarianism, however.

62 Neurath, quoted in Cartwright et al., *Otto Neurath*, p. 29.

63 Neurath, quoted in ibid., p. 37.

is as uncompromising as Marxism in requiring total collectivization, and regarding welfare socialism as entirely inadequate. In this, Neurath is far *more* left wing than he is often imagined to be today by some of his admirers in academic philosophy, for whom his radicalism consists merely in some fairly tepid ideas about the value-ladenness of scientific practice.

Neurath, having been returned to Austria, never again had the opportunity to attempt to enact full socialization. Even if, in the election of May 1919, the Social Democrats gained sole control of the Viennese government, marking the beginning of 'Red Vienna', the approach of the Austrian Social Democrats was piecemeal, in stark contrast to the all-out approach implemented in the few days Neurath served in the first and second Bavarian soviet republics. His enthusiasm for Marxism, such as it had been, also declined. In 1933, he expressed regret to Carnap that he had previously 'had the inclination to emphasize the positive side', but 'I now feel – and I very much regret it – that I did not emphasize the Marxist deficiencies. . . . One sees *how weak* the foundation was in its components. We must build [*aufbauen*] anew, for this factual work is necessary and the many-sided refusal to accept Marxist superficiality.'[64]

The Vienna Circle and the Frankfurt School

In the same year that the Schlick Circle began to meet, 1924, the Institute for Social Research was established in Frankfurt. Later to become known as the Frankfurt School, and gain a reputation as one of the most famous groupings of Marxist intellectuals in the West, the Institute grew out of the Erste Marxistische Arbeitswoche (First Marxist Work Week), held in Ilmenau in May 1923, and attended by Georg Lukács, Karl Korsch and others. It is well known that the Frankfurt School came to formulate and maintain a highly critical stance on logical positivism, one that built rejection of positivism into its Marxism. It is less well known that the Institute and the Circle share common roots, and that, as Nazism solidified its power in Europe, the two groups sought to cooperate.[65]

---

64 Neurath to Carnap, 6 April 1933, quoted in Galison, 'Aufbau/Bauhaus', p. 743.

65 An excellent account of the evolving relationship of the Frankfurt School with the Vienna Circle is given in Dahms, *Positivismusstreit*.

When the Institute was first set up – with money from Felix Weil, son of the wealthy grain merchant Hermann Weil – the man appointed as its director was Carl Grünberg. Grünberg, who had studied in Vienna, counts as one of the founders of Austromarxism, and numbered among his students its leading lights Otto Bauer, Rudolf Hilferding and Karl Renner. Not only did Grünberg come from a left-wing Viennese environment that would have been familiar to the Circle, but key members of the Institute had positivist beginnings. Max Horkheimer, who replaced Grünberg as director in 1930, wrote his doctoral dissertation under the supervision of Hans Cornelius, widely regarded as Mach's 'official representative', as did Theodor Adorno. Horkheimer, in an unpublished review of the 1927 German translation of Lenin's *Materialism and Empirio-Criticism*, while agreeing with Lenin's assessment of the empirio-criticism adopted by Bogdanov and others as signalling political resignation, still took the side of Mach and Cornelius against Lenin's accusations of subjective idealism, solipsism and fideism.[66]

In the early years of the Institute, largely appreciative reviews appeared in its house journal, *Archiv für die Geschichte des Sozialismus und der Arbeiterbewegung* (later to become the *Zeitschrift für Sozialforschung*), of works by Neurath, Frank, Carnap, Wittgenstein and Edgar Zilsel.[67] Towards the end of the 1920s, however, the Institute's allegiance to positivism began to fracture. Lukács and Korsch insisted that Marxism should be regarded as a distinctive philosophical approach with dialectic as its characteristic method, which must be insulated against any kind of empiricism, including the previously popular approach of Cornelius. The Frankfurt School in this period directed its ire not just at Machism but also at psychoanalysis, as the psychological manifestation of the same pathology. It was the Circle that, by contrast, defended Freud, who is explicitly referred to in its manifesto, even if his doctrines would have to be reconstructed

---

66 Max Horkheimer, '[Über Lenins *Materialismus und Empiriokritizismus*]', in *Gesammelte Schriften*, vol. 11.

67 Dahms, *Positivismusstreit*, pp. 49–54. Horkheimer spoke of Wittgenstein's 'excellent *Tractatus Logico-Philosophicus*', which he criticized only for its invocation of 'the mystical' (Dahms, *Positivismusstreit*, p. 53). Benjamin included a largely sympathetic discussion of Carnap's *Logical Syntax of Language*, entering only the mildly critical remark that it was peculiar that something that treated the 'form of representation of language' as a 'calculus' could carry the name 'logistic' (ibid., p. 54).

empirically due to their (in the words of Neurath) 'very many metaphysical formulations'.[68]

Both the Institute and the Circle were fundamentally extra-institutional groupings; although the Institute was linked to the still young University of Frankfurt, it made its own appointments. The Institute operated, in a phrase used by Grünberg and taken over by his successor Horkheimer, the 'dictatorship of the director'; the Circle was under the perhaps somewhat more benign leadership of Schlick, who nonetheless had sole control of its membership. Whereas Circle members tended to be closely involved with the Austrian Social Democratic Workers' Party (SDAPÖ), Horkheimer and Adorno remained aloof from politics. Horkheimer judged that the SPD 'had too many "reasons"; the Communists, who often relied on coercion, too few', and so did not join either party.[69] In an essay called 'The Impotence of the German Working Class' (published under a pseudonym in *Dämmerung* in 1931), he alleged that the Communists, while correctly diagnosing the situation of society, lacked the knowledge required to carry out the revolution successfully, whereas the Social Democrats perhaps possessed the requisite knowledge but failed to experience the urgent necessity of change.[70]

The Institute and the Circle experienced a common lot in facing the threat of closure by the Nazis, which materialized for the Institute in 1933 and for the Circle in 1934. In Germany the Nazi 'Law for the Restoration of the Professional Civil Service' came into effect on 7 April 1933; a week later, Horkheimer was removed from his professorship. Like most Institute members, Horkheimer took steps to leave Germany. Adorno, on the other hand, who 'had no personal ties at all to socialist political life', decided to stay.[71] Drawing on his experience as a music critic, he applied for a position in Joseph Goebbels's Reichsschrifttumskammer. His application was rejected on the grounds that, as a 'non-Aryan', he was not suitable for the 'administration of the German cultural heritage'.[72] He then attempted to transfer his *Habilitation* to

68 According to Marie Jahoda, Freud was himself a member of the Ernst Mach Society (Dahms, *Positivismusstreit*, p. 46).

69 Martin Jay, *The Dialectical Imagination: A History of the Frankfurt School and the Institute of Social Research 1923–1950*, p. 14.

70 The text is quoted at Dahms, *Positivismusstreit*, pp. 39–40.

71 Perry Anderson, *Considerations on Western Marxism*, p. 33.

72 See the rejection letter from the Reichsschrifttumskammer, signed on behalf of Richard Suchenwirth, dated 20 February 1935 (Bodleian Library, Oxford, Archive of the Society for the Protection of Science and Learning, MSS. S.P.S.L. 322/2).

the University of Vienna. When this failed, he instead applied, now successfully, to become an 'advanced student' working towards a second doctorate at Merton College, Oxford. There he worked from 1934 until 1937 on a (never completed) critique of Husserl, under the supervision of Gilbert Ryle.[73] The Institute moved to Geneva, then to New York.

With hindsight, it seems almost unbelievable that Horkheimer harboured plans for 'unification' (*Vereinigung*) with two positivist institutions – Neurath's Mundaneum Institute in The Hague (itself the continuation in exile of the Viennese Gesellschafts- und Wirtschafts-museum, which had been closed by the fascists) and Marie Jahoda's Wirtschaftspsychologische Forschungsstelle (Research Centre for Economic Psychology) in Vienna.[74] Opportunism would seem to be a significant explanatory factor. Horkheimer worked actively on the surface to establish collaboration with the positivists, but tacitly harboured serious reservations bordering on scorn. As early as December 1934, he wrote to the Dutch Institute member Andries Sternheim: 'The people of this tendency, who constantly emphasize that one has to stick to the facts and to do pure science, seem to limit themselves to a narrow field of expertise, so that they can talk crude nonsense about all important things.'[75] Nevertheless, Horkheimer met Neurath in Holland in January 1936 for discussions, and declared himself prepared to support the latter's conditions of life research (*Lebenslagenforschung*) in the next year with $500 from the Institute.[76] Further meetings were held in New York in October and November 1936. To these meetings, other interested parties were invited in addition to Neurath. A first such meeting was attended by Paul Tillich and Paul Lazarsfeld, a second by Sidney Hook, Friedrich Pollock, Herbert Marcuse, Leo Löwenthal, Ernest Nagel and Meyer Schapiro. At the second meeting, Hook and Neurath attacked dialectic. According to Hook's account of the meeting, to Neurath dialectic was either 'synonymous with what passed ordinarily as scientific methods' or 'a kind of hocus pocus'.[77]

---

73 A large typescript from this period ('Konvolut zu Husserl') is preserved in the Adorno Archive. Adorno's study of Husserl eventually formed the basis for his *Metakritik der Erkenntnistheorie*, as well as for an article published in English. On Adorno's stay in Oxford, see Andreas Kramer and Evelyn Wilcock, '"A Preserve for Professional Philosophers": Adornos Husserl-Dissertation 1934–37 und ihr Oxforder Kontext'.

74 Dahms, *Positivismusstreit*, p. 70.

75 Quoted in ibid., p. 81.

76 Ibid., p. 76.

77 Sidney Hook, 'The Institute for Social Research – Addendum'.

Despite these tensions about dialectic, Horkheimer wrote to Neurath on 24 November 1936 of his and his confrères' enthusiasm for occupying themselves more intensively with logical positivism. Neurath, reporting this to Carnap, scoffed: 'unfortunately Horkheimer is of the opinion that Husserl is much clearer than Mach'.[78] In addition, Neurath conveyed to Carnap that Horkheimer wanted to organize a multi-day symposium in January, which would be attended by Nagel and Hook; Carnap would get his journey paid by the Institute. Carnap replied on 28 December: 'Who is Horkheimer? I suspect he is someone from the New School for Social Research. Is that right? And what is his journal in which he wants to treat of our entire movement?'[79] (Carnap was in principle willing to participate, but later pulled out, citing a back problem.)

Privately, Horkheimer had already made up his mind to prepare an intellectual attack on logical positivism. He wrote to Adorno on 22 October 1936: 'Basically, the whole thing is only a miserable rearguard action of the formalistic epistemology of liberalism, which also in this area turns into open servility to fascism.'[80] And to Henryk Grossmann on 27 November, he wrote:

> As is well known, this is currently the most popular philosophical trend in academic circles, which derives on the one hand from the mathematical philosophy of Russell and Whitehead, and on the other hand from the empirio-criticism of Mach and the so-called Vienna Circle. One can hardly exaggerate the triumph of this direction in scientifically interested circles, especially in the Anglo-American world. It is about time that an adequate criticism is given from our side.[81]

The title of the polemical essay Horkheimer went on to produce, 'The Latest Attack on Metaphysics', refers to the positivists' attack on the metaphysical philosophy of Heidegger and others; Horkheimer claimed that, ironically, logical positivism was just as much a metaphysics as what it attacked. The essay is remarkable as an early attempt at the ideology critique of a strand of analytic philosophy. In it Horkheimer drew heavily on his correspondence with Adorno, who was feeding him

78 Dahms, *Positivismusstreit*, pp. 84–5.

79 Quoted in ibid., p. 85.

80 Horkheimer to Adorno, 22 October 1936, in Horkheimer, *Gesammelte Schriften*, vol. 15: *Briefwechsel 1913–1936*, p. 689.

81 Quoted in Dahms, *Positivismusstreit*, p. 86.

suggested lines of attack from Oxford, as an 'advanced student' of Ryle. Adorno suggested attacking, in turn, various aspects of logical positivism: the formal logic (or 'logistic') it sought to incorporate; its conception of experience; and the attempt – bound to fail, Adorno thought – satisfactorily to bring together logic and empiricism, as the movement announced it wanted to do in its very title.[82]

Fortunately for Horkheimer, he left to one side Adorno's suggested criticism of logistic, which hinged on a mistaken conception of what was at stake in Russell's Paradox, instead complaining in rather more general terms that the neopositivists' logic amounted to a 'confounding of calculatory with rational thinking'.[83] But Horkheimer did pursue Adorno's more promising suggested lines of attack focusing on the positivists' conception of experience and their difficulty bringing logic and empiricism together. Their conception of experience was said to be inherently passive, thereby engendering a tendency to resignation (or acquiescence in the status quo). Just as much as Heidegger's 'neoromantic metaphysics', neopositivism, because of its reliance on observation, subjects itself passively to 'oppression' by the 'most capital-endowed groups'.[84] Echoing Adorno's suggestions once again, Horkheimer complained that 'the two elements of logical empiricism are only superficially connected' and that 'logic is in conflict with empiricism'.[85]

Horkheimer's own preferred philosophical position, unfortunately, remained remarkably unclear. It had something to do with 'dialectic', but he was only able to talk about this in the vaguest terms:

> Dialectical thought integrates the empirical constituents into structures of experience which are important not only for the limited purposes served by science, but also for the historical interests with which dialectical thought is connected.[86]

---

82 Adorno to Horkheimer, 28 November 1936, in Theodor W. Adorno and Max Horkheimer, *Briefwechsel*, vol. 1, pp. 756–61.

83 Max Horkheimer, 'The Latest Attack on Metaphysics', in *Critical Theory: Selected Essays*, p. 180. Quotations from this translation are modified where needed.

84 Ibid., p. 140. Horkheimer's claim that the positivists' conception of observation was inherently passive might be contested on various fronts. His own argument seemed to rest on a crude misunderstanding of the opening proposition of Wittgenstein's *Tractatus*, 'The world is everything that is the case', which Horkheimer called 'the view expressed in the chief work of modern empiricism'.

85 Horkheimer, 'Latest Attack on Metaphysics', pp. 172–3.

86 Ibid., p. 162.

> In the dialectical theory, the interest in the unfolding of the general that transforms itself historically, this subjective and changeable moment, is not regarded as a sign of error, but as an inherent factor of knowledge.[87]

> Dialectical logic has reference to thought involved in the interpretation [*Nachkonstruktion*] of living reality, to thought in process, and not merely to static expression.[88]

Horkheimer's piece appeared in the Institute's *Zeitschrift für Sozialforschung* in the spring of 1937. When Neurath got sight of it in June, he was taken aback by the severity of the polemic, writing to Horkheimer: 'At first the shock rendered me speechless.'[89] Neurath's shock is unsurprising, given that Horkheimer had continued to maintain a friendly façade in correspondence. On 24 November 1936, Horkheimer wrote to Neurath: 'I can assure you that both discussion evenings you granted us were extraordinarily stimulating for me personally. You have intensified not only my desire but also the desire of the other participants to continue our engagement with logical empiricism.'[90] Friendly letters continued to pass between Horkheimer and Neurath in May and June 1937, even after Horkheimer's piece had gone to press.[91]

Neurath now sat down to compose a brief response to Horkheimer's essay.[92] His response partly misses Horkheimer's point. Horkheimer, according to Neurath, 'seems to require that one should study "dialectics"'; Neurath adds, mischievously, 'it would be helpful to know which textbook teaches the "dialectics" he advocates (the term is very ambiguous)'.[93] Neurath will have been aware that Horkheimer and his fellow would-be dialecticians would have regarded such demands to have dialectic explained, as if it could be laid out as a methodology specifiable in abstraction from what it is applied to, as hopelessly naive. Effectively, the dialogical situation between Neurath and Horkheimer was that of a standoff. Neurath felt, plausibly, that he was equipped with an answer

87 Ibid., p. 163.

88 Ibid., p. 177.

89 Neurath to Horkheimer, 21 June 1937, quoted in John O'Neill and Thomas Uebel, 'Horkheimer and Neurath: Restarting a Disrupted Debate', p. 76.

90 Max Horkheimer, *A Life in Letters: Selected Correspondence*, p. 86.

91 See Dahms, *Positivismusstreit*, p. 120.

92 This reply has now been published in English translation as Otto Neurath, 'Unity of Science and Logical Empiricism: A Reply'.

93 Ibid., p. 20.

to the question by what tribunal science was to be judged: it was *the whole of science*. There could, after all, be no enquiry other than empirical enquiry. Horkheimer, by contrast, could supply no such answer – but, whereas to Neurath this situation seemed to bespeak vice, to Horkheimer it signalled virtue.

Horkheimer point-blank refused to publish Neurath's response in the *Zeitschrift*, claiming there to have been a misunderstanding: 'Neither Pollock nor I wanted to guarantee an extension of the debate on logical empiricism in the journal through extensive discussion. Rather, we declared in the journal at the very beginning that it wasn't to provide a platform for contradictory views.'[94] He suggested Neurath publish his response in *Erkenntnis* instead, unaware that the positivists' journal had been discontinued under pressure from the Nazis.[95] Neurath persisted; Horkheimer continued to refuse. Finally, Neurath asked for the manuscript back.[96] Thus ended the sorry saga between Horkheimer and Neurath. Any prospect of significant contact or collaboration between Institute and Circle was over.

The Death of the Vienna Circle

The Vienna Circle never decisively disbanded, although the Ernst Mach Society was formally dissolved in early 1934. The Circle had already crumbled as Vienna fell progressively under the shadow of fascism. Feigl, a Jew who struggled to find employment in German-speaking countries for racial reasons, emigrated to the United States in 1930 (first temporarily, on a Rockefeller Research Fellowship at Harvard, then permanently in 1931). Hahn died in 1934. In that same year, Neurath fled to the Netherlands. (He would die in Oxford in 1945.) Carnap, who had already left Vienna for Prague in 1931, emigrated to the United States in 1936; Philipp Frank and Gustav Bergmann followed in 1938, Edgar Zilsel in 1939. Schlick was murdered by a mentally ill student in 1936. As we shall see in Chapter 5, Carnap, Frank and Feigl played a new role as progenitors of analytic philosophy in the United States, aided by Hans Reichenbach from the Berlin Circle and Alfred Tarski from

94 Horkheimer to Neurath, 29 December 1937, in Horkheimer, *A Life in Letters*, p. 128.

95 Dahms, *Positivismusstreit*, p. 180.

96 Neurath to Horkheimer, 21 February 1938, quoted in Dahms, *Positivismusstreit*, p. 181.

Warsaw. In Vienna itself, the dissolution of the Circle left a philosophical void, to be filled by the Nazi Erich Heintel, who remained in his chair into the 1980s. The future of philosophy in Vienna would be dominated by right wingers. Interest in the Vienna Circle, kindled by scholars such as Rudolf Haller and Friedrich Stadler, came into its own very late. Today, it is kept alive by the enormously productive scholarly work of the Institute Vienna Circle, producing many books on the Circle every year.

4

Ordinary Language in the Home of Dullness

Cambridge and Vienna each contributed distinct streams of what would become analytic philosophy. Oxford was, by contrast, in the period leading up to the Second World War, a receptive vessel, hesitant at first about the philosophy emanating from Cambridge and Vienna, its enthusiasm for the new developments gathering pace only in the late 1930s. It was only after 1945 that its position changed dramatically, and it became the leading centre for analytic philosophy in Britain. An internal transformation – the introduction of a new postgraduate degree, the BPhil – attracted very large numbers of students, many of them from the United States. Before long, the philosophy that had grown up in Oxford known as 'ordinary language philosophy', essentially a recalibration of the techniques of G. E. Moore, ceded to an openness to American modes of the new analytic philosophy, exemplified in the work of Donald Davidson.

As an institution, Oxford was in many ways comparable to Cambridge. Both were very old – Oxford could trace its history back to 1096, Cambridge to 1209 – and both had the same collegiate structure. Both were relentlessly male, and placed severe obstacles in the way of women's participation. At both institutions, students received one-to-one tutorials from dons (in Cambridge called 'supervisions'), in which they were interrogated about the essay they had written for the occasion. Students were subjected to the iterated deployment against them of the question, 'What exactly does this mean?', to gloomy silences, and to other techniques of intellectual intimidation supposed to engender a self-critical attitude and cultivate the crafting of suitably precise statements of the expected kind.[1]

In Oxford, however, the number of students studying philosophy, and of dons teaching it, was always large, by contrast with the tiny philosophical community in Cambridge. Again in contrast with Cambridge, philosophy was always studied in conjunction with other subjects. Initially the menu available to Oxford students who wanted to study philosophy was 'Literae Humaniores' ('Greats'), a combination of ancient history and philosophy. In 1921, the new 'Honour School' of Philosophy, Politics and Economics ('PPE') was introduced, which made it possible to study philosophy without a knowledge of Greek and Latin.

At the time of the rebellion of Moore and Russell in 1898, Oxford philosophy was, in many ways, in a similar condition to Cambridge philosophy. 'Realists', led in Oxford by John Cook Wilson, did battle with idealists. As in Cambridge, the dominance of idealism was largely imagined rather than real. But, whereas the leading 'realist' figure on the Cambridge scene, Moore, went along with Russell's enthusiasm for the 'new logic', the equivalent figure in Oxford, Cook Wilson, categorically rejected the logic espoused by Russell and others. Only later did Oxford become receptive to the new directions emanating from Cambridge and Vienna, helped by the more outward-looking attitude of two philosophers, Gilbert Ryle and H. H. Price. Price went to Cambridge in 1924 to attend lectures by Moore and C. D. Broad; in the mid 1930s Ryle sent his student A. J. Ayer to Vienna to learn about logical positivism.[2] In 1937, a group of young men began to meet regularly under the leadership of Isaiah Berlin, at that time a philosopher rather than a historian of ideas, discussing topics from Cambridge and Vienna, and from the work of the American philosopher C. I. Lewis. This group was the basis of what started to call itself 'Oxford philosophy'.

Notably, Oxford's one significant pre-Second World War contribution to the dissemination of the concept of 'analytic philosophy' itself was when R. G. Collingwood – an insightful philosopher but a remote

1 Nikhil Krishnan reports being subjected to the question 'Now what *exactly* do you mean by . . . ?' in undergraduate tutorials in philosophy at Oxford as late as 2007. Nikhil Krishnan, *A Terribly Serious Adventure: Philosophy at Oxford 1900–60*, p. 3.

2 See H. H. Price's acknowledgement in *Perception*, p. vii. I owe the information about the date of Price's visit to Cambridge to Michael Kremer.

figure in Oxford – used it pejoratively in 1933 to group together philosophers of whom he disapproved, in one of the first appearances of the expression in print. Only after the war, and Collingwood's death in 1943, could Oxford be plausibly considered a centre actively promoting analytic philosophy. It did so under the energetic reign of the man who took over from Collingwood as Waynflete Professor of Metaphysical Philosophy, Gilbert Ryle.

Ryle had been a personal friend of Wittgenstein, and drew on his work when he offered an early instance of 'ordinary language philosophy' in his 1932 essay 'Systematically Misleading Expressions'. It was J. L. Austin, however, who, modifying Wittgenstein while simultaneously denying that he had been influenced by the man he contemptuously referred to as 'Witters', turned ordinary language philosophy into a new, rigorously narrow programme in philosophy. Formed by his experience as an intelligence officer in the Second World War, Austin came to adhere to the notion that, like the intelligence work he had successfully overseen, philosophy should be carried out piecemeal and collaboratively, with each participant making some delimited contribution to the vast overall project of the clarification of uses of ordinary language.

'Ordinary language philosophy' marked itself out by subscribing to a constricted conception of philosophy as nothing but the study of the 'ordinary' usage of words. When Ernest Gellner, himself a product of PPE at Oxford, published a polemical book, *Words and Things*, attacking the movement, he won the support of Bertrand Russell but attracted the scorn of the philosophical establishment. As Gellner had predicted it would, the academic formation he attacked closed ranks on him by insisting that his critique was too crude to capture every nuance of every distinct version of 'linguistic philosophy'. No doubt they were also piqued to have been accused of engaging in 'pseudo-sociology', before being subjected to a merciless sociological analysis themselves.

After Austin's death in 1960, it did not take long for ordinary language philosophy to wither away. One descendant of it, the 'descriptive metaphysics' of P. F. Strawson, who now became one of the leading figures in Oxford, offered a road back to more traditional philosophical problems such as those raised in Kant's *Critique of Pure Reason*. But Oxford was in any case now firmly established as a philosophical centre – or, as it thought of itself, *the* philosophical centre of the world. Its many philosophers were united by their adherence to the analytic and linguistic traditions they had inherited, and opposed whatever threatened them, but never again participated in any shared, clearly enunciated programme. One of the principal features of the Oxford scene now became its capacity for attracting the elite of the American philosophical academy; intellectually, philosophy in Oxford accordingly became increasingly responsive to the agenda set by successive generations of American analytic philosophers.[3]

Realism

In Oxford as in Cambridge, there was enthusiasm at the turn of the twentieth century about 'realism', often expressed through rhetoric directed at a supposedly dominant and entrenched idealist tradition. The leading figure promoting realism in Oxford was John Cook Wilson. Cook Wilson, instead of committing his ideas to paper, cultivated an oral culture for their propagation. Such a culture was hospitable to the creation of disciples.[4]

R. G. Collingwood later claimed that the idealist 'school of Green' against which realists took themselves to be reacting was a myth propagated by Cook Wilson and his disciples. T. H. Green, the leader of the supposed school, had himself, Collingwood pointed out, died in 1882 at the age of forty-six. Other prominent idealists either left Oxford early on in their career (Bernard Bosanquet at the age of thirty-three in 1881) or died young (R. L. Nettleship, again at the age of forty-six, in 1892); F. H. Bradley, although a fellow of Merton College, never taught at the university. There is surely overreach in Collingwood's conclusion that the so-called school of Green 'never in any sense dominated philosophical thought and teaching in Oxford'.[5] He was likely right, though, that the real animus against the 'school of Green', however real or mythical that school might have been, was directed at its social progressivism. In Cambridge, the utilitarians Henry and Eleanor Sidgwick were significant promoters of women's education, whereas the idealists tended to

---

3 See Chapter 7 for the 'Davidsonic boom' that hit Oxford, and Chapter 8 for the influence of Saul Kripke and David Lewis.

4 Such writings as Cook Wilson left behind are contained in John Cook Wilson, *Statement and Inference: With Other Philosophical Papers*. Cook Wilson's realism had, however, already received a prior impetus in print from the 'first-class' cricketer and Waynflete Professor of Metaphysical Philosophy, Thomas Case, in his *Physical Realism*.

5 R. G. Collingwood, *An Autobiography*, p. 16.

be socially conservative. In Oxford, by contrast, Charlotte Green, wife of T. H. Green, was an 'indefatigable' vice-president of Somerville College, one of the two oldest women's colleges in Oxford.[6] T. H. Green's students went out into the world, Collingwood wrote, believing that 'philosophy, and in particular the philosophy they had learnt at Oxford, was an important thing, and that their vocation was to put it into practice'. As a result, 'the philosophy of Green's school might be found, from about 1880 to 1910, penetrating and fertilizing every part of the national life'.[7] According to Collingwood, then, the school of Green was influential not so much within the confines of academic philosophy in Oxford, but in terms of how it shaped students who went on to play significant roles in the British Empire.

As a mindset, Oxford realism shared much with that of the Moore and Russell of the 1898 rebellion. On matters of doctrine there were, however, large divergences: in particular, Cook Wilson was bitterly opposed to Russell's logic. Although he had studied some mathematics at Balliol College, he never became more than a competent mathematician, and saw the creation of non-Euclidean geometries as 'the mere illusion of specialists, who can't understand philosophy or metaphysics and are cocksure they do', adding: 'I long to destroy the abortion.'[8] He beat John Venn, an actual logician, in the competition to become Wykeham Professor of Logic, but himself only ever taught what was called 'ordinary' logic, innocent of the new formal rigour. In politics, Cook Wilson was a neutralist, not easily moved one way or another, who 'happily did not feel drawn to work of a semi-political semi-educational character, within or outside Oxford, confining his exuberant energy to his duties as student, teacher and citizen-soldier'.[9]

Cook Wilson's chief disciples, H. W. B. Joseph and H. A. Prichard, together made a deep and lasting mark on Oxford philosophy. The two, who were close friends, were '*the* Oxford philosophers of their generation'.[10] Both, like Moore, were highly destructive philosophers; Joseph tore into Russell, Prichard into Kant. In Joseph, Cook Wilsonian realism was united with intuitionism in ethics, just as Moore had united his own realism with such intuitionism. Whereas, for Moore, it was 'good' that was 'unanalysable' and ultimate, to be detected by the powers

6 Vera Farnell, *A Somervillian Looks Back*, p. 1.

7 Collingwood, *Autobiography*, p. 17.

8 Quoted in A. S. L. Farquharson, 'Memoir', p. xxxix.

9 Ibid., p. xxix.

10 H. H. Price, 'Harold Arthur Prichard', p. 334.

of intuition, for Joseph it was 'obligation'. The routine was essentially that of Moore's 'open question argument': 'any attempt (Naturalistic or otherwise) to *define* obligation would only result in substituting something else in its place'.[11] Both Joseph and Prichard were supreme masters of Oxford tutorial technique. The 'chill' produced by Joseph in tutorials 'proved fatal to many mental bacteria, to crude philosophic growths, and to all sloppiness of thought'.[12] Prichard liked to meet his students' statements with silence:

> He would just sit there, looking very puzzled, puffing at his pipe and relighting it when it went out . . . At last Prichard would say 'Do you mind repeating that?' By this time it was perfectly obvious that it was not worth repeating, and indeed was so confused that it should never have been uttered at all.[13]

After the First World War

The slaughter of the First World War decimated a generation of young men. Oxford philosophy after 1918 was, as a result, dominated by men who had been too old to fight: Joseph and Prichard, plus the idealists J. A. Smith and (to a lesser extent) H. H. Joachim. Exceptions were H. J. Paton and R. G. Collingwood, who had both served in the Intelligence Division of the Admiralty, and G. R. G. Mure, who fought in the Royal Horse Artillery.

Gilbert Ryle, born into a solidly distinguished family of clergymen and landowners in 1900, was too young to have fought in the war. When

11 Ibid., p. 337. The economist Roy Harrod noted that, in ethics, the 'same doctrine' as that of Moore was 'very familiar in the lecture rooms of Oxford when I was an undergraduate there (1919–1922)', and added that the arguments propounded in Oxford by the disciples of Cook Wilson 'resembled fairly closely those which appear in *Principia Ethica*'. Harrod noted, further, that in Oxford the upshot of intuitionism tended to be the reaffirmation of traditional morality, 'embodying the intuitions of wise men through the ages', whereas in Cambridge it was interpreted as 'giving fairly complete licence to judge all things anew'. Roy Harrod, *The Life of John Maynard Keynes*, p. 77.

12 Anon., 'Mr. H. W. B. Joseph'. The author of this *Guardian* obituary, designated there only as 'a pupil', is identified as a 'Mr J. Sparrow' in Prichard, 'H. W. B. Joseph, 1867–1943', p. 191. Mr Sparrow noted that in Joseph's tutorials 'there were nervous breakdowns . . . but the effort was salutary'. Among Joseph's favourite imprecations, apparently, was 'Think before you speak, and then you won't speak.'

13 Price, 'Harold Arthur Prichard', pp. 332–3.

he arrived in Oxford as a student in 1919, he found philosophy there, as he later recalled, in a sorry state: the 'philosophic kettle' was 'barely lukewarm', and logic 'in the doldrums'.[14] He now, however, educated himself in the new logic by reading Russell's *Principles of Mathematics*, and, after becoming a lecturer at Christ Church in 1924, began teaching himself German so that he could read Husserl, Meinong, Brentano, Bolzano and Frege. Husserl's earlier 'intentionalist, anti-psychologistic theory of Meaning/Nonsense' interested him, but he never became a phenomenologist.[15] He did in 1929 publish a review of Heidegger's *Being and Time*, a fact now often cited to insinuate that Ryle was sympathetic not only to the work of Husserl, the founder of phenomenology, but also to that of his more wayward student, Heidegger. Ryle's own later concept of 'knowing how' may owe something to Heidegger, and, in the review, he averred that Heidegger 'shows himself to be a thinker of real importance'; but it was hardly as if he endorsed Heidegger's approach. As he expressed his considered judgement in the review: '*quâ* First Philosophy Phenomenology is at present heading for bankruptcy and disaster and will end either in self-ruinous Subjectivism or in a windy mysticism'.[16]

In 1929, two undergraduates arrived in Oxford who would be crucial to the development of Oxford philosophy: A. J. Ayer at Christ Church, and J. L. Austin at Balliol College. Ayer came from Eton College, and was the son of a Swiss financier. Austin came from Shrewsbury School, the son of an architect turned private school bursar. A few months after obtaining a First in Greats, in 1933, Austin was ensconced in a fellowship at All Souls College – the cushiest kind of Oxford fellowship, free of teaching duties. On Ryle's suggestion, Ayer went to Vienna to acquaint himself with the Circle around Moritz Schlick. Although he could speak almost no German, Ayer sat in on the meetings of the Circle, as a result of which, in 1936, he published *Language, Truth and Logic*, setting out the doctrines of the Circle as he understood them. He had already, in 1932, presented a paper on Wittgenstein's *Tractatus*, which was, according to Ayer's later recollections, 'the first occasion in Oxford on which there had been any public discussion of Wittgenstein's work'.[17] The only other person to have troubled to look beyond Oxford had been

14 Gilbert Ryle, 'Autobiographical', p. 4.

15 Ibid., p. 9.

16 Ryle, '*Sein und Zeit*, by Martin Heidegger', p. 370.

17 A. J. Ayer, *Part of My Life*, p. 119.

H. H. Price, who had gone to Cambridge in 1924 to attend lectures by Moore and Broad at Trinity College.[18]

It was in the spring of 1937 that discussions of Cambridge and Vienna philosophy came into their own in Oxford. From this resulted what came to call itself 'Oxford philosophy'. Five young men who called themselves the 'Brethren' – Austin, Ayer, Berlin, D. G. C. MacNabb and A. D. Woozley – began to meet on Thursday evenings in Isaiah Berlin's rooms at All Souls College. Berlin was the eldest, at twenty-seven. Later joined by Stuart Hampshire and Donald MacKinnon, they continued to meet until the outbreak of the Second World War in 1939. The topics discussed were those favoured by empiricists of the traditional and more recent, 'logical' varieties: perception (or theories of sense data, as discussed by C. D. Broad in Cambridge and now by H. H. Price in Oxford); a priori truths; the verification and logical character of counter-factual statements; personal identity; and knowledge of other minds.

The influx of a 'sweeping anti-metaphysical empiricism' caused consternation among the old guard of Prichard, Joseph and Joachim.[19] Prichard and Joachim tried to ignore it or feign indifference, but Joseph was struck to the core. Berlin speculated, somewhat unkindly, that Joseph died 'in a state of intellectual despair – the truth was drowning in a sea of falsehoods, a disaster which he was never able to explain to himself'.[20] Austin, who would later become a vociferous critic of empiricism, was at this stage still 'sympathetic to the general intention' of the empiricists and the 'workshop, no-nonsense atmosphere of the Vienna Circle and its adherents'.[21]

The excitement of 'Oxford philosophy', despite its sense of involvement in the latest intellectual currents, remained remarkably untouched by the huge upsurge of interest in Marxism that occurred in Britain in the 1930s. The engagement with dialectical materialism, including by some philosophers, that did occur did not seem to leave a lasting impact. Celia Fremlin – who had obtained a Third Class degree in PPE at Somerville College, but, in spite of this result, went on to study for a BLitt (Bachelor of Letters) – was a member of the Communist Party, and published a paper on dialectical materialism in *Analysis* in 1938. The paper had resulted from a meeting of the Analysis Society at which

18 Thanks to Michael Kremer for information about the date of Price's visit to Cambridge.

19 Berlin, 'Austin and the Early Beginnings of Oxford Philosophy', p. 3.

20 Ibid., p. 4.

21 G. J. Warnock, 'John Langshaw Austin, a Biographical Sketch', p. 6.

the Cambridge philosopher G. A. Paul had also spoken about Lenin's theory of perception.[22] Fremlin did not continue in philosophy, but went on to carry out the social experiment of working as a 'char', in order to experience working-class life first-hand, and later attained fame as a writer of mystery fiction.[23] Before long, the whole idea that Oxford philosophy might have to take account of the Marxist intellectual tradition disappeared without trace.

Collingwood's Critique of Analytic Philosophy

R. G. Collingwood, one of the more interesting English philosophers of the first half of the twentieth century, was – although for many years a fellow of Pembroke College, and eventually the Waynflete Professor of Metaphysical Philosophy – a remote figure in Oxford. Ryle surmised that 'he had quite early been lacerated by the Joseph–Prichard treatment, but lacked the resilience to retaliate; and that he then, very unwisely, deemed all philosophical colleagues to be unworthy'. In any case, Ryle noted, 'philosophy got moving in Oxford without his participation'.[24]

Collingwood came from an artistically cultivated family. His father, the archaeologist and painter W. G. Collingwood, had been secretary to John Ruskin. Collingwood accompanied his father on archaeological digs, and later pursued archaeology himself, publishing *Roman Britain* in 1923. Collingwood's approach to philosophy was deeply informed by

---

22 Celia Fremlin, 'Dialectical Grammar'. As Margaret MacDonald commented in the introduction to *Philosophy and Analysis* (a later compilation of papers from *Analysis*): 'This was as near political controversy as the journal ever reached. Dialectical materialism was much discussed and seemed to need examination by analytic philosophers. A week-end meeting of the Analysis Society was held on the subject in January 1939 at which speakers from both sides took part and the papers published here [Paul and MacDonald] were among those discussed.' Margaret MacDonald, ed., *Philosophy and Analysis: A Selection of Articles Published in Analysis Between 1933–40 and 1947–53*, p. 14.

23 Celia Fremlin wrote in the preface to her book recording her experiences as a char, *The Seven Chars of Chelsea* (p. v): 'When I first embarked on the researches which led to this book I did so in that spirit of arm-chair socialism which is so prevalent among my class and generation. I thought that by coming down from Oxford and taking a series of jobs as kitchen-hand, charwoman, cook-general and so on I would get to "know" the domestic servant class; would understand and appreciate their lives and conditions of work; would find out where the mistresses were "wrong" and where the servants were "right".'

24 Ryle, 'Autobiographical', pp. 13, 14.

history, and profoundly at odds with the new modes of analysis he saw becoming dominant. He conceived the study of history as the re-enactment of past action, and the study of philosophy in terms of a question-and-answer logic: the claims of past philosophers were to be understood not as free-floating utterances but as answers to implicit questions that it was the job of the historian to reconstruct. He was, furthermore, deeply interested in the psychological dimension of philosophy, and was himself psychoanalysed.[25]

In the work he considered his best, his 1933 *An Essay on Philosophical Method*, Collingwood attacked what he called 'analytic philosophy', in what appears to be the first use of that exact phrase in print; the term continued to be rare until after the Second World War.[26]

In Chapter 7 of *An Essay on Philosophical Method*, 'Two Sceptical Positions', Collingwood discusses two kinds of scepticism regarding the possibility of establishing the proper methodology for philosophy. The first kind of scepticism he calls 'critical philosophy'. Critical philosophers strike a pose of merely showing other philosophers' positions to be self-contradictory, while affecting to hold no philosophical doctrine themselves, and to eschew all 'constructive philosophical reasoning'. But their imputation of faults to others in fact presupposes a 'standard by which to condemn existing philosophies'; and the 'idea of philosophy' in play in this standard is 'itself a philosophical idea'.

The second approach similarly eschews constructive philosophy, but does so by deferring to science and common sense. As a result, 'nothing is left for philosophy except the task of analysing the knowledge we already possess: taking the propositions which are given by science and common sense, and revealing their logical structure or "showing what exactly we mean when we say", for example, that there is a material world'.[27] This approach Collingwood calls 'analytic philosophy'. The analytic philosopher has in common with the critical philosopher that he claims to have 'no constructive or systematic theory of his own'.[28] Collingwood cites as an instance G. E. Moore's 'Defence of Common Sense', in which the propositions of common sense are simply wielded

25 J. D. Mabbott, *Oxford Memories*, p. 76.

26 The phrase 'analytic philosophy' also appears in another publication of 1933, William Pepperell Montague, 'Philosophy as Vision', p. 8. Montague, similarly, was no friend of the philosophy that he designated by this name.

27 R. G. Collingwood, *An Essay on Philosophical Method*, p. 142.

28 Ibid., p. 145.

against philosophical theory. He gives credit to Susan Stebbing for at least raising the question of how the principles of philosophical analysis are justified. In raising the questions none of her fellow proponents of philosophical analysis ever bothered to concern themselves with, Stebbing was at least 'breaking new ground'.[29] Ultimately, however, Collingwood finds Stebbing's efforts wanting. Her own offer to articulate the principles to support analysis as a philosophical method amounts to nothing better than: 'I see no reasons against it.'

Collingwood concludes by considering the possibility that, although analytic philosophy cannot state its principles, these principles are 'justified by their results'. But, he comments somewhat mockingly, 'the exponents of that method are eager to assure us that its results are very modest'.[30] Furthermore, there is no reason for accepting the results other than accepting the method, since there is no a posteriori test for establishing the correctness of an analysis – to take the example Collingwood lifts from Moore's 'Defence of Common Sense' – of 'this is a human hand' as 'there is a thing, and only one thing, of which it is true both that it is a human hand and that this surface is a part of its surface'.[31] The activity of analysis in which these philosophers engaged seemed not only vacuous and unprincipled, but even utterly capricious. The roots of what went wrong here were, according to Collingwood, in a 'defect of temper'.

The Second World War

Collingwood not only stridently attacked Cambridge analysis under the heading 'analytic philosophy' in *An Essay on Philosophical Method*, but also, in *An Essay on Metaphysics*, criticized the logical positivism reaching Oxford from Vienna through the offices of A. J. Ayer.[32] In this, Collingwood was not alone. There was opposition from those with a theological bent, to whom the strident dismissals of religious claims as 'nonsense' in Ayer's *Language, Truth and Logic* were deeply shocking. The 'Metaphysicals', a group consisting of the religiously inclined philosophers Eric Mascall, Austin Farrer, Ian Crombie, Dennis Nineham

29 Ibid.

30 Ibid., p. 146.

31 Ibid., p. 147.

32 R. G. Collingwood, *An Essay on Metaphysics*.

and Michael Foster, aimed 'to explore how far the anti-metaphysical bias of analytic (linguistic) philosophy could be resisted'.[33]

The Second World War helped to give further oxygen to those at Oxford resisting analytic modes of philosophy. The Scottish philosopher and Oxford don Donald MacKinnon, likewise uncomfortable with the trend, found himself in a position of increased influence, having remained in Oxford as a conscientious objector. (When he realized the extent of Hitler's aggression and tried to sign up, it was too late – he was then, to his consternation, turned down on medical grounds.) Others who enriched the philosophical climate in Oxford had ended up there as refugees from Nazism. Refugee scholars represented a wide range of philosophical interests. Ernst Cassirer and his son Heinz were both Kantians of a highly sophisticated kind, with a deep knowledge of the phenomenological tradition. Friedrich Waismann was a logical positivist. Fritz Heinemann's interests were in phenomenology and existentialism.[34] Raymond Klibansky and Lorenzo Minio-Paluello lectured on medieval philosophy, Richard Walzer on Islamic ethics.[35] MacKinnon later rued his own 'failure emotionally to begin to realise the enormity of what had driven' Ernst Cassirer, in particular, from Germany, perhaps intensified by his frustration with his own non-participation in the war.[36] He noted that, more generally, the refugees faced harsh treatment. Having been arrested and interned as enemy aliens for several months in 1940, they then mostly lived, in Oxford, a 'penurious hand-to-mouth existence as teachers on the fringe of faculties', with 'highly educated refugee women . . . restricted in their search for employment to domestic service'.[37]

The war brought a profound change to the philosophical scene in Oxford. The men who belonged to the rising generation of philosophers – Ryle, Ayer, Austin, Hampshire, R. M. Hare – were all away. At the same time, the undergraduate education of young men was put on hold. As a result, almost 1,000 fewer men were in residence in Michaelmas Term 1939.[38] It is significant that the female students who remained were taught by a group of teachers quite different from the Oxford

33 V. A. Demant, quoted in Clare Mac Cumhaill and Rachael Wiseman, *Metaphysical Animals: How Four Women Brought Philosophy Back to Life*, p. 228.

34 Donald M. MacKinnon, 'Philosophers in Exile', p. 15.

35 Mac Cumhaill and Wiseman, *Metaphysical Animals*, p. 71.

36 MacKinnon, 'Philosophers in Exile', p. 15.

37 Ibid.

38 Mac Cumhaill and Wiseman, *Metaphysical Animals*, p. 57.

philosophical mainstream: a combination of German and Austrian refugees, conscientious objectors such as Donald MacKinnon, and women.

Even if, unlike in Cambridge, women could by this time obtain degrees in Oxford, misogyny was similarly rife, and women had to cope with constant exclusions from aspects of university life. A statute introduced in 1927 deliberately kept the number of women students down (frozen at 840 in total), depressed the wages of women academics, and kept the women's colleges – which lacked the endowments of the men's colleges – poor.[39] Women could attend lectures unchaperoned, but groping by male academics was a persistent problem. As a precaution, if a female student was to be taught by a man, the man was often required to come into the student's women-only college rather than teach in his own rooms.[40]

According to Mary Midgley, the reason why she and a group of contemporaries studying philosophy at Oxford all of whom graduated in 1942 – Elizabeth Anscombe, Philippa Foot and Iris Murdoch – were able to flourish as they did 'was indeed', as she told the philosopher Jonathan Wolff in the pages of *The Guardian* in 2013, 'that there were fewer men about then'.[41] Another factor is that all four were, at some stage, taught by MacKinnon, and deeply marked by his approach to philosophy.[42] Murdoch said of him that 'he inspires pure devotion'; Foot that 'no one has influenced me more', and 'he *created* me'.[43] Each responded to his influence in a different way, however.

Anscombe had already marked herself out as highly individual even before arriving in Oxford in 1938. Having developed an interest in Catholic literature as a young adolescent, she horrified her nominally Anglican parents, both of them teachers in private schools in south London, by declaring an intention to convert to Catholicism. Unfazed by her parents' threats to cut her off financially if she went through with it, she obtained the Clara Evelyn Mordan Scholarship to St Hugh's College, worth £60 (about £3,300 in today's money). In her first year at Oxford, she was duly

39 Pauline Adams, *Somerville for Women: An Oxford College 1879–1993*, p. 164. Mac Cumhaill and Wiseman note that St John's was a hundred times richer than the richest of the women's colleges, Somerville College; Mac Cumhaill and Wiseman, *Metaphysical Animals*, p. 20.

40 Mac Cumhaill and Wiseman, *Metaphysical Animals*, p. 20.

41 Mary Midgley, 'The Golden Age of Female Philosophy'.

42 See Mac Cumhaill and Wiseman, 'Interrupting the Conversation: Donald MacKinnon, Wartime Tutor of Anscombe, Midgley, Murdoch and Foot'.

43 Quoted in Peter J. Conradi, *Iris Murdoch: A Life*, pp. 123, 127.

received into the Church after instruction from Fr Richard Kehoe, a Dominican. That year she met Peter Geach, a philosopher who was likewise a recent convert to Catholicism; they married in 1941. Her philosophy tutor at St Hugh's College, Mary Glover, arranged special tuition in philosophy for her from another Dominican at Blackfriars, Victor White.

Although Anscombe obtained a First Class degree in Literae Humaniores, there were not, due to the enforced poverty of women's colleges, the same college fellowships to be handed out to women as there were for men, who tended to be offered them immediately on completion of their undergraduate degrees. Lacking such prospects, Anscombe began work on a graduate thesis, studying two philosophers of crucial importance in the Catholic tradition, Aristotle and Aquinas, and their conception of the human as a rational animal. In Oxford she worked under the supervision of the refugee scholar Friedrich Waismann. As well as the Aristotelian tradition, however, she had developed a fascination with the work of Wittgenstein, and in 1942 she transferred to Cambridge, where she obtained the Sarah Smithson Studentship at Newnham College, specifically in order to be close to him. When Wittgenstein, who had been working as a hospital orderly at Guy's Hospital in London, first made his appearance in Cambridge, she felt for him, as she later recalled, 'besotted reverence'.[44] An application to renew the Smithson Studentship, despite fervent support from Waismann – who called her work 'very original' and praised her 'acute mind combined with a considerable faculty of insight into the minute structure of thought as it manifests itself in language' – was torpedoed by a negative report from John Wisdom, who sneered that 'Mrs Geach's dissertation seems to me hardly to reach fellowship standard', spoke condescendingly of her 'admirable obstinacy', and called the writer 'confused' and her arguments 'muddled'.[45] A fresh application for a research fellowship at Newnham College was again turned down, despite a reference from her hero Wittgenstein, in which he stated that Anscombe was 'undoubtedly, the most talented female student I have had since 1930, when I began to lecture', adding: 'among my male students only 8, or 10 have

44 Anscombe, 'Anecdotes about Wittgenstein'. Collegium Institute Anscombe Archive, Philadelphia, Box 1, File 259. Quoted in Mac Cumhaill and Wiseman, *Metaphysical Animals*, p. 127.

45 Letter from Friedrich Waismann to Miss Curtis in support of G. E. M. Anscombe's fellowship application, 15 May 1944; John Wisdom, 'Report to the Fellowship Electors Newnham College on Mrs Geach's (Miss Anscombe) dissertation 1944' (copy). Newnham College Archives AC/3/2.

either equalled or surpassed her'.[46] Finally, in 1946, Somerville College, back in Oxford, elected Anscombe to a research fellowship.

Anscombe's relationship to what was starting to be called analytic philosophy, inevitably complicated by her attempts to combine her interests in Aristotelian questions about rational animality with a Wittgensteinian approach, was in this period far from straightforward. In a 1948 'Mary Somerville Research Fellow Report', she proposed to 'work out my doubts about what is called analytical philosophy'.[47] She evidently resolved these doubts to her own satisfaction; however unusual her approach may have been in certain respects, in her subsequent career she would always speak of herself as an analytic philosopher.[48]

Philippa Foot, like Anscombe, was capable of holding her own, having been born into the English upper class and educated at home by governesses. Anscombe, who gave her tutorials despite being only a year and a half older, exercised a strong influence on her, and urged her to read Aquinas. In the face of Anscombe's vociferous and conservative Catholicism, however, Foot held firm in her atheism. Her work, always in moral philosophy, adopted a series of varied positions in succession, from a severe scepticism to an uncompromising defence of the objectivity of ethics. But underlying them all was a strong resistance to emotivism – the view, associated with logical positivism, that ethical statements are mere expressions of subjective emotion – which she felt was impossible to take seriously in the face of the immensity of the Holocaust. If she always opposed this particular stance characteristic of analytic moral philosophy, there was never any doubt in her mind about her allegiance to analytic philosophy itself. As late as 1981, in a fairly hostile review of Alasdair MacIntyre's *After Virtue* – a book that itself provided an excoriating critique of emotivism, but also of the wider discourse of analytic philosophy within which it played its part – far from expressing any desire to give up on analytic philosophy, she declared it to be 'early rather than late in the history of analytic philosophy's attempt to understand moral language and too early to claim a synoptic view of the possibilities'.[49]

---

46 Ludwig Wittgenstein, letter to Miss Curtis, 18 May 1945 (copy). Newnham College Archives AC/3/2.

47 Quoted in Mac Cumhaill and Wiseman, *Metaphysical Animals*, p. 183.

48 See, for example, her essay, 'Analytical Philosophy and the Spirituality of Man', in G. E. M. Anscombe, *Human Life, Action and Ethics*, which espouses highly unorthodox views while taking up the stance of 'analytical philosophy'.

49 Philippa Foot, 'Goods and Practices'.

Iris Murdoch, later to attain prominence as a novelist, developed a close friendship with Foot. Unlike either Anscombe or Foot, she was, in her student days, politically on the left, and soon after she arrived at Somerville College in 1938 joined the Communist Party. She believed at the time that society 'must be radically changed, even at the expense of some bloodshed'.[50] Again unlike Anscombe and Foot, she developed an interest in philosophers of an existentialist cast, such as Gabriel Marcel and Martin Buber, even inviting Marcel to address the Oxford Philosophical Society in 1948. This did not go down well with some; one philosopher, H. P. Grice, was 'consumed with fury that such a charlatan had been invited to address the Society'.[51] Isaiah Berlin condescendingly dismissed Murdoch as 'a lady not known for the clarity of her views'.[52]

Mary Midgley, although she came from a more left-wing family than those of Anscombe or Foot, stopped short of Murdoch's devotion to communism, instead joining the Democratic Socialist Club, a moderate breakaway from the Labour Club, when she arrived at Somerville in 1938 to read Literae Humaniores. She experienced tutorials with MacKinnon as 'an enormous stroke of luck, without which I might well have drifted away from academic philosophy altogether', and took a stance more evidently opposed to the analytic mainstream than the other three.[53] She also early on thematized the male-dominated character of philosophy, and the struggle of women within it. In 1953, Midgley submitted a radio script to the BBC that began with the sentence: 'Practically all the great European philosophers have been bachelors.'[54] It was rejected: according to the producer Aniouta Kallin, the observation concerning philosophers' marital status was a 'trivial, irrelevant intrusion of domestic matters into intellectual life'.[55] Midgley herself gave up a job at Reading University, as an assistant to H. A. Hodges – a prominent opponent of logical positivism influenced by the German hermeneutic philosopher Wilhelm Dilthey – in order to join her husband Geoffrey, also a philosopher, who had obtained a job in Newcastle.

---

50 Iris Murdoch to Ann Leech, early April 1939, in Iris Murdoch, *Living on Paper: Letters from Iris Murdoch 1934–1995*, p. 10.

51 Basil Mitchell, *Looking Back: On Faith, Philosophy and Friends in Oxford*, p. 254.

52 Quoted in Conradi, *Iris Murdoch*, p. 302.

53 Mary Midgley, *The Owl of Minerva: A Memoir*, p. 116.

54 Quoted in Mac Cumhaill and Wiseman, *Metaphysical Animals*, p. ix.

55 Midgley, *Owl of Minerva*, p. 181.

Her career would come into its own at a much later date, when she published *Beast and Man* (1978), the beginning of a sustained campaign against reductionism in biology, targeting the popularizing work on evolution of Richard Dawkins in particular. Midgley, having left the orbit of Oxford early, took herself to be striking at ideological roots shared, as she saw it, by analytic philosophy and the culture of popular science.

A New Regime

In 1945, the men returned to Oxford triumphant from the war. Ryle, Ayer, Hampshire and Austin had all worked in intelligence. Austin had played a key role in the 'life-saving accuracy of the D-Day Intelligence', as his student G. J. Warnock put it – a claim recently very fully documented by Austin's biographer M. W. Rowe.[56] R. M. Hare, by contrast, had served in the Royal Artillery, and been part of the humiliating surrender of the British to the Japanese at the Battle of Singapore in 1942.

Collingwood, meanwhile, had died in 1943, having resigned the Waynflete Professorship in 1941 for reasons of ill health. Ryle now became the new Waynflete Professor. In his inaugural lecture, 'Philosophical Arguments', he recalled his predecessor in tones of reverence, calling his 'literary productivity' during his 'brief time' as holder of the chair 'immense'.[57] There is no doubt, however, that Ryle saw himself as supplanting Collingwood's lachrymose nostalgia for the British idealists with something more peppy and in keeping with the times.

Once in post, Ryle immediately set about cleaning up and rearranging the philosophical regime in Oxford. As the official Faculty of Philosophy website tells it today, Ryle, once elected to the Waynflete chair, 'did much to raise the standard of philosophy in the University'.[58] He devised a new postgraduate degree, the BPhil, instituted in 1946. The thinking behind this was that the 'training' in philosophy offered by Literae Humaniores or PPE was too general, while that provided by

56 Warnock, 'John Langshaw Austin', p. 9; M. W. Rowe, *J. L. Austin: Philosopher and D-Day Intelligence Officer.*

57 Gilbert Ryle, 'Philosophical Arguments', in *Collected Papers*, vol. 2, p. 203.

58 'History of Oxford Philosophy', at philosophy.ox.ac.uk.

the DPhil – Oxford's PhD – was too narrow. The BPhil offered to remedy this situation by including papers across a range of topics, taken by all candidates. This was thought of as creating a lively atmosphere in which, as the conceit went, young dons could learn as much as teach. It would provide a setting, as the Oxford don J. D. Mabbott put it with a xenophobic flourish, 'as unlike German seminars as it is possible to imagine'. For Mabbott, as for many others, it was evident that Oxford was now 'the best place in the world for graduate philosophers' to study.[59] For the first time, 'training' in philosophy in Oxford would be highly professional, with, in particular, a marked increase in the study of logic, which had been a persistent black hole in the study of philosophy at Oxford since the glory days of the Middle Ages, when it was home to such logical luminaries as Robert Grosseteste, Duns Scotus and William of Ockham.

Ryle's considerable influence on the profession, in Oxford and beyond, was further bolstered by his long reign as editor of *Mind*, from 1948 to 1971. Editorial practices were very different then from anything recognizable now. Acceptance or rejection of submitted articles was entirely a matter of Ryle's personal judgement; there were no other editors, and certainly no peer review, 'blind' or otherwise. Before long, there was, as G. J. Warnock would later write, such a thing as a 'current orthodoxy' in philosophy, embodied in the pages of *Mind*, such as there could not have been before 1945. Joseph, Prichard, Collingwood, Foster and Mure were out. Austin and Ayer did not 'agree about very much', but 'neither', as Warnock put it, 'would have felt it worthwhile even to *dis*agree with, say, Joseph or Collingwood'.[60] Critics of the new orthodoxy were mostly drowned out, although a few persisted, among them Foster and Mure. Foster gave lectures attacking 'The Philosophy of Analysis' at Christ Church, Oxford, after the war.[61] In 1958 Mure published a vehement attack on the contemporary philosophical scene, and its roots in the work of Russell and others, in *Retreat from Truth*, a book expressing a 'mood of deep depression' engendered by 'the return of British philosophy to its native empiricist tradition', which now 'appeared to be reducing itself from naïveté to absurdity with such speed and conviction that I

59 J. D. Mabbott, 'Gilbert Ryle: A Tribute', p. 222.
60 G. J. Warnock, 'Gilbert Ryle's Editorship', p. 48.
61 Mac Cumhaill and Wiseman, *Metaphysical Animals*, p. 283.

began to think it might soon be time to cry stinking fish'.[62] The book fell on deaf ears.

Oxford Moral Philosophy

As the new philosophical waves broke over Oxford, the old moral intuitionism was swept aside, along with the Cook Wilsonian realism to which it was attached. Moral philosophy retreated into a 'meta' mode. The game became the analysis of moral discourse, abnegating the defence of any ('first-order') moral views themselves. Here, R. M. Hare was a leading figure, responsible for replacing the positivists' emotivism (moral discourse consists in sheer expressions of emotion, such as *boo to murder!* and *generosity, hurray!*) with prescriptivism (according to which moral discourse consists in commands like *do not murder!* and *give generously!*). Hare's theory shared with emotivism the claim that moral discourse did not consist in cognitively evaluable claims (note the exclamation marks). But it seemed to constitute an improvement, in that it could make sense of the inferential interrelationships between moral claims, relied on in arguments, for example, inferring some specific moral claim (for example, that murdering this person now is wrong) from some more general one (for example, that murder is wrong). Commands could be more or less consistent with each other, and exhibit relations of implication among themselves, as emotions could not. (To a typical analytic philosopher, emotions are just an irrational mess.)

Unlike the philosophers who had spent a pleasantly strenuous war working in intelligence, Hare had suffered indignity and defeat as a combatant in the Indian Artillery in Singapore in the Second World War. In various autobiographical texts, published and unpublished, Hare reflected on his war experiences and their impact on his moral thinking. Interestingly, nothing of the painful humiliation of the British surrender at Singapore speaks from these pages; instead, Hare gives a bloodless account of how he came to recognize the plurality of systems of moral commands. He noted that the only two Japanese prisoners the British took at Singapore, when released, 'went back to their regiments, saluted their commanding officer, and committed hara kiri to expunge the disgrace of being taken prisoner'. 'This and many

62 G. R. G. Mure, *Retreat from Truth*, p. vii.

other illustrations of cultural diversity' helped him, he reflected in a 1994 typescript preserved in the Balliol College Archives, to 'stop believing in a universal objective moral standard known by intuition without reasoning'.[63] Instead, there were various competing moral systems. Hare's own position with respect to these competing moral systems was highly individual, since he was a devout Christian. In a much earlier autobiographical typescript, written just a few years after the war, he had asked: 'So then what can I say in my argument with the Japanese? I can do nothing but ask him to choose, if he can.' He himself had chosen Christianity as his moral compass. 'The Christian is one who has chosen to be a Christian, and that is all there is to be said', he wrote, adding in pen: 'though perhaps I might add that in my opinion it is precisely this "choosing to be a Christian" which constitutes that faith by which, in St Paul's expression, we are justified'.[64] Although what Hare bequeathed to Oxford philosophy was a highly rationalistic approach to ethics, and one which eschewed the provision of ethical foundations, he personally supplied such foundations from an unshakable faith.

While Hare himself was a Christian, prescriptivism was subscribed to in Oxford by others in a secular form. But perhaps his most vociferous critic was another Christian, Elizabeth Anscombe, who saw that such a system, in the secular form in which it was promoted as 'Oxford moral philosophy', generated the implication that there was no action, however heinous, against which morality could provide an absolute prohibition. Anscombe gave dramatic utterance to her stance when she made a speech in 'Convocation' in 1956, vainly attempting to block Oxford University's conferral of an honorary degree on Harry S. Truman, who had dropped atom bombs on Hiroshima and Nagasaki – actions that Anscombe regarded as impermissible under any circumstances.[65] The only philosopher who turned up to lend support to Anscombe's speech was her friend Philippa Foot; Foot, in an effort to get other philosophers to support the cause, had telephoned Bernard Williams, who 'simply wasn't having any of it'.[66] Anscombe's behaviour

63 Hare, 'AUTOB2' (31 May 1994), p. 7. R. M. Hare Papers, Balliol College Archives, Oxford.

64 Hare, 'MORAL OBJECTIVITY' (1949/50), pp. 9–10. R. M. Hare Papers.

65 For the speech Anscombe made in Convocation, in a vain attempt to halt the proceedings, see her 'Mr Truman's Degree', in G. E. M. Anscombe, *Ethics, Religion and Politics*.

66 Philippa Foot, in a *Woman's Hour* episode on Elizabeth Anscombe, BBC Radio 4, 6 November 2001.

was at the time, far from being lauded as heroism, considered an embarrassment.

The attack on Truman had indirectly been an attack on Oxford moral philosophy and what it rendered permissible. A year later, in 1957, Anscombe attacked the philosophers directly, in a radio talk entitled 'Does Oxford Moral Philosophy Corrupt Youth?' Anscombe's approach was extremely confusing: even her producer, T. S. Gregory, drew the mistaken conclusion that Anscombe intended to exonerate, not condemn, Oxford moral philosophy. Anscombe's answer to the question of the title was 'No': Oxford moral philosophy did *not* corrupt youth. But there was heavy sarcasm in this. The answer was 'No' simply by default: such philosophy would be impotent to corrupt youth even if it tried to, since its whole function was simply to replicate, and lend credibility to, the tepid and morally spineless ideology that Oxford dons anyway shared with their students. Hare, who had got sight of Anscombe's script before the broadcast, and quite rightly saw himself as its principal target, consulted various people about what to do, including Bernard Williams. Williams wrote to Hare from New College, 'It's pretty poisonous muck, isn't it?', and advised against a reply, since such confused and provocative stuff could surely only suck Hare into a disreputable vortex he would not be able to find his way out of again.[67] Hare ignored the advice, and engaged in a controversy with Anscombe in the pages of *The Listener*.[68] When Anscombe offered to deliver a follow-up, entitled 'Principles', and the BBC refused, she took this to be for political reasons. 'I feel confident', she wrote to *The Listener*, 'that the linguistic analysis philosophers are a sufficiently strong pressure group . . . to ensure that such dreadful things will never again be allowed on the Third [Programme]'.[69]

Although Anscombe was aptly described as 'sneering', Hare was given to a comfortable smugness, reflected in his 'A School for Philosophers', a talk with which he toured various German universities in 1957, informing the Germans of the superiority of the Oxford tutorial system when compared with the educational practices in their own country.[70] In an unpublished typescript, 'Apology for Being a Philosopher', he laced his bigotry with a dose of sarcasm:

---

67 Bernard Williams to R. M. Hare, 26 January [1957]. R. M. Hare Papers.

68 See *The Listener*, 21 and 28 February, and 14 March, 1957.

69 Anscombe, letter to the editor, *The Listener*, 14 March 1957.

70 R. M. Hare, 'A School for Philosophers'.

> We are lucky to have in Oxford, in the women's colleges, a number of able and distinguished philosophers; and most of them spend quite a lot of their time attacking the views of their male colleagues. Now the interesting thing is this: with the exception of Miss Anscombe, they all, when I am the target, accuse me of paying too *much* attention to general principles and too *little* to the peculiarities of individual cases – which require to be savoured with a feminine intuition before a right moral judgment can be passed upon them.[71]

Ordinary Language Philosophy

In the 1950s, Oxford felt itself to be at the centre of the philosophical world as never before. The level of self-confidence that then reigned is bound to seem utterly mysterious today. The now forgotten Oxford philosopher Richard Robinson told another, H. J. Paton, 'in the Turl at Oxford on a summer's day': 'never has there been such a blooming of philosophy in the whole history of the world'.[72]

J. L. Austin had won out over his empiricist rival A. J. Ayer, partly because Ayer was out of the way in London, where he had taken up a professorship at University College in 1946. Austin's distinctive brand of 'linguistic philosophy', to which Ryle was sympathetic, and which in others, such as the epigones G. J. Warnock and J. O. Urmson, attracted unstinting and fawning devotion, now ruled. Linguistic philosophy, also called 'ordinary language philosophy', saw the task of philosophy as confined to the explication of ordinary language – that is, language as it is used by speakers of really existing natural languages such as English (by contrast with formal languages invented by logicians and mathematicians). The so-called problems of philosophy could all be swept aside with one great dismissive gesture. They could now be *dissolved*, as Oxford philosophers liked to say; one could be spared the trouble of trying to solve them. The task turned out to be one they were well equipped for by their classical humanistic education. Philosophy basically became philology: the study not of the world, but of words. No logic was required; indeed, logic was to be disparaged.

Austin imported into Oxford tutorials and seminars methods he had wielded with great success in the war. During the war he had directed

71 Hare, 'Apology for Being a Philosopher' (n.d.), p. 2. R. M. Hare Papers.
72 H. J. Paton, 'Fifty Years of Philosophy', pp. 350–1.

intelligence operations as an intricate cooperative effort, with each man clearly assigned his role in the overall operation. In philosophy, he likewise adopted a stance of 'high authority' combined with an aspiration to turn the enquiry into a 'co-operative pursuit'.[73] In the war, Austin worked very effectively with his juniors, but had difficulties dealing with superior officers, to whom he could be very rude. In philosophy, he was similarly adept at commanding a team, but his tendency to resort to contempt when relating to superiors was reflected in his relationship to Wittgenstein. Austin had made a close study of Wittgenstein's work, in particular the unpublished *Blue and Brown Books*, which had been circulating clandestinely in Oxford, and he derived much of his approach from Wittgenstein's careful examination of 'language games'.[74] But he took to contemptuously referring to him as 'Witters', and issuing denials that he had been influenced by Wittgenstein at all. The disposition to repeat the denial was evidently drilled into his acolytes, who liked to express outrage at the supposed misconception that Austin's linguistic philosophy could have had anything to do with Wittgenstein's language games.[75]

Austin's quasi-military operations, in which 'ordinary' English was scrutinized, took place at his 'Saturday Mornings', held in various colleges. Attendance was restricted to those junior to Austin and 'judged likely to be in sympathy with the matters in hand', and was by invitation only. No women were invited. Results were 'fairly formally reported, and records kept in writing' until, over time, the meetings became 'more informal, attendance at them more heterogenous, their aim less sharply defined'.[76]

One problem with Austin's dissection of 'ordinary language' was that it was questionable whether he was studying *ordinary* language at all. The aristocrat Bertrand Russell ridiculed Austin's approach in his essay 'The Cult of "Common Usage"' by means of the following vignette:

> The Professor of Mental Philosophy, when called by his bedmaker one morning, developed a dangerous frenzy, and had to be taken away by the police in an ambulance. I heard a colleague, a believer in 'common

73 Warnock, 'John Langshaw Austin', p. 12.

74 For evidence of Austin's study of Wittgenstein, see Daniel W. Harris and Elmar Unnsteinsson, 'Wittgenstein's Influence on Austin's Philosophy of Language'. See now also Rowe, *J. L. Austin*, pp. 145–6.

75 See, for example, John Searle, 'J. L. Austin (1911–1960)', p. 227.

76 Warnock, 'John Langshaw Austin', p. 14.

usage', asking the poor philosopher's doctor about the occurrence. The doctor replied that the professor had had an attack of temporary psychotic instability, which had subsided after an hour. The believer in 'common usage', so far from objecting to the doctor's language, repeated it to other inquirers. But it happened that I, who live on the professor's staircase, overheard the following dialogue between the bedmaker and the policeman:

Policeman. 'Ere, I want a word with yer.

Bedmaker. What do you mean – 'A word'? I ain't done nothing.

Policeman. Ah, that's just it. Yer ought to 'ave done something. Couldn't yer see the pore gentleman was mental?

Bedmaker. That I could. For an 'ole hour 'e went on something chronic. But when they're mental you can't make them understand.

In this dialogue, Russell insists, the words 'word', 'mean', 'mental' and 'chronic' 'are all used in accordance with common usage', even if 'they are not so used in the pages of "Mind" by those who pretend that common usage is what they believe in'. What linguistic philosophers were really concerned with was the 'usage of persons who have their amount of education, neither more nor less'.[77] That amount of education was indeed remarkably uniform. Of the twenty leading Oxford philosophers of the 1950s, all had received their secondary education in a 'public school' (that is, a private boys' school) except the four women and P. F. Strawson (who went to a grammar school). All twenty had received their undergraduate education at Oxford except for one, who had been to Cambridge.[78]

On the whole, criticism of linguistic philosophy was sporadic, leaving little imprint on what seemed to its participants to be an exciting and even intoxicating endeavour to be engaged in. This changed when

---

77 Bertrand Russell, *Portraits from Memory and Other Essays*, pp. 166–7.

78 Jonathan Rée, 'English Philosophy in the Fifties', pp. 16, 20*n*125. The schools were Winchester College (Michael Dummett, P. H. Nowell-Smith, G. J. Warnock), Westminster School (David Pears), St Paul's School (Isaiah Berlin), Rugby School (R. M. Hare), Stowe School (Anthony Quinton), Shrewsbury School (J. L. Austin), Repton School (Stuart Hampshire), Cheltenham College (H. L. A. Hart), Oundle School (Stephen Toulmin), Kingswood School (A. G. N. Flew, J. O. Urmson), Brighton College (Gilbert Ryle), Chigwell School (Bernard Williams) and Christ's College Finchley (P. F. Strawson). The women were educated at private schools – Sydenham High School (G. E. M. Anscombe), Badminton School (Iris Murdoch), St Swithun's School (Mary Warnock) – or at home (Philippa Foot). Stephen Toulmin was an undergraduate at King's College, Cambridge.

Ernest Gellner, himself a product of Oxford philosophy, was encouraged by the left-wing publisher Victor Gollancz to publish a polemic against it, *Words and Things*. When the book came out in 1959, its targets went on the defensive and closed ranks. Even those who privately had concerns about the mainstream of Oxford philosophy, such as Iris Murdoch and Alasdair MacIntyre, participated in the general condemnation of Gellner, who was pilloried as the ultimate *Nestbeschmutzer*.[79]

Gellner's critique is now hard to access, thanks to the strenuously enforced and still persisting consensus among analytic philosophers that it was overly harsh and also incoherent, a farrago of confusion and *ressentiment*. Few of those ready to express indignation at Gellner's book have actually read it, resting their attitude instead on the excoriations provided by authoritative figures such as the Oxford philosopher Michael Dummett, who exempted others from reading the book by issuing the declaration that it 'does not even have the smell of honest or seriously intentioned work'.[80] The most recent contributor to the general condemnation, M. W. Rowe, complains on p. 596 of his biography of Austin that Gellner was 'relentlessly unnuanced and unsympathetic' and his 300-page Pelican book 'far too long'.[81]

It is worth considering, however, what Gellner actually had to say, and against what background. A Czech Jew who had been exiled to England at the age of thirteen in 1939, his studies at Balliol College, Oxford, were interrupted by the war. After fighting in the 1st Czechoslovak Armoured Brigade, which played the major role in the siege of Dunkirk, he graduated with a First in PPE in 1947. Gellner was thus a product of Oxford philosophy; he was on friendly terms with Ryle, Murdoch, Anscombe, Berlin, Hampshire, Hare, Urmson and Pears – though not Austin.[82] Contrary to what the general condemnation might suggest, which likes to insinuate that Gellner was an ignorant outsider, his polemic was the culmination of a long-standing and well-informed engagement with Oxford philosophy. As early as 1951, he placed articles in which he criticized linguistic philosophy in four different journals recognized as prestigious by analytic philosophers.[83]

---

79 See Iris Murdoch, 'Mr Gellner's Game'; Alasdair MacIntyre, 'The Hunt Is Up!'.

80 Michael Dummett, *Truth and Other Enigmas*, p. 436.

81 Rowe, *J. L. Austin*, p. 596.

82 John A. Hall, *Ernest Gellner: An Intellectual Biography*, p. 44.

83 Ernest Gellner, 'Use and Meaning'; 'Knowing How and Validity'; 'Maxims'; and 'Analysis and Ontology'.

When, in 1957, Gellner took his criticism of linguistic philosophy into more popular venues, writing on the topic in the *Rationalist Annual* and the *Universities Quarterly*, and giving two radio talks on the BBC Third Programme, he was building on this earlier, more academic work.[84]

The publication of *Words and Things*, with a laudatory introduction by Bertrand Russell, created a minor storm in the teacup of the British intelligentsia.[85] The Oxford philosophical establishment closed ranks, just as Gellner had predicted in the book. Oxford philosophy made itself impervious to attack due to its shape-shifting nature, as Gellner had said in his book, and as it now demonstrated by its response: of any criticism, it could always be maintained that not everyone held the view in question, or that the point at issue was not a necessary component of the approach.

Although Gellner's tone could be overly snide and dismissive, he nevertheless presented a cogent argument. The most important of his four interrelated targets is what Gellner calls the 'paradigm case argument'. Michael Dummett later recalled, in the midst of his lacerating denunciation of Gellner, that he himself had written (in 1951), but never published, 'a critique of the "paradigm-case argument", which Gellner proclaimed as the cornerstone of linguistic philosophy'.[86] The 'argument from the paradigm case' fallaciously infers how expressions should be understood from how they are most typically used. An example is the attempt to discern the meaning of the word 'free' from how the expression 'I do so of my own free will' is often intelligibly used. Connected to this is Gellner's second target: the fallacy of inferring from standard usage to norms about how words *should* be used. His third target, the 'contrast theory of meaning', a counterpart to the 'paradigm case argument', presupposes that, for a term to be meaningful, there must be cases where it does *not* apply. And his fourth target is 'polymorphism', which claims, on the basis of the great variety of

84 Gellner, 'Determinism and Validity' and 'Logical Positivism and After, or the Spurious Fox'. The latter piece was reprinted in *Universities and Left Review* in 1958, leading to exchanges with the philosophers Stephen Toulmin and Alasdair MacIntyre. The radio talks were published as 'Reflections on Linguistic Philosophy'.

85 The controversy created the basis for Ved Mehta, *Fly and the Fly-Bottle: Encounters with British Intellectuals*, which reports on conversations with a number of leading philosophers. Unfortunately Mehta's book contains wild and numerous inaccuracies; it should therefore not be relied on.

86 Michael Dummett, *Truth and Other Enigmas*, p. xii.

uses of an expression, that 'general assertions about the use of words are impossible'.[87]

Thus far, Gellner's points were purely logical or methodological. He also attacked the claims of linguistic philosophy to advance no position, and its tendency instead to strike the pose of the diagnostician. This was helpful to linguistic philosophy: since it never explicitly advanced any particular doctrine, it was immune to criticism. This immunity from criticism indeed stood Oxford philosophers in good stead when it came to responding to Gellner. But even their merely diagnostic efforts were open to criticism. Linguistic philosophers claimed to leave language untouched, in line with Wittgenstein's mantra that philosophy 'leaves everything as it is'.[88] But what is the scope of 'everything'? It had better not include 'the language game known as *philosophy*', which linguistic philosophy took it upon itself to interfere with rather than leave intact.[89] But from what vantage point could such an exclusion be made? If some regions of language use were to be subjected to a 'cure', somewhere or other language had to be revised, not merely analysed. But where are the lines to be drawn between observation of usage and its improvement? As Gellner put it, 'the situation is completely indeterminate'.[90]

Gellner, who in 1949 had accepted a post at the London School of Economics as 'Assistant Lecturer in Sociology with special reference to Ethics and Social Philosophy', furthermore subjected the phenomenon of linguistic philosophy to sociological critique. He accused linguistic philosophy of cultivating 'Conspicuous Triviality', echoing Thorstein Veblen's concepts of 'conspicuous waste' and 'conspicuous consumption'.[91] It was one thing for linguistic philosophy to sustain itself in the very small social pool of Oxford by means of the tutorial and the

---

87 Ernest Gellner, *Words and Things*, p. 32.

88 Wittgenstein was specifically speaking of leaving the 'actual use of language' intact:

> Philosophy may in no way interfere with the actual use of language; it can in the end only describe it.
> For it cannot give it any foundation either.
> It leaves everything as it is.

Philosophical Investigations, §124.

89 Gellner, *Words and Things*, p. 230.

90 Ibid., p. 231.

91 Ibid., p. 273.

'esoteric discussion group'. But the effect was comic when those who had been trained in linguistic philosophy were 'condemned to teach their creed in Redbrick universities'.[92] As university education expanded, the products of Ryle's large new Oxford regime were sent all over the country to take up the new jobs. The students they were charged with teaching had first to be convinced that they suffered from various 'pathologics' characteristic of traditional philosophy, in order that the lecturer imbued with the evangelical mission of Oxford could then cure the disease.[93] This 'form of life' and its associated 'language game', as Gellner correctly perceived, laid themselves wide open to genuinely sociological investigation, by contrast with the pseudo-sociological forays of 'linguistic philosophy'.

After Austin

With Austin's death in 1960, ordinary language philosophy more or less collapsed. As P. F. Strawson put it, 'Ultimately the full tide of denunciation rolled in. The linguistic philosophers were charged with dullness, triviality, pedantry, abdication, evasion, frivolity, complacency, conservatism, and obscurity.' Although Strawson did not intend it as such, it is now difficult to read this enumeration as anything other than a fair assessment. Strawson himself developed out of his previous concern with the use of 'linguistic instruments in the course of our business with one another and the world' his own project of 'descriptive metaphysics'. This new project sought to lay out our 'actual conception of the world', transcending the limits of ordinary language philosophy, which 'cannot, by itself, satisfy the persistent philosophical craving for generality, for the discovery of unifying pattern or structure in our conception of the world'. It engendered, as Strawson put it, 'a more sympathetic understanding of the history of the subject', and a flight into the arms of Kant's *Critique of Pure Reason*, the most significant attempt yet to lay out in its entirety the conceptual scheme presupposed by human experience.[94]

Although Strawson was held in high regard among other native Oxford philosophers, the dominant influence would soon come from

---

92 Ibid.

93 Ibid., p. 274.

94 P. F. Strawson, in *Philosophical Writings*, p. 75.

the United States. More and more, the tone in Oxford would be set by the visitors, predominantly American, who came to give the prestigious annual John Locke Lectures, such as Nelson Goodman (who gave the Lectures in 1961–62), Wilfrid Sellars (1965–66), Noam Chomsky (1968–69), Donald Davidson (1969–70), Sydney Shoemaker (1971–72), Saul Kripke (1973–74), Hilary Putnam (1975–76), David Kaplan (1979–80), Daniel Dennett (1982–83), David Lewis (1983–84), Barry Stroud (1986–87) and Thomas Nagel (1989–90). Oxford continued to play its role in attracting Americans in the first place with its irresistible British prestige and its status as the oldest university in the English-speaking world, but there could be no doubt that it was increasingly the Americans themselves who were calling the shots in the exchange of philosophical ideas across the Atlantic.

5

The Making of Analytic Philosophy

Before the Second World War, there was no one thing that could be called 'analytic philosophy'. Instead, various distinct movements – those of Cambridge and Vienna, principally – marched under the banner of 'analysis'. It was after the war that a single, unified movement identifiable as 'analytic philosophy' came into being, in the United States. It established itself by 1948 or 1949; by the end of the 1950s it was dominant. This is bound to surprise many, since the standard origin myths of analytic philosophy tend to construct a unitary, continuous tradition beginning with Frege in 1879, or at the latest with Russell and Moore in 1898. Concomitantly, it was only after the war that the phrase 'analytic philosophy' began to appear regularly in print.[1]

---

1 The earliest use in print of 'the analytic philosophers' appears to have been by John Wisdom in 1931, in *Interpretation and Analysis, in Relation to Bentham's Theory of Definition*, p. 15. R. G. Collingwood and W. P. Montague, as we saw in the previous chapter, both wrote in pejorative terms of 'analytic philosophy' in 1933. The term 'analytic philosophy' must have been in wider oral use in this period, as is suggested by A. E. Duncan-Jones writing in 1937 of 'the contemporary philosophy of the people in this country who have commonly been called analytic philosophers' ('Does Philosophy Analyse Common Sense?', p. 139). A remarkably early use of 'the analytical philosophy' occurs in a summary of a meeting of the Aristotelian Society on 17 May 1915, in *The Athenaeum*, reporting a contribution made in discussion by Russell (Anon., 'Aristotelian', p. 487). Russell was responding to a defence by his niece Karin Costelloe-Stephen of the views of Bergson against his own. The context suggests that 'the analytical philosophy' referred to Russell's own approach, perhaps implicitly contrasted with 'synthetic philosophy' as defended by Costelloe-Stephen on Bergson's behalf. For discussion of the 17 May meeting, see Andreas Vrahimis, 'Sense Data and

After the end of the war, it took only a few years for analytic philosophy to establish itself as a new formation that amalgamated the Russellian and Moorean forms of analysis, logical positivism, 'Polish logic' and strands of American pragmatism. A leading role was played by logical positivist émigrés, driven from Europe by Nazism, who came to occupy significant positions in American philosophy departments. As they acclimatized to American conditions, they became newly professionalized, conceiving of themselves not as scientists with philosophical interests, as they had been in Vienna, but as exponents of a special academic discipline called 'philosophy of science'. As logical positivists became philosophers of science, their programme was shorn of its social dimension, and they now adopted a stance of political neutrality. This remarkable transformation, as the component of analytic philosophy associated with its leading founders in the United States established its fusion with kindred European and American approaches that had grown up before the war, calls for explanation.

The landscape the logical positivists entered in the United States was highly diverse. In American philosophy, as they found it, there was a proliferation of different varieties of idealism, realism and pragmatism, and also an interest in phenomenology and in some Asian philosophy. As the new analytic philosophers took over philosophy departments and journals, those other approaches were – at different rates in different places – squeezed out. Not only that, but the émigrés who secured the analytic takeover competed against émigrés from rival movements in philosophy. In particular, they had to compete for attention with the critical theorists of the Frankfurt School and with phenomenologists.[2] Again, their success calls for explanation.

The remarkably swift and successful takeover of American philosophy by analytic philosophy, and the edge which logical positivists managed to gain over rival émigrés, have recently attracted attention from analytic philosophers and historians of analytic philosophy. Their

---

Logical Relations: Karin Costelloe-Stephen and Russell's Critique of Bergson'. The first to use 'analytic philosophy' to bring the various pre-war movements under one umbrella was the American philosopher Ernest Nagel, in his 1936 article reporting his philosophical travels in Europe, 'Impressions and Appraisals of Analytic Philosophy in Europe'. In another 1936 publication, Nagel wrote of Hans Reichenbach as 'the outstanding member of the "Berlin group" of thinkers devoted to analytic philosophy'; Ernest Nagel, '*Wahrscheinlichkeitslehre*, by Hans Reichenbach', p. 501.

2 For the marginalization that phenomenology came to suffer in American philosophy, see Jonathan Strassfeld, *Inventing Philosophy's Other*.

attempts to explain these developments have, however, been hampered by the limits of their methodology, which tends to reflect the very analytic mindset whose history they are concerned with. The analytic philosophers Joel Katzav and Krist Vaesen have attempted to explain the takeover in terms of institutional mechanisms such as 'journal capture', while deliberately excluding 'external' (social and political) factors. A currently ongoing project entitled 'Exiled Empiricists' funded by the Dutch Research Council (NWO), meanwhile, seeks to explain the logical positivists' edge over their rivals largely using digital techniques.[3] These approaches bear the marks of the phenomenon they seek to analyse: the extrusion of the social, the political and the psychological, or else a reduction of these factors to the quantifiable. Although the study of such quantifiable phenomena as citation frequency can do part of the explanatory work, an adequate explanation of the rise of analytic philosophy in the post-war United States must consider the highly specific political and social conditions which obtained, and how they shaped the activities of those subject to them. A successful reconstruction of these conditions presupposes a significant effort of deliberate defamiliarization, since the world that the United States created after 1945, as the dominant Western power emerging from the war, is the world in which we live.

In the aftermath of the war, the United States found itself in a position of economic supremacy, rivalled in power only by its wartime former ally, the Soviet Union. In order to secure its position, it now worked to bolster its liberal-capitalist mode of existence, materially and ideologically. The specificity of these developments, difficult to see today thanks to their success, becomes more easily visible if we remind ourselves of the radically different situation in the decade that preceded the war: the 1930s. In the wake of the Great Depression, and with fascism on the rise, it was widely believed that the political options were now in effect limited to a choice between fascism and communism. Many American intellectuals, including professional philosophers, took the side of communism. In economics, planned economies were widely discussed, and many firmly held that socialism was the future.

The war changed all this. The diagnosis of the difficulties of liberalism remained fundamentally unchanged, but the need to build a bulwark against totalitarianism came to seem pressing. This, in turn,

---

3 'Exiled Empiricists: American Philosophy and the Great Intellectual Migration', at exiledempiricists.wordpress.com.

bolstered efforts to root out Marxism. A new group of intellectuals rose to prominence who promoted the ideology of 'neoliberalism' (to be distinguished from a later use of the same term, which associates it with the economic and social policies of Ronald Reagan and Margaret Thatcher). The term had been coined at a meeting in 1938, the Walter Lippmann Colloquium, organized in Paris by the French logical positivist philosopher Louis Rougier (later to become a *pétainiste*). The neoliberalism advocated by these influential intellectuals, economists and political figures was in no way a market fundamentalism designed to clip the wings of the state. On the contrary, its avowed mission was to safeguard a fragile liberal-capitalist order by building around it a protective shield of strong state institutions.

Much of the intense research activity that was needed in order to shore up the position of the United States in the face of the perceived threat of Soviet aggression, as well as to reinforce liberal capitalism domestically, was carried out under the auspices of the RAND Corporation. Having grown out of military facilities set up during the war ('RAND' stands for 'Research and Development'), RAND continued to be funded by the military. It provided a congenial home for analytic philosophers, who worked together with economists and others within its basic research paradigm of 'Operations Research'. As well as hosting and funding philosophers, RAND generated enthusiasm in the wider philosophical community for the burgeoning fields of rational choice theory and game theory. The philosophers Hans Reichenbach, W. V. Quine, Donald Davidson and Nicholas Rescher were all employed by RAND. Another, John Rawls, began in the same period to develop a political philosophy grounded in game theory.

RAND lent positive encouragement to analytic philosophers' engagement in Cold War efforts, cemented their identification with 'Cold War rationality', and brought them into close proximity with power elites. At the same time, philosophers were subject to pressure of a negative kind through the climate of persecution and paranoia known as McCarthyism. Ostensibly there to weed out communists who were plotting to bring down America, McCarthyism was in reality a system of compliance that largely targeted those with only the most minimal (if any) connections to any actual communism. It hit the American universities hard, including philosophers.[4] In some cases, philosophers

4 See John McCumber, *Time in the Ditch: American Philosophy and the McCarthy Era.*

were direct targets, and were called in front of its committees. But its chief work was wider and more important – and also difficult now to retrace, since what was done often subsequently remained shrouded in secrecy, and the story is even more one of what scared individuals did *not* do. It created a climate of fear through the constant threat that one might be informed on, through the elaborate procedures universities put in place to pre-empt McCarthyite committees' investigations, and through the notorious 'loyalty oaths' academics were required to sign. Analytic as well as non-analytic philosophers were affected by McCarthyism. What it shut down decisively was those who challenged the neutralism so congenial to analytic philosophy.[5]

The Formation of Analytic Philosophy

The forging of analytic philosophy, and its subsequent takeover of the American philosophical scene, took place with remarkable rapidity.[6] By 1948, the logical positivist émigré Herbert Feigl and the American philosopher Wilfrid Sellars were able to publish an anthology drawing together classic papers in what they called 'philosophical analysis' from across various pre-war traditions. A year later, in 1949, Arthur Pap, another European émigré, published the textbook *Elements of Analytic Philosophy.*

Feigl and Sellars had consulted 'about ninety teachers of philosophy in this country and in England' in order to arrive at their selection.[7] They now explicitly drew together a range of pre-war approaches, of

---

5 The story told here closely matches the accounts in George Reisch, *How the Cold War Transformed Philosophy of Science: To the Icy Slopes of Logic*, and Don Howard, 'Two Left Turns Make a Right: On the Curious Political Career of North American Philosophy of Science at Midcentury'. Curiously, though, Howard is reluctant to draw the conclusion that McCarthyism was responsible for the political neutralization of the logical positivists as they crossed the Atlantic, because he thinks to do so would involve slighting the 'sincerity of [their] protestations of neutrality'. One should remember that sincerity is a matter of only subsidiary concern in the critique of ideology.

6 Sander Verhaegh has shown that the groundwork for the takeover had been firmly laid down by the activities of Carnap and Reichenbach in the United States in the 1930s. See his two-part article, 'Coming to America: Carnap, Reichenbach, and the Great Intellectual Migration'.

7 Herbert Feigl and Wilfrid Sellars, eds, 'Preface' to *Readings in Philosophical Analysis*, p. v.

which the American philosopher Ernest Nagel had written, travelling in Europe in 1936, that they had much 'in common, methodologically and doctrinally', all of them preoccupied with 'philosophy as *analysis*', impatient with traditional philosophical systems, marked by an attitude of 'ethical and political neutrality', operating in an 'extremely unhistorical atmosphere', and subscribing to 'a common-sense naturalism'.[8] Feigl and Sellars identified 'two major traditions in recent thought' – the 'Cambridge movement' (Russell and Moore) and logical positivism (the Vienna Circle and the Berlin Circle) – as the sources of 'philosophical analysis' as they conceived it. According to them, these approaches, 'together with related developments in America stemming from Realism and Pragmatism, and the relatively independent contributions of the Polish logicians, have increasingly merged to create an approach to philosophical problems which we frankly consider a decisive turn in the history of philosophy'.[9]

The new fusion would soon start to exert its hold on American philosophy. At the same time as its institutional success grew, it crumbled intellectually at the hands of its American protagonists. W. V. Quine, one such protagonist, in 1951 published a paper that devastated the distinction between empirical truths and truths of logic on which the programme of logical positivism rested.[10] So-called analytic truths (statements true merely by definition, such as 'Bachelors are unmarried') – the logical truths – faced a problem. They relied on synonymy, which Quine persuasively showed was a far more slippery notion than one might suppose.[11] A few years later, in 1956, Sellars vitiated what he took to calling the 'myth of the given': the notion of something purely sensorily given, prior to all conceptual interpretation, on which the entire empiricist edifice rested.[12] Examples could easily be multiplied. In effect, analytic philosophy was in crisis as soon as it had asserted its presence on the American scene.[13]

---

8 Ernest Nagel, 'Impressions and Appraisals of Analytic Philosophy in Europe', pp. 6–7.

9 Feigl and Sellars, 'Preface' to *Readings in Philosophical Analysis*, p. vi.

10 W. V. Quine, 'Two Dogmas of Empiricism', in *From a Logical Point of View: Nine Logico-Philosophical Essays*.

11 Quine asserted that 'interchangeability *salva veritate*' (the condition he proposed for synonymy) 'is no assurance of cognitive synonymy of the desired type' (ibid., p. 31).

12 Wilfrid Sellars, 'Empiricism and the Philosophy of Mind'.

13 These developments are portrayed in detail in Richard Rorty, *Philosophy and the Mirror of Nature*.

The Analytic Takeover of American Philosophy

Analytic philosophy, though doomed to internal decay, moved with remarkable effectiveness to take over a series of philosophy departments. As the American philosopher Richard Rorty, himself an evangelical promoter of analytic philosophy riding the wave of conversion, later told the American Philosophical Association Western Division meeting in a 1981 retrospective,

> in the early fifties, analytic philosophy began to take over American philosophy departments. The great emigrés – Carnap, Hempel, Feigl, Reichenbach, Bergmann, Tarski – began to be treated with the respect they deserved. Their disciples began to be appointed to, and to dominate, the most prestigious departments. Departments which did not go along with this trend began to lose their prestige. By 1960, a new set of philosophical paradigms was in place.[14]

'Conversion' to analytic philosophy happened at different rates in different philosophy departments. Of elite American philosophy departments, among the quickest to convert were Harvard and Cornell, followed by Princeton. Yale and Chicago took the longest.

The Harvard department had received an early impetus from the logical positivists when Feigl of Vienna spent the year 1930–31 there. The Harvard philosopher Quine spent 1932–33 travelling in Europe, getting to know Tarski, Carnap and others. Thanks to Quine's advocacy of the European logical positivist stream, but also the native Harvard tradition of formal logic at which he himself looked askance, represented by figures such as C. I. Lewis and Henry Sheffer, the department entered the post-war period very much ready to receive analytic philosophy.

The Sage School of Philosophy at Cornell University, which had been a stronghold of idealism, began its conversion in 1946, when A. E. Murphy was appointed its chair. Murphy had spent the academic year 1936–37 in England, where he had fallen under the spell of Wittgenstein. He now hired into the department two products of Cambridge University who had been deeply marked by Wittgenstein: Max Black in 1946, and Norman Malcolm in 1947. A third philosopher, the

14 Richard Rorty, 'Philosophy in America Today', p. 214.

Constantinople-born but American-educated Gregory Vlastos, who took an analytic approach to ancient philosophy, was hired in 1948. Wittgenstein himself visited the School in 1949, attended a meeting of the Discussion Club at which Vlastos read a paper, and held 'two special meetings for graduate students alone'.[15] By 1953, it was 'the country's strongest analytical school'.[16] In that same year, it appointed John Rawls to its faculty.

In the immediate post-war years, the philosophy department at Princeton University was typical at that time in being highly diverse. The philosopher and Rawls biographer Andrius Gališanka is thus flatly wrong when he writes that 'Princeton's philosophy department in 1939 was unusual given the dominance of analytic philosophy at the time'.[17] It is indicative of the tenacity of the myths that attend analytic philosophy that such a statement could appear even in a scholarly historical work. Analytic philosophy was not yet dominant at all, except in a few departments; most were still highly diverse. At Princeton itself, the leading figures were Robert Scoon, a classicist, and Theodore Greene, an aesthetician, both of whom played a part in founding the Committee on Religious Instruction. Walter Stace, a British colonial civil servant turned professional philosopher, was a phenomenalist who had written a book on Hegel. Andrew Ushenko was a logician of catholic tastes (interested in temporal, intuitionist and Hegelian logic, as well as the logic of Russell and Carnap). To this team was added Walter Kaufmann, a Nietzsche scholar, in 1947. Not until Scoon and Stace retired in 1955, to be replaced by Vlastos from Cornell and Carl Hempel from Yale, could the department be said to be predominantly analytic.

Both Chicago and Yale continued to be overwhelmingly non-analytic in the immediate post-war period, insisting on clinging to a humanist conception of philosophy as a guide to life.[18] Their almost complete immunity to analytic philosophy is borne out by the experiences of Rorty, who was an undergraduate at Chicago and a graduate student at Yale. When, having come out of Yale with his PhD, he got a job as an assistant professor, Rorty found that he had to 'learn' analytic philosophy on the hoof.[19] There was *some* analytic presence in both departments:

---

15 Marcus G. Singer, 'Memoir', in Arthur E. Murphy, *Reason, Reality, and Speculative Philosophy*, p. xxvii.

16 Diane Davis Villemaire, *E. A. Burtt, Historian and Philosopher*, p. 78.

17 Andrius Gališanka, *Rawls: The Path to a Theory of Justice*, p. 20.

18 For Yale, see Bruce Kuklick, 'Philosophy at Yale in the Century after Darwin'.

19 Neil Gross, *Richard Rorty: The Making of an American Philosopher*.

Carnap was at Chicago from 1936 to 1952, C. L. Stevenson at Yale from 1939 to 1945. Yale refused Stevenson tenure in 1945 in spite of his having recently published his monograph *Ethics and Language*, the classic statement of ethical emotivism – for some time the dominant position in analytic 'metaethics'.[20] But the predominant figures at both Chicago and Yale were philosophers in the grand old style: Richard McKeon and Charles Hartshorne at Chicago, Brand Blanshard and Paul Weiss at Yale. Having hired Hempel as Stevenson's replacement, the Yale department in 1952 refused to promote him; allegedly, his work 'did not seem of the significance which we recognize of a full professorship'.[21] Hempel, who left for Princeton, was replaced by the mediocre positivist Pap, who on his premature death in 1959 was replaced by Sellars. Sellars's departure for Pittsburgh, which came in 1963, sent Yale into the doldrums, where it remained for decades.

A key way in which the new analytic philosophers established their dominance in the profession was by controlling the leading journals and what was published in them. As Katzav and Vaesen have documented, 'journal capture' by analytic philosophers of the most prestigious journals was rapid and successful. A particularly clear case is that of *The Philosophical Review*, edited in-house at the Sage School at Cornell. Then as now, the journal enjoyed elite status. But, unlike today, in the 1940s its output was highly diverse. In 1948, things started to shift decisively. The 1948 volume included, along with the first translation into English of Frege's 'On Sense and Reference' by Max Black and a paper by the Berlin positivist Hans Reichenbach, some remnants from a previous age: papers from a symposium on 'oriental philosophy', along with work on modern Indian philosophy. But the journal was now dominated by representatives of analytic philosophy such as Ernest Nagel, O. K. Bouwsma, Norman Malcolm and Pap. In terms of Katzav and Vaesen's categorizations, in 1944–47 fewer than one-third of the articles were analytic, whereas in 1950–55 about two-thirds were.[22] Change was somewhat slower at *The Journal of Philosophy*. It continued to be a pluralist journal until 1958, when it too became

20 Stevenson's book was clearly highly offensive to his colleagues at Yale; their stated verdict on it was that it 'evaded philosophical issues that anyone with any reasonable grounding in philosophy would be expected to appreciate'. Quoted in Kuklick, 'Philosophy at Yale', p. 324.

21 Ibid., p. 325.

22 Joel Katzav and Krist Vaesen, 'On the Emergence of American Analytic Philosophy', p. 778.

focused on analytic philosophy, 'although still open to existentialism and phenomenology'.[23] After 1963, however, existentialism and phenomenology disappeared from its pages. Katzav associates this shift with the appointment in 1964 of Arthur Danto, Sidney Morgenbesser and James J. Walsh as editors. From then on, the analytic quotient continued to rise. Whereas in the 1950s about half of the articles published were analytic, in 1962–64 about 80–90 per cent were either analytic or historical, rising to 95 per cent in 1965–69, with 'almost all' articles being analytic.[24]

In seeking to explain these transformations, Katzav draws a distinction between 'internal' and 'external' factors. He insists that McCarthyism, as an 'external contributor', 'had a limited role in driving the growth of analytic philosophy'.[25] For Katzav, analytic philosophy 'used institutional control in order to promote itself and marginalize rivals', but he wants to resist invoking social factors to explain how this institutional control was effective – in particular, the pressures of McCarthyism.[26] Apart from leaving an explanatory void – how was such institutional control facilitated? – there is an incoherence in Katzav's argument. The takeover of *The Philosophical Review* in the late 1940s, he insists – wrongly – 'predates the main pressures of the McCarthy era'.[27] This is just ignorant of the facts; McCarthyism was already exerting significant pressure in the early 1940s. And, in any case, the bulk of the conversion happened in the 1950s, when McCarthyism was at its height. But Katzav also argues that the conversion of *The Journal of Philosophy* cannot be explained by McCarthyism because the date it began, 1958, 'is already after the height of the McCarthy era'.[28] So the conversion to analytic philosophy is, according to Katzav, both too early *and* too late to be explained by the pressures of McCarthyism. In fact, as we will see, McCarthyism got going in the early 1940s and continued into the late 1950s (with after-effects still felt in the late 1960s, when a McCarthyite rationale was given for the firing of Angela Davis). Certainly, it does not play a straightforward explanatory role; for one thing, it did not simply select for analytic philosophers. But

23 Joel Katzav, 'Analytic Philosophy 1925–69: Emergence, Management, and Nature', p. 1,198.

24 Ibid., pp. 1,203–4.

25 Ibid., p. 1,199.

26 Ibid., p. 1,197.

27 Ibid., p. 1,211.

28 Ibid.

the climate of fear that worked to bolster the American order created conditions highly favourable to the takeover.

The Walter Lippmann Colloquium

The rise of analytic philosophy cannot be understood without an examination of the distinctive position of its homeland, the United States, at the end of the Second World War, and its concerted programme to reinvigorate liberal capitalism. This reinvigoration took the form not of a 'market fundamentalism', but of the creation of what the historian Quinn Slobodian has called 'the meta-economic or extra-economic conditions for safeguarding capitalism at the scale of the entire world'.[29]

One way to designate the programme by which the United States now reconfigured its place in the world is by placing it under the title 'neoliberalism'. The term is now often used to designate the policies of the deregulation of capital markets, 'globalization', privatization of public services, and the commercialization and corporatization of government departments, implemented by Ronald Reagan, Margaret Thatcher and others in the wake of the economic downturn of the 1970s. For our purposes, however, the relevant sense of 'neoliberalism' is that given to it by those who themselves coined the term in 1938.

The invention of the term 'neoliberalism' occurred at the Walter Lippmann Colloquium, a meeting held in 1938 in Paris, organized by the French logical positivist philosopher Louis Rougier, who had previously organized the Paris conference on the Unity of Science in 1935.[30] The Colloquium, which has been described as 'the birthplace of neoliberalism as an intellectual and political project', was attended by twenty-six businessmen, civil servants and economists, including F. A. Hayek, Ludwig von Mises, Michael Polanyi and Raymond Aron.[31] It took as its cue the 1937 book *The Good Society* by Walter Lippmann, an American expert on public opinion and propaganda. At the end of the colloquium, despite a range of viewpoints, the participants agreed on an 'agenda of liberalism'.

29 Quinn Slobodian, *Globalists: The End of Empire and the Birth of Neoliberalism*, p. 2.

30 Anita Burdman Feferman and Solomon Feferman, *Alfred Tarski: Life and Logic*, p. 93.

31 Hagen Schulz-Forberg, 'Embedded Early Neoliberalism: Transnational Origins of the Agenda of Liberalism Reconsidered', p. 169.

When Lippmann himself set out the 'agenda of liberalism' at the morning session of the colloquium, on 20 August 1938, its first point emphasized the demands of the individual, familiar from classical liberalism:

> 1. Economic liberalism recognizes as a fundamental premise that only the pricing mechanism functioning in free markets allows for obtaining an organization of production likely to make the best use of the means of production and to lead to the maximum satisfaction of the wants of men, such as they are truly felt and not such that a central authority pretends to establish them in their name.

The remaining points, however, were devoted to the building of strong state structures in order to secure these demands:

> 2. But the positions of equilibrium that are established in markets are affected, and can be influenced in a decisive manner by the laws of property, contracts, groupings, associations, and collective moral persons, patents, bankruptcy, currency, banks, and the fiscal system. As these laws are the creation of the State, the responsibility is incumbent on the State to determine the legal system that serves as framework for the free development of economic activities.
>
> 3. Political liberalism holds as an essential premise that the legal system [*régime*] must be determined by virtue of a pre-established procedure, implying the elaboration of the law in the course of a representative debate. The solutions applied to specific cases must result from general norms; these norms themselves having been established beforehand.
>
> 4. The determination of the legal system [*régime*] constitutes the liberal method of social control. The aim of the legal system is to ensure the maximum of utility of production within the limits that other social aims can determine. These aims must be chosen through democratic procedure, and if they do not strive toward a maximum of utility, the liberal system demands that the choice for other aims be a deliberate one.
>
> 5. The organization of production on the basis of liberal principles does not preclude the allocation of a part of the national income, diverted from individual consumption, toward collective ends. A liberal State can

and must levy through taxation a share of the national income and dedicate the resulting amount to the collective financing of:

(A) National defense;
(B) Social insurance;
(C) Social services;
(D) Education;
(E) Scientific research.

6. In this way, therefore, even though liberalism has, as a fundamental postulate, the regularization of production through the pricing mechanism on the market, the system [*régime*] that we wish for recognizes:

(A) That the prices of the market are influenced by the system [*régime*] of property and contracts.

(B) That the maximum utility is a social good, but is not necessarily the only one that must be sought.

(C) That, even when production is governed by the [market] pricing mechanism, the sacrifices that the functioning of the system entails can be put at the expense of the collective. In this case, the transfer should be made not through indirect methods, but in full light of day, and the sacrifice asked of the collective has to be expressly and consciously consented to.[32]

Clearly, the programme was for a benevolent system of control, not for laissez-faire. It became a model for the Mont Pelerin Society, created by Friedrich Hayek and Wilhelm Röpke in 1947. The American philosopher John Rawls was proposed for membership of the Society by the economist Milton Friedman in 1968.[33]

The neoliberalism of the Walter Lippmann Colloquium and the Mont Pelerin Society was not simply a reaffirmation of a liberal project according to which the autonomy of the individual was paramount. It carried over the diagnosis of the frailty of liberalism that had been characteristic of the 1930s. At that time there was a consensus, including among economists such as Joseph Schumpeter, that liberal capitalism was in a critical condition. What changed after 1945 was the loss of the

32 Jurgen Reinhoudt and Serge Audier, *The Walter Lippmann Colloquium: The Birth of Neo-Liberalism*, pp. 177–9.

33 Avner Offer and Gabriel Söderberg, *The Nobel Factor: The Prize in Economics, Social Democracy, and the Market Turn*, p. 272. Offer and Söderberg assert that Rawls was actually a member from 1968 to 1971. This claim is contested in Sophie Smith, 'Historicizing Rawls', p. 930*n*161.

sense that socialism could be the salvation of liberal societies. The power elite represented by Mont Pelerin needed to develop a new set of techniques to ensure the survival of the liberal-capitalist order. The United States, after all, had to be protected not only from the Soviet sphere of influence, but from those inside it who, it was imagined, might be following Muscovite incentives in order to attempt to bring down US liberal capitalism on American soil.

Rational Choice Theory, Game Theory, Decision Theory and the 'Rationality Project'

Lippmann was an American, but the elite team of neoliberals gathered at the Walter Lippmann Colloquium and active in the Mont Pelerin Society was highly international. They provided the intellectual underpinning for the new world order, dominated by the United States.

It was in the United States that the specific techniques were developed for the maintenance of American supremacy in the world, in particular its capacity to hold out against the Soviet Union and its sphere of influence. The development of these techniques grew out of the wartime US military programme that became 'Project RAND' in 1946.[34] According to RAND's charter, 'Project RAND is a continuing program of scientific study and research on the broad subject of air warfare with the object of recommending to the Air Force preferred methods, techniques, and instrumentalities for this purpose.'[35] RAND became a chief site of intellectual productivity in the United States. It was very attractive to academics, providing abundant money and offering, as S. M. Amadae puts it, 'a flexible work environment catering to idiosyncrasies and eccentricity, and a campus-style site without the presence of students or the burden of teaching responsibilities'.[36]

It was at RAND that rational choice theory was developed. Rational choice theory is closely related to decision theory. Where decision theory studies the 'problems involved in making optimal choices', rational choice theory studies how rational agents *ought* to behave in order to optimize outcomes under certain conditions.[37] Rational choice

34 S. M. Amadae, *Rationalizing Capitalist Democracy: The Cold War Origins of Rational Choice Liberalism*, p. 32.

35 Quoted in ibid.

36 Ibid., p. 39.

37 Kenneth J. Arrow, 'Decision Theory and Operations Research', p. 765.

theory, which can thus be characterized as *normative* decision theory, is typically concerned with what it is rational for an individual to do, considered in isolation. This is, according to the economist Michael Bacharach, 'most explicit in neoclassical microeconomics', where '*homo economicus* spends his waking hours making cool and calculated decisions designed to bring about the top outcome of a set of possible outcomes which are arranged in a clear order of preference'.[38] A subfield of rational choice theory, game theory, invented by two mathematicians, the Hungarian-American John von Neumann and the German-American Oskar Morgenstern, studies the production of a social outcome as the result of the interaction between multiple such rational agents. Von Neumann and Morgenstern built their game theory on a fundamental set of technical innovations in the theory of rational individual choice under risk. Insofar as their work on game theory consists in these more fundamental advances (effectively at the level of decision theory), the application of their work in fact 'stretches far beyond games'.[39]

Rational choice theory studies scenarios in terms of inputs and outputs. Psychology did not play a role, except insofar as it could be studied in terms of stimulus and response; the natural ally of rational choice theory in psychological science was thus behaviourism. It was evidently powerful in economics. William Riker applied it in political science.[40] James Coleman applied it to sociology.[41] Amos Tversky and Daniel Kahneman operationalized it in psychology.[42] In evolutionary biology it took the form of the theory of the 'selfish gene'.[43] In philosophy it was taken up by Patrick Suppes, Donald Davidson, John Rawls, David Lewis and others.

The signal contribution to rational choice theory, when it came to shoring up the neoliberal project against collectivism, was made by Kenneth J. Arrow. Arrow, who had been impressed by Russell's *Introduction to Mathematical Philosophy* in high school and enthusiastically took a course with Tarski on the calculus of relations as an undergraduate at City College of New York, was a summer intern at RAND

38 Michael Bacharach, *Economics and the Theory of Games*, p. 3.

39 Ibid., p. vii.

40 See Amadae, *Rationalizing Capitalist Democracy*, Chapter 4.

41 James S. Coleman, *The Mathematics of Collective Action*.

42 Amos Tversky and Daniel Kahneman, 'Rational Choice and the Framing of Decisions'.

43 Richard Dawkins, *The Selfish Gene*.

in 1948.[44] The logician Olaf Helmer, a student of Reichenbach, gave him the task of formulating mathematically the Soviet Union's collective utility function, to serve in game-theoretic strategy calculations in the case of nuclear conflict. It was as part of this work that Arrow, in July 1949, devised the first formulation of his famous 'impossibility theorem', shortly after which he received a 'top secret' security clearance (which he held until 1971).

The impossibility theorem that Arrow derived states that, when voters have three or more distinct alternatives (options), no ranked voting electoral system can convert the ranked preferences of individuals into a community-wide (complete and transitive) ranking while also meeting a set of desiderata specified by Arrow (unrestricted domain, non-dictatorship, Pareto efficiency, and independence of irrelevant alternatives). In other words, any collective decision would always have some perverse, undesirable upshot. This result was not completely new; it had been anticipated by the Marquis de Condorcet in the eighteenth century and by social welfare economists in the twentieth. But it now seemed revelatory. A consensus had emerged, in the wake of the 1929 American stock market crash and the ensuing worldwide depression, that liberalism was in crisis and should be replaced by some sort of collectivism. Arrow's impossibility theorem seemed to offer the materials needed to overturn the consensus, and to lend credibility to Lippmann's attack on the notion of collective rule in *The Phantom Public* (1925). It seemed, furthermore, that Arrow had provided an argument that democracy could be upheld while rejecting collectivism.

RAND was attractive not only to economists but to logicians and philosophers. Among those employed by RAND were Quine, Reichenbach, Davidson, Helmer, Nicholas Rescher, J. C. C. McKinsey, Abraham Kaplan and Norman Dalkey. Many later played down their experiences at RAND. Quine wrote that his 'summer job as consultant there was unprecedentedly remunerative, but apart from that it was a mistake', and that, because of a delay in getting top-secret clearance, he was 'put onto boondoggles'.[45] Davidson called his RAND activities 'diversions'.[46]

44 Patrick Suppes, 'The Pre-History of Kenneth Arrow's Social Choice and Individual Values', p. 321. Arrow proofread Tarski's *Introduction to Logic* (1941), as Tarski acknowledges in the preface, and in his own *Social Choice and Individual Values* refers to Tarski.

45 W. V. Quine, *The Time of My Life*, p. 217.

46 Donald Davidson, 'Intellectual Autobiography', p. 32.

Nicholas Rescher has given a more open and extensive account of his time at RAND.[47]

One of Quine's tasks at RAND, he recalled, 'concerned Kenneth Arrow's monograph on social reconciliation of individual preferences'. He produced four memoranda for RAND, one of them later reworked into an article jointly written with McKinsey and Krentel.[48] Davidson, who wrote his PhD at Harvard on Plato's *Philebus* but had his head turned in an analytic direction by Quine's seminar on logical positivism, in 1951 took up an assistant professorship at Stanford University.[49] Here, he co-wrote with his colleagues Suppes and McKinsey an article 'on the implications for ethical theory of decision theory'.[50] In 1957, Davidson and Suppes published *Decision Making: An Experimental Approach.*

Reichenbach's work for RAND was perhaps the most serious, directly involved as it was with anti-Soviet strategy. He 'initiated several studies', concerned respectively with 'the problem of combining evidence', 'the aggregation of values' and 'decisions under risk'.[51] These were not merely academic 'boondoggles', to borrow Quine's term for his RANDiana. As the titles of two papers from 1949 indicate – 'General Form of the Probability for War' (RAND D-515) and 'Rational Reconstruction of the Decision for War' (RAND D-539) – Reichenbach was, ostensibly, attempting to lay the groundwork for real-life calculations to be made in the supposedly always impending war with the Soviet Union.

Rawls did not work for RAND. He encountered game theory, however, as an instructor at Princeton in the early 1950s.[52] As he wrote in

47 Nicholas Rescher, *Instructive Journey: An Essay in Autobiography*, Chapter 8.

48 Quine, *Time of My Life*, p. 217. See the list in Paul Erickson, *The World the Game Theorists Made*, p. 283*n*16: 'A Theorem on Parametric Boolean Functions', RAND RM-196, July 27, 1949; 'Commutative Boolean Functions', RAND RM-199, August 10, 1949; 'Notes on Information Patterns in Game Theory', RAND RM-216, August 17, 1949; 'On Functions of Relations with Especial Reference to Social Welfare', RAND RM-218, August 17, 1949. For the joint article, see W. D. Krentel, J. C. C. McKinsey and W. V. Quine, 'A Simplification of Games in Extensive Form'.

49 Davidson, 'Intellectual Autobiography', p. 22.

50 Ibid., p. 31. The paper appeared as Donald Davidson, J. C. C. McKinsey and Patrick Suppes, 'Outlines of a Formal Theory of Value, I'.

51 Norman Dalkey in Hans Reichenbach, *Selected Writings 1909–1953*, vol. 1, pp. 51–2.

52 Andrius Gališanka, 'Just Society as a Fair Game: John Rawls and Game Theory in the 1950s', p. 301.

his 1951–52 lectures, 'it is profitable to view society as a game, even as a number of games'.[53] In Rawls's view, 'the point is that we can achieve an objective by getting people to follow certain rules – even an objective of *justice* when they are all *egoistic* – provided we *design* the *rules correctly*'.[54] 'The game analogy warns us that we must not oppress self-interest – it's a poor game in which nobody wants to play.' The rules should not 'stamp out' self-interest, which is the 'motor of society'. 'Under certain conditions, "the *free* play" of self-interest achieves a rational order.'[55] Rawls's 1958 paper, 'Justice as Fairness', sets out both his proximity to, and deviations from, von Neumann and Morgenstern's theory of games. Eventually, in 1971, Rawls would engender an extraordinary rebirth of political philosophy within analytic philosophy with the publication of his *A Theory of Justice*, which he had been working on for decades. A crucial factor in this would be the dry-as-dust game-theoretical basis of Rawls's attempted vindication of a social contract theory of society.

The Machinery of McCarthyism

Analytic philosophers received much sustenance, financial and otherwise, from the incentives of 'Cold War rationality'. A more insidious form of encouragement in the direction of conformity to the demands of the political powers of the day came from the climate of fear generated by McCarthyism. Despite the name, this was a much larger phenomenon than just the work of Senator Joseph McCarthy, and was driven by the work of a panoply of quasi-legal committees, and even more so by a system of intense surveillance under the auspices of J. Edgar Hoover's FBI. Its hold on Hollywood is best known; academia was another major sphere of operation.

As Ellen Schrecker, the foremost historian of McCarthyism in the universities, has put it, McCarthyism 'produced one of the most severe episodes of political repression the United States ever experienced'.[56]

53 John Rawls, 'Society as a Game', quoted in ibid., p. 302.

54 Ibid., p. 303. Emphases in original.

55 Ibid.

56 Ellen W. Schrecker, *No Ivory Tower: McCarthyism and the Universities*, p. 9. Schrecker's book is the most authoritative treatment of McCarthyism in the universities to date. See also David Caute, *The Great Fear: The Anti-Communist Purge Under Truman and Eisenhower*, which has a somewhat wider remit, but is in places less

On Schrecker's analysis, McCarthyism was a 'process', consisting of two stages: 'First, the objectionable groups and individuals were identified – during a committee hearing, for example, or an FBI investigation; then they were punished, usually by being fired.'[57] At the first stage, those who were called before McCarthyite committees were technically witnesses, not defendants; but they were treated as if they were the accused in a court of law. If found (in effect) guilty, their academic institution then took care of the second stage: dismissal.

It might seem at first blush that membership of the Communist Party, though somewhat unfortunate in the eyes of the witch-hunters, could not, since it was not illegal, have been a fireable offence. Firings, however, could be rationalized by associating membership of the Communist Party with unfitness to uphold a university's basic mission to promote the free dissemination of knowledge. According to the precepts of McCarthyism, a communist was, by definition, a puppet controlled by Moscow, incapable of independent thought; *ergo* a communist could not be a university professor. The Whiteheadian philosopher Victor Lowe helpfully put the argument into premise-conclusion form in the pages of *The Journal of Philosophy*: 'Professor *X* is a Communist; a Communist has no respect for freedom of inquiry or for objectivity in teaching; to put it positively, he indoctrinates for the party line and the Soviet dictatorship; therefore *X* is not fit to be a professor.'[58] The argument's first premise ('Professor *X* is a Communist') was very easy to satisfy. There was no need for decisive proof that Professor *X* was a member of the Party, or indeed *was* any other kind of communist; suspicion was enough. The second premise consisted of the supposedly definitional (or 'analytic') truth that to be a communist was to be controlled from Moscow. Putting these together, the conclusion followed immediately that Professor *X* was – in truth – no professor.

Academics could be hauled in front of one of various committees. The best-known, the House Un-American Activities Committee (HUAC), was in operation as early as 1938. The smaller Rapp–Coudert Committee operated in New York from 1940 to 1942, and the Canwell Committee in Washington State in 1948. These committees constituted

---

accurate than Schrecker's book. For the impact of McCarthyism on philosophy, see John McCumber, *Time in the Ditch: American Philosophy and the McCarthy Era*, and *The Philosophy Scare: The Politics of Reason in the Early Cold War*; George A. Reisch, *How the Cold War Transformed Philosophy of Science: To the Icy Slopes of Logic.*

57 Schrecker, *No Ivory Tower*, p. 9.

58 Victor Lowe, 'A Resurgence of "Vicious Intellectualism"', p. 438.

the sharp end of McCarthyite 'Red hunting'. Many suspects of the inquisition never ended up there, since universities themselves pre-emptively implemented measures designed to prevent their academics from appearing before them, in particular through 'loyalty oaths' that they compelled their employees to sign (or – strictly speaking – on the voluntary signing of which they made employment conditional).

The effect of these procedures on academics was chilling; McCarthyism achieved its tremendous influence chiefly through the threat of persecution hanging over potential victims rather than through actual persecution. Informants were everywhere, and suspicions high. No academic was unaffected. Those in any way involved in its machinations were not only secretive at the time, but were later motivated to continue to draw a veil over their precise role, in collective self-interest. The intellectual historian George Reisch has written that, judging by memoirs such as those of the former communist turned Red-hunter Sidney Hook, 'many wounds never healed and scores were still being settled in the 1990s'.[59] Even now, many blithely go on as if not much happened. Thomas Pogge, a German-American philosopher and student of Rawls who continues to hold a number of prestigious appointments at Yale University, has written that the two years (1950–52) his mentor spent as an instructor at Princeton were 'the time of the McCarthy accusations and hearings, from which Princeton was, however, largely insulated'.[60] In fact, Princeton was nothing like insulated. One of the finest physicists of the time, David Bohm, was driven from Princeton by McCarthyism in 1950.[61] Others have been motivated to deny the penetration of McCarthyism into the universities outright. The reactionary literature professor Allan Bloom even wrote, in his diatribe *The Closing of the American Mind*, that 'professors were not fired, and they taught what they pleased in their classrooms'.[62] In reality, professors, including philosophy professors, *were* fired. And, if they were Marxists, what they taught in their classrooms was intensely scrutinized.

The loyalty oaths that universities required their employees to sign, containing a specific clause relating to non-membership of the Communist Party, were not some formal nicety; failure to sign them could have very serious consequences, as is made apparent by the case of Jacob

59 Reisch, *How the Cold War Transformed Philosophy of Science*, p. 21.

60 Thomas Pogge, *Rawls: His Life and Theory of Justice*, p. 16.

61 Schrecker, *No Ivory Tower*, pp. 142–4.

62 Allan Bloom, *The Closing of the American Mind*, p. 324.

Loewenberg. Loewenberg had given thirty-five years of service to the University of California, Berkeley, when he was fired in 1950 for refusing to sign a loyalty oath. A Latvian émigré who, after studying with the idealist Josiah Royce at Harvard, had developed his own 'problematic realism', he was no Marxist. He simply took a principled stance, and was summarily fired along with the thirty-seven other faculty members who did so, across different departments. Some philosophers turned down appointments in order to avoid having to sign loyalty oaths. Rudolf Carnap turned down two speaking invitations at Berkeley and UCLA's Flint Visiting Professorship, out of a principled opposition to signing loyalty oaths, and only accepted a teaching position at UCLA, to succeed Hans Reichenbach, after the oath requirement had been lifted.[63] Carnap seems to have been fairly exceptional. Certainly Reichenbach at UCLA and Alfred Tarski at Berkeley complied and signed the oath. Perhaps, as a Pole, Tarski was motivated by antipathy to Stalinist rule of his native country; or perhaps he just thought expediency should prevail in such matters.

The FBI could go to extraordinary lengths when it came to keeping tabs on academics. Reisch has examined the FBI files on Vienna Circle members Philipp Frank and Rudolf Carnap, both of them rather moderate leftists before the war. J. Edgar Hoover wrote to the Pentagon's chief of national security in 1952 that 'an allegation has been made that captioned individual [that is, Frank] came to the United States for the purpose of organizing high level Communist Party activities'.[64] A scrupulous search of records revealed that Frank was friends with his Harvard colleague, the astronomer Harlow Shapley, himself apparently a 'concealed communist'.[65] But that was more or less it. Hoover failed to connect Frank with any actual communist activity, and the investigation was closed in April 1954. However, an informant in Indianapolis who had known Frank in Prague provided a tip-off that sparked a new investigation. In Prague, the informant revealed, Frank had been in contact with a man by the name of Rudolf Carnap. Hoover now instructed the Newark field office to investigate Carnap; over time, FBI offices in Washington, DC, Chicago, Indianapolis and Los Angeles were drawn into the investigation. Newark agents visited Carnap about ten times at the Institute of Advanced Study in Princeton in the autumn

63 Reisch, *How the Cold War Transformed Philosophy of Science*, pp. 277–8.

64 Quoted in ibid., p. 268.

65 Ibid., p. 269.

of 1954, but could not turn up any evidence of communist agitation. What they discovered was that Carnap, as well as having been seen with Shapley at a dinner party, had a penchant for signing statements in support of various (from a Red-hunters' perspective) dubious causes. He favoured clemency for Julius and Ethel Rosenberg, convicted of spying for the Soviet Union and due to be electrocuted at Sing Sing prison. Carnap did not support the Rosenbergs' actions by any means, but averred that 'the severity of the sentence is out of proportion to the actual damage which could possibly have been done'.[66] On ten occasions, Carnap lent his signature to statements in the communist *Daily Worker* supporting leftist causes. He publicly opposed the McCarran Act in the *New York Herald Tribune*, supported the American Committee for Protection of the Foreign Born in the *Daily Worker*, signed an open telegram to the attorney general in support of deportees, called for official recognition of the People's Republic of China, and gave his name five times in support of the American Peace Crusade. His support could even be monetary, as when he donated $5 to MIT mathematician Dirk Struik's defence after his indictment under the anti-communist McCarran Act. Nothing decisive could be pinned on Carnap, however, and the case was dropped.

Philosophers Before the Inquisition

McCarthyism and its climate of fear left no philosophy professor untouched. It did not operate simply by weeding out leftists who were opposed to the new liberal consensus. Logical positivists were targets as well as phenomenologists or Marxists. Nevertheless, its chilling effect encouraged conformism and severely hampered those with the most radical agendas in philosophy.

Albert Blumberg, who had collaborated with Feigl on the paper that introduced logical positivism to America, was an early victim, called to appear before HUAC in 1940.[67] Born in Baltimore in 1906 to Russian parents, he studied at various American universities and the Sorbonne in Paris, received his doctorate under Schlick in Vienna, and from 1931 to 1937 taught philosophy at Johns Hopkins University back in Baltimore.

66 Quoted in ibid., pp. 271–2.

67 Albert E. Blumberg and Herbert Feigl, 'Logical Positivism: A New Movement in European Philosophy'.

He held a range of leadership positions in the Communist Party, and helped found the journal *Science & Society* in 1936. At a party banquet in 1942, he was introduced, according to his FBI file, as 'not only a Doctor of Philosophy and a good Party leader, but a fighter and an organizer and a political leader of whom you can all be proud'.[68] After appearing before HUAC, Blumberg was fined and given a suspended sentence of thirty days in prison. He subsequently gave courses at the Communist Party's New Worker's School in Manhattan on such topics as 'What Is Philosophy?', 'World Politics' and 'The Negro in America'. In 1958 he left his radical political life and returned to academia, teaching at Rutgers University from 1965 to 1977, where he ardently supported student protests against the Vietnam War.

In 1941, Howard Selsam was called before the Rapp–Coudert Committee. A grocer's son from Harrisburg, Pennsylvania, he had been a graduate student at Columbia University, where he wrote a master's thesis on the eighteenth-century French materialist d'Holbach and a PhD dissertation on the British Idealist T. H. Green. Selsam took 'an active part in the social struggles of his day on the side of the communist movement', and participated in anti-war events on campus.[69] He published in *New Masses* under the pseudonym 'Paul Salter', and was an editorial board member of *Science & Society*. As a teacher, he was careful not to impose his political views on students. When called before the Rapp–Coudert Committee, he refused to testify, as a consequence of which he faced contempt charges and was forced to resign his position at Brooklyn College. He never again held an academic appointment; instead, he participated in alternative educational institutions. He co-founded the School for Democracy in New York, associated with the Communist Party, and in 1944 became director of the Jefferson School of Social Science, a Marxist adult education institute, closed down in 1956.

Selsam's political commitments were pursued in his academic works, such as *What Is Philosophy? A Marxist Introduction* (1938), *Socialism and Ethics* (1947), *The Negro People in the United States: Facts for All Americans* (1953) and *Philosophy in Revolution* (1957). Herbert J. Phillips, a professor at the University of Washington who was called before the Canwell Committee, by contrast, did not publish on Marxist topics

68 Quoted in Reisch, *How the Cold War Transformed Philosophy of Science*, p. 97.

69 Dirk Struik, 'Howard Selsam 1903–1970', p. 225.

but was a Marxist by conviction, and told his students to take this into account.[70] The case against him, such as it was, rested entirely on his membership of the Communist Party. Raymond B. Allen, president of the University of Washington, concluded that Phillips and his co-defendant Joseph Butterworth were 'by reason of their admitted membership of the Communist Party . . . incompetent, intellectually dishonest, and derelict in their duty to find and teach the truth'.[71] This is the basis on which Phillips was fired. The dismissal of Phillips and others from the University of Washington established the 'Allen Formula', according to which mere Party membership led directly to dismissal. Phillips was now unable to get another academic position, and scraped by in a variety of odd jobs, working for a while on a construction site, and later on an assembly line in a furniture factory. By the time he could have returned to the academy, in the early sixties, he was on Social Security.[72]

The case of another philosopher called before the Canwell Committee, Melvin Rader, indicates just how far McCarthyism could go. Like Phillips, Rader was accused simply of membership of the Communist Party, having been informed against by another man in front of the Committee. According to Rader's account, however, he was never in fact a member of the Party, and he was later exonerated.[73]

Barrows Dunham, called before HUAC in 1952, was, by contrast, decidedly a Party member *and* a Marxist philosopher.[74] Like many others, he had been radicalized in the 1930s, and published in *New Masses* under the pseudonym 'Joel Bradford'. Having joined the Communist Party in 1938, he left in 1945, largely in protest at the expulsion of his friend Samuel Adams Darcy. When called before HUAC, Dunham invoked the Fifth Amendment, designed to protect witnesses from incriminating themselves. He refused to answer all questions other than to state his name, age and home address. This made him HUAC's most uncooperative witness thus far. As a result of his performance, he

70 Schrecker, *No Ivory Tower*, pp. 44–5, 100.

71 Quoted in ibid., p. 103.

72 Ibid., pp. 104, 283.

73 For an account of the witch hunt, see Melvin Rader, *False Witness*.

74 The main source on Dunham is the highly detailed dissertation by Fred Zimring, 'Academic Freedom and the Cold War: The Dismissal of Barrows Dunham from Temple University: A Case Study'. See also the website by Jordan Ricker, storymaps.arcgis.com, and Howard L. Parsons, 'The Philosophy of Barrows Dunham: The Progress of an American Radical'.

was suspended from his position at Temple University. The university's president, Robert L. Johnson, explained to him that his 'lack of cooperation' was 'inconsistent with your obligations as a teacher and your responsibilities to all members of Temple University, and to the society of which it is a part'.[75] Temple set up its own internal Loyalty Committee in the spring of 1952. Dunham later described his new inquisitors as 'more loathsome' than those of HUAC, and as 'cowards, cowards'.[76] Attorneys hired by the university's trustees to write up an opinion duly recommended Dunham's dismissal. Since the decision to fire him rested entirely on his invocation of the Fifth Amendment, they could claim it involved 'no issue of academic freedom and no question concerning the political opinions of Dr Dunham'. Dunham was acquitted in 1955, but not reinstated by Temple. It was only in 1981 that Temple University restored Barrows Dunham to the faculty.[77]

The insidious pressures of McCarthyism are well illustrated by the vacillations on the part of the respected pragmatist philosopher John Dewey when it came to Dunham's book *Man Against Myth*. When approached for an endorsement of the book, Dewey eagerly obliged, and the book appeared with the following text on its dust jacket: 'Dr Dunham has written a remarkable book . . . for me, it is most decidedly the book of the year – and in the interest of good sense and intelligent clearheaded action one can hope for many years to come.'[78] Soon after the book's appearance, however, Dewey dramatically changed his mind. The millionaire businessman Albert C. Barnes, founder of the Barnes Foundation, had written to Dewey to instruct him that Dunham's book was 'a phony', 'in the class of communistic tracts'. Dewey was moved to write to Dunham to tell him that he was 'disturbed by the reports that my endorsement of your book carried with it an endorsement of that part of your economic [views] which agree with those of the PCA, Wallace and other Pro-Soviet partisans'. He then wrote to the publisher withdrawing his endorsement.[79]

When Stanley Moore, a fellow Marxist philosopher at Reed College in Portland, Oregon, was called before HUAC in June 1954, he, like

75 Schrecker, *No Ivory Tower*, pp. 209–10.

76 Quoted in ibid., pp. 210–11.

77 Ibid., p. 338.

78 Quoted in Zimring, 'Academic Freedom and the Cold War', p. 138.

79 Ibid., pp. 139–41. Zimring's source for Dewey's letter to the publisher, Little, Brown and Company, is an FBI informant's report.

Dunham, 'took the Fifth'.[80] On 13 August he was fired by the College's Board of Trustees, even though he was a full professor with tenure.[81] Moore, like Dunham, had joined the Communist Party in the 1930s, but had left by the time of his HUAC appearance. In an open letter released the day after his hearing, he directly criticized the Allen Formula. If the reason for firing communists were really that they were incapable of independent thought, then they would never have acquired the faculty positions they were fired from in the first place. 'Behind the falsehood that no Communist is qualified to teach', Moore wrote in his open letter, 'lies the truth that all Communists get fired.'[82] Moore was duly fired. After a series of temporary jobs, he taught at the University of California, San Diego, from 1965. On 14 January 1978, the Reed College Board of Trustees decreed that it had made a mistake in firing him.[83]

Dunham and Moore had taken the principled stance of invoking the Fifth Amendment before HUAC in order to remain entirely silent in the face of the inquisition. A lighter, and more successful, version of this approach was adopted by David Hawkins and William T. Parry, who chose to speak freely about themselves but remain silent on all questions concerning others' involvement with communism. Unlike Dunham and Moore, neither of them was a social philosopher of a Marxist stripe, but they had both been involved with communism in the 1930s. Hawkins, called before HUAC in 1950, had majored in philosophy at Stanford, before going to Berkeley in 1936 to work on a PhD dissertation entitled *A Causal Interpretation of Probability.* He joined the Communist Party in 1938, but dropped out after a few years. In 1943 he was recruited by his friend J. Robert Oppenheimer to work at the Manhattan Project's Los Alamos Laboratory, where he was Oppenheimer's administrative assistant, and responsible for selecting the Alamogordo area as the location for the Trinity nuclear test. Although his appearance before HUAC generated much controversy, Hawkins retained his job at the University of Colorado at Boulder. His junior colleague Morris Judd was not so lucky. Judd was considered the

80 On Moore, see Michael Munk, 'Oregon Tests Academic Freedom in (Cold) Wartime: The Reed College Trustees Versus Stanley Moore'; Floyd J. McKay, 'After Cool Deliberation: Reed College, Oregon Editors, and the Red Scare of 1954'.

81 Munk, 'Oregon Tests Academic Freedom', p. 263; Schrecker, *No Ivory Tower*, p. 236.

82 Quoted in Schrecker, *No Ivory Tower*, p. 239.

83 Ibid., p. 338.

department's most promising instructor, and had been unanimously recommended for promotion to assistant professor. He was, like Hawkins, called before HUAC, and told the committee he was not then a communist, but refused to answer any other questions about his politics. The University of Colorado at Boulder, perhaps in order to expiate the sin of retaining Hawkins, offered up Judd as a lamb to the slaughter. He was fired, and never worked as a philosopher again, instead running a junkyard.

When Parry, a logician, was called before HUAC in 1953, he adopted a similar policy to that of Hawkins, talking freely about himself, but not others.[84] He had been radicalized in 1932 after witnessing fascist rioting at the University of Vienna, where he was spending time before handing in his PhD, completed that same year under Whitehead at Harvard, on the topic of implication. He solidified his grasp of communism by reading Lenin's *State and Revolution*. In 1933 he joined the Communist Party USA, in 1936 became a founder and the first managing editor of *Science & Society*, and in 1937 organized the Harvard unit of the Communist Party.[85] He left the Party in 1946, but continued to publish in the journal.[86] After appearing before HUAC, Parry remained employed by the University of Buffalo, but had his tenure revoked and was 'placed on annual appointment as associate professor'.[87] His tenure was not restored until 1961.

Parry's work was of signal importance in modal logic, seemingly removed from anything to do with communism. Nonetheless, Parry did not keep his logical interests entirely insulated from Marxism. In 1948 he published a paper, 'The Unity of Opposites: A Dialectical Principle', jointly with V. Jerauld McGill, who would later become another victim of the 'great fear'. When McGill was fired by Hunter College, New York, in October 1956, his crime was not that of remaining silent about his brief period in the Communist Party in the 1930s (which he freely admitted), but his refusal to name others.[88] Although, like Parry, McGill had gained his PhD from Harvard, he was a quite different kind of philosopher, immensely broad in range. He had used a Sheldon Traveling Fellowship in 1925–26 to study with both G. E. Moore in

84 On Parry, see Irving H. Anellis, 'Parry, William Tuthill (1908–88)'.

85 On Parry as organizer of the Harvard unit, see Robert W. Iversen, *The Communists and the Schools*, p. 164.

86 Peter H. Hare, 'William Tuthill Parry 1908–1988', p. 314.

87 Schrecker, *No Ivory Tower*, p. 207.

88 Caute, *Great Fear*, p. 445.

Cambridge and Edmund Husserl in Freiburg, and in the early 1930s published monographs on August Strindberg and Arthur Schopenhauer. In 1940 he co-founded the International Phenomenological Society, and joined the editorial staff of its organ, *Philosophy and Phenomenological Research*.[89]

Sometimes a professor could be fired even without the involvement of a McCarthyite committee. The African American philosopher Forrest O. Wiggins was fired by the University of Minnesota simply for making a speech in January 1951 in which he directly criticized the US government. In the speech, entitled 'The Ideology of Interest', Wiggins argued that 'capitalism did not emerge from the last depression by any natural causes indigenous to capitalism itself', and (concerning the Korean War) that 'it is the capitalists and the militarists in the United States who want war'.[90] Wiggins's appointment had been greeted by a certain amount of fanfare. Having obtained a PhD from the University of Wisconsin in 1938, he had worked at a series of colleges in the South – including Morehouse College, Johnson C. Smith University and Howard University – before the University of Minnesota hired him in 1946 as an instructor in philosophy, making him the first African American to be given 'a regular full time teaching appointment with the rank of instructor at a state university', a historical first celebrated in *Atlantic Monthly* in an article entitled 'Chosen for Ability'.[91] Wiggins, as vice-president of the Minnesota Progressive Party, campaigned for the Progressive Party nominee Henry A. Wallace's presidential bid in 1948, openly attacking capitalism, racism and imperialist war.[92]

On 7 December 1951, Wiggins received a letter from the University of Minnesota's president, James L. Morrill, informing him that his contract would not be renewed. The chairman of the philosophy department, George P. Conger, protested, and students immediately mobilized. They amassed 2,035 signatures for a petition they sent to Morrill requesting clarification of the 'grounds on which Dr Wiggins

89 Today *Philosophy and Phenomenological Research* is, despite its title, an analytic-only journal.

90 Forrest O. Wiggins, 'The Ideology of Interest', Forrest O. Wiggins Papers, University of Minnesota, Box 1, Folder 1.

91 'Biographical Sketch of Forrest O. Wiggins (1907–82)', at archives.lib.umn.edu; Fred G. Wale, 'Chosen for Ability'.

92 John H. McClendon III and Stephen C. Ferguson II, *African American Philosophers and Philosophy: An Introduction to the History, Concepts, and Contemporary Issues*, p. xv.

has been considered incompetent'. Morrill issued a statement declaring that Wiggins's dismissal was based solely on deficiency in professional competence and scholarship. This was surprising, since Wiggins was highly regarded by his colleagues. According to the historian David Caute, he had in fact been 'dogged by the FBI' and 'harassed by rumors ranging from homosexuality to having had relations with white female students'.[93] Eight hundred students met under the aegis of the Student Action Committee, and issued a statement. The Minnesota branch of the American Association of University Professors investigated the case; as was characteristic of its investigations, it managed to detect no violation of academic freedom. The National Association for the Advancement of Colored People (NAACP) and the American Civil Liberties Union (ACLU) stepped in to support Wiggins. All this was to no avail. After being fired, no school would have him, until he finally found employment at a black religious institution, Allen College in Columbia, South Carolina. After Allen College dismissed him in 1957, Wiggins taught at various other small colleges in the South until his retirement in 1971. According to Caute, some of the students who had stood up in defence of Wiggins 'were subsequently rejected for state employment'.[94]

The Case of Angela Davis

In the universities, McCarthyism was largely about academic freedom. The image of free academic enquiry it upheld was, clearly enough, a sham, the mirror of its deranged notion about communists' – or would-be communists', or suspected communists' – slavish devotion to dictates emanating from Moscow. Its effect was to place severe limits on any freedom of thought that involved deviation from the demands of American neoliberalism.

In 1969, long after the death of Senator Joseph McCarthy, the philosopher and activist Angela Davis was subjected to what she described as 'an inquisition à la McCarthy' at the University of California, Los Angeles (UCLA).[95] The Angela Davis affair made freedom of speech on campus the absolutely central issue.

93 Caute, *Great Fear*, p. 421.

94 Ibid.

95 Angela Y. Davis, *An Autobiography*, p. 217.

Davis's hiring by UCLA was preceded by overtures from, of all places, the Princeton philosophy department, by now an analytic stronghold. The chair of the department, Donald Davidson, made moves to hire Davis to teach a class on the early Marx, and had her interviewed for a position. This was 1968: an exceptional moment in which not even analytic philosophy departments could remain impervious to the charged political atmosphere. Davis's background and intellectual orientation would seem to have made her entirely antithetic to the analytic approach in philosophy. Born in Birmingham, Alabama, into a family of black activists, she had majored in French at Brandeis University, where her interest in philosophy was stimulated by Herbert Marcuse, the most politically radical member of the Frankfurt School, who was then teaching there. Marcuse resolved to 'teach her philosophy' in a series of one-to-one meetings, remarking that Davis was 'the best student I ever had in the more than 30 years I have been teaching'.[96] After graduating from Brandeis in 1965, Davis went, on Marcuse's recommendation, to work with Theodor Adorno in Frankfurt. When she returned to the United States in 1967, Marcuse had been pushed out of his position at Brandeis, and was now teaching at the University of California, San Diego, where Davis now began work on a PhD supervised by him on 'the problem of violence in German idealism'.[97] Progress on the PhD was slow, but Davis's fame was spreading sufficiently for Davidson to have become aware of her.[98] Unfortunately, when Davis came to be interviewed at Princeton, as Davidson later recalled events, 'the department faculty was unimpressed, and she wasn't appointed'.[99] Although Davidson thought it 'would have been better if Angela Davis had been there to teach it', he himself took charge of the class on the early Marx, but 'let the students do most of the preparing and talking', in line with the general tendency at Princeton and elsewhere at this time towards student autonomy and informality.[100] Davidson, however, wrote to the philosophy department at UCLA to inform them of Davis's 'interest in a teaching position', noting that both Princeton and Swarthmore had

96 Marcuse quoted in 'Personality: The Fugitive', *Time Magazine*, 31 August 1970.

97 Donald Kalish and David Kaplan, 'A Statement of Facts Concerning the Appointment and Threatened Dismissal of Professor Angela Davis, Provided by the UCLA Department of Philosophy, September 29, 1969'.

98 Davis's PhD seems never to have been completed.

99 Davidson, 'Intellectual Autobiography', p. 47.

100 Ibid., pp. 48, 47.

been sufficiently interested to invite her to interview.[101] When interviewed at UCLA, Davis scraped through, with 'only a bare majority' voting in favour of her appointment.[102] Nonetheless, on 21 April 1969 she was appointed to a two-year position at the rank of acting assistant professor.

It was not long before the campaign to oust Davis from her position began. On 1 July 1969, a student called William Divale, who was acting as an undercover agent for the FBI, wrote in UCLA's *Daily Bruin* newspaper that the philosophy department 'has recently made a two-year appointment of an acting assistant professor. The person is well qualified for the post, and is also a member of the Communist Party.' On 9 July the *San Francisco Examiner* named the person as Angela Davis, adding that she was a 'known Maoist, according to US intelligence reports, and active in the SDS and the Black Panthers'. As a result, the chancellor's office sent a letter to Davis on 16 July, stating: 'I am constrained by Regental policy to request that you inform me whether or not you are a member of the Communist Party.'[103] In reply, Davis openly declared that she was, at the time of writing, a member of the Communist Party, adding:

> While I think this membership requires no justification here, I want you to know that as a black woman I feel an urgent need to find radical solutions to the problems of racial and national minorities in white capitalist United States. I feel that my membership in the Communist Party has widened my horizons and expanded my opportunities for perceiving such solutions and working for their effectuation.[104]

On 19 September, in response to Davis's statement, the regents of the University of California adopted the following resolution:

> WHEREAS, on October 11, 1940, the Regents adopted a Resolution stating that 'membership in the Communist Party is incompatible with membership in the faculty of a State University'; and
>
> WHEREAS, on June 24, 1949, the Regents reaffirmed and amplified that policy with a Resolution stating, in part, 'pursuant to this policy,

101 Kalish and Kaplan, 'Statement of Facts'.
102 Bettina Aptheker, *The Morning Breaks: The Trial of Angela Davis*, p. 2.
103 Kalish and Kaplan, 'Statement of Facts'.
104 Quoted in ibid.

> the Regents direct that no member of the Communist Party shall be employed by the University'; and
>
> WHEREAS, in an action reported March 22, 1950, the Academic Senate, Northern and Southern Sections, concurred in the foregoing policy by adopting a resolution that proved members of the Communist Party are not acceptable as members of the faculty; and
>
> WHEREAS, on April 21, 1950, the Regents adopted a Resolution confirming and emphasizing their policy statements of October 11, 1940, and June 24, 1949; and
>
> WHEREAS, it has been reported to the Regents that Angela Y. Davis was recently appointed as a member of the University faculty, and subsequently she informed the University Administration by letter, stating, among other things, that she is a member of the Communist Party;
>
> NOW, THEREFORE, the Regents direct the President to take steps to terminate Miss Davis' University appointment in accordance with regular procedures as prescribed in the Standing Orders of the Regents.[105]

The philosophy department staunchly defended Davis, led by its chair, Donald Kalish, who was physically attacked by a man who broke into the department building.[106] Kalish, an outstanding logician, had strong left-wing sympathies, and had himself in 1950 been under investigation by a 'loyalty oath committee' – but, thanks to his statement that 'the philosophical foundations of Marx's Communism are balderdash', no action was taken.[107] Davis recounted in her *Autobiography* that she was under constant attack from racists and anti-communists. 'Bomb threats were so frequent that after a while the campus police stopped checking under the hood of my car for explosives. Of necessity, I had to learn the procedure myself.'[108]

Despite the support Davis received from her department, the regents ploughed ahead with determination. On 3 October they adopted a further resolution, declaring that 'during the Fall quarter of 1969 Miss Davis shall be assigned no teaching duties, and that she shall not be authorized to give instruction in any course under the jurisdiction of any school, college, department or other academic agency approved by

---

105 *University Bulletin*, 29 September 1969, p. 29.

106 Davis, *Autobiography*, p. 219.

107 'Summary of Loyalty Oath Hearings and Recommendations, Los Angeles Campus (June, 1950)', at oac.cdlib.org.

108 Davis, *Autobiography*, p. 220.

The Regents'.[109] But the resolution was declared unconstitutional by the Superior Court of California, so that UCLA's chancellor had to write to the registrar: 'you are hereby constrained to accept regular enrollments in Philosophy 99 to which Prof. Davis had previously been assigned as instructor by the chairman of the Dept. of Philosophy'.[110] The regents now regrouped to find a new rationale for dismissing Davis. They appointed an ad hoc committee, and on 19 June 1970 approved by a vote of fifteen-to-six the committee's report setting out its findings. The committee presented itself in its report as having entirely ignored 'the membership of Angela Davis in the Communist Party or the circumstances in which previous actions were taken by the Board relating to her membership in the Communist Party'.[111] Instead, it had devoted its attentions exclusively to three 'allegations against Miss Davis':

> 1. That she has utilized her position in the classroom for the purpose of indoctrinating students;
> 2. That her extra University commitments and activities interfere with her duties as a member of the faculty; and
> 3. That her public statements demonstrate her commitment to a concept of academic freedom which substantiates the first two charges and would ultimately be destructive of that essential freedom itself.[112]

The committee stated that, while they had found no substantiation for the first two charges, they found the third to be substantiated; and anyway, the third charge was formulated in such a way as to entail substantiation of the first two. The committee took as its evidence four speeches Davis had made around various California campuses between October 1969 and February 1970, which it evaluated against the American Association of University Professors' Statement on Professional Ethics, stating that a professor 'respects and defends the free inquiry of his associates', 'shows due respect for the opinions of others' and 'has a particular obligation to promote conditions of free inquiry and to further public understanding of academic freedom'.

Clearly Davis, the committee found, had violated these aspects of the ethics code. She had quite unacceptably 'denounced' a 'professor who,

109 *University Bulletin*, 13 October 1969, p. 39.
110 Quoted in *University Bulletin*, 27 October 1969, p. 49.
111 Quoted in *University Bulletin*, 29 June 1970, p. 197.
112 Ibid., p. 198.

after years of study, published a lengthy article outlining an hypothesis that certain kinds of learning abilities vary in measurable degrees between races and are due primarily to genetic rather than social factors'; she had, again quite unacceptably, called him 'a racist and an "exploiter" of academic freedom'.[113] Davis had a tendency to be 'less than fair in her characterization of the views of fellow scholars whom she has denounced' – for example, calling the scholars who voted not to fire (or *not renew the contract of*) the radical anthropology professor Bill Allen 'senile'. Her whole notion of how academics should behave seemed seriously off. The committee expressed its consternation by quoting Davis's own words on academic freedom, which she considered 'an empty concept which professors use to guarantee their right to work undisturbed by the real world, undisturbed by the real problems of this society', not realizing 'that they are also unconscious perhaps . . . accomplices in the exploitation and oppression of man'. For Davis, academic freedom was meaningless unless used to 'unveil the predominant, oppressive ideas and acts of this country'; otherwise, she said, it was a 'real farce'. A lot of her language just seemed too 'extravagant and inflammatory', 'distasteful and reprehensible', as when she referred to the police as 'pigs' (although the committee admitted that such language did not really imperil academic freedom).[114] As the committee reported, the philosophy department endorsed Davis's reappointment, with fourteen voting in favour and three abstentions.[115] The dean of the Division of Humanities and the dean of the College of Letters and Science tried the manoeuvre of pleading that there was no money to reappoint Davis, claiming it would require 'special funding' to do so; but the Budget Committee flatly contradicted this. In any case, the committee's mind was made up: Davis's statements in her speeches were 'so extreme, so antithetical to the protection of academic freedom and so obviously deliberately false in several respects as to be inconsistent with qualification for appointment to the faculty of the University of California'.[116] The problem seemed to be Davis's views themselves, in particular her attack on what she considered sham academic freedom, the committee itself admitting that the intemperate nature of Davis's speeches could not, of itself, contribute to undermining 'standards' of academic freedom.

113 Ibid., p. 199.
114 Ibid.
115 Ibid.
116 Quoted in ibid., p. 200.

Challenges of the kind posed by Davis to liberal conceptions of free speech have subsequently made little impact on analytic philosophy – not because university regents have stepped in to protect analytic philosophers from such challenges, but simply because they are never heard in the first place. Such rhetoric, if it is aired on university campuses, is heard only outside the philosophy seminar. Angela Davis was never to cross paths with analytic philosophy again. In the 1970s the world of American academic philosophy settled down, and resumed its liberal slumber.

6

Analytic and Continental

As it works to sustain and reproduce its hegemony in the academy, analytic philosophy expels its challengers. Its most important out-group consists of those nourished on the post-Kantian philosophical tradition that analytic philosophy circumvents in order to take things up where David Hume left them: what analytic philosophers have called 'continental philosophy'.[1] Today, the categories of 'analytic philosophy' and 'continental philosophy' have been naturalized to the point that, to students of philosophy, it seems almost unquestionable that there simply are two such traditions. From the student's point of view, the analytic–continental 'divide', if it has not *always* been there, is certainly so long-lived a feature of the philosophical landscape as not to come in for questioning.

We have seen that analytic philosophy did not constitute itself as the unified entity we now know until the late 1940s. The *self*-constitution of 'continental philosophy' is a much later affair still. Use of the term 'continental philosophy', as a contrast to Anglo-Saxon philosophy, in play already in the nineteenth century, grew in the early twentieth century, and became entrenched after the Second World War. The self-conscious description of philosophers as 'continental', however, did not

1 As the opening sentence of the article 'Philosophie continentale' in French Wikipedia states in lapidary fashion, '"Continental philosophy" is a term originally used by Anglophone philosophers of language, especially those belonging to analytic philosophy, to designate various philosophical traditions from continental Europe (especially Germany and France)' – at fr.wikipedia.org.

happen until much later, in the 1980s, principally in the United States and the rest of the Anglosphere.[2]

The reasons for the late entrenchment of 'continental philosophy' as an academic and social formation are not far to seek. Analytic philosophy was a fusion of what, before the Second World War, had been a set of autonomous movements. Continental philosophy has not even been that. The very idea of 'continental philosophy' is an analytic philosopher's fiction. Not only are the movements and approaches it lumps together – phenomenology, existentialism, hermeneutics, structuralism, deconstruction – diverse, but some of them (deconstruction in particular) challenge the very idea of *philosophy* itself in a way that does not even occur to analytic philosophers as a possibility. Continental philosophy, in one sense, is just a fiction; it does not exist. In another, more important sense, it does. Analytic philosophers have made it so. This is a social reality, one that self-professed 'continental philosophers' have more recently helped to sustain. Continental philosophers now have their own journals, conferences, sometimes departments. They, too, cite their own kind and move in their own circles.

In recent decades, analytic philosophers have been much given to attempts to dismiss the distinction between analytic and continental philosophy as mistaken or no longer useful. The usual tactic is to point out that, as is immediately obvious, 'continental' is a geographical designation, whereas 'analytic' is not. As we saw in previous chapters, many analytic philosophers were from the continent of Europe. The point is often made by repeating a quip made by Bernard Williams: 'it is like classifying cars as Japanese and front-wheel drive'.[3] In other words, the analytic–continental distinction involves a 'cross-classification between the methodological and the geographical'. But Williams's quip falls flat. Such cross-classification could, conceivably, be a problem if there was a real chance someone might fail to recognize that two different distinctions (one geographical, the other methodological) were in play. No one is really fooled, however.[4]

---

2 A Google Ngram confirms that use of the term 'continental philosophy' shot up in the 1980s.

3 Bernard Williams, *Philosophy as a Humanistic Discipline*, p. 201.

4 Consider the retort to Williams's quip by Peter Dews, highlighting the ability of what analytic philosophers like to call 'competent users of English' to handle such cross-classifications without much trouble: 'Williams's remark is no more persuasive than the claim that a Danish pastry can't be distinguished from a croissant, since

In the first place, analytic philosophers seem to handle the contrast with ease, and without any apparent confusion. The contrast was available more or less as soon as the concept 'analytic philosophy' became widely accepted. This is evinced, for example, by the Jesuit historian of philosophy Frederick Copleston, writing in 1953: 'In my opinion both the Americans and ourselves have something to learn from modern continental philosophy. On the other hand some of the continental philosophers might profit by giving some serious attention to linguistic analysis.'[5] This is not surprising, since the label 'continental philosophy' was invented precisely to mark out a contrast with analytic philosophy (or, as Copleston calls it, 'linguistic analysis').

If today analytic philosophers like to announce that the conflict with continental philosophy is over, things look like that, to them, because they have successfully colonized their 'other'. Anil Gomes, an analytic philosopher at the University of Oxford, has written that 'analytic philosophy has moved into the places where Continental philosophy once reigned supreme: reading its thinkers, writing on its topics, pushing it to the margins'. Gomes applies to this process the epithet 'gentrification', and comments that, 'for some of us' (that is, presumably, Gomes is thinking, analytic philosophers), 'the coffee now tastes better'.[6] Gomes's witticism is tellingly apt.

Post-war England

The association of 'continental philosophy' with dark, threatening European ideas apt to disturb the placid English mind is older than analytic philosophy. It has its precedents in the nineteenth century, when the importation of German ideas to the islands under British rule by Samuel Taylor Coleridge and Thomas De Quincey invited the outrage of such right-thinking Englishmen as John Stuart Mill.[7] Even at this date, it is notable that 'continental philosophy' functioned as an

---

croissants are also produced in Copenhagen.' Peter Dews, letter to *London Review of Books*, 18 March 2021.

5 Frederick C. Copleston, '*Philosophic Thought in France and the United States*, edited by Marvin Farber', p. 363.

6 Anil Gomes, letter to *London Review of Books*, 1 April 2021.

7 John Passmore, *A Hundred Years of Philosophy*, pp. 14–16. Compare, for John Stuart Mill's use of the term 'continental philosophy', his essay 'Coleridge', in *Dissertations and Discussions*, vol. 2.

ideological marker, not a merely descriptive geographical term. Mill did not apply it, for instance, to the positivism invented by the Frenchman Auguste Comte – an important inspiration for his own version of empiricism.

New fuel was added to the anti-continental fire in post–Second World War Britain.[8] A. J. Ayer was probably the most vociferous anti-continental campaigner. Relying on his credentials as a fluent French speaker, thanks to his descent from French Swiss on his father's side and from the French Citroën family on his mother's, with the supposed implication that he would be friendly to French culture if anyone was, he made it his business to denigrate French philosophy, in particular the work of Sartre. In a talk delivered at the first UNESCO conference in Paris in 1946, he began by dividing contemporary philosophers into two classes: the 'pontiffs' and the 'journeymen'. The pontiffs, Ayer said, challenge the claim of scientists to 'give a complete and definite account of "ultimate" reality'. According to the journeymen – 'technicians' who 'deal piecemeal with a special set of problems' – 'this "ultimate" reality is a fiction'. The pontiffs know this somewhere, and so 'tend to desert reason and even to decry it'. Hegel had at least 'claimed the support of reason for his fantasies', but, with Heidegger, 'the leading pontiff' of the day, we are 'in a country from which the ordinary processes of logic, or indeed reasoning of any kind, appear to have been banished'. Heidegger simply appealed, Ayer pontificated, to the experience of anguish, 'provided that it is always an anguish without any special object'. This anguish reveals 'the Nothing'. Ayer admitted that Heidegger did seem to have an argument for this, but since it depended 'upon the elementary fallacy of treating "nothing" as a name, it is hardly to be taken seriously'.[9]

On several occasions, Ayer delivered critiques of Sartre, the most important existentialist in the wake of Heidegger, that affected to be based on close scrutiny of his texts. Here too, however, what Ayer

---

8 This terrain has been well covered by Thomas L. Akehurst in a series of writings: 'The Nazi Tradition: The Analytic Critique of Continental Philosophy in Mid-Century Britain', 'British Analytic Philosophy: The Politics of an Apolitical Culture', and *The Cultural Politics of Analytic Philosophy: Britishness and the Spectre of Europe*. Unfortunately, Akehurst's approach tends to the reductionistic, seemingly seeking to explain away his protagonists' ideas through an uncovering of their covert political motivations. See also Andreas Vrahimis, *Bergsonism and the History of Analytic Philosophy*, which gives greater credence to the philosophy but lacks Akehurst's sense for the social.

9 A. J. Ayer, 'The Claims of Philosophy', p. 52.

actually offered in the guise of critique was a series of flippant put-downs. About Sartre's doctrine that existence precedes essence, he wrote: 'It is just as necessary that a tea-pot should exist if it is actually to contain tea as that a man should exist if he is actually to have the character of being rational.'[10] One device was simply to quote a passage from Sartre followed by such a statement as: 'This is a typically Existentialist piece of reasoning and one that I find very difficult to follow.'[11] The profession 'I do not understand this', if aimed by the right person at the right target, counts as a powerful objection in analytic philosophy.

Royaumont

Ayer never met Sartre, who was of the opinion that 'Ayer est un con'.[12] He did meet Georges Bataille and Maurice Merleau-Ponty.[13] On the whole, analytic philosophers and their continental counterparts were experts at avoiding each other. This was so even at the International Congress of Philosophy, a mammoth meeting of philosophers held every few years (and at the first instalment of which Russell had made the personal acquaintance of Louis Couturat and Giuseppe Peano). Write-ups of such congresses in the philosophy journals record the rift. A report of the Eleventh Congress (Brussels, 1953) speaks of 'the deep cleavage between Anglo-American philosophy on the one side and Continental philosophy on the other', and adds: 'the Continentals do their philosophizing by themselves without any reference to or interest in the Anglo-American group, and vice versa; the two groups move in parallels that never meet'.[14] At the Twelfth Congress (Venice and Padua, 1958), 'the familiar empiricist versus existentialist and metaphysical gulf was still evident'; it was not that 'the average British analysts *scorn* Continental philosophy – they merely *ignore* it'.[15]

---

10 A. J. Ayer, 'Some Aspects of Existentialism', p. 5.

11 Ibid., pp. 8–9.

12 Olivier Todd, *Un fils rebelle*, p. 105.

13 For the details, see Andreas Vrahimis, *Encounters Between Analytic and Continental Philosophy*, Chapter 3.

14 Max Rieser, 'Remarks on the Eleventh International Congress of Philosophy', p. 100.

15 Paul W. Kurtz, 'International Congresses and International Tensions', p. 1,137.

Also in 1958, a group of French philosophers staged a significant attempt to arrange an encounter across the divide, inviting a set of leading representatives of what was now widely coming to be known as 'analytic philosophy' to speak at a conference at Royaumont Abbey, near Paris.[16] Most of the speakers were from Oxford: J. O. Urmson, Bernard Williams, Gilbert Ryle, P. F. Strawson, J. L. Austin and R. M. Hare. W. V. Quine was invited from America. Also on the analytic team were Leo Apostel from Belgium and Evert Willem Beth from the Netherlands.

The attempt to achieve mutual understanding, if that is what it was, was a failure. One of the participants, the then twenty-six-year-old Canadian philosopher Charles Taylor, described it as 'a dialogue that didn't come off, a *dialogue de sourds*'.[17] Taylor, a bilingual Québécois, acted as a translator back and forth between English and French speakers, screening out some of the more offensive remarks as he went; J. L. Austin was the only Anglophone philosopher to present his talk in French.[18] Few among the French knew much about analytic philosophy, although Jean Wahl, who presided, had written on British and American philosophers, as well as on Hegel and Kierkegaard.[19] The tragic failure to achieve full engagement is well recorded in the proceedings, in which edited versions of the discussions are printed following the papers themselves. There were some attempts to establish convergences and sympathies, but also insults – the Dominican logician Józef Maria Bocheński elicited laughter, as the proceedings record, by suggesting that, as far as he was concerned, Quine's view might be said to be 'simplistic, absurd, mythological, etc.'[20] There were subtle digs in both directions. Merleau-Ponty, who had been persuaded to grace the symposium with his presence by a last-minute telephone call from Jean Wahl, commented in one session that he 'had the impression, listening to Mr Ryle, that what he was saying was not so foreign to us', but also that, 'if there are any distances, it is he who is establishing them'.[21] According to an unfortunate myth, which has its origins in the preface written for the published proceedings by Leslie Beck, an English

16 The proceedings were published as L. J. Beck, ed., *La philosophie analytique*.

17 Charles Taylor, '*La Philosophie analytique*', p. 132.

18 Conversation with Charles Taylor, 24 May 2024.

19 See Jean Wahl, *Les philosophies pluralistes d'Angleterre et d'Amérique*, and *Vers le concret. Études d'histoire de la philosophie contemporaine. William James, Whitehead, Gabriel Marcel.*

20 Beck, *La philosophie analytique*, p. 185.

21 Conversation with Charles Taylor; Beck, *La philosophie analytique*, p. 93.

Descartes scholar with strongly anti-analytic leanings, Ryle had responded to Merleau-Ponty's well-meaning question 'Is our programme not the same?' with the disparaging 'I hope not'. Ryle *did* utter the words 'I hope not', but in response to a quite different question from Merleau-Ponty – whether Ryle's work in philosophy was 'always in strict agreement' with the programme set out by Russell and refined by Wittgenstein.[22] Ryle, who had entitled his paper 'Phenomenology Versus *The Concept of Mind*', had not been *that* brusque.

But Ryle had, in his paper, been deliberately offensive. He accused Husserl of wanting to 'puff philosophy up into the Science of sciences'. By contrast, English philosophers had, he went on,

> been immunised against the idea of philosophy as the Mistress Science by the fact that their daily lives in Cambridge and Oxford Colleges have kept them in personal contact with real scientists. Claims to Fuehrership vanish when postprandial joking begins. Husserl wrote as if he had never met a scientist – or a joke.

Ryle's claims were absurd, as well as offensive, on several counts. The reference to 'postprandial joking' was supposed to reflect that Oxford dons came into daily contact with real scientists at college dinners. As Husserl's student Herman Van Breda was quick to point out in the discussion of Ryle's paper, however, it was extraordinary for him to suggest that Husserl had never met any scientists: Husserl, who had done his PhD in mathematics, in fact had close relationships with Georg Cantor, David Hilbert and Max Planck.[23] If anything, it was Husserl who knew about science, something of which Ryle, Ayer and Austin, all of whom had received a classical education at Oxford, remained ignorant. Ryle might have been right about Husserl lacking a sense of humour. But the reference to 'Fuehrership' was remarkably crude and distasteful. As Ryle surely knew, Husserl was a Jew who had suffered at the hands of the Nazi regime, devastated by the actions taken against him by his former student at Freiburg University, Martin Heidegger, when Heidegger was appointed rector of the university in 1933. Another strange feature of Ryle's approach was that, since he had presented his characterization of Husserl's thought explicitly as a 'caricature', he took himself to be thereby exempt from having to be

22 Ibid., p. 98.
23 Ibid., p. 85.

accurate about Husserl.[24] In the discussion, mobilizing the analytic philosopher's trope of not being fussed about historical details, he expressed impatience at the idea that 'this debate' might 'degenerate into another colloquium on Husserl'.[25]

Derrida

Much of the time, analytic and continental philosophers have simply ignored each other, cultivating a studied mutual ignorance and distrust. Some continental philosophers, however, have been just too famous, or too notorious, to ignore. A prime example is Jacques Derrida, who has been a focus for the idea that has gripped some analytic philosophers that continental philosophy is fundamentally fraudulent.[26]

The ire Derrida could incite is well documented by a letter a group of analytic philosophers sent to *The Times* of London in 1992 to protest the decision of the University of Cambridge to award him an honorary doctorate. They included W. V. Quine, the historian of logical positivism Rudolf Haller, the logician Ruth Barcan Marcus, and the Australian materialist philosopher David Armstrong. Analytic philosophers pride themselves on their fairmindedness. That was not strongly in evidence

24 Gilbert Ryle, 'Phenomenology Versus "The Concept of Mind"', in *Collected Papers*, vol. 1, p. 188.

25 Beck, *La philosophie analytique*, p. 87.

26 The analytic philosopher Kit Fine gave expression to this attitude in an interview conducted by Pablo Carnino, then an undergraduate student at the University of Geneva, an institution where analytic philosophy has been vociferously promoted by one of its prime Francophone evangelists, Pascal Engel. When Carnino asked Fine his opinion of 'non-analytical philosophy', the response was: 'I despise it.' When Carnino requested 'precisions' or 'motivations', Fine offered: 'I don't want to say that it's all bad. I'm sure there were good Nazis.' He went on: 'The main thing that I dislike about it is that it's fraudulent. I genuinely believe that many of the people who are doing it, and indeed who are quite famous, are frauds. That, for me, is the main objection I have to it. I probably feel more strongly about this than is healthy. But, I mean, if one was kind to these people you'd think they know no better. But I think you can actually almost demonstrate that there are cases when they do know better and decide to engage in fraudulent intellectual activity.' 'Kit Fine on the Armchair 2', at youtube.com. When the interview was published in French translation, the comment about Nazis was delicately replaced with: 'je suis sûr qu'il y a de bonnes choses'. To Fine's imputation of deliberate fraudulence, the editors added a footnote: 'La rédaction préfère suspendre son jugement sur cette question'. 'Interview de Kit Fine', *iphilo* no. 4 (Printemps 2011), p. 16 – pdf available at phileasunige.wordpress.com.

when the writers snidely commented that 'Derrida describes himself as a philosopher, and his writings do indeed bear some of the marks of writings in that discipline', sarcastically adding that 'he has shown considerable originality'. They went on to say that 'in the eyes of philosophers, and certainly among those working in leading departments of philosophy throughout the world, M. Derrida's work does not meet accepted standards of clarity and rigour'. The letter itself, however, appeared to have exempted itself from these 'accepted standards'. It alleged that 'many of' Derrida's writings 'seem to consist in no small part of elaborate jokes and puns ("logical phallusies" and the like)'.[27] Derrida nowhere, in fact, talks about 'logical phallusies'; the letter writers' own addiction to rigour had not extended to checking whether Derrida had ever employed such a phrase. Perhaps they had in mind the word 'phallogocentrism', which does not rely on a pun.

In Oxford, fascination with Derrida had taken a different form. There he was subjected several times to analytic cross-examination – in 1967, 1977 and 1999. The first of these summons to Oxford occurred during an extraordinary year for Derrida, in which he published three important works, *De la grammatologie*, *L'écriture et la différence*, and *La voix et le phénomène*. In Oxford he presented an early version of another key text, 'La Différance'.[28] In 1977 the philosopher Alan Montefiore and the literary critic Jonathan Culler invited him back to Balliol College to speak at a seminar on philosophy and literature. Writing about the latter occasion, Derrida linked it with his 1967 appearance, recalling 'the embarrassed silence, the injured politesse, and the faces of Ryle, Ayer, and Strawson'.[29] In 1999, the British continental philosopher Simon Glendinning staged another encounter with Derrida in Oxford. Derrida on this occasion again recalled the 1967 event:

> I was totally mad to go to Oxford then to give that lecture! On that occasion the *silence* which followed it was obviously eloquent. Eloquently saying: 'There is no arguing here and there is no prospect of arguing with this man, or with this discourse.' Strawson was there – and very politely kept silent. Ryle was there – didn't say a word. It was very embarrassing

27 Letter to *The Times*, 9 May 1992, 'From Professor Barry Smith and others', at ontology.buffalo.edu.

28 The version Derrida gave to the Société Française de Philosophie on 27 January 1968, and published in the Société's *Bulletin*, was reprinted in Jacques Derrida, *Marges de la philosophie*.

29 Jacques Derrida, *The Post Card: From Socrates to Freud and Beyond*, p. 14.

for me, a very embarrassing situation. Ayer started arguing – but it didn't improve the situation.[30]

Later, Derrida recalled: 'the thing was not very well received: icy consternation, rather than objection and critique, but an angry outburst from Ayer, the only one to lose his cool there among Ryle, Strawson, and so forth.'[31] There are small differences between these accounts.[32] But they all basically say the same thing: Derrida was met with silence, except for Ayer – always more excitable than others when it came to 'engaging' with French philosophy.

At the 1999 meeting itself, the atmosphere was more conciliatory. The analytic philosophers Adrian Moore and Jonathan Dancy tactfully debated Derrida, who, in turn, at one point declared: 'I am an analytic philosopher.'[33] Moore has more recently given Derrida a sympathetic treatment in a chapter of his 2012 book *The Evolution of Modern Metaphysics*.[34] This is a far cry from the acrimony that attended an exchange in the 1970s between Derrida and the American philosopher John Searle. In his 1971 paper 'Signature événement contexte', Derrida had the audacity to make play with the work of J. L. Austin. When published in English translation in the first issue of the periodical *Glyph* in 1977, it was accompanied by an acid reply, under the testy title 'Reiterating the Differences', from Searle, who had been in Oxford in the 1950s and regarded himself as having been anointed as Austin's philosophical heir. Derrida wrote a reply to Searle's reply, entitled 'Limited Inc, a b c', published in his collection *Limited Inc*. Since Searle refused permission for his reply to be reprinted there, alongside writings by Derrida, *Limited Inc* printed its own summary of Searle's argument instead.

Searle was outraged at just how inaccurate Derrida managed to be about Austin and how his text could be vitiated by basic logical errors throughout. Searle fumed: 'Derrida's Austin is unrecognizable. He bears almost no relation to the original.'[35] At points, Searle had trouble controlling his exasperation: 'Does one really have to point this out?'[36]

30 Jacques Derrida in Simon Glendinning, ed., *Arguing with Derrida*, pp. 52–3.

31 Jacques Derrida, *Without Alibi*, p. 127.

32 Andreas Vrahimis, *Encounters Between Analytic and Continental Philosophy*, pp. 160–1.

33 Derrida in Glendinning, *Arguing with Derrida*, p. 83.

34 A. W. Moore, *The Evolution of Modern Metaphysics*, Chapter 20.

35 John R. Searle, 'Reiterating the Differences: A Reply to Derrida', p. 204.

36 Ibid., p. 205.

'I find so many confusions in this argument of Derrida that I hardly know where to get started on it.' Derrida confused 'no less than three separate and distinct phenomena: iterability, citationality, and parasitism'.[37] Derrida, on the other hand, just could not get over Searle's lack of humour, relentlessly teasing him about his insistence on writing 'Copyright © 1977 by John R. Searle', and referring to him as 'Sarl – or the self-made, auto-authorized heirs of Austin'.[38] SARL is an acronym standing for the French equivalent of 'limited company'; Derrida was poking fun at Searle for his acknowledgement of 'H. Dreyfus and D. Searle for discussion of these matters' (D. Searle was Searle's wife, Dagmar).[39] Derrida's deliriously playful text goes on for eighty-two pages, a maddening exercise in the performativity of speech acts. This was all too much for Searle, or Sarl, or whatever he chose to call himself.

The Student Movement

Searle, the self-anointed inheritor of Austin's legacy, managed the feat of turning the inventive theory of speech acts into just another piece of routine analytic philosophy.[40] Another area in which he is supposed, according to a consensus among analytic philosophers, to have contributed to philosophy is the analysis of the social world. It cannot be said, however, that Searle possessed a particularly fine understanding of social reality. A book he published in 1972 on student unrest bears this out in particularly excruciating form.[41]

In the book, Searle's apparently sympathetic and patient approach to his subject matter thinly veils an overweening condescension and irritation. After trying to establish necessary and sufficient conditions for the student movement, Searle launches into what he takes for social analysis. He tells his readers that one of his 'basic "methodological assumptions"' is that 'student revolts exhibit certain formal mechanisms'.[42] Students are full of anger and anxiety, Searle proffers, and they have something akin to a religious urge. 'The most striking tactical device of this generation of student activists is the conversion of student

37 Ibid., p. 206.
38 Jacques Derrida, *Limited Inc*, p. 37.
39 Searle, 'Reiterating the Differences', p. 208.
40 John R. Searle, *Speech Acts: An Essay in the Philosophy of Language*.
41 John R. Searle, *The Campus War: A Sympathetic Look at the University in Agony*.
42 Ibid., p. 14.

anxieties and aspirations on national and international moral questions into hostility against universities and university authorities.'[43] As a result, they form the bizarre and incomprehensible idea they are 'taking a meaningful action against racism or militarism by throwing a brick through the window of the office of a college administrator'.[44]

It is hard not to feel that Searle gives himself away as the kind of liberal incapable of appreciating that he is not the radical he supposes himself to be. As the Welsh socialist philosopher Colwyn Williamson pointed out in a review of the book, 'it is part of Searle's "liberal" ideology that he is able to see himself as defending the rights of dissenting minorities'.[45] In the late 1980s, Searle took his identification with the oppressed to a new pitch of grotesque absurdity when he and other landlords petitioned the Berkeley rental board to raise limits on the rents they could charge under the city's 1980 rent stabilization ordinance. After the petition was rejected, Searle filed suit. This resulted in the 1990 'Searle Decision' by the California Supreme Court, which upheld Searle's argument in part, and led to substantial rent increases between 1991 and 1994. Searle held forth, a wretched landlord of the earth: 'The treatment of landlords in Berkeley is comparable to the treatment of blacks in the South . . . our rights have been massively violated and we are here to correct that injustice.'[46]

Some analytic philosophers had greater sympathy for the student movement. As we saw in Chapter 5, Donald Davidson, for instance, had considerably more time for the students' demands than did Searle. Nonetheless, many analytic philosophy professors gravitated towards comforting themselves with the illusion of being upholders of freedom, while imagining liberal freedom to be the only freedom anyone could possibly want. In an interview in 1986, Iris Murdoch avowed that she had 'moved to the right', and now thought that 'a lot of time can be wasted during one's education on left-wing politics'. For the student protesters of 1968 she could summon up only scorn: 'We found them all sitting round watching propaganda films on Cuba. It was such an unnecessary protest in a free place like Oxford.'[47]

43 Ibid., p. 21.

44 Ibid., p. 22.

45 Colwyn Williamson, 'Searle's Idea of a University', p. 18. As Williamson also says, 'When it comes to his own ideology Searle would probably claim that he is a "liberal", which means that he is a conservative of the petit-bourgeois variety' (p. 17).

46 Quoted in Stephen E. Barton, 'The Success and Failure of Strong Rent Control in the City of Berkeley, 1978 to 1995'.

47 Murdoch in Edward Whitley, *The Graduates*, pp. 63, 66.

Radical Philosophy

In Britain, a group of philosophers including Sean Sayers, Jerry M. Cohen, Jonathan Rée and Scott Meikle in 1972 founded the Radical Philosophy Group, which railed against the constrictions of institutional philosophy and aligned itself with the demands of the student movement. In its founding statement the group declared:

> Contemporary British philosophy is at a dead end. Its academic practitioners have all but abandoned the attempt to understand the world, let alone to change it. They have made philosophy into a narrow and specialised academic subject of little relevance or interest to anyone outside the small circle of Professional Philosophers . . .
>
> As well as exposing the poverty of so much that now passes for philosophy, we shall aim to understand its causes. We need to ask whether its barrenness is the inevitable consequence of its linguistic and analytic methods as opposed to, for example, their application to trivial 'problems'. We shall examine the historical and institutional roots of recent British philosophy and investigate its ideological role within the wider culture.[48]

The opening pages of the first issue of the group's publication, *Radical Philosophy*, deliberately framed more as a magazine than an academic journal of the traditional kind, contained a criticism by Jonathan Rée of the dominant philosophical culture. In a response to Rée, Benjamin Gibbs added to Rée's indictment of 'examinational tyranny' an exposé of 'the institution of weekly one-hour tutorials with one or two undergraduates', as an 'absurdly expensive institution' which is 'the basic medium of philosophical teaching at Oxford, Sussex (which in this respect has modelled itself on Oxford), and elsewhere'.[49]

Attitudes to analytic philosophy varied among early members of the Radical Philosophy Groups set up across the country, and, by extension, contributors to *Radical Philosophy*. Some saw a need to transform analytic philosophy so as to realize its potential; others were intent simply to crush it. The situation was complex, in both social and institutional

48 *Radical Philosophy* 1 (1972), frontispiece.

49 Jonathan Rée, 'Professional Philosophers'; Benjamin Gibbs, 'Academic Philosophy and Radical Philosophy'.

terms. The dominance of analytic philosophy meant that those who came to the Radical Philosophy Groups generally shared the experience of having been trained in it. Indeed, some of those who became the most vocal advocates of non-analytic philosophy had been formed in heavily analytic departments: Gillian Rose at Oxford, Howard Caygill and Peter Osborne at Bristol.

In keeping with its alignment with the student movement, early issues of the magazine contained extensive reports from various local groups based at different universities across the country. Issue 2 (Summer 1972) included a report from Cambridge. Following a sit-in by students protesting against the university's handling of proposals for exam reform in economics, philosophy students had held a well-attended open meeting with faculty members to discuss the reform of courses and examinations. Changes were proposed that involved the scrapping of compulsory exams, with students given the option of submitting a 'portfolio' of work instead, with 'no restriction on the form or content of the portfolio'. All class marks were to be abolished, and replaced by a pass/fail system. Although, at a second meeting, attendees voted 'overwhelmingly in favour' of the proposals, they were then rejected by the Faculty Board.

In the meantime, the Knightbridge Professor of Philosophy at Cambridge, Bernard Williams, addressed the demands of *Radical Philosophy* in his final lecture of the term – with an audience five times the size of that which had shown up for the preceding lectures. Williams's tactics were classic analytic philosophy. He began by distinguishing between 'two possible motives behind the radical assault': *either* 'dissatisfaction with the *present* state of academic philosophy' *or* 'scepticism about academic thought in *general*'. The first could be dismissed, since Williams could easily agree with it himself. But the second option, Williams opined, seemed to reject academic thought altogether, 'in favour of "Life as against Theory"'. That was all very well, but Williams could not see 'how thinkers such as Kierkegaard and Nietzsche' – proponents of Life as against Theory – 'could be institutionalised'. And Williams expressed his amusement that this party of Life, as he insisted on portraying it, seemed so keen on 'that most academic and theoretical of philosophers, Hegel'. By the time he had got to the end of his lecture, Williams had thrown so much sand in the eyes of the radicals that they were at a loss how they might respond.[50] Cambridge philosophy reverted to its usual course.

50 Williams had earlier used a similar tack dealing with the undergraduate upstart Perry Anderson at Oxford. Williams accused Anderson of unclarity about

A rare document of the British philosophical scene in 1972 is a series of six one-hour films about Oxford philosophy entitled *Logic Lane*, directed by Michael Chanan, later to become a Marxist filmmaker but then a young graduate student of Isaiah Berlin. The films were produced by Chanan's elder brother Noel, and the first of the series incorporated a commentary written by Christopher Hitchens. The funding had come from a private investor, Oliver Stutchbury, who had been one of Chanan's philosophy tutors when he was an undergraduate at the still very young University of Sussex, and would later become a major fundraiser for the Labour Party. They were bought by a company called New Yorker Films, which distributed them in the United States in a package with Roberto Rossellini's *Socrate*, a fictionalized reconstruction of the last days of Socrates. They were never distributed in Britain, and only became available to a wide audience when they were posted to YouTube.

The first episode of *Logic Lane* was done in the standard documentary style of the day, with a narrative overview of Oxford philosophy by A. J. Ayer; the remaining, more innovative episodes consisted almost entirely of long discussions between pairs of philosophers, plus some coverage of tutorials and lectures. Perhaps most significant in terms of the social history of Oxford philosophy are some segments of discussion among graduate students, presided over by a young don, the Canadian philosopher William Newton-Smith. In one segment of discussion, Newton-Smith expresses himself in an instructively confusing way on the topic of the sense that might be made of Oxford philosophy in sociological terms. Newton-Smith opines that 'an ordinary person using a concept . . . in one sense . . . understands it because he gets it right – he picks out people who are in love and those that aren't, say'. But this ordinary person, wielding the concept 'love', 'doesn't see what's involved in that concept'. Here, apparently, 'the Oxford philosopher might be able through analytic techniques to present a clear picture of what's involved, what implications his using that concept has. And then he may decide, "I'm not going to use that concept".'[51] Newton-Smith seems to be suggesting that 'a sociological explanation about Oxford's position in British society' will illuminate why more of such correction

---

his precise target: was it English philosophy, philosophy as such, or 'smugness' in philosophy? See Bernard Williams, 'The Hatred of Philosophy', and Chapter 1, above.

51 *Logic Lane*, episode 1, at 50:23, at youtube.com.

of how ordinary people use concepts does not take place. Curiously, the highly implausible idea that such correction could in the first place be workable – or desirable – does not come in for questioning.

Institutional Challenges to Analytic Hegemony

Oxford University was not the only place where philosophy was taught in the United Kingdom, although it could seem so to those inside its bubble. But it was utterly dominant. Beyond Oxford, Cambridge and London, there were the 'English civic universities' (Durham, Leeds, Manchester, Liverpool, Birmingham, Sheffield, Bristol, Reading, Nottingham and Southampton), as well as Welsh and Scottish universities and Queen's University in Belfast. In 1992, the number of British universities was significantly increased as polytechnics became universities.

Oxford was the main producer of professional philosophers, who were then sent out to other universities to teach, so that its particular style of analytic philosophy was uniformly spread across the system. Where this was challenged, as by the Radical Philosophy Groups, this occurred largely in the polytechnics (or, as they became, 'post-1992 universities'). Such challenges were not easy to sustain. During the Thatcher years, seven philosophy departments were closed in Britain: Newcastle, Leicester, Aberystwyth, Bangor, City, Surrey and Exeter.[52] In 2010, the Centre for Research in Modern European Philosophy, founded at Middlesex University in 1995 by Jonathan Rée and Peter Osborne, was closed down. A slimmed-down version of the Centre was then reopened at Kingston University, another former polytechnic, in south-west London.

In the United States, although continental philosophy is widely disseminated, often outside philosophy departments, the stranglehold of analytic philosophy on the philosophy departments is secure. As John Searle jingoistically put it, 'without exception, the best philosophy departments in the United States are dominated by analytic philosophy, and among the leading philosophers in the United States, all but a tiny handful would be classified as analytic philosophers'.[53] The Ivy League schools – Harvard, Yale, Penn, Princeton, Columbia,

52 Duncan Wilson, *The Making of British Bioethics*, p. 215*n*84.

53 John R. Searle, 'Contemporary Philosophy in the United States', p. 1.

Brown, Dartmouth and Cornell – are all analytic strongholds.[54] Outside such socially elite schools there is room for departments with a strong 'continental' tendency, such as Penn State, the New School, Boston University, DePaul, Duquesne, Emory, Fordham, Georgetown, Marquette, Northwestern, Purdue, SUNY (at Binghamton, Buffalo and Stony Brook), Syracuse, Temple, UC Irvine and Villanova. As in Britain, however, many 'continental' philosophers operate in other academic departments. To take a prominent example, Judith Butler, who received a PhD from the philosophy department at Yale University in 1984, has long taught in the departments of comparative literature and rhetoric at the University of California, Berkeley.

Some have engaged in attempts, limited and liable to failure, to shake things up from within the structure of the American Philosophical Association. In 1971, occasional 'political resolutions' put forward to be voted on by members provoked a petition from 690 philosophers (representing about a quarter of the APA's 3,000-strong membership at the time) urging the APA 'to bar political resolutions from their deliberations'. These philosophers wrote: 'A philosopher or teacher of philosophy does not join the APA in order to use it as a vehicle for his political opinion. He does not give the APA, by joining it, a mandate to make political pronouncements in his name.'[55] The resolutions that sparked concern opposed 'activities that make our universities instruments of injustice', opposed discrimination against women, condemned the Leningrad trials of Soviet Jews, favoured 'recruiting Negro scholars as philosophy teachers' and 'sending observers from the association to the trial of Angela Davis', and committed the Association to guarantee support for three years to jobless PhDs and some PhD candidates. Among the 'concerned' philosophers were the seasoned Red-hunter Sidney Hook, as well as Paul Oskar Kristeller, Brand Blanshard, Nelson Goodman and Harry Frankfurt. Of course, the sense in which the APA was politicized at all was negligible. It did eventually come out against the Vietnam War, but only after the tide had already turned that way.

In 1978, continental philosophers in the United States attempted a rebellion in order to gain a foothold in the power structure of the discipline, at the Eastern APA meeting. This became known as the 'pluralist rebellion'. The strategy was to obtain transparency about how

---

54 As will be seen in Chapter 8, the dominance of Harvard in the analytic sphere was matched, and even outstripped, by that of Princeton in the 1970s.

55 '690 Philosophers Oppose Radicals', *New York Times*, 30 May 1971.

nominations were made to key APA positions, at the usually somnolescent business meeting of the APA, and then get the continental philosophy advocates who had turned up to the meeting to elect each other to positions. As a result, continental philosophers briefly secured key positions: John Smith was president; Quentin Lauer and John McDermott were elected to the Executive Committee. Once the tactics of the Committee on Pluralism were understood, however, their ruse failed. By 1980 the rebellion was over, and analytic philosophers regained control of the APA.[56]

A unique history, when it comes to the contest between analytic and continental philosophy, is that of the University of Sydney. Like many other universities, Sydney was rocked by campus unrest. Within its philosophy department, however, events took an unusual turn.[57] Some faculty members, as well as students, demonstrated enthusiasm for putting Marxism on the curriculum. Wal Suchting, a Marxist philosopher, and Michael Devitt, an analytic philosopher with left-wing political views, proposed courses in Marxism–Leninism for the year 1972–73, taking in Stalin, Ho Chi Minh, Mao and Che Guevara. Suchting's and Devitt's radicalism was matched by fierce reaction from their colleagues David Armstrong and David Stove. Armstrong, a proponent of a hard-line materialism ('Australian materialism'), was right wing enough to have zero tolerance for sit-ins and other forms of disruption, and earned the nickname 'the Beast' after snatching a microphone from a student who tried to challenge the first secretary of the South Vietnamese embassy at a meeting. If Armstrong was hard line enough, Stove was still further to the right politically; not content with opposing feminism, he published vociferously misogynistic articles claiming that women were less intelligent than men.

The department approved the Marxism courses by ten votes to three; when Armstrong tried to veto this, he had his veto overturned by another vote, which went eight-to-four against him. As a compromise, one course on Marxism went ahead. Meanwhile two graduate students, Jean Curthoys and Liz Jacka, proposed a course on 'The Politics of Sexual Oppression'. When approvals of the course by the department and the Faculty of Arts were overturned by the Professorial Board, a

---

56 See Bruce Wilshire, *Fashionable Nihilism: A Critique of Analytic Philosophy*, Chapter 3; Lawrence Cahoone, 'The Pluralist Revolt: Forty Years Later'.

57 James Franklin, *Corrupting the Youth: A History of Philosophy in Australia*, Chapter 11.

strike of staff and students ensued. The strike was successful, and the course was approved (under the title 'Philosophical Aspects of Feminist Thought').

As the tensions continued, Keith Campbell, a moderate, proposed to split the department in two. As a result, Sydney acquired two rival philosophy departments. General Philosophy (the name devised for the Marxist department) was the larger department, with some 750 students. It implemented full democracy, with staff and students given the right to speak and vote on course content, assessment and appointments, and eliminated formal exams. Traditional and Modern Philosophy (the analytic department) was smaller, with about 200 students, and maintained standard academic practices. Eventually, in 2000, Traditional and Modern Philosophy was closed. There was now effectively one department again. The Sydney department today is a thoroughly analytic department.

7

The Linguistic Turn and the Myth of Frege

As we have seen, the movements fused together to make analytic philosophy after the Second World War had been diverse and distinct prior to the fusion. They had differed over doctrines and over methodology. There had never been a single, unified 'classical programme of analysis'.[1] Nor would the fusion that was analytic philosophy bring into being any such programme.

Nonetheless, in the distinctively ahistorical atmosphere of analytic philosophy there was plenty of room for retrospective fictionalized histories to take hold. A priority for such narratives was to lend unity to analytic philosophy, so as to shore up its credentials as the most rigorous and respectable way of doing philosophy. According to the most prominent and enduring narrative, it was marked out by the 'linguistic turn', an intellectual event that had set it on its distinctive path. Despite widespread agreement that such a turn had occurred, there has been little agreement, or precision, about what this meant. Somehow a 'concern with language' was 'central'. But central in what sense? Was it a question of applying a distinctive linguistic method to the problems of philosophy? Was the idea to show that what had been considered to be philosophical problems were instead merely verbal puzzles? Did it involve a reform of language use? All of these notions are routinely suggested, but they are not equivalent, and there has been little effort to

1 I borrow this phrase from P. F. Strawson's paper to the Royaumont conference, 'Analysis, Science, and Metaphysics', in Richard Rorty, ed., *The Linguistic Turn: Essays in Philosophical Method, With Two Retrospective Essays*, p. 318.

settle which of them talk of 'the linguistic turn' is meant to capture. Nor has there been agreement about when precisely the linguistic turn was supposed to have been 'taken'. One prominent candidate has been Wittgenstein's *Tractatus*, published in 1921; another, Frege's much earlier *Foundations of Arithmetic*, published in 1884. Some proponents of the story of the turn are less specific, and consider Moore and Russell, and perhaps others still, to be at its heart.

Confusion over the meaning of the term 'linguistic turn' affected even its inventor, the Vienna Circle émigré Gustav Bergmann, who himself used it in a disconcerting variety of different ways during the course of the 1950s.[2] In some sense, the confusion is understandable. What could it *possibly* mean for philosophy to have become 'linguistic' in a way it was not before? Surely, philosophers had always expressed themselves in language, and dealt with problems concerning the meaning of terms? What was the difference between Aristotle's careful considerations of how terms are used, on the one hand, and those of 'linguistic' philosophers, on the other?

It might be concluded that no single, decisive linguistic turn ever took place. But this would be a mistake. One way to be sure that a linguistic turn has been carried out is to establish that it has been given its most uncompromising form possible. This Wittgenstein did in his *Tractatus*. When Wittgenstein spoke of philosophy as 'critique of language', he did not have in mind piecemeal clarification, or reform, of language.[3] For the early Wittgenstein, philosophy was critique of language, because there was nothing for the world to be but a logical structure. The world was, as the opening proposition of the *Tractatus* announced, the totality of facts, not of things. There was no stepping outside of the logical structure in order to examine something independent of it, with which to compare it. An implication of this view was that the propositions of philosophy, which attempted – *per impossibile* – to talk about this

2 The origins within analytic philosophy of the idea of the 'linguistic turn' can now easily be lost sight of. Jürgen Habermas spoke (in a lecture given at the Royal Institute of Philosophy in London in 1998) of what he considered to be parallel 'linguistic turns' in Wittgenstein and Heidegger, with an ancestry in Wilhelm von Humboldt (Jürgen Habermas, 'Hermeneutic and Analytic Philosophy: Two Complementary Versions of the Linguistic Turn?'). Arguably, a linguistic turn analogous to that of Wittgenstein's *Tractatus* was carried out by the founder of structuralist linguistics, Ferdinand de Saussure (see Roy Harris, *Language, Saussure and Wittgenstein: How to Play Games with Words*). Another, quite different, meaning is given to the term 'linguistic turn' in the field of history.

3 Ludwig Wittgenstein, *Tractatus Logico-Philosophicus*, 4.0031.

structure as if from outside, were nonsense (and so the book itself was mostly nonsense). Wittgenstein's message was enthusiastically received in the Vienna Circle, where the idea of preserving a professional space for philosophers to occupy, distinct from scientific activity, was not pressing. The members of the Circle were, after all, mostly practising scientists themselves. Beyond this milieu, however, in those places where the credentials of a distinct discipline called philosophy were to be nervously guarded, the message was threatening.

So much for Wittgenstein's uncompromising linguistic turn, according to which any theory of meaning (including the one the *Tractatus* itself advances) is nonsense. In the post–Second World War period, a different, less austere conception of the linguistic turn emerged. An alliance between American and British philosophers was crucial to this ('British' in this period meant, more or less, 'Oxford', given Oxford's preeminent status after Ryle's institution of the BPhil had made it into a Mecca of philosophy).[4] Donald Davidson, in America, promoted the idea that there was a highly technical programme to be carried out ('Davidson's programme', or 'the Davidsonian programme', as it became known) of providing a 'theory of meaning' for a natural language (such as English) modelled on a truth theory for formalized languages, as devised by the Polish logician Alfred Tarski. In the meantime, the English philosopher Michael Dummett had begun an intensive exploration of the work of Gottlob Frege that had the result of instituting the nineteenth-century German mathematician as a philosopher of language, concerned with the theory of meaning. Dummett now brought the project he attributed to Frege under the heading of the 'linguistic turn', meaning by that something quite different from what Wittgenstein had carried out in the *Tractatus*. According to Dummett, Frege had initiated analytic philosophy by taking the linguistic turn, where this meant that philosophy of language (or the theory of meaning) was now 'first philosophy' – a revolution comparable to Descartes's replacement of metaphysics by epistemology as first philosophy.[5] According to Frege, as Dummett imagined him, philosophers had to get their philosophy of language straight before they could proceed to anything else in philosophy: it was the portal through which all philosophers must pass.[6]

4 See Chapter 4, above.

5 See René Descartes, *Meditations on First Philosophy*, in *The Philosophical Writings of Descartes*, vol. 2.

6 Arguably, Frege's work, as Wittgenstein read it, provided a precedent for the Wittgensteinian linguistic turn. It seems plausible that Frege admits of different

The efforts of Davidson and Dummett had a mutually supporting function. Dummett's reinterpretation of Frege helped encourage Davidson in the idea that he was building on Frege's work. Meanwhile, Davidson gave Oxford philosophers, bereft of a project after the demise of ordinary language philosophy, technical work to do: the construction of a theory of meaning for English. It had turned out that the linguistic turn, rather than tending to put the task of philosophy into question, as in Wittgenstein's *Tractatus*, instead had created a field of work for an autonomous discipline: the philosophy of language. The interpretation of Frege with which Dummett helped to support this project was a falsification. Contrary to Dummett's central claim, Frege had never been a philosopher of language in the sense Dummett imagined. His interpretation of Frege, and its concomitant institution of Frege as the founder of analytic philosophy, was nonetheless successful, for a time, in shoring up a conception of analytic philosophy's task instrumental in securing its prestige.

It is important that Frege enters the story recounted in this book only at this late stage, as the object of a mythical reconstruction. Russell and Wittgenstein, of course, had earlier drawn deep from the well of Frege's thought, as had Carnap and others in the Vienna Circle. But the construction of Frege as the 'father' of analytic philosophy, which succeeded largely due to the efforts of Dummett, is a key element in a wider myth, according to which analytic philosophers (or the participants in the 'ancestor movements' of analytic philosophy) had always been concerned with the 'problem of meaning'. That is simply not true.[7]

The issues Dummett presented, under the banner of a 'linguistic turn' supposedly initiated by Frege, as the crucial problems for philosophers

---

readings on this point, as his own central concerns were neither Wittgenstein's nor Dummett's. Dummett writes in *Origins of Analytical Philosophy* that 'the first clear example' of the linguistic turn 'occurs in Frege's *Die Grundlagen der Arithmetik* of 1884' (p. 5). Later in the same book, he writes that 'if we identify the linguistic turn as the starting-point of analytical philosophy proper', then 'to however great an extent Frege, Moore and Russell prepared the ground, the crucial step was taken by Wittgenstein in the *Tractatus Logico-Philosophicus* of 1922' (p. 27).

7 The American philosopher of science Greg Frost-Arnold provides strong evidence that what he calls 'second-phase, mid-century justifications' of analytic philosophy, according to which it had always been concerned with the problem of meaning, are flatly contradicted by the statements of those who are supposed to be covered by such justifications (in particular, pre–Second World War Cambridge philosophers). See Greg Frost-Arnold, 'The Rise of "Analytic Philosophy": When and How Did People Begin Calling Themselves "Analytic Philosophers"?'.

to work on – concerned with how words mean what they do, or how language 'hooks onto' the world – were among just those problems that Wittgenstein's linguistic turn had marked out as pseudo-problems. The peculiarities that resulted from this reimagining of the linguistic turn were brought out in a debate between Dummett and another Oxford philosopher, John McDowell, about how Davidson's suggestion of providing a theory of meaning for English could be realized. Dummett thought such a theory had to *explain* what it is speakers understand when they speak a language – something McDowell held to violate a proscription against attempting to explain language 'as from outside'. McDowell was effectively seeking to reinstate, or hold onto, Wittgenstein's linguistic turn.

The Davidsonian programme encouraged much frenetic activity on the part of Oxford philosophers, with their classical or at least humanistic education encouraging them to fetishize technical devices they did not fully understand. All this, nevertheless, came to nothing. Dummett's alternative proposals for a theory of meaning fared no better. As McDowell quit the scene for the University of Pittsburgh in 1986, his fellow Oxford philosophers continued in the spirit of high technicality they had imbibed from Davidson. The linguistic project of first philosophy attributed by Dummett to Frege was gradually forgotten; instead the problem of 'meaning', or 'aboutness', became just another scholastic issue analytic philosophers 'worked on' without being sure why.

The genuine linguistic turn, as undertaken by Wittgenstein, holds the promise of a difficult and important insight: that there is no outside to the languages by means of which we communicate. This has the potential to transform our social self-understanding. Yet the putative 'linguistic turn' which the myth of Frege and the elaboration of the 'Davidsonian programme' have served to promote has turned out to be little more than a means of validating a conception of philosophy that seems highly technical and rigorous but serves no purpose at all. This has resulted in a research community that is oddly at sea, with little prospect of connecting meaningfully with the concerns that matter on dry land. It is an odyssey with no promise of return.

What Might the Linguistic Turn Be?

It was the 1967 publication of an anthology called *The Linguistic Turn*, edited by Richard Rorty, that helped to entrench the use of the term to characterize analytic philosophy as a whole. In his editorial introduction, Rorty, a convert to analytic philosophy after his non-analytic education at Chicago and Yale, wrote with the breathless enthusiasm characteristic of a neophyte of what the turn had accomplished as 'the most recent philosophical revolution', driven by what was 'considered by many of its proponents to be the most important philosophical discovery of our time, and, indeed, of the ages'. This 'methodological revolution' inaugurated 'linguistic philosophy', which was, according to Rorty, 'the view that philosophical problems are problems which may be solved (or dissolved) either by reforming language, or by understanding more about the language we presently use'.[8] The turn would seem to be a break with all previous philosophy that, for the first time, brought philosophy into its own and gave philosophers a previously unheard of importance. But just what sort of altered relationship to language did Rorty have in mind?

The phrase 'linguistic turn' had been coined by Gustav Bergmann, a Jewish member of the Vienna Circle who had escaped from Austria in 1938 and obtained a position at the University of Iowa. He first used the term in 1950, and then employed it, with varying senses, in a series of subsequent writings. In 1950 he wrote of 'the linguistic turn of Logical Positivism', which he said could be connected 'with the rise of modern or mathematical Logic, which began around the middle of the last century'.[9] In 1952 he wrote that 'the causes of [the] linguistic turn . . . are many, in part diffuse and anonymous as well as very complex', but singled out 'the influence of three men, Moore, Russell, and Wittgenstein'.[10] The turn, Bergmann's story now continued, subsequently split into two branches: the 'formalists' and the 'antiformalists' (or what became known as 'ideal language' and 'natural language' linguistic philosophers). Bergmann downplayed the differences between the formalists and the antiformalists: it was 'gray against gray, not white against black'. For formalists and antiformalists alike, there was

---

8 Rorty, *Linguistic Turn*, pp. 3–4.

9 Gustav Bergmann, *The Metaphysics of Logical Positivism*, p. 18.

10 Gustav Bergmann, 'Two Types of Linguistic Philosophy', p. 417.

nothing that could decide between rival positions such as phenomenalism and realism, since, Bergmann averred, 'all philosophical problems are verbal'.[11] Here, the net was cast especially wide, capturing a large group of philosophers, and the linguistic turn was given a particularly stark characterization, in terms of the dissolution of philosophical problems by language. In 1953, Bergmann attributed the linguistic turn specifically to Wittgenstein, writing that the logical positivists 'all accept the linguistic turn Wittgenstein initiated in the *Tractatus*'.[12] In 1960, he wrote of 'the linguistic turn' as 'the fundamental gambit as to method, on which ordinary and ideal language philosophers agree', and characterized it in terms of the following claim: 'All linguistic philosophers talk about the world by means of talking about a suitable language.'[13]

It is difficult to avoid the impression Bergmann never really straightened out what he meant by the term 'linguistic turn'. This reflects the general confusion that has surrounded the idea. There must be more to it than reflection on language; philosophers have always engaged in that. But, if it is some special 'gambit as to method', what can that gambit be, exactly? What entitles the philosopher to be clarifying, or instead reforming, language in any certifiably useful way? Must language not, after all, be checked against reality? And then have we not lost the whole point of the supposed linguistic turn?

Wittgenstein

While Bergmann sometimes cited Wittgenstein as being one among others who contributed to the linguistic turn, sometimes he credited him as the person who carried it out singlehandedly. The case that such a turn occurs in Wittgenstein's *Tractatus* is certainly strong. Wittgenstein's investigation of logical form led him to the principled stance that there could be no meaningful study of the relationship between the logical form of what can be said about the world and the world itself. Such form, while it provided for the shape of all those things that could be 'said', could itself only be 'shown'. There was no stepping

11 Ibid., p. 418.

12 Gustav Bergmann, 'Logical Positivism, Language and the Reconstruction of Metaphysics'.

13 Gustav Bergmann, 'Strawson's Ontology', p. 607.

outside the language in which such form was exhibited in order to talk about that language from outside it.

According to the *Tractatus*, the world was 'the totality of facts, not of things'.[14] The traditional philosophical conception of the world was to be replaced by that of 'the facts in logical space'.[15] There was, then, no gap between logic and the world; 'logic pervades [*erfüllt*] the world: the limits of the world are also its limits'.[16] Since, for Wittgenstein, logic was, as P. M. S. Hacker has written, 'the transcendental condition of representation', and therefore 'the depth-grammar of *any* possible language', philosophy could take the form of 'critique of language' as such.[17] Philosophy was clarificatory in function.

There were, as the *Tractatus* spelled out, different ways for the world to be; this was a matter of the arrangement of the components ('objects') that made up facts. This arrangement was logical. Through the arrangement of components, language 'pictured' the world. An implication was that the propositions of philosophy, which attempted to talk *about* logical form, rather than exhibiting it, were nonsense. Hence the propositions of the *Tractatus* were also nonsense.[18] The analysis of propositions that philosophy performs yielded no new truths about the world, only clarifications of other propositions and the exposure of metaphysical nonsense.

Wittgenstein's approach, as his student Elizabeth Anscombe pointed out, is in many ways 'more akin to ancient, than to more modern philosophy'.[19] His central preoccupation was not what seems the central

---

14 Wittgenstein, *Tractatus*, 1.1.

15 Ibid., 1.13.

16 Ibid., 5.61.

17 P. M. S. Hacker, 'The Linguistic Turn in Analytic Philosophy', p. 932.

18 Wittgenstein wrote:

> My propositions are elucidatory in this way: he who understands me finally recognizes them as nonsensical, when he has climbed out through them, on them, over them. (He must so to speak throw away the ladder, after he has climbed up on it.)
>
> He must surmount these propositions; then he sees the world rightly. (Wittgenstein, *Tractatus*, 6.54).

This has been read in varying ways by different interpreters. For a *locus classicus* of the 'resolute' reading according to which the propositions of the *Tractatus* really are nonsense, see Cora Diamond, 'Throwing Away the Ladder', in her *The Realistic Spirit: Wittgenstein, Philosophy, and the Mind.*

19 G. E. M. Anscombe, *An Introduction to Wittgenstein's* Tractatus, p. 13.

concern given a more empiricist picture such as Russell's – that of discerning *how* thought and experience relate to the world – but the logical structure that must be in place for that relationship to be as it is. Thus he was exercised by questions, raised in texts such as Plato's *Theaetetus* and *Sophist*, of how it is possible to judge of something not real. For Wittgenstein, this could not involve comparing thought with what it is thought of. Reflecting this, what Wittgenstein's linguistic turn involves is precisely *not* an 'emphasis on language', as the loose characterizations of the linguistic turn in vogue among analytic philosophers have it. Instead, its point is to clear away language as the obstruction it would otherwise be.

A large part of Wittgenstein's later work, *Philosophical Investigations*, is concerned with criticizing his own earlier view in the *Tractatus*. He now came to see his earlier conception of the logical structure of language as seriously deficient. The uses of language were far more varied, subtle and contextual than the formal structure outlined in the *Tractatus* could allow. The actual use of language, moreover, seemed to reveal a sovereign command of subtle intricacies on the part of speakers. The notion of philosophy as a critique of language remained in place, but philosophy now became 'a battle against the bewitchment of our intellect by means of our language', to be executed through the careful delineation of 'language games' modelling people's actual linguistic activities.[20] This left the status of the linguistic turn less unequivocal than in the *Tractatus*, with its promise of absolute transparency. Furthermore, if people's actual use of language were to be clarified using the methods proposed in the *Investigations*, by what canons was this to be accomplished? Merely inspecting 'language games' would not, of itself, decide whether what now needed to happen was to actively clear up a confusion or to respect the intricacies of the existing language use modelled by the game.[21]

In the *Tractatus*, Wittgenstein had offered no 'theory of meaning', if that meant a theory of how words mean what they do; according to its precepts, there could precisely be no such theory. Gilbert Ryle, who had fallen under the influence of Wittgenstein after meeting him in 1929, wrote in the paper that turned his own philosophy 'linguistic',

20 Ludwig Wittgenstein, *Philosophical Investigations*, §109 (Anscombe's translation modified).

21 Consider, as an example, when Wittgenstein writes: 'The concept of "seeing" makes a tangled impression. Well, it is tangled' (*Philosophical Investigations*, p. 200).

'Systematically Misleading Expressions' (1932), that there was something 'very odd' about the 'attempts of philosophers to thrash out "what it means to say so and so"'.[22] 'For', Ryle reasoned, 'if the expressions under consideration are intelligently used, their employers must already know what they mean and do not need the aid or admonition of philosophers before they can understand what they are saying.'[23] All that it could make sense to do, in clarifying what was meant, was to make internal comparisons on the side of language – for instance, between the use of more and less general terms – to draw attention to possible confusions. Language was here compared with itself, not with 'the world'.

The Myth of Frege

Wittgenstein had certainly acknowledged, in the preface to the *Tractatus*, the 'stimulation' he had received from 'the great works of Frege'.[24] But there is a reading of the 'linguistic turn', promoted by Michael Dummett, which makes Frege its originator in a way that is profoundly at odds with Wittgenstein's version (and, by implication, with the way Wittgenstein understood himself to be building on Frege's 'great works').

Dummett was born in London in 1925, the son of a silk merchant, and the maternal grandson of Sir Sainthill Eardley-Wilmot, former Inspector-General of Indian Forests. After attending the elite boarding school Winchester College, Dummett won a scholarship to Christ Church, Oxford, in 1943. He only took up his place in 1947, after war service in the Royal Artillery, at the Wireless Experimental Centre outside Delhi (an outpost of Station X at Bletchley Park) and in Malaya. Dummett took the PPE course, and, when he came to his Finals in 1950, chose a paper that had been set by J. L. Austin, encompassing a series of texts stretching from Plato's *Theaetetus* to Frege's *Grundlagen der Arithmetik* (*Foundations of Arithmetic*). Austin had specially translated Frege's text into English for the purposes of the paper. Dummett later recalled: 'I was bowled over by the *Grundlagen*: I thought, and still think, that it was the most brilliant piece of philosophical writing of its

22 Gilbert Ryle, *Collected Papers*, vol. 2, p. 41.

23 Ibid.

24 Wittgenstein, *Tractatus*, p. 29.

length ever penned.' In 1951, he 'settled down to read everything that Frege had written'.[25]

The degree to which Dummett was a pioneer in the serious study of Frege's work is now difficult to appreciate fully. As a result of his tremendous efforts, the idea of Frege's importance is now part of the unquestionable ideological furniture of analytic philosophy. At the time Dummett began his work, however, hardly any of Frege's work had even been translated into English. Apart from Austin's brand new translation of *Foundations of Arithmetic*, the only works by Frege available in English at the time were Johann Stachelroth and Philip Jourdain's translation of selections from *Fundamental Laws of Arithmetic*, published in *The Monist* in three instalments (1915, 1916, 1917) and Max Black's very recent translations in *The Philosophical Review* of 'On Sense and Reference' (1948) and of a selection from *Fundamental Laws* Volume II (1950). When Black, together with Peter Geach, brought out *Translations from the Philosophical Writings of Gottlob Frege* in 1952, even this fairly capacious sample of Frege's writings included only a part of Frege's early masterpiece *Begriffsschrift*, which was not translated in its entirety until 1967.[26] Even in the original German, *Begriffsschrift* was extremely difficult to get hold of.[27]

Dummett's spirit of questing heroism was not confined to his excavations of Frege. He devoted himself with enormous energy to combating racism in Britain, laying his philosophical work aside for extended periods in order to concentrate on this. Together with his wife Ann Dummett, he helped in 1967 to found the Joint Council for the Welfare of Immigrants, an organization that today continues to campaign on behalf of immigrants in the United Kingdom. This involved, uncharacteristically for university professors, driving to British ports such as Dover and Heathrow to plead personally on behalf of immigrants when immigration officers tried to block their entry. When Tony

---

25 Michael Dummett, 'Intellectual Autobiography', p. 10.

26 Translation by S. Bauer-Mengelberg, in Jean van Heijenoort (ed.), *From Frege to Gödel: A Source Book in Mathematical Logic, 1879–1931*. In 1972 Terrell Ward Bynum published another: Gottlob Frege, *Conceptual Notation and Related Articles*.

27 See Bynum's editorial introduction to Frege, *Conceptual Notation*, p. vii. When Quine came to write his textbook *Mathematical Logic* (1940), 'the need to acknowledge sources' led him 'to examine Frege, whose slim *Begriffsschrift* of 1879 I soon discovered as the real beginning of mathematical logic'. There was no copy of the text available in America; instead Quine 'recovered its content' from a review by Russell's student P. E. B. Jourdain. W. V. Quine, *The Time of My Life*, p. 144.

Blair's New Labour government awarded Dummett a knighthood in 1999, it was 'for services to Philosophy and to Racial Justice'. His views on immigration could suffer, however, from a certain hauteur. Like most liberals, he tended to frame the central question of immigration politics as: How many of *them* should *we* let in? The authority of the liberal nation-state to pose such a question in the first place was left unquestioned. Ultimately, according to Dummett, there was a limit to be placed on immigration – an 'indigenous culture' was not to be 'submerged'.[28] The word 'submerged' was deliberately chosen to avoid, as he put it, the 'more emotive' connotations of 'swamped', as in Margaret Thatcher's notorious statement in a 1978 television interview that 'people are really rather afraid that this country might be rather swamped by people of a different culture'.[29] The point was – whether it was submersion or swamping from which the 'indigenous culture' was to be saved – nonetheless the same in structure.

A major problem with Dummett's approach to Frege is that he preferred to make grand, far-reaching claims, to the detriment of careful historical scholarship. When the results of his labours were finally made public in 1973 in his first book on Frege, running to 700 pages, it bore the title *Frege: Philosophy of Language*. Frege was principally presented, remarkably, not as the mathematician he had understood himself to be, but as an innovator in a field he himself had never heard of: philosophy of language. Dummett claimed that Frege had been 'the first to have fashioned a genuine theory of meaning'.[30] Consideration of Frege as a philosopher of mathematics was relegated to a second, slimmer volume, *Frege: Philosophy of Mathematics*, which came out in 1991.

Frege was a tremendous innovator, of profound importance for the development of twentieth-century philosophy. But his innovations were not those Dummett foisted on him. Frege's actual achievement was a revolution in logic, achieved from within mathematics. Although he

---

28 Michael Dummett, *On Immigration and Refugees*, p. 15.

29 Ibid., p. 14.

30 Dummett, 'Intellectual Autobiography', p. 24. Compare *Frege: Philosophy of Language*, p. 669: 'the theory of meaning is the fundamental part of philosophy which underlies all others. Because philosophy has, as its first if not its only task, the analysis of meanings, and because, the deeper such analysis goes, the more it is dependent upon a correct general account of meaning, a model for what the understanding of an expression consists in, the theory of meaning, which is the search for such a model, is the foundation of all philosophy, and not epistemology as Descartes misled us into believing.'

frequently touched on philosophical issues, and published some of his work in philosophy journals, it would have been utterly surprising to him to be portrayed as foremost a philosopher. As Rudolf Carnap, probably the only philosopher of any significance apart from Gershom Scholem to have experienced Frege as a teacher, reported:

> Although Frege gave quite a number of examples of interesting applications of his symbolism in mathematics, he usually did not discuss general philosophical problems. It is evident from his works that he saw the great philosophical importance of the new instrument which he had created, but he did not convey a clear impression of this to his students.[31]

Frege's most important theoretical contribution did not consist of the late essays on which Dummett concentrated, broaching topics in the philosophy of language, but in his path-breaking early work, *Begriffsschrift* (1879), written when he was a thirty year-old, unsalaried and obscure instructor in mathematics at the University of Jena. This eighty-eight-page booklet set out, as its title indicates, a 'conceptual notation', whose purpose was to render mathematical proofs into a formal language that would make their validity evident to the eye, and thus susceptible to mechanical checking. The notation was cumbersome, involving two-dimensional arrays that were nearly impossible to typeset, and was never used by anyone other than Frege himself. The technical innovation it represented was, however, of supreme importance.

Frege's motivation for devising his conceptual notation is clear. As he states in the preface to *Begriffsschrift*, his starting point was arithmetic.[32] Just how could one demonstrate that certain chains of reasoning in arithmetic are valid, and others not? In order to do so, any psychological element had to be eliminated – in other words, there should be no appeal to intuition in getting from one step to the next. All such gaps in which intuition could wreak havoc should be closed. 'So that nothing intuitive could intrude here unnoticed, everything had to depend on the chain of inference being free of gaps.'[33] This could only be achieved

31 Rudolf Carnap, 'Intellectual Autobiography', p. 5.

32 This important preface was omitted in Geach and Black's *Translations from the Philosophical Writings of Gottlob Frege*. It was thus not available to English readers until the appearance of van Heijenoort's anthology *From Frege to Gödel* in 1967.

33 Gottlob Frege, *Begriffsschrift*, in *The Frege Reader*, p. 48.

by constructing a purely logical language, one that could be used as an 'optical instrument', so that the eye could inspect chains of inference for validity.[34]

Frege proposed various innovations designed to counter the way in which 'logic hitherto has always followed ordinary language and grammar too closely'.[35] One such innovation consisted in eliminating from logic the concepts 'subject' and 'predicate', imported from grammar, and replacing them with 'argument' and 'function', borrowed from mathematics. While the distinction between subject and predicate had its place in grammar, its logical insufficiency could be brought out by considering a pair of statements each reporting the outcome of the Battle of Plataea in 479 BCE: 'the Greeks defeated the Persians', and 'the Persians were defeated by the Greeks'. In the first statement, the place of the subject is occupied by 'the Greeks', in the second by 'the Persians'. The statements, then, differed from each other grammatically. But, Frege urged, logically they were surely equivalent. The distinction between subject and predicate was therefore excluded from Frege's 'representation of a judgement'.[36] Instead, the defeat of the Persians by the Greeks was to be captured logically in terms of a function (*defeat*) with two 'argument places', one for the victor, one for the loser.

Another key innovation introduced in *Begriffsschrift* was that of quantification, which again helped in the effort to get away from grammatical appearances. The statement 'Félicette purrs', grammatically, has the same form as 'All cats purr'. In each of them a predicate (*purr*) is ascribed to a subject: in the first to a unique subject (the cat bearing the name Félicette), in the second to a plural subject (the totality of cats). But, in terms of logical form, a statement such as the second, Frege points out, differs from the first. The form of the first corresponds to its surface appearance: it straightforwardly says of Félicette that she purrs. The second does not say of some much larger thing than Félicette (the thing called 'all cats') that that thing purrs. Instead, it is a conditional statement governed by the universal quantifier 'for all *x* . . .'. It is to be rendered as: 'for all *x*: if *x* is a cat, then *x* purrs'.

The entirety of Frege's basic logical framework is set out in *Begriffsschrift*. It was not until much later that he brought out a series of papers on which Dummett's interpretation hinges: 'Function and

34 Ibid., p. 49.
35 Ibid., p. 51.
36 Ibid., p. 53.

Concept' (1891), 'Sense and Reference' (1892) and 'Concept and Object' (1892). These papers, rather than forming a self-standing philosophical contribution, are tasked with a clean-up operation dealing with various deficiencies of the programme set out in *Begriffsschrift*. As the Frege scholar Roy Cook has pointed out, 'each of these papers was aimed at solving a particular problem in Frege's original logic as laid out in *Begriffsschrift*'.[37] 'Function and Concept' brought concepts and relations under the category of mathematical function. 'Sense and Reference' worked at clarifying the issue of identity. 'Concept and Object' dealt with problems stemming from the type of distinctions Frege used in his higher-order logic.

Dummett helped to institute the idea – very much to the advantage of professional philosophers – that these late papers by Frege carry out a revolution in philosophy, establishing a theory of meaning. Their chief interest, however, is not their unprecedented positive contribution (as Dummett imagines this), but their careful, and ultimately unsatisfying, treatment of *problems* generated by Frege's earlier logical work.

Frege's contribution is, in fact, particularly unpromising when it comes to the theory of meaning. He notes that we must distinguish between the 'sense' and 'reference' of expressions. (This replaces earlier talk of 'judgeable contents'.) The statement 'Hesperus is Phosphorus' is informative; 'Hesperus is Hesperus' is not. This is so even though the 'reference' of both 'Hesperus' and 'Phosphorus' (the object 'out in the world' talked about in each case) is the planet Venus. So there must be something more in play than mere reference. But Frege is able to say nothing more definite about the 'sense' of the expression than to characterize it in a vague way as its *Art des Gegebenseins* (its 'way of being given'). Things get worse when it comes to whole sentences. All true sentences have just one referent, 'the True' (for all false sentences, it is 'the False'). That may not seem so bad; it can be left up to sentences' *senses* to do the work of differentiating them from each other, even if their *references* all meld into one. But, here again, Frege is pushed into a troubling vagueness. The senses of sentences, he says, are 'thoughts' (*Gedanken*) that are not psychological (their home is not in anyone's minds), but instead inhabit a nebulous 'third realm' (*drittes Reich*) about which he has nothing further to say. Philosophically, then, all Frege has to offer in terms of a patch-up of his earlier work is an array of implausible and unsatisfactory notions about his dual notions of meaning

37 Roy Cook, 'Frege's Logic'.

('sense' and 'reference'). This situation may be excusable given the depth of the philosophical difficulties here, but it gives the lie to Dummett's notion of Frege as a great innovator in precisely these areas.

That Dummett obtained anachronistic results, constructing, in the name of his hero, a web of ideas far removed from those of the historical Frege, seems not entirely surprising given his almost ostentatiously cavalier approach to scholarship. In writing the massive *Frege: Philosophy of Language*, he apparently 'forgot' to supply any bibliographical references at all to Frege's own writings to support his interpretation.[38] He had instead 'adopted the policy of writing from memory, seldom pausing to look up a passage'.[39]

More amazing than Dummett's ability to get away with such scholarly standards is that his influence was such that his seriously misleading reading of Frege became known as the 'standard interpretation' – so influential, in fact, that even his detractors were stuck with having to call it that.[40] Frege had never spoken of a 'theory of meaning', or presented himself as a philosopher of language at all. But, thanks to Dummett's accomplishment, the onus was now on those wishing to contest his reading to show this. Few had the energy to see this through, not least since Dummett's reactions tended to be unsparingly hostile. It had somehow become impossible to see Frege as the mathematician he was. The effects of what Dummett had wrought, even those who sought to resist his anachronisms, were profound. Hans Sluga, a German who had been introduced to the work of Frege by the logician Wilhelm Britzelmayr while studying at the University of Munich, and had then become a graduate student of Dummett's at Oxford, launched a concerted scholarly attack on Dummett's reading in his book *Gottlob Frege* (1980). Sluga was anxious not to have Frege leap from Zeus's head fully formed, and strenuously opposed foisting a concern with 'theory of meaning' on him.[41] Nevertheless, in his very efforts to correct Dummett's reading, Sluga

38 Dummett, *Frege: Philosophy of Language*, p. xiv.

39 Ibid. In the second edition of the book, this oversight was corrected, and references to Frege's works were printed in the margins.

40 See, for example, the repeated use of this phrase in Joan Weiner, 'Frege and the Linguistic Turn'.

41 'If logic is meant to be a theory of meaning or a theory of truth, then there can really be no such thing . . . Frege's thoughts are not unlike those we find in Wittgenstein's *Tractatus*. There, too, the possibility of a semantic meta-theory for our language is rejected. As Wittgenstein puts it: "Logic must take care of itself"'. Hans D. Sluga, *Gottlob Frege*, p. 116.

tellingly fell into the trap of seeking Frege's intellectual context in the work of *philosophers* of the time, such as Hermann Lotze, who were in fact relatively unimportant to Frege. It is an understandable professional deformation of philosophers, responsive to the demands of academic life, to conceive Frege as a philosopher who must have been influenced, if by anyone, by other philosophers. But the results are deceptive, and significant in their replication of a closed community of philosophers who can only speak to each other, closed off from all other forms of enquiry.

Dummett's reimagining of Frege powerfully served the agenda of a new vindication of the task of philosophy, according to which philosophy of language was 'first philosophy'. Philosophers, it turned out after all, had something to do.[42] Frege's lighting of the way to philosophy of language as first philosophy, Dummett maintained, set him apart from Husserl, who had been occupied with similar issues but had not managed to take the linguistic turn as Frege had. Dummett liked to emphasize, as he did in a set of lectures given at the University of Bologna in 1987 (later published in revised form as *Origins of Analytical Philosophy*), how close together Frege and Husserl had once been: he compared them to the mighty European rivers the Rhine and the Danube, which have their sources only some 150 km apart but flow out into seas at opposite ends of the continent (the North Sea and the Black Sea, respectively).[43] Where, with one hand, Dummett gestured to a rapprochement between analytic and 'continental' philosophy, with the other he underlined the superiority of analytic philosophy as putting philosophy for the first time on its proper footing by recognizing that philosophy of language was first philosophy. The gesture has been effective: in Italy, especially, Dummett has had a loyal following that has exercised considerable influence in its university departments.[44]

42 The American philosopher Eric Schwitzgebel persuasively links insistence on a distinctive task for philosophers conceived in terms of the 'linguistic turn' with 'philosophy's need to distinguish itself from rising empirical disciplines'. As he points out, this 'could only work' when psychology was 'dominated by a behaviorist focus on simple behaviors and reinforcement mechanisms' ('The Linguistic U-Turn', *The Splintered Mind*, 30 July 2008, at schwitzsplinters.blogspot.com). Of course, as Richard Rorty has written, the whole idea that 'there is an autonomous discipline called "philosophy", distinct from and sitting in judgment upon both religion and science, is of quite recent origin' (Richard Rorty, *Philosophy and the Mirror of Nature*, p. 131).

43 Dummett, *Origins of Analytical Philosophy*, p. 26.

44 Especially important has been Eva Picardi, who, having studied with Dummett in Oxford, was professor of philosophy of language at the University of Bologna for forty years.

Davidson's Programme and the Theory of Meaning

Dummett helped to carve out a space for a 'philosophy of language' ostensibly derived from Frege.[45] This was the preserve not of mathematicians or logicians, but of professional philosophers. It was when combined with an impetus provided by the work of Donald Davidson that such an approach to philosophy attained supreme professional dominance. In the 1970s, Davidson exerted a massive influence on Oxford philosophy, captured in the phrase 'the Davidsonic boom' (apparently coined by Bernard Williams). This influence lasted for some time; as late as the mid 1980s, when the English philosopher Ian Rumfitt was a student in Oxford, 'Donald Davidson loomed larger over the philosophical scene than any other living thinker'.[46]

From early on, Davidson had a predilection for technical approaches to philosophy. In the 1950s, while Dummett was immersing himself in Frege, Davidson had, in addition to work in game theory, made a study of Carnap's 'method of extension and intension', as set out in his *Meaning and Necessity*. What Carnap proposed was a highly technical semantic theory, whose purpose really *was* to show how words meant what they did. So, for Davidson, the question became: 'What is meaning?'[47] As he pursued this question, he developed a hunch. The Polish logician Alfred Tarski had in 1931 presented a truth theory for formalized languages.[48] This introduced what became known as 'Convention T'. Truth for a formal language could be defined in a metalanguage.

---

45 I am here using 'philosophy of language', in scare quotes, as contrasting with the genuine linguistic turn executed by Wittgenstein. In Chapter 6 of *Philosophy and the Mirror of Nature*, Rorty makes a similar distinction, but using different terminology. Rorty calls what I call the genuine, Wittgensteinian linguistic turn 'pure philosophy of language'; the Dummettian project I call 'philosophy of language', Rorty calls 'impure philosophy of language'. Rorty characterizes the former as 'de-epistemologized', the latter as 'epistemologized'. Rorty is happy to place Davidson in the former camp. Given Davidson's stylistic and philosophical evasiveness, it is difficult to be sure if Rorty is right about this. In any case, the interest of the discussion here is the *use* made of Davidson's work by those adhering to what Rorty calls the 'epistemologized' conception.

46 Ian Rumfitt, '*The Structure of Truth: The 1970 John Locke Lectures*, by Donald Davidson', p. 1,027.

47 Donald Davidson, 'Intellectual Autobiography', p. 33.

48 Alfred Tarski, 'The Concept of Truth in Formalized Languages'.

Instances of such definitions could be illustrated using examples such as the following:

'Snow is white' is true if and only if snow is white.

Davidson's hunch was that Tarski's truth theory could be repurposed as a theory of meaning. This could then be used as the basis of a formal semantics for a language such as English, and thereby answer the question he had inherited from Carnap: 'What is meaning?' The reason this seemed plausible was the natural-seeming idea that what it was to know what 'Snow is white' meant was a matter of grasping the conditions under which 'Snow is white' is true. Somewhat miraculously, a metalanguage could be dispensed with: the truth conditions for meaning in English could be stated in that language itself.

Davidson's proposal was supposed to have various attractions. It was clear that speakers have only limited vocabulary at their disposal, but are capable of generating an infinite number of sentences using these materials. The proposed theory could help with this, by aiming to explain the meaningfulness of the sentences, and speakers' ability to grasp this meaningfulness, in terms of rules of composition. That bit of the task could be accomplished using established techniques.[49] Beyond this, however, the theory was supposed to do more. It was supposed to explain what speakers were, in some sense, 'doing' when they uttered meaningful statements: 'what it was' to use language

49 Among such techniques was the use of 'truth tables' (popularized by Wittgenstein, but used earlier by C. S. Peirce and by Frege). Truth tables exhibited the truth or falsity of statements involving logical 'connectives' such as 'and', 'or' and 'not'. A simple example is a truth table for 'not':

p	not-*p*
true	false
false	true

Or a truth table for 'or':

p	*q*	*p* or *q*
true	true	true
true	false	true
false	true	true
false	false	false

meaningfully. Here, however, the theory threatened to replace vices it was supposed to avoid with vices of its own. The theory was, thankfully, free of the vice of 'mentalism': that is, it did not try to explain meaning in terms of what went on in speakers' minds.[50] Mentalistic theories suffered from the problem that they made meaning private, thereby making it a mystery how speakers were able to communicate. How did the meanings get from the mind of the speaker into the mind of the hearer? Again, the Davidsonian style of theory was free of the vice of treating meanings, implausibly, as 'entities'.[51] But, in combating these tendencies, it engendered a highly dubious tendency of its own to resort to talk of linguistic 'behaviour' that, though it did not make language problematically private, reduced it to the making and hearing of noises – and so to something less than meaningful communication.

Davidson's influence was secured by a two-way exchange. Several Oxford philosophers, including Dummett, had come to Stanford, where Davidson was working, in the 1950s and 1960s.[52] Back in Oxford, mimeographed copies of Davidson's 'Truth and Meaning', eventually published in 1967, were pored over along with other papers by Davidson. The exchange went both ways. When Davidson came to Oxford to give the John Locke Lectures in 1970, setting out the 'Davidsonian programme', he was rapturously received.[53] In 1973–74 he returned to

---

50 John Locke put such a theory in especially stark form: 'Words in their primary or immediate Signification, stand for nothing but the Ideas in the Mind of him that uses them' (John Locke, *An Essay Concerning Human Understanding*, 3.2.2).

51 Among the many who lampooned the notion of meanings as entities, Wittgenstein issued some of the more memorable indictments. For instance: 'You say: the point isn't the word, but its meaning, and you think of the meaning as a thing of the same kind as the word, though also different from the word. Here the word, there the meaning. The money, and the cow that you can buy with it.' (*Philosophical Investigations*, §120.) And: 'When I think in language, there aren't "meanings" going through my mind in addition to the linguistic expressions: the language is itself the vehicle of the thinking.' (*Philosophical Investigations*, §329 – Anscombe's translation modified.)

52 'An early influence on my thinking was Michael Dummett, who lectured on Frege and philosophy of language several times at Stanford University while I was there in the fifties.' Donald Davidson, *Inquiries into Truth and Interpretation*, p. xx. In his 'Intellectual Autobiography' (p. 30), Davidson mentions as visitors to Stanford, at his invitation, in the time he was there (1951–67): Gilbert Ryle, Peter Strawson, Michael Dummett, Elizabeth Anscombe, Peter Geach, David Wiggins, David Pears and Paul Grice.

53 The Locke Lectures have since been published as Donald Davidson, *The Structure of Truth: The 1970 John Locke Lectures.*

Oxford as a visiting fellow at All Souls College, spending time with the younger Oxford philosophers Derek Parfit, John McDowell and Gareth Evans. Parfit and Evans had come to Oxford from English boarding schools (Eton College and Dulwich College, respectively); McDowell from the University College of Rhodesia and Nyasaland. As Davidson later reported, 'Gareth and John McDowell were determined to prove to the "Americans" that they had learned how to apply formal methods to the study of natural language, and they put together a fine volume, *Truth and Meaning*.'[54]

Evans's and McDowell's 1976 volume, whose title replicated that of Davidson's own 1967 paper, showed a high level of enthusiasm for the level of technicality that Davidson had introduced into the philosophy of language. It also laid bare a fault-line between Dummett and McDowell. Dummett had argued in his 1974 lecture 'What is a Theory of Meaning?' that 'a theory of meaning has to give an account of . . . what it is that someone knows when he knows the language', and that 'to know a language is to be able to employ a language'.[55] He complained that, in light of these demands that a theory of meaning must (according to Dummett) meet, Davidson's theory was 'a modest theory', that is, a theory that 'would be intelligible only to someone who had already grasped' the concepts whose meaning it was the theory's task to explain.[56] Dummett followed this up with 'What is a Theory of Meaning? (II)', published in Evans and McDowell's collection. As Davidson reported, this second essay 'had been produced in the course of a seminar on truth that Michael [Dummett] and I gave during that year. The seminar was apparently viewed by the Oxford community as a sort of gladiatorial contest, and a large crowd turned out.'[57]

It is not known what Davidson's contributions to this 'gladiatorial' contest were; his published contributions on the subject evince, ultimately, a studied evasiveness on the question of 'modesty'. McDowell, however, went into print with a defence of 'modesty'. Dummett was frustrated by the circularity involved in saying that a speaker's understanding of 'Snow is white' amounted to their knowing the conditions under which it was true (namely, snow's being white). McDowell

54 Davidson, 'Intellectual Autobiography', p. 53.
55 Michael Dummett, 'What Is a Theory of Meaning?', pp. 99, 101.
56 Ibid., p. 103.
57 Davidson, 'Intellectual Autobiography', p. 53.

insisted, against Dummett's demand for something more when it came to explaining what a speaker understood, that there was simply no way to provide a theory 'as from outside' of what it was for the speaker to understand what she was saying.[58] The only prospect there could be for such a theory had to take a 'philistine' form, along the lines of the behaviourism favoured by Quine.[59] Quine was able to avoid talking about 'meanings' as mysterious entities, but at the price of having to conceive of communication as the making and hearing of noises. When McDowell blocked Dummett's calls for a 'full-blooded' theory of meaning that would explain *how* words are meaningful with an insistence that such a theory could only ever be 'modest', this was effectively the revenge of Wittgenstein's linguistic turn against Dummett's invented pseudo-Fregean 'linguistic turn'.

The great flurry of technical work that went into the 'Davidsonian programme' and associated attempts at a 'theory of meaning' came to nothing. It served to professionalize a group of philosophers, and to cement Oxford's reputation as a philosophical powerhouse. But all that has survived of it is a certain relentless technicality and the glorification of the febrile 'gladiatorial' atmosphere evoked by Davidson. Gareth Evans's life was cut short by cancer at the age of thirty-four. It is difficult to know where his highly original work might have led him if he had lived. In the unfinished monograph, *Varieties of Reference*, edited from the materials Evans had left behind by his friend John McDowell and published posthumously, there were signs of his breaking out of the confines of analytic philosophy into a kind of phenomenological enquiry that treated the thinker as nothing other than an embodied agent in the world.[60] Following Evans's death in 1980 and McDowell's departure for Pittsburgh in 1986, to pursue a Kantian and even a Hegelian turn, among those left behind in Oxford pseudo-problems concerning how language 'hooked onto' the world continued to be attacked with great vigour.

In the eyes of many analytic philosophers the purported problem of meaning only gained in seeming importance the more it became a self-standing concern no longer apparently requiring anything to motivate it. Paul Horwich has even spoken – despite professing to be, of all things,

58 John McDowell, 'In Defence of Modesty', in *Meaning, Knowledge, and Reality.*

59 John McDowell, 'On the Sense and Reference of a Proper Name', in *Meaning, Knowledge, and Reality*, p. 181.

60 For hints along these lines, see Charles Taylor, 'Dwellers in Egocentric Space'.

a Wittgensteinian – of the supposed 'urgency' of the pseudo-problem of how words mean what they do:

> What is meaning? Why are some sounds imbued with it and others not? How, for example, does it come about that the word 'dog' means precisely what it does? How is it possible for those intrinsically inert ink-marks (or some associated state of the brain) to reach out into the world and latch on to a definite portion of reality: namely, the dogs? This issue, which might perhaps strike some as small and arcane, is on the contrary one of the most urgent of philosophical questions.[61]

Others have given relentlessly technical treatments of what is now routinely called 'aboutness'. Stephen Yablo, a professor of philosophy at MIT who has written a monograph on the topic, calls it 'the relation that meaningful items bear to whatever it is that they are *on* or *of* or that they *address* or *concern*'.[62] 'Aboutness' has become an industry.

Representationalism

The Davidson–Dummett flurry of activity around the 'theory of meaning' did not just represent a travesty of Wittgenstein's linguistic turn. It was also regressive with respect to the more expansive conception of language that Wittgenstein's later work, and the work of Austin, had helped to open up. For the later Wittgenstein and for Austin, language possessed not merely a 'constative' use, but many others: it was used to command, to promise, to coax, and much else.

In 1980, at a time when the Dummett–McDowell debate was still live, Charles Taylor, himself a product of Oxford, gave a lecture on 'Theories of Meaning' in London, in which he urged that the debate rested on a constricted conception of language which three post-Enlightenment Germans – Herder, Humboldt and Hamann (or, as Taylor ominously called them, 'HHH') – had already criticized. The Germans had insisted, in their criticism of the highly naturalistic theory of the eighteenth-century French philosopher Condillac, that language does not merely represent, but also expresses. The

61 Paul Horwich, *Meaning*, p. 1.

62 Stephen Yablo, *Aboutness*, p. 1.

meaningfulness of language could therefore not be restricted to what a representational model allowed for.[63]

If Taylor was right, no truth-conditional semantics could plausibly claim to show how language worked in full (whether the theory was 'modest' or 'immodest'). Furthermore, the restriction of language to representation on which such a conceit rested was historically specific. Michel Foucault had argued in *The Order of Things*, one of the works in which he sought to carry out 'archaeology of knowledge', that a representationalist paradigm had become ascendant in what he called *l'âge classique* (the seventeenth and eighteenth centuries), shored up by the prime logical text of the time, the *Port-Royal Logic* of Antoine Arnauld and Pierre Nicole, and permeating intellectual life.[64] Foucault's treatment did not suggest any way back from the representationalist predicament; his historical story certainly did not point in the direction of the 'expressivism' that Taylor located in the age of HHH – and a fourth H, Hegel.[65] But it is difficult not to read his historical analysis of the age of representation, in which 'language has withdrawn from the midst of beings themselves and has entered a period of transparency and neutrality', without experiencing this as a confinement.[66] The confinement is analogous to that effected by 'theories of meaning', modest or immodest – and the cry of language for its own liberation similarly resonant.

---

63 McDowell complained that Taylor seemed 'too willing to make his Enlightenment opponents a present of the notion of representation' (McDowell, *Meaning, Knowledge, and Reality*, p. 107). However, the point that expression is something over and above representation could surely not be contested.

64 Michel Foucault, *The Order of Things*, Chapter 3.

65 As Taylor wrote in his study of Hegel, a new view emerging at the end of the eighteenth century 'needed . . . a theory of meaning in which linguistic meaning, the meaning of signs, was not sharply marked off from other forms of meaning, but was rather continuous with the expressive meaning of art' (Charles Taylor, *Hegel*, p. 18). Taylor related this issue to contemporary theories of meaning later in the book (pp. 565–6).

66 Foucault, *Order of Things*, p. 56.

8

Modal Logic and the Return of Metaphysics

In the 1970s metaphysics, long ostracized and maligned, staged a remarkable comeback in analytic philosophy – the principal action taking place, as was by now to be expected, in the United States. In fact, it took place largely in the philosophy departments of the most elite American universities, in particular Harvard and Princeton. The task of this chapter is to explain how this could have happened. As a leading analytic metaphysician, Timothy Williamson, has pointed out, the return of metaphysics, facilitated by the work of the American philosophers Saul Kripke and David Lewis, and pursued by their numerous disciples, followers and imitators, is far more astonishing, given the prior history of analytic philosophy, than is generally acknowledged.[1]

The reassertion of metaphysics as a legitimate field of enquiry in philosophy was not simply a matter of philosophers rediscovering a taste for metaphysical speculation. It was instead the outcome of a set of developments in what might seem a more or less unconnected discipline: logic. The resurgence of metaphysics cannot be understood in isolation from the triumph of modal logic, or the logic of necessity and possibility, and thus from the activities of logicians. Before the rise of the 'new logic' of Frege, Peano, Russell and others, logic had, for much of its history, concerned itself not just with which statements about what is the case can be validly inferred from which other statements about what is the case, but also with valid inference between statements about

1 Timothy Williamson, *The Philosophy of Philosophy*, p. xvii.

what is necessarily or possibly so, and with more or less necessary kinds of entailment. In the medieval period in Europe, for example, a substantial part of logic was occupied with 'modality' ('ways' or 'modes' for things to be, such as *necessarily* and *possibly*).[2] The logic that animated the work of Russell and Whitehead, the Vienna Circle, and others, however, tended to suppress modality. The formal techniques it wielded – techniques of unprecedented power – had been born out of a revolution whose success depended (for reasons that will become clear in this chapter) precisely on this exclusion.

It might seem eccentric to try to explain the return of metaphysics in terms of social history, and even more so if the driving explanation is to be a social history of logic. But the notion that there could be a social history of logic, and in particular of modal logic, is not entirely without precedent. The New Zealand logician Max Cresswell, in an informal talk to the Australasian Association for Logic in 2022, entitled 'Why Did W. V. O. Quine Hate Ruth Barcan Marcus?', suggested that the history of modal logic in the twentieth century had a political dimension.[3] Cresswell outlines the story of Quine's vociferous attempts to halt, or at least frustrate, progress in modal logic, noting along the way that modal logicians were often of a different political persuasion to Quine. They tended to be considerably to the left of Quine: Cresswell mentions Quine's teacher C. I. Lewis, the American logicians W. T. Parry and Ruth Barcan Marcus, and the New Zealander Arthur Prior. Rudolf Carnap, Quine's youthful hero who subsequently went dangerously modal, was, as we have seen, a member of the Independent Social Democratic Party in Germany, and attracted suspicion from J. Edgar Hoover's FBI because of his expressed leftist sympathies.[4] Oskar Becker, a key continental figure in modal logic who had been a student of Husserl, was an ardent Nazi.

A proper grasp of the history, building on the suggestive hints contained in Cresswell's narrative, requires us to go back several centuries. In the eighteenth century, Leibniz had drawn up an ambitious plan (in keeping with his tendency to draw up grand schemes in many different areas) for a formal logic – that is, a logic using repeatable symbols. That

2 'Necessary' and 'possible' are interdefinable, in the following way: what is necessarily the case is not possibly not the case, what is possibly the case is not necessarily not the case.

3 A recording of the talk is available at youtube.com: 'Max Cresswell – Why Did W. V. O. Quine Hate Ruth Barcan Marcus?'

4 See Chapter 5, above.

plan informed many subsequent attempts to get such a formal logic off the ground. No such plan succeeded, however, until the work of the English mathematician George Boole in the nineteenth century. An important reason why Boole could make this breakthrough where others had failed was that, as a mathematician, his priorities significantly differed from those of Leibniz and his other philosophical predecessors in the field of logic. Boole's logic was able to subvert a complex set of questions because, for him, those questions simply did not come up. Among these were the questions raised by modality.

In the wake of Boole's breakthrough, formal logic proceeded in an 'extensional' vein (that is, it excluded 'intensional' notions, modality among them). Extensional notions are those such as class membership – they can do their work pointing to things 'in the world' without having to give consideration to 'intensions' (the meanings of terms or the contents of thoughts). The work of Frege, and that of Russell and Whitehead, operated with a basically extensional conception of logic. A lone, unconventional and socially marginalized voice raised in protest against this was that of Hugh MacColl, a secondary school teacher in Boulogne who had been born the son of a shepherd in the Scottish Highlands. MacColl argued the need for a logic that integrated modality, but to little avail. In the United States, the young C. I. Lewis, a student of the idealist Josiah Royce at Harvard University, who had become fascinated by logic through Royce's teaching, renewed MacColl's onslaught on extensionalism. Lewis was more successful than MacColl because he was in a position to utilize, for his attacks on Russell's extensionalism, the formal apparatus of Russell and Whitehead's *Principia Mathematica*, the first volume of which had appeared in 1910, the year after MacColl's death.

The division between extensionalism and intensionalism (where extensionalism means the exclusion of intensional notions from logic, intensionalism their inclusion) runs deep. Lewis observed that 'British logicians, when really original, have always thought in terms of extension; Continental ones in terms of intension.' He added, in parentheses: 'Some psychologist with an eye for history ought to investigate this.'[5] A sketch of a psychosocial history is given in this chapter.

In the wake of Boole, and then of the work of Frege and Russell, all of it extensionalist in spirit, progress in modal logic could be made only by those willing to flout orthodoxy. MacColl and Lewis were two such

5 C. I. Lewis, 'Logic and Pragmatism', p. 33.

iconoclasts. Arthur Prior was helped partly by his geographical location in New Zealand, remote from both Europe and America, and partly by an unusual background, steeped in the medieval Christian tradition as well as socialism. Ruth Barcan Marcus, an American raised in the Bronx, shared Prior's disregard for orthodoxy, but also seemed to be boosted in her dogged determination by the relentless obstinacy with which Quine, the keeper of extensionalism, opposed her every move in modal logic.

The story presented here should be understood as that of a series of heroic assaults – with Lewis, Parry, Marcus and Prior as protagonists – upon the fortress of extensionalism. To attack extensionalism was effectively to strike at the core of analytic ideology. The figures who mounted such attacks were not exactly outsiders, but they were, in a significant sense, iconoclasts. As the story proceeds, the impact that Prior and Marcus achieved is overshadowed by two figures who came to dominate late-twentieth-century analytic philosophy: Saul Kripke and David Lewis. Quine had seen his successive attempted arguments against Marcus turn to dust, until he was left only with the general charge of 'Aristotelian essentialism' – something for which Quine was capable of summoning up a seemingly bottomless dislike. Kripke, in a series of lectures delivered at Princeton University in 1970 entitled 'Naming and Necessity', mounted a triumphant defence not only of modality, but of the very essentialism Quine despised. Lewis pursued a different policy. Having inherited a sympathy for extensionalism from his teacher Quine, he turned his ingenuity to squeezing modal notions back into an extensionalist framework. Either way, something extraordinary had happened. Whether one accepted Kripke's unashamed essentialism or Lewis's accommodation of modal metaphysics to a Quinean paradigm, the damage was done. Metaphysics was back. Efficiency at putting the right things in the right boxes – to which the extensionalist paradigm helped to reduce philosophy – had given way to the resurgence of the old metaphysical questions about what kinds of things constitute reality. Institutionally, it was now Princeton that was the centre of analytic philosophy, no longer the Harvard of Quine.

There is no doubt that, since the impetus given by Kripke and Lewis in the early 1970s, metaphysics is now a core part of analytic philosophy. Every undergraduate degree now has at least one course called 'Metaphysics', which, it is claimed, will acquaint students with the nature of reality. But how could this reimportation of metaphysics into philosophy have been accepted by the analytic establishment in the first place? Quine, Kripke and Lewis, although their approaches diverged sharply, had in common a high level of methodological scrupulousness. Quine modelled ontological theory choice after the natural sciences; Kripke depended on what he took, unabashedly, to be an 'intuitive' standpoint (though often differing widely from what most analytic philosophers thought were the intuitions of the 'ordinary person'); Lewis characterized his method in terms of 'cost-benefit' analysis. The underlying ideologies are not difficult to read off. Quine and his student Lewis were liberals in a Humean tradition: there was, for them, a world of inert 'matters of fact' with which the autonomous subject was confronted. Kripke, by contrast, was happy to embrace substantive theses that often conformed to traditional Aristotelian or Cartesian views, in a 'take it or leave it' mode. The vast majority of contemporary metaphysicians, by contrast, though they claim to draw their fire from Quine, mediated by developments brought about by Kripke and Lewis, seem to be in a state of severe methodological confusion. They blithely claim to be engaged in 'speculative ontology', without having any response ready to the charge that philosophy then rests on dogmatism (that is, on mere assertion, and thus on nothing at all). The term 'armchair methods' is used – as if this were anything other than a veil to obscure a lack of methodological probity.

In the new era of analytic metaphysics which Kripke and Lewis helped birth, their legacy is strangely double. The rigour and intellectual brilliance to be found in their own work have secured them their place in the pantheon of analytic philosophy. But their many followers have tended to forget the great methodological troubles to which they went, instead deriving from them a smooth professionalism, accompanied by the myopia that comes with working on tiny, isolated problems. Although Lewis, in particular, towers over the discipline, Lewisianism as a social formation seems sadly lacking in the philosophical verve that marked the man himself. The idea that philosophical theses could be weighed up by means of a 'cost-benefit analysis', as if the profession of philosophy was a kind of subgroup of engineering, seems to form the dreary bulk of his legacy. It ought to surprise us, furthermore, that today's metaphysicians, while making claims to the special rigour ostensibly associated with analytic philosophy, base their arguments on their own intuitions, conceived 'in the armchair'. The next chapter will focus more closely on this greater strangeness.

The Development of Logic

Logic is the study of valid inference; of what follows from what. Aristotle inventoried the valid and invalid forms of the syllogism, and thereby created a formal framework within which logic in the European-Christian and Islamic traditions was to move for many centuries. The resources that this Aristotelian framework offered were, however, severely limited. Arguments that could be assessed for validity were restricted to those conforming to a particular pattern: a predicative conclusion drawn on the basis of two predicative premises.[6] It is a commonplace that no major innovation was made in logic after Aristotle until technical developments that occurred in the nineteenth century. The commonplace is highly misleading, in that it ignores the considerable innovations made in the medieval Aristotelian tradition, building partly on Stoic logic. Nevertheless, efforts to bring such innovations into a satisfactory formal order were limited and fitful.

One of the chief projects of the German polymath Gottfried Wilhelm Leibniz was the attainment of peace in Europe between warring religious factions. Another was that of a logic that could be employed to solve all of the problems of science. It would have to be rigorous, not only by reliably distinguishing between valid and invalid inference, but also through an entirely transparent and unambiguous notation of a kind not achievable in natural languages such as German, French, Latin or English. Logic, then, required both a *calculus ratiocinator* and a *characteristica universalis*.

Leibniz envisaged his project, plausibly enough, as having to be assigned to a great army of researchers to carry out jointly, rather than as something that could be accomplished by one man such as himself. The project never took off, for intellectual as well as practical reasons. Leibniz's concern with intension, as well as extension, was a major factor here. The contrast between extension and intension can be best illustrated by considering what it takes for two expressions to be extensionally equivalent or, by contrast, intensionally equivalent. The expressions 'the morning star' and 'the evening star' are extensionally equivalent, because they both 'refer to' the same object: the planet Venus. They are not, however, intensionally equivalent, because the two

6 By a 'predicative' statement is meant one of the form 'S is P' (where 'S' stands for 'subject' and 'P' for 'predicate'); for example, 'Socrates is wise'.

expressions do not *mean* the same thing, or have the same sense. It is a substantive astronomical discovery to realize that the Morning Star (so-called because it appears in the sky in the morning) and the Evening Star (so-called because it appears in the sky in the evening) are not two different celestial bodies, but one. 'Intensional contexts' are types of statement in which this difference becomes relevant. So, for example, it does not follow from 'George knows that the Morning Star is the Morning Star' that 'George knows that the Morning Star is the Evening Star'. A correct logic should be able to account for the invalidity of this inference.

When a breakthrough in formal logic was finally made, it was achieved by someone who ignored intensional contexts altogether. This was the English mathematician George Boole, with whose work a continuous history of symbolic logic has its beginning.[7] Boole had the distinct advantage that, as a mathematician, his thinking naturally moved along extensional lines. Where he discussed intensional notions such as 'necessary' (as in his formal treatment of Spinoza's *Ethics*), he simply treated them as adjectives on a par with non-intensional notions such as 'blue' and 'red'.[8] He was thereby able to make progress with the calculus of 'the relations of concepts or classes' undeterred by the issue of how to accommodate intensions that had delayed, and ultimately defeated, Leibniz.

The 'Boole–Schröder Algebra' that resulted from the refinements to Boole made by the German mathematician Ernst Schröder, and the logic of Peano and Frege that supplanted it, were extensional. A subclass of intensional notions ruled out by this approach were modal notions – those concerning what is necessarily or possibly the case, what must be and what might have been. Frege explicitly dismissed modal notions as irrelevant to logic: 'If I call a proposition necessary, I thereby give a hint as to my grounds for judgement. *But since this does not affect the conceptual content of the judgement, the apodeictic form of a judgement has no significance for us.*'[9] As the historians of logic William and Martha

---

7 Bertrand Russell, *Our Knowledge of the External World as a Field for Scientific Method in Philosophy*, pp. 49–50; C. I. Lewis, *A Survey of Symbolic Logic*, p. 51; John Passmore, *A Hundred Years of Philosophy*, p. 125.

8 See, for example, Boole's attribution to Spinoza of a division of things into 'things free, *f*, and things necessary, *f*''. George Boole, *An Investigation of the Laws of Thought, On Which Are Founded the Mathematical Theories of Logic and Probabilities*, p. 213.

9 Gottlob Frege, *Begriffsschrift*, §4, in *The Frege Reader*, p. 55. Emphasis in original.

Kneale put it, for Frege what is wrong with words like 'necessary' and 'possible', when it comes to logic, is that they 'involve a covert reference to human knowledge for which there is no place in pure logic'.[10]

Russell vacillated somewhat on the issue of modality. In *The Principles of Mathematics*, he took up a position 'intermediate between pure intension and pure extension', unlike his French counterpart Couturat, who, in his study of Leibniz, blamed the failure of Leibniz's logical efforts on his infatuation with intension.[11] Elsewhere, Russell took a hard line against the notions of necessity and possibility. In a paper entitled 'Necessity and Possibility', which he read to the Oxford Philosophical Society in 1905, he claimed that since, 'so far as appears, there is no one fundamental logical notion of *necessity*, nor consequently of *possibility* . . . the subject of modality ought to be banished from logic, since propositions are simply true or false, and there is no such comparative and superlative of truth as is implied by the notions of contingency and necessity'.[12]

Hugh MacColl

The general direction in which logic travelled in the nineteenth century, then, was extensional. A lone voice railing against the extensionalism that dominated formal logic was that of Hugh MacColl. His voice was not entirely ignored; Russell engaged with him in the pages of *Mind*, and briefly addressed what he called MacColl's 'important series of papers' in *The Principles of Mathematics*.[13] Nevertheless, it was effectively drowned out.

MacColl was a startlingly marginal figure, born in 1837 in Strontian in Argyllshire, in the Scottish Highlands, the son of a shepherd.[14]

10 William Kneale and Martha Kneale, *The Development of Logic*, p. 548.

11 Bertrand Russell, *The Principles of Mathematics*, p. 66. Compare Louis Couturat, *La Logique de Leibniz, d'après des documents inédits*, p. 387, where Couturat writes: 'L'échec final de son système [that is, that of Leibniz] est donc extrêmement instructif, car il prouve que la Logique algorithmique (c'est-à-dire en somme la Logique exacte et rigoureuse) ne peut pas être fondé sur la considération confuse et vague de la compréhension; elle n'a réussi à se constituer qu'avec Boole, parce qu'il l'a fait reposer sur la considération exclusive de l'extension, seule susceptible d'un traitement mathématique.'

12 Bertrand Russell, 'Necessity and Possibility', in *The Collected Papers of Bertrand Russell*, vol. 4, p. 520.

13 Russell, *The Principles of Mathematics*, p. 12.

14 The main source on MacColl's life is Michael Astroh, Ivor Grattan-Guinness and Stephen Read, 'A Survey of the Life of Hugh MacColl (1837–1909)'.

His father died when MacColl was three years old. His mother only spoke Gaelic. Hugh's elder brother Malcolm, thanks to the patronage of a wealthy lady, gained a place at Oxford University, eventually becoming a noted public figure and friend of William Gladstone. But his hopes of helping Hugh into Oxford fell through after Malcolm, who was addicted to controversy, became involved in the dispute within the Episcopal Church over the proper interpretation of the Eucharist in 1857–58. Hugh MacColl never had a university education, and did not obtain a degree until he was nearly forty, when he was awarded a BA in mathematics as an external student of the University of London. From 1865, he lived in Boulogne-sur-Mer, teaching mathematics and English at the Collège Communal. Although his contact with other logicians was largely in writing, it appears that the greatest of all nineteenth-century American logicians, Charles Sanders Peirce, visited him in Boulogne in 1883.[15] Outside his logical work, MacColl subscribed to conventional theological pieties and metaphysical idealism. He thus shared little with Russell in terms of either social background or general outlook. They did have in common, however, that each had lost his father at the age of three, and both tried their hand at fiction, both producing heavily autobiographical work of a low literary standard.[16]

Between 1880 and 1906 MacColl published a series of eight papers in *Mind*, under the title 'Symbolic Reasoning'. Much of this work was integrated into his monograph *Symbolic Logic and Its Applications* (1906), of which Russell published two reviews (a more popular one in *The Athenaeum* and a more learned one in *Mind*). In the first of the eight papers, MacColl paid tribute to Boole, as 'the first person to show that symbolical reasoning might also be employed with advantage in the investigation of matters usually considered altogether beyond the sphere of mathematics'. He described 'logicians', however, as seeing 'their hitherto inviolate territory now for the first time invaded by a foreign power, and with weapons which they had but too much reason to dread'.[17]

---

15 That a visit took place is implied in Peirce's correspondence with MacColl. See Astroh, Grattan-Guinness and Read, 'Survey of the Life of Hugh MacColl', p. 86.

16 MacColl published two novels, *Mr Stranger's Sealed Packet* (1889) and *Ednor Whitlock* (1891), both concerned with the academic travails of a man who loses his father at an early age. For an assessment, see Stein Haugom Olsen, 'Why Hugh MacColl Is Not, and Will Never Be, Part of Any Literary Canon'.

17 Hugh MacColl, 'Symbolical Reasoning', p. 46.

MacColl noted that 'other logicians generally divide logic into two parts: the logic of *class inclusion* and the logic of *propositions*'.[18] The logic of class inclusion is inherently extensional. Class inclusion, after all, is merely a question of what elements are members of larger things containing them. There is no place here for questions of what is necessarily or possibly so, or issues about the meanings of expressions, to get a foothold. But the logic of propositions, MacColl thought, was not obviously purely extensional. For one thing, the claim that some proposition *entails* another seems to say something about what *must* be. What is more, MacColl was resolute in his commitment to devising a logic that could do duty as *both* a logic of class inclusion *and* a logic of propositions: what he proposed was 'one simple homogeneous system'.[19]

MacColl placed modality at the very heart of his symbolic system. For 'implies', he introduced his own symbol ':' (so that 'A implies B' is written 'A : B'). This symbol, he wrote, 'asserts that *the statement following it must be true, provided the statement preceding it be true*'.[20] Note the 'must': MacColl's notion of implication is inherently modal. He was also adamant that this symbol must not be taken as equivalent to symbols used by other logicians to stand for implication, in particular Peirce's $-\!\!<$. Convinced of the superiority of his system, and embittered by the lack of appreciation with which it was met, he wrote, with a mixture of stridency and resignation:

> Human nature being what it is, and professional prejudices being what they are, and what they can hardly help being, such a general recognition of the superiority of my system is hardly to be expected just yet; but I think it will come in time – after I have dropped into my place among the silent people of the past.[21]

That MacColl treats modal notions as on a par with other logical notions is brought out by his notation. In the second paper of the series, he abandons his earlier notation, inherited from Boole, of '1' (for 'is true') and '0' (for 'is false'), which are replaced by ε (for 'is certain') and η (for 'is impossible'). To these are added the further operators θ (for 'is

18 Hugh MacColl, 'Symbolic Reasoning (V)', p. 355.

19 Ibid.

20 MacColl, 'Symbolical Reasoning', pp. 50–1.

21 MacColl, 'Symbolic Reasoning (V)', pp. 356–7.

variable'), τ (for 'is true', read as *not* necessarily certain) and ι (for 'is false', read as *not* necessarily impossible).[22] All of these operators represented by Greek letters are on the same logical footing (each can modify a statement in the same way), and they can be concatenated. So, for example, $A^{\eta\iota\varepsilon\varepsilon}$ is to be read (with the superscript operators read from right to left): 'It is certain that it is certain that it is false that it is impossible that A is true.'[23]

MacColl left many questions unanswered. However, he already drew attention to the issue that there appears something illicit in Peirce's symbol $\prec$ leaving its natural home (the extensional logic of class inclusion) in order to do duty in a logic of propositions (which involves implication). In a logic of class inclusion, $A \prec B$ is used 'to assert that *every individual of the class* A *belongs also to the class* B'. But logicians who use this symbol, when they are doing the logic of propositions, 'abandon this definition and use the same symbol to assert that *either* A *is false or* B true'. These, however, are clearly different. More worryingly, the proposition that *either* A is false *or* B is true seems to *mean* something different from the proposition that A *implies* B. MacColl's symbol : is not like this, he insists: 'I use the symbol A : B in always one and the same sense, namely, to assert that *it is certain that either* A *is false or* B true.' And so 'my symbol A : B is formally stronger than and implies their symbol $A \prec B$ . . . Thus, my symbol A : B never coincides in meaning with their symbol $A \prec B$, when A and B are propositions'.[24] MacColl raised the issue that 'A : B' is not equivalent to 'either not-A or B' as a problem for Russell's *Principles of Mathematics* in the pages of *Mind* in 1908.[25] Although Russell did take the trouble to reply, no fruitful discussion ensued. A real advance concerning such issues did not occur until the young American philosopher C. I. Lewis took them up, equipped with the technical resources of Russell and Whitehead's *Principia Mathematica*, the first volume of which came out in 1910, a year after MacColl's death.

---

22 Hugh MacColl, 'Symbolic Reasoning (II)', p. 497.

23 Hugh MacColl, 'Symbolic Reasoning (III)', p. 75.

24 MacColl, 'Symbolic Reasoning (V)', p. 357.

25 Hugh MacColl, '"If" and "Imply"'.

C. I. Lewis

Clarence Irving Lewis was born in 1883 in Stoneham, Massachusetts, the son of a shoemaker, and grew up in a socialist household. His father was involved in the temperance movement, something that was approved by the community. His later involvement in the Knights of Labor, by contrast, 'did not meet with similar approval'.[26] As a result of his agitation in this proto-trade union movement, Lewis *père* lost his job and his home. He subsequently became a Fabian socialist. Lewis *fils* read Marx's *Capital*, and went to meetings with the leading trade unionists Samuel Gompers and Eugene Debs.[27] At Harvard he became a student of the idealist philosopher Josiah Royce, whose 'ponderous cogency' enraptured him, but whose 'metaphysical conclusions' he rejected.[28]

In 1910–11, Lewis was Royce's teaching assistant for two courses in logic, and thereby got his hands on the newly published Volume 1 of Russell and Whitehead's *Principia Mathematica*. Not long after, in 1912, he published his objections to the theorems that resulted from the authors' treatment of the 'material conditional' ('if *p*, then *q*') as equivalent to 'either not-*p* or *q*'.[29] Among the consequences of Russell and Whitehead's treatment were that a false proposition implies any proposition, and that a true proposition is implied by any proposition.[30]

Statements involving 'or' are called by logicians 'disjunctions'. In his 1912 article, Lewis noted that there are two different kinds of disjunction. An example of the first kind is 'Either Caesar died or the moon is made of green cheese'. An example of the second kind is 'Either Matilda does not love me or I am beloved'.[31] A feature possessed by the second kind that the first lacks is that it can be read off the statement that one

26 C. I. Lewis, 'Autobiography', p. 1.

27 Ibid., p. 2.

28 C. I. Lewis, 'Logic and Pragmatism', p. 32.

29 C. I. Lewis, 'Implication and the Algebra of Logic'.

30 These are the two best-known 'paradoxes of material implication'. According to Lewis, they were merely two among a wild profusion of such paradoxes. In another paper he listed thirty-five theorems of *Principia* that he considered appropriate for *Alice in Wonderland*, and claimed that there were actually infinitely many such bizarre theorems. C. I. Lewis, 'Interesting Theorems in Symbolic Logic', p. 241.

31 Lewis, 'Implication and the Algebra of Logic', p. 523.

of the disjuncts (either 'Matilda does not love me', or 'I am beloved') must be true, for the reason that to deny the one is to affirm the other. (Suppose Matilda *does* love me: then I am loved by someone, and so beloved. Suppose I am *not* beloved: it follows that Matilda, just like everyone else, does not love me.) Lewis, on the basis of this difference between extensional disjunction (the first kind, where the disjuncts are, so to speak, indifferent to one another) and intensional disjunction (the second kind, where the disjuncts, so to speak, matter to each other), now proposed to define implication in terms of intensional disjunction only. This is 'strict implication'. The result is a system in which the paradoxes do not appear.

Across a series of papers, Lewis started to build a systematic formal logic that contained intensional as well as extensional elements. In his first full presentation of such a system, contained in his largely historical book, *A Survey of Symbolic Logic*, he wrote that 'the fundamental ideas of the system are similar to those of MacColl's *Symbolic Logic and its Applications*'.[32] Here, 'the theorems of *Principia* hold as consequences of Strict Implication whether the method of proof used in *Principia* is regarded as legitimate or not'.[33] In the later *Symbolic Logic*, co-authored with Cooper Harold Langford, a series of five systems of modal logic were set out (ever since known as S1, S2, S3, S4 and S5). Lewis now favoured S2 over the system set out in *A Survey of Symbolic Logic* (here designated S3). Modal logic was thereby set on a formally secure footing.

Politically, Lewis was a characteristic progressive of his time – suspicious of unfettered markets, in favour of regulation by experts, progressive taxes on income and rent, public ownership of utilities, and eugenics.[34] In Europe, meanwhile, a significant contribution was made to modal logic by Oskar Becker, who had obtained his doctorate in mathematics in 1914, and then, after serving in the First World War, studied philosophy with Edmund Husserl and Martin Heidegger. Becker's *Mathematische Existenz*, which took an existential approach to the foundations of mathematics inspired by Heidegger, formed pp. 439–809 of Volume 8 of the *Jahrbuch für Philosophie und phänomenologische Forschung* edited by Husserl; the remainder of the volume, pp. 1–438, was taken up with the original publication of Heidegger's *Sein und Zeit*.

32 Lewis, *Survey of Symbolic Logic*, p. 292.

33 Murray Murphey, *C. I. Lewis: The Last Great Pragmatist*, p. 93.

34 Ibid., p. 103.

Becker's 'Zur Logik der Modalitäten' ('On the Logic of Modalities', 1930), concerned to fuse the tradition of MacColl and Lewis with a phenomenological approach, was a key reference point for all those who were to pursue modal logic after him, including W. T. Parry.[35] Becker was a devoted Nazi, who published several contributions to the journal of Nazi racism *Rasse: Monatsschrift der Nordischen Bewegung* in the late 1930s, and presented as one of the *Kriegsvorträge* ('war lectures') at the University of Bonn in 1942 a disquisition on Nietzschean 'rank ordering'. Needless to say, Becker's reputation was tainted by this – suffering in particular, during the post-war years, in the eyes of those who had fled Nazi persecution.

Quine the 'Confirmed Extensionalist'

Lewis and those following him who wanted to develop modal logic had fierce opposition to contend with. The most immovable of their opponents was also one of the most influential and powerful philosophers in the United States, Willard Van Orman Quine. Born in Akron, Ohio, the son of a businessman who would go on to found a tyre mould company, he styled himself variously as W. V. Quine or W. V. O. Quine. Quine obtained his PhD from Harvard under Alfred North Whitehead, before spending time in Europe learning the ideas of Carnap and Tarski. From 1936 on, he taught at Harvard (interrupted by war service in naval intelligence from 1942 to 1945).

Quine's attachment to extensionalism was extreme. Late in his career, he called himself 'a confirmed extensionalist', and extensionalism a 'policy' that he 'clung to through thick, thin, and nearly seven decades of logicizing and philosophizing'.[36] For him, as for Frege and Tarski, logic was non-modal all the way through; the notions of necessity and possibility had to be vociferously eliminated. Logic was also tenseless, so notions of past, present and future had to be kept out too. In clinging to extensionalism, Quine saw himself as reacting against a native Harvard tradition. American philosophers, he noted, thought of Harvard as embodying a great tradition of logic because of its association with Whitehead, Henry M. Sheffer and C. I. Lewis, and, before them,

35 For Parry's sufferings at the hands of McCarthyism, see Chapter 5 above.

36 W. V. Quine, 'Confessions of a Confirmed Extensionalist' (2001), in *Confessions of a Confirmed Extensionalist and Other Essays*, p. 498.

Peirce and Royce.[37] But they were wrong. Whitehead, Lewis and Sheffer were all 'soft on intensions and introspective meanings', and 'really the action was in Europe'.[38] It was Quine's role, as he saw it, to set American logic right.

It caused Quine considerable upset when he witnessed his great hero Rudolf Carnap, of all people, go 'soft' on intensions. After visiting Carnap in Prague in 1933, Quine would see him as 'the dominant figure in philosophy from the 1930s onward, as Russell had been in the decades before', and as his 'greatest teacher'.[39] The Carnap under whose spell Quine had fallen was a devout extensionalist, in the line of Frege, Gödel, Church and Tarski. As the 1930s progressed, however, and Carnap developed his 'principle of tolerance', it turned out to Quine's consternation that among what Carnap proposed to tolerate were modal, and more generally intensional, languages. In his *Logische Syntax der Sprache* (1934), Carnap's tolerance still took the form of advocating the translation of intensional sentences into extensional ones.[40] But, as the decade went on, it sounded more and more like tolerance extended to allowing in actual intensional talk – not merely in an 'as if' mode, accompanied by an assurance of translatability into extensional talk. By 1938, Quine was getting nervous. He now wrote to Carnap: 'I fear your principle of tolerance may finally lead you even to tolerate Hitler.'[41]

Quine continued to be vociferous in his opposition to allowing in modal and other intensional ingredients. In one place, he expressed some tolerance for modal logic that 'stops short of quantification theory', but warned that, when it was extended to include quantification theory, 'serious obstacles to interpretation are encountered – particularly if one cares to avoid a curiously idealistic ontology which repudiates

---

37 Peirce notably never acquired a teaching position at Harvard, for complex personal reasons, but he was associated with the university in various ways throughout his life.

38 W. V. Quine, 'Two Dogmas in Retrospect' (1991), in *Confessions of a Confirmed Extensionalist*, p. 391; W. V. Quine, 'Autobiography', p. 9.

39 Quine quoted in Ádám Tamás Tuboly, 'The Early Formation of Modal Logic and Its Significance: A Historical Note on Quine, Carnap, and a Bit of Church', p. 290.

40 Ibid., p. 294; Rudolf Carnap, *The Logical Syntax of Language*.

41 Quine to Carnap, 4 February 1938, in W. V. Quine and Rudolf Carnap, *Dear Carnap, Dear Van: The Quine-Carnap Correspondence and Related Work*, p. 241. Carnap marked the final comment about Hitler with '!' in the margin (editorial note on p. 243).

material objects'.[42] In the end, he wrote in another paper, the complaint was that modal logic constituted a 'reversion to Aristotelian essentialism'.[43] The implied distinction between 'essence' and 'accident' (between those properties that attach to something necessarily, and those that do so only contingently), however 'venerable' thanks to its Aristotelian lineage, was, Quine was happy to state without argument in his monograph *Word and Object*, 'surely indefensible'.[44]

Quine's opposition to modality seemed almost unabashedly an aesthetic preference. He professed 'a taste for desert landscapes', as he said in what came to be regarded among analytic philosophers as a path-breaking paper, 'On What There Is'. The comment comes in the course of Quine's animadversions against a fictionalized philosopher, 'Wyman', whose ontology includes, horror of horrors, 'unactualized possibles'. (The horror could be invoked, Quine thought, by rhetorically asking: What would be the means of deciding whether the possible fat man in the doorway and the possible bald man in the doorway were one and the same man?!) Quine, evidently enough, liked to keep things clean and tidy. As he warned: 'Wyman's slum of possibles is a breeding ground for disorderly elements.' While 'some effort might be made at rehabilitation', it would be 'better simply to clear Wyman's slum and be done with it'.[45]

Strangely, Quine's 'On What There Is' has come to be widely misunderstood by later analytic philosophers as contributing to the rehabilitation of metaphysics. It is true that the paper establishes a test for working out what the ontological commitments of a theory are – that is, it proposes a procedure for answering the question: Given some theory, what are the things that the theory says *exist*? Quine's proposal is to model the question of 'ontological commitment' in general on the technique Russell used in his theory of descriptions. Russell could 'analyse away' the phrase 'the present king of France' as it figured in the statement 'The present king of France is bald' by replacing the troublesome expression 'the present king of France', which only *seems* to name an object, with a 'bound variable' (the x in the analysis 'there exists some x such that x . . .'). Quine proposed that all talk of entities could be analysed in this way, so that ontological commitment could be

42 W. V. Quine, 'The Problem of Interpreting Modal Logic', p. 43.

43 W. V. Quine, 'Reference and Modality', in *From a Logical Point of View: Nine Logico-Philosophical Essays*, p. 155.

44 W. V. Quine, *Word and Object*, p. 183.

45 W. V. Quine, 'On What There Is', in *From a Logical Point of View*, p. 4.

captured in the slogan 'To be is to be the value of a variable'.[46] None of this, however, helps with the question of *which* theory should be adopted in the first place, which Quine treated only in the closing pages of the paper. There, Quine suggested that 'acceptance of an ontology' was 'similar in principle to our acceptance of a scientific theory, say a system of physics: we adopt, at least insofar as we are reasonable, the simplest conceptual scheme into which the disordered fragments of raw experience can be fitted and arranged'.[47] He did not specify how claims to simplicity were themselves to be assessed; today's analytic metaphysicians might take note that their hero Quine had claims as to the correctness of an ontological theory rest on nothing other than the emulation of natural science.

Modality in the Antipodes

Quine opposed the idea of allowing into logic tensed statements (statements true at one time, but not at another) as much as he resisted allowing in the modal operators 'necessarily' and 'possibly'. The chief proponent of tense logic, closely analogous to modal logic, was Arthur Prior, a moral philosopher turned logician working in relative obscurity and isolation in New Zealand.

Prior, who had been born into a Methodist family on the small North Island town of Masterton in 1914, soon after he began his studies at the University of Otago on the South Island became a Presbyterian and joined the Student Christian Movement, which in New Zealand at the time had 'a very strong political and social conscience'.[48] One of his first publications was 'Maurice's Kingdom of Christ' (1935) in the *New Zealand Journal of Theology*, on the nineteenth-century Christian socialist and one-time Knightbridge Professor of Moral Sciences at Cambridge, F. D. Maurice. Prior would later lose his religious faith, but he would remain a socialist to the end. In 1969, the year of his death, he declared: 'I am left wing, [and] won't go to America again till the Vietnam war is over.'[49]

Prior's early interests were in ethics. Remarkably, he became a logician of the first rank having become interested in the subject only in his

46 Ibid., p. 15.
47 Ibid., p. 16.
48 Anthony Kenny, 'Arthur Norman Prior, 1914–1969', p. 322.
49 Quoted in ibid., p. 321.

late thirties. While working on a mammoth manuscript called *The Craft of Formal Logic*, he immersed himself in medieval logic, developing the work of Peter of Spain, Boethius and Walter Burleigh, and then in the Stoic logic of Diodorus Chronos, 'who had defined modal notions in terms of temporal notions, the possible being what either is or will be true, the impossible what both is and always will be false'.[50] Prior now set himself, with encouragement from J. N. Findlay, a wide-ranging philosopher then in New Zealand, to developing a calculus with temporal operators analogous in function to the operators of modal logic.[51] In 1954, Gilbert Ryle visited New Zealand. Evidently impressed by Prior, he invited him to give the 1956 John Locke Lectures at Oxford. Prior's friend Jack Smart, an Australian philosopher strongly under the influence of Quine, tried in the strongest terms to dissuade him from his plan to lecture on tense logic.[52] Prior ignored the advice. The work that resulted, *Time and Modality*, made tense logic and its modal cousins more difficult to ignore than it had been.

Ruth Barcan Marcus

A significant innovator in modal logic after C. I. Lewis and Rudolf Carnap was Ruth Barcan Marcus, born Ruth Barcan in New York in 1921. Her parents, Sam and Rose Barcan, were Russian Jewish immigrants who had settled in the Bronx. The household was socialist (though not communist); as in Lewis's parental home, Eugene Debs was a 'sainted' figure.[53] Young Ruth attended the Red Falcons ('Marx for tots').[54]

Barcan followed an unconventional path. She herself attributed this to the death of her father in 1930, which left her part of a 'family of four females' in which there was no 'strong male presence' to try to dissuade her from her ambitions.[55] She studied mathematics and philosophy at Washington Square College of New York University, graduating in

50 Ibid., p. 336.

51 To see the analogy, consider the functional similarity between the pairs of operators 'necessarily' and 'possibly', on the one hand, and 'always' and 'sometimes', on the other.

52 David Jakobsen, 'In What Sense is J. N. Findlay the Founding Father of Tense-Logic?', p. 180.

53 Ruth Barcan Marcus, 'A Philosopher's Calling', p. 18.

54 Ibid., p. 19.

55 Ibid.

1941. At the same time, she received private instruction in logic from J. C. C. McKinsey, through which she became interested in modal logic, and worked (unsuccessfully) to prove the completeness of Lewis's system S3. On the advice of her teachers McKinsey and Sidney Hook, she avoided Harvard, where the arch-enemy of modal logic, Quine, reigned, and went instead to Yale to do her graduate work, with Frederic Fitch.

Yale placed significant obstacles in the way of female students. Housing for women was subject to 'house rules, a curfew, and a housemother', so Barcan lived outside of university accommodation. Women were not allowed in undergraduate classrooms, and were not welcome in the section of the library housing contemporary fiction and criticism, which was 'furnished like a comfortable men's club'. Barcan protested against this, and was told that 'books women wanted would be passed out to be read elsewhere'. When she was elected president of the philosophy club, and received a letter from the chair of the department suggesting that she renounce the role, she simply ignored the letter.

In modal logic, too, Barcan similarly ignored those who would stand in her way. Supposed 'insurmountable difficulties of interpretation' did not deter her, and she pressed ahead with the task of introducing quantification into modal logic.[56] Her 1946 paper 'A Functional Calculus of First Order Based on Strict Implication' opened with the announcement: 'The following system is an extension of the Lewis calculus S2 to include quantification.'[57] This system was not simply a mélange of non-modal quantified logic with non-quantified modal logic, as already existed, but genuinely established a quantified modal logic. One of its axioms was the now famous 'Barcan Formula', which states that if there *can* be something that has a certain property, there *is* something that can have that property. Barcan's paper met with strenuous opposition from Quine. Quine first claimed to have technical objections, but these turned out to be technically unsound. Although there was a widespread perception that Quine had (or *must* have had) strong arguments against modal logic, his role was in reality, as she later put it, that of a 'gadfly'.[58] Every time Barcan published something, Quine would be ready with an attack, 'as if such efforts needed to be nipped in the bud'.[59]

56 Ibid., p. 25.

57 Ruth C. Barcan, 'A Functional Calculus of First Order Based on Strict Implication', p. 1.

58 Marcus quoted in Tuboly, 'Early Formation of Modal Logic', p. 297.

59 Marcus, 'A Philosopher's Calling', p. 29.

In 1942, Ruth Barcan became Ruth Barcan Marcus, on her marriage to the physicist Jules Alexander Marcus.[60] Remarkably, between 1948 and 1963, she had no affiliation with a university department, and did not apply for one, instead performing her domestic duties as wife and mother, producing logic in her spare time.[61] Only in 1963 did this change, when she became the founding chair of the new department of philosophy at the University of Illinois at Chicago. She subsequently held positions at Northwestern University and, finally, at Yale, where she campaigned ardently against proposals to grant Jacques Derrida – a frequent visitor to the comparative literature department – a foothold in the philosophy department.[62]

During her years of domestic production of logic, away from academic institutions, Marcus gave a crucial paper, 'Modalities and Intensional Languages', to a meeting of the Boston Colloquium in Philosophy of Science in 1962. This event is of historical importance, as it has since given rise to controversy about the ownership of key ideas in modal logic. Here, Marcus defended the view that proper names were mere 'tags', devoid of descriptive content, and referring directly to objects in the world. Views of this kind were, at the time, highly unorthodox; they only became widely accepted thanks to the subsequent work of Saul Kripke, who had attended Marcus's paper and contributed to the discussion that ensued. Kripke was then twenty-one years old.

In 1994 an obscure and irascible American philosopher, Quentin Smith, who was teaching at Western Michigan University in Kalamazoo, ignited a controversy about the relationship between Marcus's ideas and those of Kripke at the American Philosophical Association's landmark annual conference (its 'Eastern Division Meeting'). Smith claimed that Marcus 'originated many of the key ideas of the New Theory of Reference that have often been attributed to Saul Kripke and others'.[63] To say this was to accuse Kripke of plagiarism. The

60 According to Timothy Williamson, it was under pressure from Alonzo Church, the editor of *The Journal of Symbolic Logic*, that Ruth Barcan switched to publishing under her married name, Ruth Barcan Marcus. Timothy Williamson, 'Laudatio: Ruth Barcan Marcus (1921–2012)', p. 13.

61 Ibid.

62 This earned Marcus a footnote in Derrida's book *Limited Inc*, where she and John Searle are described as 'members of an academic Interpol' (p. 159). For more on Derrida and Searle, see Chapter 6, above.

63 Quentin Smith, 'Marcus, Kripke, and the Origin of the New Theory of Reference', p. 179.

controversy that ensued has served unhelpfully to shroud the real issue – whether Marcus's ideas have been given their due. Smith had severely overstated his case. His charge that Kripke *plagiarized* Marcus was easily rebutted, by showing either that Kripke had given proper credit to Marcus's ideas insofar as he took them over in his own work, or that his ideas were significantly distinct from Marcus's.[64] The controversy about plagiarism is, however, a distraction from the more important issue. Even if it can be allowed that Kripke did not plagiarize Marcus, it remains true that, as she herself pointed out, for a long time her work in intensional and modal logic was not properly recognized or acknowledged.[65] Kripke's work, by contrast, was received with adulation.

The Rise of Saul Kripke

Saul Kripke was a phenomenon, the archetype of the child prodigy. He was born in New York in 1940, the son of a rabbi and the grandson of a Polish-born bottle and barrel salesman. In the highly cultivated home environment that Rabbi Myer S. Kripke and his wife Dorothy provided for their three children, Saul had read the complete works of Shakespeare by the age of ten, and by eighteen had mastered modal logic so fully that he could publish a paper in *The Journal of Symbolic Logic* stating a completeness theorem for S5.[66]

Kripke's formal work in modal logic quickly led him to a set of views deeply at odds with cherished notions in analytic philosophy. They were enunciated with remarkable verve by the twenty-nine-year-old Kripke, who then held a position at the Rockefeller University, in three lectures under the title 'Naming and Necessity', given at Princeton University in January 1970. Two of Kripke's contemporaries on the faculty of the Princeton department, Gilbert Harman and Thomas Nagel, transcribed the talks, delivered *extempore* without any notes; the result, padded out

64 Two philosophers, Scott Soames and Stephen Neale, predictably went for the jugular in mounting rebuttals of Smith's claims along these lines. See Scott Soames, 'Revisionism about Reference: A Reply to Smith'; Stephen Neale, 'No Plagiarism Here'.

65 She wrote: 'There remain lengthy bibliographies and historical accounts of intensional and modal logic as well as interpretations of modalities where reference to my work is absent, but that is gradually being corrected.' Marcus, 'A Philosopher's Calling', p. 27.

66 Saul A. Kripke, 'A Completeness Theorem in Modal Logic'.

with footnotes supplied by Kripke, was published in 1972. When the lectures were reissued as a monograph in 1980, Kripke pointed out in the preface that the ideas in them dated as far back as 1963–64, when he was still in his early twenties – the immediate aftermath of Marcus's landmark Boston paper.[67]

The basic ideas of Kripke's lectures were simple but powerful. Russell had been wrong to understand names (such as 'Aristotle') as disguised definite descriptions (such as 'Plato's best student' or 'the teacher of Alexander the Great'). This is the 'descriptive theory of names'. Its falsity was easily brought out by considering modal claims. One of Kripke's more extreme examples to illustrate this was the claim that Hitler might never have gone into politics. Suppose 'Hitler' is to be analysed, as per Russell's descriptive theory, as, for example, 'the man who killed more Jews than anyone else'. Then the claim that Hitler might never have gone into politics amounts to the claim that the man who killed more Jews than anyone else might never have gone into politics. But this is simply not, Kripke insisted, what is meant. To claim that *Hitler* might never have gone into politics is not to claim that whoever it was who killed more Jews than anyone else (who would then have been someone else) might never have gone into politics; it is to claim that *this very man* might, instead of going into politics, have led a quite different life, perhaps churning out mediocre paintings in obscurity. A less controversial example is that of the prophet Jonah. Biblical scholars agree that none of the things that Jonah is famous for are things that *Jonah* actually did. He was not swallowed by a big fish; he did not even go to Nineveh to preach. If the 'descriptive' theory of names were correct, Jonah's sad failure to do any of the things he is reputed for would imply that there was not so much as any individual referred to by the name Jonah at all. But clearly, Kripke insisted, the name Jonah does pick out exactly one individual – *that very guy* of whom the scholars deny that he was swallowed by a big fish or went to Nineveh to preach, or did anything else we ostensibly know about at all.[68]

Kripke appealed to modal scenarios to make his case against the descriptive theory of names. The case for his own positive view about naming again appealed to modal notions. Names refer to what they refer to *in every possible world*. We already saw this in the examples of Hitler and Jonah. There is one individual – Hitler – referred to across

67 Saul Kripke, *Naming and Necessity*, p. 3.

68 Ibid., p. 67.

all the counterfactual claims we might make about things Hitler might or might not have done. Similarly for Jonah. In Kripke's terminology, these names are 'rigid designators'. A designator (which might be a name or a description) is rigid 'if in every possible world it designates the same object'; otherwise it is nonrigid, or accidental.[69]

What is remarkable about Kripke's approach is that he does not merely mount objections to some theses widely held by analytic philosophers; he calls a whole picture into question. As he says of the descriptive theory, 'the whole picture given by this theory of how reference is determined seems to be wrong from the fundamentals'.[70] A mistake that he diagnoses throughout the lectures is the assumption, deeply embedded in analytic philosophy, that objects can be picked out in a merely 'qualitative' manner. Although Kripke makes only brief and oblique comments about possible 'ideological' motivations or prejudices in the text, these comments might be elaborated by pointing out that the tendency to try to resort to picking out objects merely qualitatively, that is, by listing properties – paradigmatically by means of a description – belongs to a Humean mindset.[71] To the Humean, the world is an inert mosaic of 'matters of fact', which the mind must go to work on. Kripke fundamentally dislodges this picture. Not only can the mind simply refer to *that man, Aristotle,* without going via qualitative sorting; but it had better eschew the qualitative route. Attempting to go through any such route, it will never get to *Aristotle,* such that statements such as 'Aristotle might not have been Plato's best student' are so much as articulable.

Now that Kripke has been successfully absorbed into the analytic mainstream, it is difficult to recover the drama of his 1970 lectures, and the sense in which they, as Richard Rorty put it, 'set analytic philosophy on its ear'.[72] In addition to the eccentricity, by the standards of previous analytic philosophy, of the claims themselves, there is the question of Kripke's method. Kripke refused to advance any theory spelled out in terms of necessary and sufficient conditions, on the grounds that philosophical theories of this type all eventually turn out

69 Ibid., p. 48.

70 Ibid., p. 93.

71 Ibid., pp. 99, 155*n*77. This Humean mindset is, incidentally, inherited by Kant, who plays up more starkly than Hume does the contrast between a 'receptivity' associated with the merely sensorily given and the 'spontaneity' of the autonomous agent, doing the active work of the mind.

72 Richard Rorty, 'Kripke Versus Kant'.

to be wrong.[73] This refusal he associated with his adherence to Bishop Butler's dictum, 'Everything is what it is and not another thing', which can be given, Kripke says, 'the nontrivial sense that philosophical analyses of some concept like reference, in completely different terms which make no mention of reference, are very apt to fail'.[74]

Kripke's method, such as it was, was avowedly nothing other than appeal to intuitions. These intuitions, however, are distinct from those that analytic philosophers usually ascribe to what they think of as the 'ordinary person'. This comes out particularly clearly in Kripke's arguments against physicalism (the view that mental entities are identical to physical entities).[75] If physicalists *really* think that mental entities are identical to physical entities, he argued, they will need to show they can rebut the premise of a Cartesian argument. Descartes argues as follows:

The mind could exist without the body. (Cartesian premise)
so The mind is distinct from the body. (Cartesian conclusion)

Physicalists, in holding that the mind and body are identical, assert the negation of the Cartesian conclusion. If Descartes's reasoning is valid, as it seems to be, they must then also hold the negation of the Cartesian premise. But, Kripke insists, the Cartesian premise is entirely intuitive: it is very easy to think of pains without thinking of them being embodied in any way, and one could easily think of a body without a mind (a corpse).

Analytic philosophers have generally taken it for granted that the 'ordinary person' (so-called) adopts something like the liberal–empiricist worldview. Kripke seemed to find a quite different view intuitive. For him, something close to Cartesian dualism was common sense. Kripke's views might well, in fact, be closer to the views people hold before being subjected to the 'philosophical education' about which he expresses considerable suspicion.[76] More recent contributions to

73 Kripke, *Naming and Necessity*, pp. 64, 93.

74 Ibid., p. 94.

75 There are various ways of stating the view, and Kripke considers a few of them in turn. According to the one he focuses on ('type–type identity'), pain is identical to the stimulation of C-fibres (Kripke, *Naming and Necessity*, p. 148).

76 See Kripke, *Naming and Necessity*, p. 81: 'It is a tribute to the education of philosophers that they have held this thesis for such a long time.' And p. 84: 'But it may seem to many of you that this is a very odd example, or that such a situation occurs rarely. This also is a tribute to the education of philosophers.'

'experimental philosophy' have lent support to the idea that ordinary people are much more likely to be dualists (or, in other words – by the lights of analytic philosophers – philosophically 'sophisticated') than has long been supposed.[77]

Kripke never worked out a detailed positive theory of how naming by rigid designation works. What he did say, however, brings out the social character of naming in a way that once again goes against the paradigmatic ideology of analytic philosophy. It is not a matter of the autonomous individual doing the work, accomplishable in solitude, of projecting descriptions into an inertly present reality, with anything social to be understood as the result of interactions between in principle solitary subjects. Instead, the necessity of communal work is written in from the start. The 'fixing' of a reference (that the name shall henceforth pick out such-and-such an object) occurs in an initial act, akin to baptism. It is then passed 'from link to link as if by a chain'. The obvious example to invoke is the naming of a baby. The parents typically bestow a name – say, 'Saul' – on the baby, then 'talk about him to their friends', and gradually the reference of the name to that human being radiates through the community.[78]

What is remarkable about Kripke's legacy is that, far from being repelled by analytic philosophy, his ideas have been successfully absorbed into it. This is despite his insistence on relying on a mixture of Aristotelian and Cartesian intuitions that have been anathema to analytic philosophers of all stripes. It would seem as if something more powerful than intellectual probity were at work.

David Lewis

David Kellogg Lewis was an almost exact contemporary of Kripke. He, too, was a child prodigy. The modal notion of possible worlds would be central to his work, as to Kripke's. It was Lewis, however, who more effectively than Kripke paved the way for modality to be accepted and, in the wake of this acceptance, for metaphysics to be revived. Lewis did this not by overturning the extensionalist paradigm, but by ingeniously squeezing modal logic back into it. Lewis's unique way of doing so involved the acceptance of a view, modal realism, that no one else was

77 For more on 'experimental philosophy', see Chapter 9, below.

78 Kripke, *Naming and Necessity*, p. 91.

prepared to accept. Accordingly, it was not in his own way of accommodating the modal that his influence lay, but in the smooth elegance with which he demonstrated it was possible to operate. Philosophy could be highly technical and, more importantly, weigh up the relative merits of theories in a manner uncannily like that so successful in the natural sciences.

Lewis was, like Quine, a child of Ohio, born in Oberlin in 1941, the son of John D. Lewis, a professor of government at Oberlin College. J. D. Lewis was a moderate Democrat and a liberal who admired Thomas Jefferson and John Stuart Mill, was baffled by Arendt, and strongly disliked Marcuse.[79] The young David Lewis during his high school years regularly went to undergraduate chemistry classes at Oberlin, and at fifteen started a degree in chemistry at Swarthmore College. As part of his studies, he spent a year abroad in Oxford, where he developed an enthusiasm for philosophy, receiving tutorials from Iris Murdoch and attending lectures by Ryle, Strawson, Austin and Grice.[80] Remarkably, although Lewis's interest in philosophy was awakened in Oxford at the time when ordinary language philosophy was at its height, exposure to its leading figures seemed to leave no mark on him. Both in Oxford and on his return to Swarthmore, where he now turned from chemistry to philosophy, he pursued philosophy in his own way.

Like Kripke's, Lewis's principal ideas and approach to philosophy were formed early, while he was still in his twenties. He obtained his PhD from Harvard in 1967, with Quine as his supervisor. At this time, he was still opposed to modal talk about possible worlds, unless appeal to them was very thoroughly circumscribed. He wrote to Quine on 1 October 1968: 'up to about a year ago, I took for granted that possible worlds were *entia non grata* unless reduced to state descriptions, maximal consistent sets of sentences, or the like'.[81] He now saw things differently, however, and had made up his mind about how to proceed so that talk of possible worlds could be reconciled with the extensionalism to which he, like Quine, was devoted. About this he was

79 Email from Harlan Wilson, J. D. Lewis's successor at Oberlin College, 29 February 2024.

80 Stephanie R. Lewis, 'Intellectual Biography of David Lewis (1941–2001): Early Influences', p. 8.

81 Lewis to Quine, 1 October 1968, quoted in Frederique Janssen-Lauret, 'The Quinean Roots of Lewis's Humeanism', p. 258. 'State description' is a term of art employed by Carnap; each state description is a complete non-modal specification of possible states of a world.

remarkably candid in his paper from that same year, 'Counterpart Theory and Quantified Modal Logic':

> We can conduct formalized discourse about most topics perfectly well by means of our all-purpose extensional logic, provided with predicates and a domain of quantification suited to the subject matter at hand. That is what we do when our topic is numbers, or sets, or wholes and parts, or strings of symbols. That is not what we do when our topic is modality: what might be and what must be, essence and accident. Then we introduce modal operators to create a special-purpose, nonextensional logic. Why this departure from our custom? Is it a historical accident, or was it forced on us somehow by the very nature of the topic of modality?
>
> It was not forced on us. We have an alternative. Instead of formalizing our modal discourse by means of modal operators, we could follow our usual practice. We could stick to our standard logic (quantification theory with identity and without ineliminable singular terms) and provide it with predicates and a domain of quantification suited to the topic of modality. The new predicates required, together with postulates on them, constitute the system I call *Counterpart Theory*.[82]

The plan, then, was this. Although it *seemed* like modality forced the abandonment of 'our usual practice' – that is, adherence to an extensionalist logic that expelled modal notions – there was, after all and in spite of appearances, a way of 'sticking with' the old procedure. Instead of conceiving of possible worlds, as Kripke and others had done, as alternative scenarios (*ways* the world might have been), they could be treated as *other worlds*. The alternative scenario in which I had never set my mind to writing this book becomes instead another world in which my writing the book *does not happen*. Note that there is nothing modal in 'does not happen': in the other world, things simply do or do not happen, just as in this one. A peculiarity of Lewis's view is that it is not *I* in the other world who does not do this, but a 'counterpart' of me (hence 'counterpart theory'). The counterpart is very like me, but is not me.

The view (which Lewis called 'modal realism', because of its claim that the other worlds, beside the actual world, *exist* as concrete entities)

82 David Lewis, 'Counterpart Theory and Quantified Modal Logic', in *Philosophical Papers*, vol. 1, p. 26.

is extremely strange. It requires *all* logically possible worlds to exist.[83] (This is a far greater number of worlds than the number of worlds – of a quite different kind – required by the 'many worlds interpretation' of quantum mechanics.[84]) The view is not that all the worlds exist in one spacetime. Each is a totality, sealed off from the others; there is no 'travel' between them, and no 'looking' at one from another by means of 'telescopes'. (Again, this way in which worlds are hermetically sealed from each other is a contrast with 'many worlds' in physics.) In an important sense, the phrase 'possible worlds' is a misnomer for Lewis's worlds: they *exist* – *simpliciter*, rather than possibly. The contrast between the *actual world* and other, possible but not actual worlds, is, for Lewis, simply the contrast between the world we happen to be in, and all the others. This notion is completely relative: to those in *other* worlds, *theirs* is the actual world, ours merely possible.

Analytic philosophers have almost universally rejected modal realism as too bizarre. But Lewis himself regarded it as a theory answering to the highest virtues of parsimony. Lewis's proliferation of worlds was no slum, like Wyman's, requiring clearance. After all, it required the positing of only one *kind* of thing: worlds. And it solved a great many problems. In fact, it was the perfect way to maintain an extensionalist picture. According to this picture, there is no necessity in the world. The world, instead, is 'a vast mosaic of local matters of particular fact, just one little thing and then another'. 'All else', Lewis added, 'supervenes on that.' That is to say, whatever other distinctions there are to be made about reality, they track nothing but distinctions in 'the arrangement of qualities' – in other words, in how the mosaic is composed.[85]

Lewis's genius was to absorb the advances in modal logic and defuse the threat they posed to analytic philosophy by somehow accommodating them within the very framework that they threatened. In that sense,

83 Lewis's theory is often compared to that of Leibniz. There is a very crucial difference. Leibniz envisages God determining which out of an infinity of logically possible worlds to create; God only creates one. There is no precedent in the history of philosophy for Lewis's notion that all possible worlds exist. Note also that Lewis's understanding of what a world is places a restriction on the totality of logically possible worlds: worlds are composites of physical items. There are no non-physical worlds. By contrast, Leibniz's God presumably could contemplate creating a world composed entirely of disembodied angels thinking their thoughts, or the like.

84 Although Lewis's modal realism should not be confused with 'many worlds' in physics, there are nonetheless analogies. See, for example, Brian Skyrms, 'Possible Worlds, Physics and Metaphysics'.

85 Lewis, 'Introduction' to *Philosophical Papers*, vol. 2, pp. ix–x.

his own work was the product of analytic ideology writ large. Somehow, the totality of possible worlds could now figure as an inert Humean mosaic for the liberal, autonomous subject to face. Lewis's strategy was, however, unique. It is Lewis's style in philosophy that has been highly influential in the profession. Not only was Lewis smooth, precise and technical; more importantly still, all philosophical discussion was a matter of give and take, cost and benefit. This allowed a fantasy of consummate ease to take hold. No objection was ruled out of court; everything was dealt with patiently. Proper procedures were followed, and confidence could be high that the appropriate verdict would be reached. In Lewis's own writing, the sense of sovereign command went together with a gesture of absolute inclusiveness. The opening words of *On the Plurality of Worlds* signal this: 'The world we live in is a very inclusive thing.'[86] There was nothing not dreamt of in Lewis's philosophy. The inclusiveness is, of course, an illusion. Lewis, for one thing, made no bones about being in thrall to a vulgar materialism (renamed 'physicalism').

By the time Lewis's life was tragically cut short by kidney failure resulting from diabetes in 2001, his influence within analytic philosophy was colossal. In 2013, Kieran Healy, a professor of sociology at Duke University, reported that, in the two preceding decades, discussion in four 'top' journals, *The Philosophical Review*, *The Journal of Philosophy*, *Mind*, and *Noûs*, 'was dominated by two philosophers: Saul Kripke and David Lewis'.[87] Of the two, Lewis was far ahead: Lewis's works were cited 934 times, Kripke's 242 times.[88] When the Italian scholars of analytic philosophy Valerio Buonomo and Eugenio Petrovich examined articles published between 1985 and 2014 in five journals (Healy's four plus *Philosophy and Phenomenological Research*) Lewis was found to have been cited 2,119 times, more than twice as frequently as the second author on the list, W. V. Quine (921 times).[89] (Here Kripke appears in tenth place.) Lewis's hold on the profession was supreme.

---

86 David Lewis, *On the Plurality of Worlds*, p. 1.

87 Kieran Healy, 'Lewis and the Women', 19 June 2013, at kieranhealy.org.

88 Ibid. I have added up the numbers in the tables showing citations of Lewis and Kripke per work.

89 Valerio Buonomo and Eugenio Petrovich, 'Reconstructing Late Analytic Philosophy: A Quantitative Approach', p. 164.

Beyond Lewis

In the period since 1970, David Lewis has been far and away the most influential figure in analytic philosophy. In metaphysics, while a story is routinely told according to which Quine made ontology respectable again, with both Kripke and Lewis building on Quine's achievement, it is clear that it is Lewis whose influence has been dominant. Quine was far more circumspect about ontology than the standard self-understanding of contemporary analytic metaphysics, and its accompanying origin story, suggests. And hardly anyone is sympathetic to Kripke's approach of building metaphysics on Cartesian and Aristotelian intuitions. It was Lewis's demonstration that a basically Humean spirit could be preserved, all while engaging in metaphysics, that did the crucial work of reconversion to metaphysics. What has sprung forth is the growth of a kind of metaphysics deeply implicated in the essentialism Quine so deeply feared, and which Lewis still combated in his name. Perhaps due to the extreme professionalization and specialization of the discipline, this does not seem to disturb anyone greatly: the metaphysicians are just left to get on with their metaphysics.

For a time, anti-metaphysical wariness still induced analytic philosophers to frame their lurch towards their old foe metaphysics by appeal to the notion of 'supervenience', which had been popularized by Lewis, for whom everything supervened on the 'Humean mosaic' of the point-like physical bits that made up the fundamental totality of reality. Supervenience was highly prized, as ostensibly supplying the ultimate 'ontological free lunch'. The idea was simple – even if the term sounds fancy. Something supervened on something else wherever, when the first thing had some property F, there was a property G such that, if the second thing had G, it also had F.[90] A principal use of supervenience was to try to shore up physicalism. The idea was, as Alyssa Ney puts it in her widely used textbook on metaphysics, 'to express the claim that although mental and other properties are not strictly identical with physical properties, they are, as it is frequently put, *nothing over and above* physical properties'.[91] Supervenience apparently made it possible

---

90 For a classic statement, see Jaegwon Kim, 'Concepts of Supervenience'. Kim's distinction between weak, strong and global supervenience does not matter for present purposes.

91 Alyssa Ney, *Metaphysics: An Introduction*, p. 194.

to talk about mental properties without being committed to a substantive metaphysical thesis as to their existence. But it was all a mirage, as free lunches tend to be. It turned out, as anyone might have noticed before even sitting down to lunch, that physicalism demanded a demonstration that the mental *depended* on the physical, rather than that it merely coincided with it.

Analytic metaphysics, although inspired by Lewis, now looks very different from anything he himself advocated. The dead end of 'supervenience' has been supplanted by the question of 'what grounds what'. The mental is to be 'grounded' in the physical, and truths in 'truthmakers'. No one knows what truthmakers are, except that they are what truths depend on. The trouble with grounding is that, even if it seems to be 'needed', as Jonathan Schaffer claims, it is 'primitive' and 'unanalyzable' – fancy analytic philosophy talk for: assumed dogmatically, without argument.[92]

Analytic metaphysicians now routinely engage in what they call 'armchair', 'a priori', or even 'speculative' metaphysics. A classic of this approach is the 2001 monograph *Four-Dimensionalism*, by Schaffer's colleague at Rutgers, Theodore Sider, which argues for 'an ontology of the material world according to which objects have temporal as well as spatial parts', and which Sider characterizes as 'a work in speculative ontology'.[93] Sider says his metaphysics is not 'descriptive', because four-dimensionalism does not fit 'our ordinary conceptual scheme'. But neither is it 'prescriptive': prescription cannot be done from the armchair, and should be left to scientists. Instead, Sider is, he says, 'after the truth about what there is, what the world is really like', and he urges that 'the quickest scan through this book will make it clear that the reasons I provide for my conclusions are largely a priori'. His approach accords with that of the descriptive metaphysician in 'taking ordinary belief about metaphysical matters seriously', but that of the prescriptive metaphysician 'in aspiring to more than autobiography'. Sider thinks this approach is 'common to many of the practitioners of contemporary analytic metaphysics', but, unfortunately, he shares with them 'the lack of a good answer to a very hard follow-up question:

92 'Grounding should . . . be taken as *primitive*, as per the neo-Aristotelian approach . . . Grounding is an unanalyzable but needed notion – it is *the primitive structuring conception of metaphysics*.' Jonathan Schaffer, 'On What Grounds What', p. 364.

93 Theodore Sider, *Four-Dimensionalism: An Ontology of Persistence and Time*, pp. xiii, xiv.

why think that a priori reasoning about synthetic matters of fact is justified?'[94]

Effectively, Sider *has* no methodology. Although he professes to have 'no good epistemology of metaphysics to offer', that does not make his approach worthless, he thinks, because no epistemology can be established for any enquiry before embarking on it. And so we have to make do with what Sider calls 'a familiar give and take' between 'ordinary' beliefs and stuff from science. Sider assures us that he will assume that 'modern logic's quantificational apparatus mirrors the structure of reality'. As he adds: 'I assume an ontology of *things*'. He also assumes 'that there is a single, objective, correct account of what things there are'. A lot of these assumptions fly in the face of science, but Sider is presumably unperturbed by this since, as he says, 'only ordinary beliefs tie down the inquiry'.[95]

The analytic metaphysicians of today like to say that they 'carve nature at the joints'.[96] They have no method for achieving this, other than reporting the findings of science, unless and until these are to be overruled by common sense or 'ordinary' beliefs, as the particular philosopher sees fit. This methodological decrepitude has not gone unnoticed, and the armchair metaphysics of the likes of Schaffer and Sider has attracted criticism from some quarters within analytic philosophy. James Ladyman and Don Ross have written that analytic metaphysics 'fails to qualify as part of the enlightened pursuit of objective truth, and should be discontinued'.[97] James Maclaurin and Heather Dyke ask an apt question: 'What is analytic metaphysics *for*?' Their own response is negative: it doesn't seem to be (good) *for* anything.[98]

On the whole, analytic metaphysicians fall back into a peculiar combination of appeal to common sense and deference to science. One wonders what the institutional and social mechanisms are that serve to maintain the remarkable lack of methodological self-scrutiny that allows this to continue. There are some exceptions to the general rule – philosophers who are forthright and self-questioning about their

---

94 Ibid., p. xv.

95 Ibid., pp. xv–xvi.

96 The phrase derives from Plato. In *Phaedrus*, Socrates speaks of an ability to 'cut up each kind according to its species along its natural joints, and to try not to splinter any part, as a bad butcher might do' (265e).

97 James Ladyman, Don Ross, David Spurrett and John Collier, *Every Thing Must Go: Metaphysics Naturalized*, p. vii.

98 James Maclaurin and Heather Dyke, 'What Is Analytic Metaphysics For?'

methodology. Timothy Williamson, Wykeham Professor of Logic at Oxford University since 2000, for one, is prepared to defend in explicit terms his controversial conception of philosophy as, like the natural sciences, an enquiry engaged in inference to the best explanation (or 'abduction').[99] There are notorious problems that go with the notions of 'fitting the evidence' and 'approximation to the truth' involved in this abductive picture. But few others will engage in anything like the principled defence of their approach that one would expect of a philosopher. There is just too much metaphysical business to be got on with.

99 Williamson, *The Philosophy of Philosophy.*

9

Intuitions and Moral Mathematics

The ancestor movements of analytic philosophy, such as the various forms of Cambridge analysis or the logical positivism of the Vienna Circle, were highly methodologically self-conscious. This was not true of analytic philosophy as it constituted itself after 1945. The notion of methodological unity it retrospectively built for itself in terms of the 'linguistic turn' was a myth (see Chapter 7). As metaphysics reasserted itself, analytic philosophy went into methodological free-fall (Chapter 8). It now fell back on a surprising methodology for a supposedly rigorous form of philosophy: that of reliance on intuitions. If anything is today the most prominent characteristic of how analytic philosophers conduct themselves, it is the frequency with which they invoke intuitions as a guide to what to think. Some even think that reliance on intuitions provides analytic philosophy with a distinctive methodology that secures its status as a respectable field of enquiry.[1] Reliance on intuitions is heavy, widespread and astonishingly casual. This would seem to conflict with analytic philosophy's fetishization of 'rigour'.

As we already saw in the previous chapter, the metaphysics that grew up in the wake of Kripke and Lewis was content to rely on intuitions, but such reliance on intuitions is not confined to analytic metaphysics. Analytic philosophers have been overt about this. Often, the reliance on

1 See Gary Gutting, '"Rethinking Intuition": A Historical and Metaphilosophical Introduction', p. 7: 'In contemporary analytic discussion . . . "intuition" has become the name for whatever it is that might provide philosophy with a distinctive method and hence preserve it as a separate (in principle) intellectual domain.'

intuitions follows a highly specific pattern. 'Cases' are constructed (usually in the form of thought experiments involving concocted and more or less plausible counterfactual scenarios, sometimes in the form of scenarios thought to be already familiar). These cases are then used to elicit intuitions ('intuition pumping'). The intuitions are considered to be experimental results, and are often described as 'data'. Those data may then be fed into further philosophical reflection. One prominent use of 'intuition pumping' is in order to elicit the 'application' of some term, such as 'knows'. The audience is confronted with a case, and asked whether it is a case in which 'S knows that *p*'.[2] Another use is in order to discern what 'our' moral intuitions are, where these can embody mini-theories. For example, a scenario in which the audience is asked to decide whether or not to turn a runaway train whose brakes have failed onto a side track to limit the resulting human death toll might be used in order to find out whether 'we' are utilitarians.

The use of fanciful thought experiments might be questioned on the grounds that they are unrealistic, or tell us nothing about the real world. That need not be so – thought experiments have been productively used in philosophy, physics and elsewhere in order to stretch the intellectual imagination. Some of Einstein's most significant breakthroughs were closely connected to his use of thought experiments. What is concerning about analytic philosophers' 'intuition pumping' is not the use of such scenarios per se, but the methodological assumptions – generally unarticulated – that are in play. These assumptions have the effect that here thought experiments, instead of expanding the philosophical imagination, constrict it. The scenarios are not only unrealistic, although they are that; as imaginative exercises, they encourage and reinforce the impoverishment of thought.

Intuition pumping is rife throughout analytic philosophy – from metaphysics to ethics. When 'normative' ethics freed itself from the preoccupation with 'metaethics', it quickly latched on to producing scenarios designed to elicit 'our intuitions'. The credence given to intuitions in ethics has been criticized by some, such as the Australian philosopher Peter Singer.[3] Notably, these critics tend to find themselves – in their detachment from psychology, culture and history – thrown back

2 'S' here stands in for some subject of knowledge, '*p*' for some proposition.

3 Compare, for a systematic working out of the critique of the use of intuitions in moral philosophy and its replacement by an uncompromising utilitarianism, Peter K. Unger, *Living High and Letting Die: Our Illusion of Innocence.*

into an extremely crude eighteenth-century style of reasoning: utilitarianism. The lowest common denominator here is a lack of philosophical imagination.

When analytic philosophers use thought experiments as intuition pumps, they almost always rely on an amorphous 'we'. The reader – imagined, invariably, as another analytic philosopher – is co-opted for inclusion into this undefined 'we', freed of subjectivity. Where membership of the 'we' is made explicit, it is the class of 'competent speakers of English' (or possibly, at the fringes, some other language). There is good reason to wonder about what this assumes.[4] On what basis do analytic philosophers speak on behalf of the population of those who can speak a language? To put the question another way: what sort of social group is it that can unreflectively take itself to be speaking for language users at large, while failing to inspect their own title to do so?

Reliance on the notion that the analytic philosopher can act as a stand-in for all competent speakers of a language has been counteracted by the 'experimental philosophy' that arose in the 2000s. Instead of pontificating on the basis of their own intuitions, experimental philosophers conduct philosophy by questionnaire, to see what competent language users *actually* say. This is a modification of the method of cases: cases are now presented to unsuspecting members of the public, rather than to other analytic philosophers. Experimental philosophy has been salutary in throwing into doubt some of analytic philosophers' cherished, and often condescending, notions about what 'ordinary' people believe. It has also taken on the (rather obvious) insight that the answers people give depend on context (such as what order questions are asked in, what affect they have been loaded with, and so on). It has, however, retained the atomistic–referential conception of language of the 'armchair philosophy' it seeks to correct. Furthermore, it is assumed that the audience simply 'grasps' the scenario – *even if* it is allowed that their responses might be culturally conditioned. Here, experimental philosophy collides with the psychology that it wishes, to some degree, to elucidate. 'Grasping' the scenario is a matter of 'correctly' applying what turns out to be, for one thing, a highly gendered conception of what such scenarios can be, and how they might function.

Thought experiments are, potentially, great imaginative resources. Their exploration can, not least, bring to light significant philosophical

4 Similar concerns were raised about ordinary language philosophy in Chapter 4, above.

questions about just what we might learn from them. Plato, for instance, considered how a sophist might think to deploy the thought experiment of the 'ring of Gyges', but then sought to show that the sophist's notion of how it might work rested on being mistaken about something else – here, about what justice is. In physics, thought experiments have often been used in order to bring out the paradoxes in some theory, so as to drive forward theory revision. Perhaps some thought experiments can be used to clarify what our intuitions are. But what then? Should we not have to consider what the status of such intuitions is, and what they are good for?

Notably, analytic philosophers have not given much attention to the methodological issues *underlying* the use of the method of cases as an instrument of 'intuition pumping'. The trend instead, in the growing literature on 'metaphilosophy', has been towards denialism. The Oxford philosopher Timothy Williamson, together with Herman Cappelen, a Norwegian philosopher working in Hong Kong, and others, have expended considerable energy on attempting to demonstrate that, even though analytic philosophers constantly *claim* they are relying on intuitions (what Cappelen calls 'Centrality'), they are wrong to do so. According to Cappelen, analytic philosophers' tendency to say that they rely on intuitions is nothing more than that; it is, he says, a mere 'verbal tic'.[5] The denialists go to great lengths to cast doubt on the idea that it is really *intuitions* that are in play. The general strategy is adopted of specifying many different senses of 'intuition', and then rhetorically presenting believers in 'Centrality' with the question: *Which* sense of intuition do you mean? Or we are told that what are called 'intuitions' are really 'common-sense beliefs' or 'judgements'. None of this matters. Whether it is 'intuitions' or 'common-sense beliefs' on which those calling themselves philosophers rest their arguments, they show themselves to be giving in to arbitrariness, and therefore dogmatism. This is the antithesis of philosophy.

Reliance on intuitions is so endemic in contemporary analytic philosophy that, for the most part, it is not remarked on, but simply assumed as part of ordinary procedure (or, in the kind of imagery analytic philosophers are apt to use, part of the 'toolkit'). This is highly

---

5 Herman Cappelen, *Philosophy Without Intuitions*, p. 22. Edouard Machery criticizes reliance on the 'method of cases', but, like Williamson and Cappelen, insists that philosophers' self-understanding as relying on intuitions is mistaken. The method of cases is to be understood in terms of reliance on judgements, not intuitions. Edouard Machery, *Philosophy Within Its Proper Bounds*.

significant, since such reliance on intuitions robs philosophy of its critical power. The results are unsurprising: a 'philosophy' whose wheels spin idly in the service of well-entrenched patterns of thought. Here analytic philosophy wears its social function on its sleeve. Opting for 'common sense' as its ultimate basis, its practitioners speak with one voice in order to feed their own ideology back to themselves. The alternative is a deference to natural science. In common between these alternatives is a failure to feel the fundamental human impulse to expand the imagination.

The Rise of Intuitions

While reliance on intuitions has a considerable history in analytic philosophy, in recent decades it has 'exploded', to borrow the term used by James Andow, an 'experimental philosopher' at the University of Manchester. Andow has found that, in the decade 1900–09, around 22 per cent of philosophy articles indexed on the digital journal archive JSTOR 'indulg[ed] in intuition talk', whereas in the decade 2000–09 around 54 per cent did so.[6] Intuition talk grew in philosophy as a whole (not just analytic philosophy), and across other disciplines too, but the steepest growth was in analytic philosophy, as a study of three leading analytic journals shows. Between the 1950s and the 2000s, the percentage of articles engaging in 'intuition talk' in *The Philosophical Review* rose from 31.2 per cent to 86 per cent; in the same period, those in *Mind* rose from 25.9 per cent to 67.2 per cent; in *Noûs*, they rose – from the first decade of its existence, 1967–1976, to the 2000s – from 46.7 per cent to 83.9 per cent.[7]

Although Andow's data merely indicate the increased use of a word, and he notes that use of the word 'intuition' has grown elsewhere too, analytic philosophers have also increasingly made explicit statements that they rely on intuitions in their philosophical work. According to Alvin Goldman, a leading epistemologist whose work has long been standard reading for undergraduates,

> One thing that distinguishes philosophical methodology from the methodology of the sciences is its extensive and avowed reliance on intuition. Especially when philosophers are engaged in philosophical

6 James Andow, 'How "Intuition" Exploded', p. 190.

7 Ibid., p. 203.

> 'analysis', they often get preoccupied with intuitions. To decide what is knowledge, reference, identity, or causation (or what is the concept of knowledge, reference, identity, or causation), philosophers routinely consider actual and hypothetical examples and ask whether these examples provide instances of the target category or concept. People's mental responses to these examples are often called 'intuitions', and these intuitions are treated as evidence for the correct answer. At a minimum, they are evidence for the examples' being instances or non-instances of knowledge, reference, causation, etc. Thus, intuitions play a particularly critical role in a certain sector of philosophical activity.
>
> The evidential weight accorded to intuition is often very high, in both philosophical practice and philosophical reflection. Many philosophical discoveries, or putative discoveries, are predicated on the occurrence of certain widespread intuitions.[8]

The practice is widespread: 'Most philosophers do it openly and unapologetically, and the rest arguably do it too, although some of them would deny it. What they all do is appeal to intuitions in constructing, shaping, and refining their philosophical views.'[9] It is even, we are told, the standard procedure, definitive of what analytic philosophy *is*: 'It can seem that analytic philosophy without intuitions just wouldn't be *analytic* philosophy.'[10]

There are various ways analytic philosophers rely on intuitions, as these quotations begin to indicate. They speak of leaving as many of 'our' intuitions untouched as possible, or making their claims consistent with pre-existing intuitions.[11] They base arguments on intuitions. And they use thought experiments as 'intuition pumps' to yield intuitions as 'data'.

Intuitions tend to be pumped by means of the 'method of cases'. A scenario is sketched, often in the form of a thought experiment. A question

8 Alvin I. Goldman, 'Philosophical Intuitions', p. 1.

9 Hilary Kornblith, quoted in Cappelen, *Philosophy without Intuitions*, p. 2.

10 Justin Weinberg, quoted in ibid., p. 3.

11 David Lewis was particularly forthright about this: 'One comes to philosophy already endowed with a stock of opinions. It is not the business of philosophy either to undermine or to justify these preexisting opinions, to any great extent, but only to try to discover ways of expanding them into an orderly system.' David Lewis, *Counterfactuals*, p. 88. Again, according to Lewis, a view is preferable if it 'demands less frequent corrections of what we want to say'. David Lewis, *Papers in Metaphysics and Epistemology*, p. 419.

is then asked about the scenario in order to elicit the wanted intuitions. Often, the question is whether the case presented is one in which a certain term 'applies'. For example, a scenario is outlined that specifies that a subject, *S*, has some belief (the belief that some proposition, *p*, holds), and how *S* has come by the belief that *p*. The question is now put: 'Does S know that *p*?' Whether the imagined audience takes the term to apply or not is then taken as 'evidence', intuitions to the effect that *S* does or does not know that *p* being taken as 'data' elicited by the thought experiment. These data can then be fed into further philosophical reflection.

Sometimes, the idea is to settle the case by appeal to intuitions. Sometimes it is to use the case in order to elicit intuitions. In the former case, intuitions are taken as analogous to data, fed into the experiment as 'inputs'; in the latter, they are data in the sense of 'outputs', or observations to be read off the experiment. Sometimes the intuitions elicited as outputs are thought to be reflective of a so-called folk theory that the person whose intuitions have been elicited implicitly holds.[12] As the Australian philosopher Frank Jackson has written, 'my intuitions about possible cases reveal my theory of free action – they could hardly be supposed to reveal someone else's! Likewise, your intuitions reveal your theory.'[13] Intuitions seem to do many jobs. Some special credence is given to their power. But if they are merely being fed in, or being observed as outputs, how can this be?

Intuitions can, of course, conflict. It then seems eminently sensible to try to bring them 'into equilibrium', as David Lewis suggests. But what constitutes an equilibrium is itself dependent on common sense. 'If our official theories disagree with what we cannot help thinking outside the philosophy room', according to Lewis, 'then no real equilibrium has been reached.'[14] There is no escaping the vortex of intuition.

It is not difficult to see that reliance on intuitions is a symptom of philosophical degeneracy. It is a form of dogmatism, and thus the antithesis of philosophy. Philosophy advances grounds for claims. To appeal to intuitions is to admit that explanation has run out, and that we are merely relying on something for which no better support can be

12 Use of the phrase 'folk theory' used to be widespread in analytic philosophy, and parallel currents in psychology, but has understandably fallen out of fashion.

13 Frank Jackson, *From Metaphysics to Ethics: A Defence of Conceptual Analysis*, pp. 31–2.

14 David Lewis, *Philosophical Papers*, vol. 1, p. x.

given than that it is intuitive, or what I, or you, or some group, think anyway – and this is no support at all if philosophy is what is supposed to be happening. As Michael Della Rocca – a professor of philosophy at Yale University and a rare outspoken critic of the reliance on intuitions from within analytic philosophy – declares: 'the starting points in common sense are arbitrary'.[15] As he rightly points out, such arbitrariness is bound to underwrite an intellectual conservatism. David Lewis does indeed, with admirable intellectual honesty, describe his approach as 'theoretical conservatism'.[16]

Thought Experiments

Intuition pumping by means of the method of cases is a highly specific instance of the use of thought experiments. A way to bring out its specificity is to contrast it with other – more imaginative, expansive, productive – things that a thought experiment might be.

The term 'thought experiment' (*Gedankenexperiment*) was given currency by the physicist-philosopher Ernst Mach. Mach was not thinking of intuition pumps. Although he had in mind two types of user of thought experiment – on the one hand, 'the dreamer, the builder of castles in the air, the poet of social or technological utopias'; on the other, 'the respectable merchant' or 'the devoted inventor or researcher' – it is basic to Mach's conception that the 'method of the thought experiment is just like that of a physical experiment, namely, the method of variation'.[17] As with the thought experiments carried out by Galileo and Einstein, 'by varying the circumstances (continuously, if possible) the range of validity of an idea (expectation) related to these circumstances is increased'.[18] The background of physics, which means that a set of theoretical assumptions can be held fixed, means that thought experiments can have a highly productive function.[19]

Beyond the realm of physics, there have long been thought experiments in philosophy, such as Plato's 'ring of Gyges', Descartes's 'evil

15 Michael Della Rocca, *The Parmenidean Ascent*, p. 269.

16 David Lewis, *On the Plurality of Worlds*, p. 134.

17 Ernst Mach, 'On Thought Experiments', p. 451.

18 Ibid., p. 453.

19 See the thought experiments concerning the movement of bodies in Galileo Galilei, *Dialogue Concerning the Two World Systems*, 'The First Day', and in Albert Einstein, *Relativity: The Special and the General Theory*, Chapters 9–11.

demon' and Locke's 'prince and the cobbler'. It is significant that none of these are intuition pumps.

The American-born and Oxford-educated philosopher Cora Diamond has drawn attention to the narrative structure of Plato's use of the thought experiment of the ring of Gyges, which has the magical power of rendering its wearer invisible.[20] This narrative structure is often missed. In *Republic*, Plato does not simply ask his readers to imagine what they would do if they had the ring – would they use it in order to get away with heinous acts undetected? When one of the participants in the dialogue, Glaucon, introduces the scenario early on in the discussion, in Book II, he does so in the following terms:

> Let's suppose, then, that there were two such rings, one worn by a just and the other by an unjust person. Now, no one, it seems, would be so incorruptible that he would stay on the path of justice or stay away from other people's property, when he could take whatever he wanted from anyone he wished, kill or release from prison anyone he wished, and do all the other things that would make him like a god among humans. Rather his actions would be in no way different from those of an unjust person, and both would follow the same path.[21]

Glaucon does not merely introduce a thought experiment about someone wearing the ring, but speaks of *two* people each having the ring. His prediction about what these two people would do seems highly surprising: the just person will act just as nefariously as the unjust person, and exploit the ring's power. It is crucial here that the background of the discussion is one in which (as Plato sees things) the correct conception of justice is not yet in play. What Glaucon is doing is representing what a sophist, who gets justice wrong, thinks the outcome of the thought experiment with the two wearers of the ring will be. The point of this is made clear only much later, when Socrates returns to discussion of such ring wearing in Book X. Socrates now asks rhetorically: 'haven't we found that justice itself is the best thing for the soul itself, and that the soul – whether it has the ring of Gyges or even it together with the cap of Hades – should do just things?'[22] What Plato has tried to do with

20 See Cora Diamond, 'What If x Isn't the Number of Sheep? Wittgenstein and Thought-Experiments in Ethics'.

21 Plato, *Republic* II, 360b, in *Collected Works*. Glaucon was the name of Plato's elder brother.

22 Plato, *Republic* X, 612b. The cap of Hades also made its wearer invisible.

the ring of Gyges is to show, as Diamond puts it, that 'this thought-experiment cannot be carried out properly . . . by anyone with a vulgar conception . . . of what it is to be just'.[23] Plato's use of the ring is not as an intuition pump, but in the service of a comparative analysis of where one's imaginative resources take one if one has a skewed, confused, mistaken conception of justice (the sophist's) or, alternatively, the correct one (Socrates' own). For the person who knows what justice is, the ring is a mere piece of jewellery, and leaves his pattern of action unaffected.

Descartes's 'evil demon' scenario is nothing like an intuition pump, but the background to a philosophical demonstration.[24] Descartes invites each of us who read his *Meditations on First Philosophy* to engage in meditating for ourself.[25] When I, the meditator, attempt to subject my thought that I myself exist to the 'hyperbolic doubt' engendered by my supposing that 'some malicious demon of the utmost power and cunning has employed all his energies in order to deceive me', I quickly find that I cannot, for 'if I convinced myself of something' (even if the something is my own non-existence), 'then I certainly existed'. So my very attempt to doubt my own existence issues unavoidably in my recognition that 'this proposition, *I am, I exist* [*ego sum, ego existo*], is necessarily true whenever it is put forward by me or conceived in my mind'.[26] Descartes secures his result by means of some kind of demonstration, not by eliciting an intuition.[27]

Locke introduces into philosophy a new technical use of the term 'person', defined as 'a thinking intelligent Being, that has reason and reflection, and can consider it self as it self, the same thinking thing in different times and places', and asks 'wherein *personal identity*

23 Diamond, 'What If x Isn't the Number of Sheep?', p. 230.

24 *Pace* Daniel Dennett, who blithely assumes that 'Descartes's "cogito ergo sum" thought experiment' is an intuition pump (Daniel C. Dennett, *Elbow Room: The Varieties of Free Will Worth Wanting*, p. 18). He seems to miss that Descartes, in securing his conclusion, does not appeal to intuitions at all.

25 Compare Iris Murdoch's journal, 17 March 1946, Iris Murdoch Collections, Kingston University London, KUAS202/1/3: 'Talk with Pippa [Philippa Foot] about her conversation with Elizabeth [Anscombe] about the cogito. The cogito as a proof which one can "only do for oneself". "Now *you* do it". Example of the man who comes up to me in a dream and says *cogito ergo sum*. (To which I reply, "oh, no you don't pal!")' As quoted in Iris *Murdoch Newsletter* No. 14 (Winter 2000), p. 2.

26 René Descartes, *Meditations on First Philosophy*, AT VII 22, 25, in *The Philosophical Writings of Descartes*, vol. 2.

27 Just what kind of demonstration has, of course, been much discussed.

consists' – that is, what makes sameness of person across time.[28] In the course of the discussion, Locke imagines the soul of a prince entering the body of a cobbler:

> But yet the Soul alone in the change of Bodies, would scarce to any one, but to him that makes the Soul the *Man*, be enough to make the same *Man*. For should the Soul of a Prince, carrying with it the consciousness of the Prince's past Life, enter and inform the Body of a Cobler as soon as deserted by his own Soul, every one sees, he would be the same Person with the Prince, accountable only for the Prince's Actions: But who would say it was the same Man? The Body too goes to the making the Man, and would, I guess, to every Body determine the Man in this case, wherein the Soul, with all its Princely Thoughts about it, would not make another Man: But he would be the same Cobler to every one besides himself.[29]

Locke uses the case to illustrate a point he has already made. Sameness of 'person' consists not in sameness of 'man' (that is, the sameness of a certain corporeal being), but in sameness of 'soul' (that is, the continuity of a certain consciousness). Person, not man, is the locus of agency. And so, should the soul of a prince enter the body of a cobbler, it will be the *prince* who is responsible for the actions now performed by (or by means of) the cobbler's body.

In these examples from Plato, Descartes and Locke, the thought experiment is an adornment to a philosophical argument. But a thought experiment might be something different again – namely, a starting point for philosophical exploration. An instance of such thought experimentation is the 'No-Space world' explored in P. F. Strawson's *Individuals*, written at the end of the 'ordinary language philosophy' era, as its author transitioned into his Kant-inspired project of 'descriptive metaphysics'. Strawson's overall aim in the book was to delineate the conceptual scheme presupposed by our ability to have intelligible experiences of the world, and to find our way in it. In considering this, Strawson found himself wondering what would happen if we cut out one of Kant's two pure forms of intuition (space), leaving only the other (time) to orientate us. How would subjects orientate themselves? Could they do so at all? Is there something in a no-space world sufficiently

28 John Locke, *An Essay Concerning Human Understanding*, 2.27.9.

29 Ibid., 2.27.15.

analogous to the re-identifiable spatial 'particulars' by which we orientate ourselves in space?

Strawson had inherited a love of English literature from his parents, who had met while they were both studying the subject at Goldsmith's College, London; he himself had got into Oxford on a scholarship to study English before switching to Philosophy, Politics and Economics.[30] What he is doing with 'No-Space world' is not pumping intuitions from his readers, but stretching his own and their imaginative capacities to somewhere near or beyond their limit. His imaginative scenarios, he says explicitly, are not 'for the purpose of speculation about what would really happen in certain remote contingencies', but 'models against which to test and strengthen our own reflective understanding of our own conceptual structure'.[31] The interest of Strawson's thought experiments is precisely that their upshot is difficult to determine – with the result that his readers are directed not back to their intuitions but away from them.[32] In this, they resemble the thought experiments in a work of 'continental' philosophy such as Sartre's *Being and Nothingness*, which invite the reader to embark on a philosophical exploration, not to press a button that has the effect of making intuitions ooze out.

Gettier Cases and Other Intuition Pumps

Intuition pumping, by contrast with the use of thought experiments in Plato, Descartes, Locke or Strawson, simply presents us with a scenario, briefly sketched, and then invokes an expected intuitive response in order to settle a question concerning it.

One of the earliest deployments of this approach is a three-page paper published in *Analysis* in 1963 by Edmund Lee Gettier III, then a young teacher of philosophy at Wayne State University in Detroit.[33] The paper, as analytic philosophers routinely comment, has sparked a huge industry of 'Gettier cases'. Gettier began by noting that some philosophers thought that necessary and sufficient conditions for knowledge could be stated as follows:

---

30 P. F. Strawson, 'Intellectual Autobiography', p. 3.

31 P. F. Strawson, *Individuals: An Essay in Descriptive Metaphysics*, p. 86.

32 In case it needs saying, Strawson nowhere speaks of 'intuitions' in *Individuals*.

33 Edmund Gettier, 'Is Justified True Belief Knowledge?'

S knows that *p* if and only if (i) *p* is true,
(ii) S believes that *p*, and
(iii) S is justified in believing that *p*.

In analytic philosophy class, this is known as the 'JTB analysis of knowledge' (JTB stands for 'justified true belief'). Undergraduates are routinely taught that the JTB analysis is the 'standard definition' of knowledge, found in Plato and many others. In fact, it is easy to show that Plato never held it, and very few others have done so. The 'JTB analysis' is the sort of thing analytic philosophers thirst for: a definition in terms of a set of necessary and sufficient conditions. If your conditions for *x* are both necessary and sufficient, you have established an equivalence relation: you have managed to state what *x is*. An analysis in terms of necessary and sufficient conditions, once it is on the table, furthermore provides the (to analytic philosophers) mouth-watering prospect of indefinitely permuted tinkering with the conditions.

Gettier started the ball rolling on the 'Gettier industry' in his paper by arguing that conditions (i)–(iii) were not, in fact, jointly sufficient for S's knowing that *p*. You could meet all three conditions and still not know that *p*. All that needed to be done was to supply a case where conditions (i)–(iii) were met, but S did not know that *p*. This might seem strange to outsiders to analytic philosophy. How could the carefully crafted technical definition of knowing that *p* be made to collapse so easily? It was a matter, somehow, of *intuitively knowing* that S did not know that *p*.[34]

In the first of two cases Gettier presented, two work colleagues, Smith and Jones, have both applied for a job that has come up in the company they work for. The company's president has assured Smith that Jones will get it. As it happens, Smith has, ten minutes previously, counted the number of coins in Jones's pocket, and found there to be ten coins. (Don't ask what business Smith had fumbling in Jones's pocket.) Smith, therefore, has 'strong evidence' that the man who will get the job has ten coins in his pocket. And his belief that the man who will get the job has ten coins in his pocket is true. So it looks, 'by JTB', that Smith knows this. But, as it happens, the hiring process takes an unexpected turn and Smith himself, who likewise has ten coins in his

34 Gettier himself did not use the language of intuition, but his successors usually have. For discussion, see Timothy Williamson, *The Philosophy of Philosophy*, Chapter 6.

pocket, gets the job. And so surely, Gettier reasons, Smith does not *know* that the man who will get the job has ten coins in his pocket.

Where Gettier only implicitly relies on his reader sharing his own intuitions, Harry Frankfurt, then a colleague of Saul Kripke at the Rockefeller University, in a 1969 paper designed to combat an argument for 'hard determinism' (the view that there can be no free will in a deterministic world), explicitly relied on intuitions in deploying a similar approach to Gettier's.[35] Frankfurt's paper seeks to undermine the 'principle of alternate possibilities' ('PAP') to which, he says, arguments for hard determinism appeal. According to PAP, someone is 'morally responsible for what he has done only if he could have done otherwise'. (If determinism is true, the hard determinist maintains, then no agent ever acts freely, because she could not have acted otherwise than she does.) Frankfurt offered a case that purported to show that someone 'may well be morally responsible for what he has done even though he could not have done otherwise', thereby undermining 'PAP'. Such cases have become known in analytic discussion as 'Frankfurt cases'.

In Frankfurt's key case, Black wants Jones to do something.[36] When coercing people to do things, Black does not like to show his hand. So he waits until Jones is about to decide for himself whether what he will do is the thing Black wants or not. Black, all the while, is prepared to 'take effective steps' to ensure Jones does what he (Black) wants him to do. These steps might involve placing Jones under a 'terrible threat', or under hypnosis, or – in more extreme versions – somehow gaining complete control of the workings of Jones's brain. Since it turns out Jones himself resolves to do the thing Black wanted him to do, Black never has to show his hand or take these steps. Jones could not have done otherwise; if he had tried do, Black would have coerced him to do what he does. And yet he is responsible for his action. How could, Frankfurt asks, whether or not Black steps in to coerce Jones make a difference to whether Jones is responsible for his action? Jones was responsible if Black did not step in; how could the mere fact of Black's stepping in so radically upset our understanding of what Jones was going to do anyway?[37]

35 Harry G. Frankfurt, 'Alternate Possibilities and Moral Responsibility'.

36 In the paper, this is $Jones_4$, the protagonist of the fourth of a series of cases.

37 Frankfurt, 'Alternate Possibilities', p. 836. The argumentative move is similar to that of the classic empiricist 'argument from illusion'. Whether I really see the dagger before me, or it is a mere hallucination, could surely make *no difference*,

Frankfurt's presentation of his cases is curiously abstract: he does not fill in any detail about the kinds of action we are to imagine being carried out or the extremely far-fetched ways in which Black might manipulate the workings of Jones's brain. Ultimately, they are extremely hard to adjudicate, because the ways in which Black is supposed to be ready to control Jones's action need to be highly far-fetched: a kind of control exceeding what is possible – in the case of imagined brain control, down to the manipulation of synapses – or at the least what happens in any known situation.

Similar difficulties attend a host of the intuition pumps favoured by analytic philosophers. In 1973, Hilary Putnam, a professor of philosophy at Harvard University, asked his readers to imagine a planet called 'Twin Earth', where everything is the same as on Earth (down to English, French, and so on, being spoken, in countries exactly like the United States, Canada, etc.), except for one thing. On Twin Earth, the water that comes out of the taps, fills the lakes, and so on, has a different chemical formula. Whereas on Earth, water is H_2O, on Twin Earth it is XYZ. Putnam asks: does 'water' mean the same on Twin Earth as it does on Earth?[38] To Putnam, it was clear that it did not: as he liked to say in summing up his point, 'meanings just ain't in the head'. But who knows?

In 1978, Putnam's student Ned Block, then an associate professor of philosophy at MIT, devised the 'China brain' thought experiment. The idea was basically the same as in the Soviet cyberneticist Anatoly Dneprov's 1961 short story 'The Game'.[39] Where Dneprov's thought experiment involved imagining 1,400 young mathematicians in a stadium, in Block's version it was the one billion inhabitants of China. (The number one billion was helpfully roughly equivalent to the number of neurons in the brain.) Block asked: if the individual Chinese people all used walkie talkies to send messages to each other, as neurons send 'messages' to each other in the brain, would the Chinese nation be conscious?

---

the argument goes, to what it is like to have the visual perception of the dagger. This argumentative strategy, a stock in trade of analytic philosophy, has been powerfully challenged in John McDowell, 'Criteria, Defeasibility, and Knowledge', in his *Meaning, Knowledge, and Reality.*

38 Hilary Putnam, 'Meaning and Reference'.

39 Ned Block, 'Troubles with Functionalism'. For Dneprov's story, in the original Russian with English and Bulgarian translation, see 'Anatoly Dneprov. The game. Knowledge – Power 1961; No. 5, pp. 39–41' – available at q-bits.org.

A further Chinese-themed variation on Dneprov's idea, developed shortly after Block's, was John Searle's 'Chinese Room'.[40] It was as a description of what Searle was up to here that one of the official respondents to his paper, Daniel Dennett, invented the term 'intuition pump'.[41] In the Chinese Room, someone is locked up in solitary confinement and given the task of answering questions written in Chinese that are given to him, with answers also written in Chinese. He does so successfully, without any knowledge of Chinese, but on the basis of a complicated set of instructions. The intended analogy is with the operations performed by a computer on the basis of a program. Does the person in the Chinese Room understand Chinese?

Searle was adamant that, since the person does not understand Chinese, the programme of 'strong AI' advanced by Roger Schank and others must be misconceived. In the official responses, Block objected that Searle had simply assumed, not shown, that his intuitions could not be overruled; Dennett that different, contrary intuitions could be generated. Searle countered these objections with the declaration: 'When I now say that I at this moment do not understand Chinese, that claim does not merely record an intuition of mine, something I find myself inclined to say. It is a plain fact about me that I don't understand Chinese.'[42]

Stand-offs of this kind, in which a philosopher of the distinction of John R. Searle resorts to question-begging, is perhaps just what one should expect where intuitions are made to stand in for philosophical grounds.

Ethics Against Intuition

In this book, I have up to this point said little about ethics. This ought not to surprise. Analytic ethics has been a sorry saga. It took ethics in the analytic tradition a long time to recover from the onslaught of positivism, most of whose adherents regarded ethical statements as mere expressions of emotion – they *appeared* to have cognitive content, but this really was only an appearance. Accordingly, analytic ethics was, in the period immediately after the Second World War, largely confined

40 John R. Searle, 'Minds, Brains, and Programs'.

41 Dennett, in ibid., p. 429.

42 Ibid., p. 451.

to 'metaethics'. Analytic philosophy continues today to operate a conceptual and disciplinary division between 'normative' (or 'first-order') ethics and 'metaethics'. 'Normative' ethics contains doctrines about how to act. Metaethics, by contrast, studies the status of moral discourse. In a highly fragmented and professionalized discipline, some have metaethics as their 'area of specialization'; others, ethics itself. There is an obvious problem here: such a conception supposes that it is intelligible to study what 'moral discourse' is, just as it is given, awaiting a set of 'meta' questions to be asked of it. It takes a bizarre kind of alienation from one's own nature as a human being to be capable of entertaining this supposition, as if the philosophical community were no human community.

When normative ethics did make a comeback, a prevalent strand was utilitarianism. Whatever else may be said about utilitarianism, it is marked out by a rejection of 'our moral intuitions'. The Australian utilitarian philosopher Peter Singer has explicitly argued against reliance on intuitions; Philippa Foot, always an opponent of utilitarianism, wrote in a *Festschrift* for another Australian utilitarian, J. L. Mackie, that 'non-utilitarian principles are apparently deeply embedded in our ordinary morality'.[43]

Utilitarianism is a calculative approach to ethics. As its eighteenth-century inventor, Jeremy Bentham, wrote,

> by the principle of utility is meant that principle which approves or disapproves of every action whatsoever, according to the tendency it appears to have to augment or diminish the happiness of the party whose interest is in question: or, what is the same thing in other words, to promote or to oppose that happiness.[44]

This might sound egoistic, but another influential formulation of the principle of utility going back to Francis Hutcheson, an Irish philosopher of the early eighteenth century, was in terms of 'the *greatest Happiness* for the *greatest Numbers*'.[45] Utilitarianism operates with a 'hedonic calculus': measurements of the consequences of projected

43 Philippa Foot, 'Morality, Action, and Outcome', in her *Moral Dilemmas*, p. 88.

44 Jeremy Bentham, *An Introduction to the Principles of Morals and Legislation*, p. ii.

45 Francis Hutcheson, *An Inquiry into the Original of Our Ideas of Beauty and Virtue*, vol. 1, p. 177.

actions in terms of imagined units ('hedons') are compared against each other, and that which yields the greatest quantity selected.

In recent decades, utilitarianism has been rebranded 'effective altruism'. The units of utility are now called 'QALYs' (quality-adjusted life-years).[46] Effective altruism, like all utilitarianism, makes ethics into a system of calculation.[47] It teaches that what people care about is not what matters ethically. People care about those close to them; they care about the here and now. But caring for those you are acquainted with, rather than strangers, is a callous and misplaced prejudice. Furthermore, the priority should be to make things better for those who may exist in the distant future – there is, after all, so much more of that than there is of the now.

The founding scripture of effective altruism is a paper by Peter Singer published in the first volume of the journal *Philosophy and Public Affairs* in 1972.[48] The journal had been founded by a group of analytic moral philosophers who had become occupied by 'real world' issues. Singer argued that anyone who recognized the moral demand to save a drowning child from a shallow pond they happened to be walking by, in spite of the inconvenience of dirtying their clothes, should just as much see it as a requirement to send money to faraway starving or diseased children, via charities, in spite of the inconvenience of thereby being less able to indulge frivolous urges like buying new clothes for themselves. For Singer, the apparatus of charity under capitalism was a given.

Following Singer's line, effective altruists have reasoned that, since utilitarian decision-making is a matter of calculating outcomes, people should make the maximum amount of money they can, so as to be in a position to give away as much as possible to charity. Effective altruists have therefore got involved with those who have amassed the greatest fortunes in neoliberal capitalist society. Two of the movement's leading lights, the Swede Nick Bostrom and the Scot William MacAskill, have received the blessing of Elon Musk.[49] The movement's least fortunate

46 See Amia Srinivasan, 'Stop the Robot Apocalypse'.

47 The Oxford philosopher Derek Parfit actually used the phrase 'moral mathematics'. Derek Parfit, *Reasons and Persons*, Chapter 3. Parfit was a kind of utilitarian, and a fan of effective altruism, who eventually came to believe that all moral theories apparently not his own agreed with what he had to say. See Derek Parfit, *On What Matters*.

48 Peter Singer, 'Famine, Affluence, and Morality'.

49 On 3 August 2014, Musk tweeted: 'Worth reading Superintelligence by Bostrom. We need to be super careful with AI. Potentially more dangerous than

liaison has probably been that with Sam Bankman-Fried, the founder of the FTX cryptocurrency exchange who was convicted of fraud in 2023.[50] Investment levels in 'EA' have been high. In 2021 the 80,000 Hours website boasted: 'How much funding is committed to effective altruism (going forward)? Around $46 billion.'[51]

Effective altruism is now a large-scale movement with many chapters all over the world. It reaches into universities, where undergraduates form Effective Altruism Societies, in which normal student activism seeking to change society is replaced with the ideology of wealth redirection. Many of its institutes have been based at Oxford University: the Future of Humanity Institute, founded in 2005 by Bostrom; Giving What We Can, founded in 2009 by Toby Ord and William MacAskill, and absorbed into the Centre for Effective Altruism in 2012; the Global Priorities Institute, founded in 2018. The Future of Humanity Institute was shut down in April 2024. In the same month, a luxurious retreat at Wytham Abbey in Oxfordshire, where effective altruists brainstormed about how most efficiently to maximize utility, also ceased operation.

Effective altruism is overwhelmingly white and 70 per cent male.[52] When it folded in 2024, the Future of Humanity Institute had no women at all in its hierarchy above the level of PhD students and 'affiliates'.[53] In the United States, a culture of sexual harassment has been documented in the movement's research centres. As the *Time* magazine writer Charlotte Alter has recorded, on the basis of the testimony of seven women, many of the men try to sleep with as many of the women as possible, serving their fantasy that they can be fuckboys *and*

---

nukes.' On 29 April 2022, Musk tweeted, about MacAskill's book *What We Owe the Future*: 'Worth reading. This is a close match for my philosophy.' This prompted a quote tweet from MacAskill: 'So, er, it seems that Elon Musk just tweeted about What We Owe The Future. Crazy times! You might wonder: Where do we agree and disagree?'

50 The 80,000 Hours website features the following message: 'November 17, 2022 1:00 pm GMT: Until recently, we had highlighted Sam Bankman-Fried on our website as a positive example of someone ambitiously pursuing a high-impact career. To say the least, we no longer endorse that.' Benjamin Todd, 'Is Effective Altruism Growing? An Update on the Stock of Funding vs People', 28 July 2021, at 80000hours.org.

51 Ibid.

52 David Moss, 'EA Survey 2020: Demographics', 20 May 2021, at forum .effectivealtruism.org.

53 'Team: Leadership', at shorturl.at/XHesu.

'ethical' while they are at it. Women who refuse to enter a 'polycule' are shamed, on the basis that monogamy is 'a lifestyle governed by jealousy', and polyamory 'a more enlightened and rational approach'. As one person put it, 'Under the guise of intellectuality, you can cover up a lot of injustice.' One woman recalled being 'groomed' by a powerful older man 'who argued that "pedophilic relationships" were both perfectly natural and highly educational'. A woman who reported her experiences of harassment on an online EA forum in November 2022 was told by other contributors to the forum that her post was 'bigoted', would 'pollute the epistemic environment' and was 'net-negative for solving the problem'.[54]

Effective altruism has evident cult-like features. Apart from sexual abuse of power, entrants to the movement are encouraged to leave their intuitions at the door, as per utilitarian ideology.[55] As the user Nathan_Barnard instructs his readers on the Effective Altruism Forum: 'Be less trusting of intuitive arguments about social phenomena'![56] Become part of the superior ethical-calculative community, in which reason will prevail.

The Bloomberg journalist Ellen Huet has pointed out, in a piece on effective altruism based on the testimony of eight women, how the culture of EA is reflective of, and realizes, the way its ideas imagine the world. Nick Bostrom, in a 2003 paper, imagined a scenario in which an artificially intelligent system tasked with making paperclips took things into its own hands and started turning absolutely everything in the world into paperclips.[57] This is the so-called 'paperclip-maximizer' thought experiment. As Huet wrote,

> Every AI safety researcher knows about the paper clip maximizer. Few seem to grasp the ways this subculture [EA] is mimicking that tunnel vision. As AI becomes more powerful, the stakes will only feel higher to

54 Charlotte Alter, 'Effective Altruism Promises to Do Good Better. These Women Say It Has a Toxic Culture of Sexual Harassment and Abuse', *Time*, 3 February 2023.

55 Compare the saying of the purported Messiah, Jesus of Nazareth, weaponized by Christian cults in order to gain control of their victims: 'If any man come to me, and hate not his father, and mother, and wife, and children, and brethren, and sisters, yea, and his own life also, he cannot be my disciple' (Luke 14: 26).

56 Anonymous, 'Be Less Trusting of Intuitive Arguments about Social Phenomena', 18 December 2022, at forum.effectivealtruism.org.

57 Nick Bostrom, 'Ethical Issues in Advanced Artificial Intelligence', available at fhi.ox.ac.uk.

those obsessed with their self-assigned quest to keep it under rein. The collateral damage that's already occurred won't matter. They'll be thinking only of their own kind of paper clip: saving the world.[58]

Ethics by Intuition

Outside of effective altruism, which seeks to shake off intuition in its pursuit of rational calculation, analytic moral philosophy is, by contrast, deeply involved with intuitions. Philosophers of the intuition-loving kind themselves state:

> The appeal to intuitions is a pervasive strategy in contemporary philosophical discourse. A good philosophical theory is widely taken to be one that gives an adequate account of our intuitions. Ethical theory is no exception.[59]

> Anyone who reflects on the way we go about arguing for or against moral claims is likely to be struck by the central importance we give to thinking about cases. Intuitive reactions to cases – real or imagined – are carefully noted, and then appealed to as providing reason to accept (or reject) various claims.[60]

> Many moral theorists have relied on intuitions in both building up and challenging theories.[61]

Again, the notion that intuitions serve as 'data' is invoked:

> Many contemporary ethicists like to treat moral intuitions as evidence, akin to experimental data that are to be explained by theories.[62]

> It appears that in moral reasoning, moral intuitions play the same role which observations do in science: we test general moral principles and

---

58 Ellen Huet, 'The Real-Life Consequences of Silicon Valley's AI Obsession', Bloomberg, 7 March 2023, at bloomberg.com.

59 Robert Audi, quoted in Tomasz Herok, 'Intuitions Are Never Used as Evidence in Ethics', p. 1.

60 Shelly Kagan, quoted in ibid., p. 2.

61 Frances Kamm, quoted in ibid.

62 Paul Thagard, quoted in ibid.

> moral theories by seeing how their consequences conform (or fail to conform) to our moral intuitions about particular cases.[63]

Intuitions are also invoked as a way of choosing between ethical theories. 'How would you choose among consequentialism, Kantianism, contractarianism, and virtue theories without appealing to moral intuitions at some point in some way?'[64]

The Trolley Problem

One might think that in ethics, at least, analytic philosophers would try to go in for the imaginative exploration of thought. But, again, a very basic and crude use of intuition pumps is prevalent.

Probably the most prominent use of intuition pumping by means of thought experiments, in ethics, is in the form of countless versions of the 'trolley problem'. A vast literature on 'trolley cases' grew from a relatively casual suggestion made by Philippa Foot in a 1967 paper into a proliferation of morally challenging scenarios, real and imagined. After contemplating an example in which 'a pilot whose aeroplane is about to crash is deciding whether to steer from a more to a less inhabited area', Foot added as an afterthought: 'it may rather be supposed that he is the driver of a runaway tram which he can only steer from one narrow track on to the other; anyone on the track he enters is bound to be killed'.[65] This became the 'trolley problem' in the American philosopher Judith Jarvis Thomson's 1976 paper, 'Killing, Letting Die, and the Trolley Problem'. Foot's original case was now presented as follows:

> Edward is the driver of a trolley, whose brakes have just failed. On the track ahead of him are five people; the banks are so steep that they will not be able to get off the track in time. The track has a spur leading off to the right, and Edward can turn the trolley onto it. Unfortunately there is one person on the right-hand track. Edward can turn the trolley, killing the one; or he can refrain from turning the trolley, killing the five.[66]

---

63 Richard Boyd, quoted in ibid.

64 Walter Sinnott-Armstrong, Liane Young and Fiery Cushman, quoted in ibid.

65 Philippa Foot, 'The Problem of Abortion and the Doctrine of the Double Effect', in her *Virtues and Vices*, p. 23.

66 Judith Jarvis Thomson, 'Killing, Letting Die, and the Trolley Problem', p. 206.

Thomson proceeds from here to cycle through an enormous array of different variations on the case. The reader's intuitions are pumped at every stage. Scenarios to be imagined include a surgeon transplanting organs without people's consent, a 'fat man' being pushed off a bridge to stop a runaway train, buttons being pressed to pulverize bombs in the sky, picnics arranged for pensioners only for them to be blown off the tracks, a disobedient schoolboy ploughed into, and so on. A novel kind of absurdity is attained when Thomson introduces a case concerned with benefit rather than harm, that of the 'Health-Pebble':

> Suppose there are six men who are dying. Five are standing in one clump on the beach, one is standing further along. Floating in on the tide is a marvelous pebble, the Health-Pebble, I'll call it: it cures what ails you. The one needs for cure the whole Health-Pebble; each of the five needs only a fifth of it. Now in fact that Health-Pebble is drifting towards the one, so that if nothing is done to alter its course, the one will get it. We happen to be swimming nearby, and are in a position to deflect it towards the five. Is it permissible for us to do this? It seems to me that it is permissible for us to deflect the Health-Pebble if and only if the one has no more claim on it than any of the five does.

Thomson's intuitions cut through this entirely improbable and intractable set-up to tell her that whoever owns something has a right to it: 'If the one alone owns it, or if we have promised it only to the one, then he plainly has more claim on it than any of the five do; and we may not deflect it away from him.'[67] Perhaps that ought not to surprise. American university professors presumably attach a high value to what one owns.

Thomson, looking back on her career in her John Dewey Lecture, delivered to the Eastern Division meeting of the American Philosophical Association in 2012, mused: 'I came to think that the main, central problems consist in efforts to explain what makes certain pre-philosophical, or nonphilosophical, beliefs true.'[68] Unfortunately, these 'pre-philosophical, or nonphilosophical, beliefs' might not be true in the first place.

In case it needs saying, the affective dimension of human beings' intuitive responses to moral scenarios is nowhere given any attention.

67 Ibid., p. 209.

68 Judith Jarvis Thomson, 'How It Was', p. 115.

The Calculative Model

The proliferation of 'trolley cases' has become notorious among analytic philosophers. Intuition pumping by what they affectionately call 'trolleyology' follows an obviously set pattern, relying on a calculative mindset, locked within a constricted conception of what psychology could possibly be. There is, from within analytic philosophy, no means to secure a critical vantage point on this sorry situation.

The model presupposed by the deployment of 'trolley cases' is well brought out by considering the work of the American psychologist Lawrence Kohlberg, who extended Jean Piaget's work on stages of child psychological development to the question of children's moral development, and the response to it of the psychologist and feminist theorist Carol Gilligan. Gilligan, who began her career working with Kohlberg at Harvard University, came to question the presuppositions baked into Kohlberg's analyses of children's responses in the interviews he devised to evaluate their evolving moral development.

An exemplar of Kohlberg's approach was the 'Heinz Dilemma'. The child is presented with the following scenario. A woman suffers from a rare and aggressive form of cancer. Her husband is intent on getting the money together to pay for the only known treatment, which uses a recently discovered from of radium, but the man who discovered it and knows how to turn it into medicine sells it at $2,000 per small dose, which the couple cannot afford. The husband implores the discoverer to let him have the drug (on which he makes a $1,800 profit) for less money – but the druggist insists on his right to profit from his discovery and be paid the full asking price. The child is now asked whether Heinz may (or indeed should) steal the medicine in order to save his wife's life.

Gilligan reported that, when she put the Heinz Dilemma to her own test subjects, the girls she asked gave markedly different answers from the boys.[69] An eleven-year-old boy, Jake, answered confidently, arriving swiftly and logically at the conclusion that Heinz should steal the medicine. He availed himself of a simple argument: life is worth more than money, so Heinz should steal the medicine. For this argument to work, it must of course be, as Jake assumes, that there are here two quantities

69 I will not here enter into the controversies surrounding the nature of Gilligan's feminism and its defensibility, instead confining my interest to the very notion that different responses to the Heinz Dilemma are possible.

amenable to being measured against each other. As Jake told Gilligan, mathematics was 'the only thing that is totally logical'.[70] Amy, a girl of the same age, answered in a much more hesitant manner. At first she proffered, in response to the question whether Heinz should steal the medicine: 'Well, I don't think so'. She then explored a series of considerations, slaloming around the challenge of giving a direct, decisive answer. She wondered if Heinz could find the money some other way, but then also insisted 'his wife shouldn't die either'. If Heinz stole the medicine, he would likely go to prison, and thereby be rendered incapable of procuring more of the medicine for his wife if her health deteriorated again. All this led Amy to the conclusion that 'they should really just talk it out and find some other way to make the money'. As Gilligan writes, for Amy, Heinz's Dilemma was 'not a math problem with humans but a narrative of relationships that extends over time'.[71]

Jake's response could readily be made sense of in terms of Kohlberg's metrics for moral development: he was exhibiting the clear-sightedness to be expected at his age. By those standards, Amy's response seemed hopeless, providing 'an image of development stunted by a failure of logic, an inability to think for herself'.[72] To Gilligan, this suggested there was something wrong with Kohlberg's metrics. For this, Gilligan got it in the teeth from the analytic philosopher Roy Sorensen. In his book *Thought Experiments*, Sorensen seemed unable to restrain himself from misrepresenting, and sneering at, Gilligan. For Sorensen, it was all very simple: 'Carol Gilligan's females respond to a hypothetical forced choice by searching for loopholes.' Sorensen was happy to extend to Gilligan permission to draw her obviously misguided conclusions: 'Gilligan is free to admire her subjects' evasiveness as a sign of resourcefulness, sensitivity, or some other virtue.' But, he added, somewhat bafflingly, 'to assume that all virtues rest on an ethical *insight* is to overintellectualize morality'.[73] Was Sorensen seriously suggesting that it was *Gilligan* who overintellectualized morality in suggesting that Amy's responses manifested moral intelligence rather than sheer incomprehension?

For Sorensen, the response of 'Gilligan's females' simply manifested a failure to see how the method of cases works. You have to accept what

70 Carol Gilligan, *In a Different Voice: Psychological Theory and Women's Development*, p. 26.

71 Ibid., p. 28.

72 Ibid., pp. 27–8.

73 Roy A. Sorensen, *Thought Experiments*, p. 259.

is stipulated, or you just didn't 'get it'. It may *seem*, as Cora Diamond has written, as if the subject who questions the stipulations must just be immature, no better than the schoolboy who responds to the mathematical stipulation 'Let *x* be the number of sheep' with, 'But, Sir, what if *x* isn't the number of sheep?' But what, Diamond asks, is in fact to be gained by insisting on the stipulation in considering moral cases? After all, it is not at all clear 'how the stipulated case is relevant to moral life, if it is relevant at all'.[74] If it is not clear how it is relevant to moral life, then it is also not at all clear why a child's ability to handle such stipulated cases would be a guide to her stage of *moral* development. In our moral life, what we have to deal with are not stipulations. Instead, we are called on to be responsive and imaginative. If anything, Amy does better on this score than Jake does. Jake may handle stipulative thought experiments more deftly – but what does that show, other than his skill with basic logic puzzles of a certain sort?

There is a deep lesson in Gilligan's assessment. The method of cases brings into play capacities representing only a limited sector of human thought, and applicable only to a constricted range of its exercises. It is these exercises that analytic philosophers are good at. Unfortunately this means there are, at best, no good grounds to think they will be good at moral philosophy. At worst, analytic philosophy ricochets between a misguided confidence in the salutary effects of intuition pumping, with potentially monstrous results, and the calculative performances of the utilitarians, who think they know better than to pay attention to intuition – with, if anything, worse results still.

Experimental Philosophy

By the early 2000s, the notion that philosophers (meaning analytic philosophers) 'rely on' intuitions was entirely commonplace. In 2004, a Princeton PhD student, Joshua Knobe, wrote an article for the British publication *The Philosophers' Magazine*, intended for a non-academic audience, entitled 'Intuitions in the Test-Tube'. Knobe began by noting that it was 'common practice' in analytic philosophy to 'appeal to intuitions about particular cases'. 'Typically', Knobe told his readers, 'the philosopher presents a hypothetical situation and then makes a claim of the form: "In this case, we would surely say . . ." This claim about

74 Cora Diamond, 'What if x Isn't the Number of Sheep?', p. 238.

people's intuitions then forms a part of an argument for some more general theory about the nature of our concepts or our use of language.'[75]

Knobe now proceeded to argue that it was 'puzzling' that philosophers should make such claims without empirically checking what people's intuitions actually were. Here, he saw an opportunity. As an undergraduate at Stanford University, he had already become interested in the 'folk psychology' of concepts such as 'intentional action'. In 1997, having gained his BA only the year before, Knobe published a paper jointly with Bertram Malle, a psychologist who had just been awarded his PhD from Stanford.[76]

By 2004, Knobe was calling the approach he took over from Malle and others, and repurposed for philosophy, 'experimental philosophy'. In a four-page paper in *Analysis*, Knobe reported on an experiment he carried out on seventy-eight people in a New York park, transforming the method of cases into philosophy-by-questionnaire. Half of Knobe's experimental subjects were given the following vignette:

> The vice-president of a company went to the chairman of the board and said, 'We are thinking of starting a new program. It will help us increase profits, but it will also harm the environment.'
>
> The chairman of the board answered, 'I don't care at all about harming the environment. I just want to make as much profit as I can. Let's start the new program.'
>
> They started the new program. Sure enough, the environment was harmed.

The other half of Knobe's experimental subjects were given a different version of the vignette, in which all mentions of 'harm' were replaced by 'help'. The subjects in each group were then asked whether the chairman intentionally harmed/helped the environment. Of those who had been given the 'harm' version, 82 per cent said that the chairman intentionally harmed the environment; of those who had been given the 'help' version, 77 per cent said that the chairman had not intentionally helped the environment.[77] This difference is now known in the analytic philosophy literature as the 'Knobe effect'.

75 Joshua Knobe, 'Intuitions in the Test-Tube', p. 37.

76 Bertram F. Malle and Joshua Knobe, 'The Folk Concept of Intentionality'.

77 Knobe, 'Intentional Action and Side Effects in Ordinary Language', pp. 191–2.

Experimental philosophy has, as its literature points out, a 'negative' and a 'positive' programme.[78] Both suffer from irremediable problems. The negative programme might seem to offer a helpful corrective to 'armchair' philosophers of an amorphous 'we'. It is not clear, however, why one is supposed to think that the 'intuitions' elicited by going up to people in the street and firing questions at them out of the blue are of any greater use in philosophy. Meanwhile, the positive programme has been a failure even on its own terms. In 2001, Jonathan Weinberg, Shaun Nichols and Stephen Stich published a paper claiming to have empirical evidence that East Asians had different intuitions from Westerners about Gettier cases.[79] When others tried to replicate the results presented by these teams, as per the imperatives of true empirical science, they failed. East Asians now had the same intuitions as Westerners.[80] The project seems, at best, questionable in its methodological robustness. Even if it were not vitiated by internal failure, however, one ought from the first to have expected little insight from a field of enquiry that presupposes an unrealistic atomistic conception of how linguistic units mean what they do, compounded by a crude programme in psychology that treats the subjects of psychological experiments in abstraction from any appreciation of the dynamics of the mind. One wonders why anyone would think that simply thrusting 'intuition pumps' into the hands of an unsuspecting general public would yield any kind of insight – psychological, philosophical, or of any other kind.

Experimental philosophy does not show much, other than the failures produced by a crude conception of how to elicit what people think about things that pays no heed to any of the developments since Freud in the understanding of the mind. Attempting to ask people whether they believe 'that *p*' without any attention to context has, it turns out,

---

78 See, for example, the distinction between 'EXPERIMENTALISM–' and 'EXPERIMENTALISM+' in Antti Kauppinen, 'The Rise and Fall of Experimental Philosophy', p. 97.

79 Jonathan M. Weinberg, Shaun Nichols and Stephen Stich, 'Normativity and Epistemic Intuitions', pp. 441–3. According to Weinberg's team's statistics, of the Western subjects, seventeen said the subject of the Gettier case 'really knows', forty-nine that he 'only believes'; of the East Asian subjects, thirteen said she 'really knows', ten that she 'only believes' (p. 458). (Yes, the numbers really are that small.)

80 See Minsun Kim and Yuan Yuan, 'No Cross-Cultural Differences in the Gettier Car Case Intuition: A Replication Study of Weinberg *et al.* 2001', citing in turn other failures to replicate the purported results reported by Weinberg, Nichols and Stich.

wild results. One would think that those who have attempted such projects would now take the next step and learn about the mind and about culture. But, trapped in their simplistic empiricist paradigm for psychology, they just keep on with their questionnaires. Remarkably, experimental philosophy, while the wave of enthusiasm that greeted it in some quarters in the 2000s and 2010s may have subsided, ploughs on.[81]

81 For the latest, see Joshua Knobe and Shaun Nichols, eds, *Oxford Studies in Experimental Philosophy*, vol. 5 (2024).

10

Colonizing Philosophy

Analytic philosophy has long insulated itself from social, cultural and political questions. Insofar as it has come to occupy itself with political philosophy – a development kick-started by the publication of John Rawls's *A Theory of Justice* in 1971 – its approach has tended to be highly abstract and schematic, with a studied disregard for the historically conditioned social and cultural dimensions of the political.

Philosophy departments have, not unrelatedly, long remained dominated by privileged white males, and a hostile environment for others. Those who do not fit the traditional white, masculine mould of the philosopher, if they do gain a foothold in philosophy departments, are very unlikely to stay. As Kristie Dotson, one of very few Black women philosophers holding academic positions in the United States, has written, philosophy departments have 'an extraordinarily leaky pipeline when it comes to retaining the small number of diverse people it manages to attract'.[1] Partly responsible for this, as Dotson points out, is the 'culture of justification' to which anyone coming with an alternative approach is subjected.[2] Although the underlying mechanisms of exclusion, including a culture of misogyny, are not confined to analytic

1 Kristie Dotson, 'Concrete Flowers: Contemplating the Profession of Philosophy', p. 403.

2 Kristie Dotson, 'How Is This Paper Philosophy?' The title of Dotson's paper evokes the culture of justification, encapsulated in the question posed ad nauseam to those whose approach to philosophy appears discomfortingly unfamiliar to upholders of accepted norms.

philosophy, the problems have been stark there.[3] The culture is shifting inside analytic philosophy, as it is elsewhere. Thanks to the tireless work of individuals acting in concert, and of more formal organizations such as the Society for Women in Philosophy, the environment within analytic philosophy is becoming less hostile for those who are not white men, even if the problems are far from removed.

As part of a general shift in culture, analytic philosophers have also begun to heed calls to decolonize and demasculinize the curriculum that they teach to their students. An increasing contingent draw on the intellectual work of feminists and critical race theorists. An analytic feminism has been on the rise, as has 'critical philosophy of race' (a reconfiguration of critical race theory). But there are limits to what analytic philosophy can do – limits set by its own ideological constraints. The ways in which analytic philosophy inevitably constrains itself will be the topic of this chapter.

It is possible to imagine, by contrast with the narrative to be presented in this chapter, that analytic philosophy is today undergoing a transformation by which it will ultimately empower itself to transcend, rather than imprison itself within, these limits. Analytic philosophy might seem today to be experiencing – as Kevin Richardson, an assistant professor at Duke University, has suggested – a 'social turn'. Richardson himself, in a blog post on the analytic philosophy website *Daily Nous*, signalled the importance he attached to this 'social turn' by comparing it to the 'linguistic turn':

> Of course, the linguistic turn is over. We partied hard, got hungover, and now we're trying to live as respectable adults. When our kids (students) ask about this period, we pretend we didn't partake. Today, a new revolution is brewing. Analytic philosophy is in the midst of a *social turn.*

The idea of the linguistic turn was that of a seismic methodological shift in how philosophy was done.[4] To effect the linguistic turn was to enable philosophy to be carried out by linguistic means (even if no one could exactly spell out what this meant). Every philosophical question

---

3 For the culture of misogyny, see Sally Haslanger, 'Changing the Ideology and Culture of Philosophy: Not by Reason (Alone)'.

4 See, however, Chapter 7, above, for criticism of how the 'linguistic turn' has been understood in analytic philosophy.

was, thanks to the linguistic turn, supposed to be put on a linguistic footing. The 'social turn', so-called, cannot claim to be something of that type – a revolution presaging a recasting of the very way in which philosophical questions are put. Richardson lists a number of subfields of analytic philosophy, and associated chief practitioners, as exemplary of the alleged 'social turn': the social philosophy of language of Quill Kukla; the social epistemology of Kristie Dotson, Miranda Fricker and Jennifer Lackey; the feminist philosophy of mind of Keya Maitra; and social ontology, a field 'thriving more [than] ever, thanks to the work of philosophical giants like Sally Haslanger'.[5] Contrary to what Richardson's analogy with the linguistic turn suggests, however, the activity in these fields does not involve a methodological turn: analytic philosophy has not itself turned social. The figures he mentions are analytic philosophers in a traditional mould, continuing methodologically as they were before, but now applying the methods and 'tools' of analytic philosophy to subject areas that analytic philosophy had previously ignored. In a sense, the situation is the opposite of that which the 'linguistic turn' was supposed to represent: in the case of the linguistic turn, the subject matter was to remain the same even as the methodology was supposed to be radically reinvented.

Richardson himself underlines some of the dangers attending this new attention to social subject matter on the part of analytic philosophers, in particular that of 'philosophical Columbusing'.[6] The concept of 'Columbusing' is particularly apt, given its reference to Christopher Columbus's claim to have 'discovered' the so-called New World in 1492. The danger is not merely what Richardson means to advert to: passing off what many already know as if it were a newly discovered insight. There is a risk that conforms even more closely to what the actions of Columbus himself symbolize: the subjection of an entire world to an imperialist logic. The danger that attends analytic social philosophy is not merely that of reinventing the wheel, and doing so badly, but of selling the wheel back to its original inventors after having subjected it to analytic refurbishment.

The ideology of analytic philosophy is that of liberalism. Accordingly, participants in its discussions are conceived of as entering a liberal marketplace of ideas. Circulation on the market is the mechanism by

---

5 Kevin Richardson, 'The Social Turn in Analytic Philosophy: Promises and Perils', 8 August 2023, at dailynous.com.

6 Ibid.

which the best ideas win out.[7] It is presupposed that each participant may enter the market as they see fit, and take full part in the process of exchange. Entry conditions are not considered – it is taken for granted that all are free, sovereign individuals. The maintenance of the fiction of equal entry, of course, just as in the case of the commercial marketplace, serves the interests of those who in fact exercise power.

Analytic philosophers have been effective in subjecting a series of successive radical, non-liberal currents of thought to liberal marketization. In the 1970s, the Canadian philosopher G. A. Cohen, educated at Oxford University, invented analytic Marxism. In the 1990s, Sally Haslanger, Rae Langton and others established the credentials of analytic feminism – a peculiarly narrow form of feminism, constrained by the highly historically contingent framework set by the American lawyer and anti-pornography campaigner Catharine MacKinnon. Where it has drawn on the Marxist tradition of feminist standpoint theory, it has worked to neutralize this tradition politically. Philosophy of race in the analytic mould was, again in the early 1990s, given its initial impetus by Kwame Anthony Appiah, a denier of the reality of race and opponent of the black radical tradition represented by W. E. B. Du Bois. Among those analytic philosophers who have drawn on critical race theory, the most influential figure, Charles Mills, worked hard to lead that fundamentally anti-liberal tradition back into the field of liberalism.

Thanks to these developments, analytic philosophers now have greater exposure to radical traditions. They face grave difficulties, however, giving those traditions' critical power their due, thanks to their blindness to their own tendency to neutralize and defang them. This is brought out in particularly egregious form by efforts to decolonize the philosophy curriculum in those places where analytic philosophy holds sway. Here, it engages in a peculiar act of double forgetfulness. It forgets that it is itself a tradition among others; and it forgets, perhaps even more remarkably, that it is not coeval with 'Western philosophy'. It thereby equates decolonization with exposure to 'non-Western philosophy' – that is, traditions alternative to the tradition of Western philosophy. In this vanishing act, in which it itself goes missing from the picture, it again insulates itself from the critical power of decolonial thought. The tradition that is none cannot be touched, just as whiteness, the colour that is none, cannot be seen.

---

7 For the *locus classicus* of this view, see John Stuart Mill, *On Liberty*, Chapter 2.

Analytic Marxism

The work of Karl Marx is the *fons et origo* of the radical critique of liberalism and its ideology. Today, however, Marx himself has been appropriated by liberals, in order to shore up their ideology of the sovereign, autonomous individual, exercising preferences and maximizing utility.

In Italy and France, some of the finest philosophical minds were drawn to Marxism (in the 1960s, Louis Althusser and Lucio Colletti respectively; before that, Maurice Merleau-Ponty and Galvano Della Volpe). In Britain, this was not so: here, it was notably historians, not philosophers, who were the leading intellects of Marxism.

When Marxism entered mainstream Anglophone philosophy, it was as 'analytic Marxism', the creation of one man, Gerald Allan ('Jerry') Cohen. Cohen had grown up in a Jewish communist household in Montreal, in which he had ardently imbibed Marxist ideas. In 1961 he came to Oxford to take the BPhil degree, and, as he later put it, 'under the benign guidance of Gilbert Ryle . . . learned British analytical philosophy'.[8] Cohen later recalled that in the 1960s 'almost all politically committed students' were hostile to analytic philosophy. By contrast, he felt in his own case that, since he had already become a committed Marxist in his youth, it was 'not difficult to take analytical philosophy on board'.[9] In 1978 he published *Karl Marx's Theory of History: A Defence*, a book that performed the extraordinary task of defending a hyper-orthodox technological-determinist Marxism in the style of analytic philosophy. As the Marxist historian Ellen Meiksins Wood has commented, the book is 'less a re-interpretation of Marx than an uncompromising defence of the most orthodox interpretation'. It is also curiously ahistorical. Its 'law' of history is 'so diluted that it has no explanatory value'.[10] What Cohen defends is not a historical theory of capitalism – the social order of a specific epoch – but a theory of history as such. Cohen's version of Marx is thus useless for explaining capitalism; unsurprisingly, that task, as Wood points out, is relegated by Cohen to a purely moral form of explanation. Marx gives way to a traditional liberal-bourgeois form of philosophizing.

8 G. A. Cohen, 'Introduction to the 2000 Edition', in *Karl Marx's Theory of History*, p. xx.

9 Ibid., p. xxi.

10 Ellen Meiksins Wood, 'Happy Campers'.

Shortly after the publication of his book, Cohen formed a group with two like-minded parties, the Norwegian social scientist Jon Elster and the American economist John E. Roemer. Having first met in September 1979, they called themselves the 'September Group'. Elster had arrived in Paris to do a PhD on Marx in 1968, just as Althusserianism was at its height, but chose to work instead with the right-wing philosopher Raymond Aron. He came to the view that Marx employed two methods: methodological individualism and methodological collectivism. The first was correct, the second a deep mistake. It was 'extraordinary', Elster reported, how Marx could shift from one to the other within the same work (for example, his *Grundrisse*).[11] When Marx himself, 'on numerous occasions', as Elster admitted, 'invoked the "dialectical method" as a privileged approach to the analysis of social phenomena', it tended to be 'in such general, even vapid terms', that it was hard to see what implications dialectic could have 'for more specific analyses'.[12] So much for Marx's own understanding of what he was up to. Roemer's *A General Theory of Exploitation and Class* (1982) sought to explain exploitation in terms of game theory. It need hardly be pointed out that this was to attempt to dismantle the master's house using the master's tools. The rational agents assumed by game theory could not possibly do the work expected of them *unless* they hoisted themselves over the barriers imposed by class.

Cohen liked to call the approach shared by the members of the September Group 'non-bullshit Marxism'. The 'bullshit' in 'non-bullshit' was, in part, what Cohen detected in the work of Althusser. He complained that the theses of Althusserians were either so impenetrable that it was impossible to tell if they were true, or, where they were intelligible, admitted of only two interpretations, one of which made them trivial, and the other obviously false. 'Bullshit' was partly equated with 'dialectic'. It was never made clear, Cohen protested, what dialectical reasoning was, leading him to conclude that the notion of 'dialectic as a *rival* to analysis thrives only in an atmosphere of unclear thought'. Analytic Marxism was not merely 'non-bullshit', but involved a positive commitment to analysis, a commitment conceived as standing in opposition to holism. Social formations had to be understood in terms of the behaviour of their component parts. The commitment to analysis – both in the 'non-bullshit' sense and the individualist sense – was,

11 Jon Elster, *Making Sense of Marx*, p. 4.

12 Ibid., p. 37.

according to Cohen, 'unrevisable'. Any resistance to the techniques of analysis was 'irrational obscurantism'.[13]

As time went on, Cohen himself, as the philosopher of the September Group, strayed away from Marxism. He followed in the line of his mentor, Isaiah Berlin, and Berlin's successors John Plamenatz and Charles Taylor, to become Chichele Professor of Social and Political Theory at Oxford University (a post he held from 1985 to 2008). In later work, his concerns were the traditional themes of liberalism, and his arguments became indistinguishable from those of moral philosophers. Cohen, who seemed genuinely troubled that his life as an Oxford professor and fellow of All Souls College might be somehow dissonant with continued professions of Marxism, had left the communism of his Montreal youth far behind.

The Creation of Analytic Feminism: Haslanger and Langton

In the 1990s, the remarkable phenomenon of 'analytic feminism' came into being – remarkable because, prior to that time, the idea of the noun 'feminism' being modified by the adjective 'analytic' had seemed unimaginable. The great theoretical flowering that feminism experienced in its 'second wave', at its height in the 1960s, was something in which analytic philosophy did not, and could not, take any part. Analytic philosophy, fussing about logic and language, had no truck with women's issues. Those who might have feminist proclivities were considered by the men of analytic philosophy radical, threatening, and inevitably 'hysterical'. Things could turn ugly, as they had in Sydney, where the patriarchy had actively hit back against its critics.[14] The small contingent of women operating in philosophical environments where the analytic tradition prevailed, insofar as they were drawn to feminist causes and ideas, needed to look beyond the analytic tradition. To be a feminist philosopher was to throw in one's lot, for better or worse, with 'continentals' of various stripes. Prominent feminist philosophers in this period who had got PhDs in philosophy departments, such as Iris Marion Young and Judith Butler, found academic jobs in departments outside philosophy.

Before 1990, to be a feminist philosopher was to be out in the wilderness as far as analytic philosophy was concerned: there was, as yet, no

13 Cohen, 'Introduction', pp. xxi–xxiv.

14 See Chapter 6, above.

analytic feminism.[15] In the 1980s, some philosophers trained in the analytic tradition did publish significant feminist works.[16] But it was still necessary in this period for feminist philosophers to reach outside the analytic tradition. Thematically, the emphasis in the 1980s was on the question of the masculinity of reason.[17] That theme was bound to sit uncomfortably with analytic philosophy. If reason was somehow masculine, where did that leave the rationality of women, and thus their ability to wield the tools of analytic philosophy? Should women in philosophy be content to think of themselves as more 'emotional' than their male colleagues, or was that to make a fatal concession?

The feminist field within which analytic philosophers could operate changed dramatically in the 1990s, as the notion gained pace that there could be a distinctively analytic feminism capable of tackling such questions head-on. In 1991, the logician Virginia Klenk founded the Society for Analytical Feminism as a subgroup of the American Philosophical Association. The most influential figures in the development of the new analytic feminism, Sally Haslanger and Rae Langton, had met in the late 1980s in Princeton University's philosophy department, where Haslanger was an assistant professor and Langton a doctoral student. Haslanger was an American whose work so far had been on the metaphysics of persistence and change. Langton, born in India to missionary parents, had attended the University of Sydney – where, having spent time between its two philosophy departments, she settled for the analytic department, or 'Traditional and Modern Philosophy' as it was called – and was now writing her PhD on Kant's *Critique of Pure Reason*.[18] Haslanger and Langton would later be reunited at one of the most prestigious of all American institutions, MIT, where Haslanger gained a position in 1998 and Langton in 2004. Haslanger has remained at MIT; Langton now holds the prestigious Knightbridge Professorship at the University of Cambridge in England.

---

15 It is debatable precisely when analytic feminism got underway. My concern, however, is with analytic feminism as an institutionally viable formation with significant momentum, and with significant recognition in the broader sphere of analytic philosophy.

16 See, for example, Alison M. Jaggar, *Feminist Politics and Human Nature*.

17 See, for example, Genevieve Lloyd, *The Man of Reason: 'Male' and 'Female' in Western Philosophy*.

18 The Princeton department initially failed Langton's PhD dissertation, although it was already under contract with Oxford University Press as *Kantian Humility*. See Langton's section on 'career lowlights' on her personal page at newn.cam.ac.uk.

In the early 1990s, Haslanger and Langton turned from their previous concerns – with metaphysics and with Kant, respectively – to produce a series of key writings that would put analytic feminism on the map. Throughout these writings, their point of departure was the work of the American legal scholar and feminist activist Catharine MacKinnon. MacKinnon's work was particularly well suited to analytic treatment. A concern central to her activism – counteracting the effects of pornography on women – took on a highly specific form dictated by the contingencies of the US legal context within which she was working.[19] In the United States, pre-existing debates concerning the legal regulation of pornography were framed in terms of First Amendment rights to free speech, with pornography treated as if it were a form of speech. MacKinnon and her collaborator Andrea Dworkin devised a feminist response to free-speech arguments defending the production of pornography that turned such arguments on their head, directing attention to the way in which pornography was capable, as they conceived things, of infringing women's speech rights. In 1983 they drafted a feminist ordinance that would make it possible for women to bring civil lawsuits against pornographers on the basis that their civil rights had been infringed; though considered in various cities, including Minneapolis and Indianapolis, the ordinance was never implemented. The nature of MacKinnon's approach – especially as framed in terms of speech – lent itself to further elaboration in terms of the speech act theory of J. L. Austin, a possibility that Langton was a pioneer in exploiting.

Despite the appropriateness of the specifically American legal arguments put by MacKinnon for being recast in Austinian form, in other ways MacKinnon's work makes a startling choice of source and reference point for analytic feminism.[20] It is difficult to convey the nature of her writing to those who have not encountered it at first hand. Her style is highly impassioned and her views extremely uncompromising. Many

---

19 Another crucial concern of MacKinnon's was sexual harassment. It is largely due to MacKinnon's tireless efforts that both the term 'sexual harassment' itself, and the problem it stands for, have the recognition they do today. This aspect of MacKinnon's work has been less important for analytic feminists than it has been for the world at large.

20 MacKinnon's continuing status as the key reference point for analytic feminists is reflected in Kate Manne, *Down Girl: The Logic of Misogyny*, a recent book popularizing analytic feminism. MacKinnon's is the first proper name mentioned in the body of the text.

of her best-known texts are, as she liked to emphasize, 'unmodified' printings of lectures. One such text, very frequently cited by analytic feminists, is 'Francis Biddle's Sister', given as the 1984 Francis Biddle Memorial Lecture at Harvard Law School. MacKinnon urged her audience to reflect that Francis Biddle, the chief American judge at the Nuremberg trials, 'had a sister', and that 'we don't know a thing Francis Biddle's sister said, much less in her own words'.[21] Here, she defined pornography (in close conformity to the ordinance she had co-written with Andrea Dworkin),

> as the graphic sexually explicit subordination of women through pictures or words that also includes women dehumanized as sexual objects, things, or commodities; enjoying pain or humiliation or rape; being tied up, cut up, mutilated, bruised, or physically hurt; in postures of sexual submission or servility or display; reduced to body parts, penetrated by objects or animals, or presented in scenarios of degradation, injury, torture; shown as filthy or inferior; bleeding, bruised, or hurt in a context that makes these conditions sexual.[22]

For MacKinnon, the difference between rape and other kinds of heterosexual acts was a subtle one within 'rape culture' – which is how she understood advanced capitalist society as a whole. The very relationship between men and women in such a society was one of 'subordination', and that subordination was inherently 'eroticized'. It is important to realize how specific these claims are: for MacKinnon, the subordination to which women are subject is, of its nature, (hetero-)sexual.

That MacKinnon should have provided the foundational texts for analytic feminism is startling in a number of ways. Apart from her uncompromising and impassioned rhetoric, far removed from the bloodless pedantry of analytic philosophy, her vociferously anti-liberal strain of Marxism made it a considerable feat to repurpose her ideas for a set of liberal arguments, as Langton would go on to do. These efforts by analytic philosophers to take on MacKinnon's insights, furthermore, coincided with the emergence at just this time of third-wave feminism, which challenged MacKinnon's approach in fundamental ways. The

21 Catharine A. MacKinnon, 'Francis Biddle's Sister', in *Feminism Unmodified: Discourses on Life and Law*, pp. 195–6.

22 Ibid., p. 176.

'sex positivity' of much of the third wave provided a challenge to the idea of women as inherently subordinated by male eroticization. The 'intersectionality' pioneered by the activist and legal scholar Kimberlé Crenshaw worked to complicate things further. Intersectionality would set large traps for analytic philosophers, whose efforts to evacuate themselves from the varieties of concrete lived experience subjected them to the constant risk of reducing intersectionality to a metric of abstract 'axes' of oppression. Further challenges were posed by the queer theory likewise rising up in this period. Here, the challenges seem insurmountable: the straight reading of texts is so baked in to analytic philosophy that it would be difficult to imagine how its practitioners might even attempt to counteract it.

As Langton and Haslanger set to work bringing MacKinnon's second-wave ideas into the analytic fold, they produced a series of papers setting the tone for the new analytic feminism. Langton's first feminist publication, in 1990, was 'Whose Right? Ronald Dworkin, Women, and Pornographers', published in analytic philosophy's home for 'applied' philosophy, *Philosophy and Public Affairs*. Ronald Dworkin – no relation, either familially or intellectually, of Andrea Dworkin – was a well-heeled establishment liberal professor equally at home in Harvard and Oxford. Langton turned Dworkin's liberal defence of the right to produce and consume pornography on its head, aiming to show, by working 'entirely within the Dworkinian theoretical system' and using arguments 'modeled closely on Dworkin's own', that the 'radical feminist' argument against the legality of pornography 'is not only consistent with Dworkin's liberalism, but is . . . demanded by it'.[23] The paper ingeniously overturned Dworkin's argument by appeal to MacKinnon's 'feminist civil rights argument about pornography'.[24] Even in its appeal to MacKinnon, however, the approach remained confined within liberal parameters: the argument to show that women's civil rights win out over the rights of the producers and consumers of pornography was couched entirely in terms of the status of the relevant rights as conceived in liberal theory.

In a second article for *Philosophy and Public Affairs*, 'Speech Acts and Unspeakable Acts', published in 1993, Langton brought J. L. Austin into the picture – Austin and MacKinnon, as she put it, 'emerging as close,

23 Rae Langton, 'Whose Right? Ronald Dworkin, Women, and Pornographers', pp. 312–13.

24 Ibid., p. 331.

if unlikely, cousins'.[25] Containing the classic exposition of Langton's claim that pornography not only subordinates but also silences women, the paper is now a set piece of analytic feminism given to undergraduate students wherever analytic philosophy reigns. The claim is meant quite literally: it is not that the production, dissemination and/or consumption of pornography have the further effect, somewhere down the line, of subordinating and silencing women; pornography itself does so. The identification of pornography with speech is crucial to this – in the words with which Langton opens the paper: 'Pornography is speech.'[26] The squaring of Austin with MacKinnon is felicitous, in that, just as agents *do* certain things by performing speech acts, rather than merely bringing them about as effects, so pornography – when defined as performing speech acts – can be said to *do* such things as subordinate and silence women. Such speech acts have, in Austin's terminology, 'illocutionary' force: they bring about what they state. Speech can perform the 'illocutionary act' of subordination; for instance, someone invested with the authority to declare that 'blacks are not permitted to vote' not only *says* something subordinating, but, in saying it, 'subordinates blacks'.[27] As Langton points out, MacKinnon uses a 'striking list of illocutionary verbs' when talking about pornography: 'Pornography sexualizes rape, battery, sexual harassment . . . and child sexual abuse; it . . . *celebrates*, *promotes*, *authorizes* and *legitimates* them.'[28] Not only that, but pornography performs what Langton calls 'illocutionary disablement'.[29] Pornography silences women by making it the case, Langton argues, that a woman's saying 'no' to sex is an instance of illocutionary disablement: because her authority has been removed, her saying it fails to have illocutionary force. Pornography does this: 'The felicity conditions for women's speech acts are set by the speech acts of pornography.'[30]

Langton had made MacKinnon fit Austin's theory by imagining pornography as constituted by speech acts – a regimentation with which MacKinnon herself would show impatience.[31] In the same year,

25 Rae Langton, 'Speech Acts and Unspeakable Acts', p. 297.

26 Ibid., p. 293.

27 Ibid., p. 302.

28 MacKinnon, 'Francis Biddle's Sister', quoted in ibid., p. 307 (Langton's emphases).

29 Langton, 'Speech Acts and Unspeakable Acts', p. 315.

30 Ibid., p. 324.

31 Lorna Finlayson, 'How to Screw Things with Words', adverts to MacKinnon's criticisms of Langton in the course of a critique of Langton.

1993, as Langton's classic Austinian paper, Haslanger's first published work of analytic feminism, 'On Being Objective and Being Objectified', appeared in a collection of essays edited by Louise Antony and Charlotte Witt entitled *A Mind of One's Own: Feminist Essays on Reason and Objectivity.* As the subtitle of the collection makes clear, the masculinity, or otherwise, of reason was here still a central theme. Haslanger's contribution examined one of MacKinnon's most ambitious claims: that there was, in MacKinnon's words, a 'relation between objectification, the hierarchy between self as being and other as thing, and objectivity, the hierarchy between the knowing subject and the known object'. As MacKinnon went on to say about her own feminist theory of the state,

> Epistemology and politics emerged as two mutually enforcing sides of the same unequal coin. A theory of the state which was at once social and discrete, conceptual and applied, became possible as the state was seen to participate in the sexual politics of male dominance by enforcing its epistemology through law.[32]

Haslanger set out in her essay to evaluate MacKinnon's claim that objectification is sustained by the epistemological ideal of objectivity. Having taken over MacKinnon's notion that (in Haslanger's words) 'one is a man by virtue of standing in a position of eroticized dominance over others; one is a woman by virtue of standing in a position of eroticized submission to others', she now asked whether MacKinnon was, further, right to claim (in MacKinnon's words) that 'objectivity is the epistemological stance of which objectification is the social process, of which male dominance is the politics, the acted-out social practice'.[33] Haslanger found the premises of MacKinnon's argument for this claim to be 'seriously overstated' and her basic strategy 'deeply flawed'.[34] Objectivity was, according to Haslanger, only 'weakly masculine'. In particular, an ideal of 'assumed objectivity' (comprising neutrality and aperspectivity) served to shore up men's social role. Objectivity was not, however, as MacKinnon would have it, 'strongly masculine': the ideal of

32 Catharine A. MacKinnon, *Toward a Feminist Theory of the State*, p. xi.

33 Sally Haslanger, 'On Being Objective and Being Objectified', in *Resisting Reality: Social Construction and Social Critique*, pp. 59 and (quoting MacKinnon) 63–4.

34 Ibid., p. 77.

objectivity was not 'sufficient for being a sexual objectifier'.[35] Nowhere did Haslanger's argument make contact with social reality; nowhere were MacKinnon's claims that what it is to be a woman is to suffer eroticized domination at the hands of men seriously scrutinized. Curiously, in an essay whose theme is conceptions of reason as neutral, Haslanger commented, without apparent irony: 'I will try to remain as neutral as possible on the issue of what counts as reason or rationality.'[36]

Haslanger's later work has dropped MacKinnon's concern with ideals of objectivity. But it retains the conception of women as defined by subordination. To analytic philosophers, Haslanger's message that to be a woman is to perform a social role, and that the concept 'woman' is a social construct, appears revelatory. To them, it is confounding that anything socially constructed could be real; after all, for them, the paradigm of what is real is small physical items like atoms, or bigger physical items like pieces of furniture, not people or institutions.[37] Haslanger's treatment of 'woman' as socially constructed, however, finds itself ill-served by her reliance on schematic notions, inherited from MacKinnon, of what this might mean. In a 2005 paper, 'What Are We Talking About?', Haslanger began to speak of her project as 'ameliorative'. Her principal question, 'What is a woman?' was to be understood, she claimed, not in terms of mere analysis of the concept as used, or the refinement of the concept through empirical study, but as an enquiry into uses to which the concept might be better put than it had been hitherto.[38] What better use is the concept 'woman' to be put to? Haslanger cannot say, having trapped herself in MacKinnon's predicament, which does not afford any indication of how to progress beyond the critical claim that women are subordinated.

The root of the difficulties MacKinnon has freighted Haslanger with here can be traced back to MacKinnon's claim that the society in which

35 Ibid., p. 76.

36 Ibid., p. 38.

37 At this point, the analytic philosopher will typically express wonder at the fact that a $10 bill really is worth $10, even though it is just a piece of paper.

38 Sally Haslanger, 'What Are We Talking About?', in *Resisting Reality*, p. 367. In a footnote, Haslanger noted that the idea of amelioration was modelled on what Quine called an 'explicative' definition. Quine had written in 'Two Dogmas of Empiricism', in a passage that Haslanger quotes, that the point of an explicative definition is 'to improve upon the definiendum by refining or supplementing its meaning'. W. V. Quine, *From a Logical Point of View: Nine Logico-Philosophical Essays*, p. 25.

we live is 'one in which some fuck and others get fucked and everybody knows what those words mean'.[39] Since MacKinnon *defines* women as those who, because they are the fucked, are thereby subordinated, and for her society is divided into the two categories of those who fuck and those who are fucked, what are women to do?[40] A deeper issue, when it comes to its ability to imagine alternatives, is that MacKinnon's theory is too divorced from the complexities of social reality for such imaginative work to get going. In MacKinnon's world, women had best run to the Law to protect themselves, as if running to the Father. (MacKinnon is the daughter of the distinguished lawyer and Republican congressman George MacKinnon.)

MacKinnon's tendency to portray the social world in frightening terms, remote from the complexity of lived experience, imbues her Marxism with a strange hollowness. That hollowness comes back to haunt the project of 'social ontology' that Haslanger has developed out of it and established as a core part of analytic metaphysics.[41] The German scene of 'critical theory' today welcomes analytic philosophers with open arms, and so finds itself on the receiving end of what the latter have made of social ontology. In 2023, Sally Haslanger was invited to give the Walter Benjamin Lectures in Berlin. She opened her first lecture as follows:

> Here I am, an analytic metaphysician, who was an activist for a while, and here I am on this stage. It kind of blows my mind. And it wouldn't really have happened but for Robin [Celikates] and Rahel [Jaeggi], who have transformed me into a critical theorist. Oh my gosh! *Anything* is possible, I guess.[42]

These informal remarks signalling the new amity between analytic philosophy and critical theory – something Neurath and Horkheimer

---

39 MacKinnon, *Toward a Feminist Theory of the State*, p. 4.

40 As the American legal scholar, philosopher and activist Drucilla Cornell wrote, 'in MacKinnon's world of "fuckees" and "fuckors", an obviously heterosexual social reality, the only possible alternative to being a "fuckee" is to be a "fuckor".' Drucilla Cornell, *Beyond Accommodation: Ethical Feminism, Deconstruction, and the Law*, p. 132.

41 See, again, the influential textbook treatment given in Alyssa Ney, *Metaphysics: An Introduction*, Chapters 5–6.

42 'Sally Haslanger: Benjamin Lecture 1 – Who's in Charge Here? Micro, Meso, Macro Interactions', at youtube.com.

had been unable to achieve – disguise the fact that, in reality, Haslanger had not been transformed into a critical theorist at all. Instead, a Marxist tradition, having travelled to America, was being sold back to its inheritors having suffered a reduction to the status of analytic philosophy. Haslanger set out to teach her Berlin audience that 'our contemporary social order is a complex system with multiple co-integrated subsystems'. Full of insights into the complex ways efforts to resist or subvert that system in its multiply complex and interrelated functioning can themselves be rechannelled by the system in its own interests, the lectures were nonetheless even more lacking in concrete cultural, historical, economic material than what is found in MacKinnon's work. The Berlin audience was being sold, not a new critical theory, but the old analytic philosophy in new clothes.

Standpoint Theory and Epistemic Injustice: Fricker

In the wake of Haslanger and Langton's pioneering work in the 1990s, the most notable contribution to analytic feminism has been that of the British philosopher Miranda Fricker, whose *Epistemic Injustice* (2007) has been highly influential in analytic philosophy circles and beyond.[43] The book is concerned with two principal ways in which someone can be wronged in their capacity as a 'knower' – testimonial injustice, where a speaker is not taken as seriously as they should be, and hermeneutical injustice, where an agent experiences an epistemic deficit thanks to structural social factors that impede their capacity to form a proper understanding of their own situation.

Having studied modern languages and philosophy at Oxford, Fricker found her love of literature trumped by her predilection for philosophical analysis. After taking an MA in women's studies at the University of Kent, she returned to Oxford for a doctorate in philosophy.[44] She now devoted her efforts to attempting to rescue feminism from the clutches of 'postmodernism'. Since then, Fricker has held a series of positions in British and American universities, culminating in the Julius Silver Professorship at New York University.

---

43 According to Google Scholar, the book has been cited 10,762 times (as of 22 May 2024). David Lewis's *Convention* had (as of the same date) been cited 10,198 times, his *On the Plurality of Worlds* 10,119 times, and Kripke's *Naming and Necessity* 19,893 times.

44 This was the UK's first MA in women's studies, launched in 1980.

Fricker has taken a more sceptical approach to MacKinnon than have Langton and Haslanger, instead repurposing feminist standpoint theory, which shares with MacKinnon's work a Marxist and anti-liberal orientation, for liberal purposes.[45] In her classic exposition of feminist standpoint theory, the American political scientist Nancy Hartsock had offered to 'set off from Marx's proposal that a correct vision of class society is available from only one of the two major class positions in capitalist society'. Analogously to the lives of proletarians for Marx, she argued, 'women's lives make available a particular and privileged vantage point on male supremacy, a vantage point which can ground a powerful critique of the phallocratic institutions and ideology which constitute the capitalist form of patriarchy'.[46] In support of this thesis, Hartsock drew on a wealth of material, from the psychoanalytic work of Nancy Chodorow to the literary studies of Georges Bataille.

In *Epistemic Injustice*, a book that initiated its own body of literature within analytic feminism, Fricker limited her acknowledgement of this background in the work of Hartsock and feminist standpoint theory more generally to one page.[47] In an earlier paper, however, she had credited the idea of 'epistemic oppression' to Hartsock, and explicitly discussed how she sought to modify Hartsock's standpoint theory. She urged there that 'there are problems with the Marxist formulation that impede the insight's having the epistemological impact it deserves', and offered to free the topic of epistemic injustice from the dead hand of 'such a monolithic and even moribund theory as Marx's'.[48]

Fricker objected to Hartsock's treatment of women, on the Marxist model, as a class. To Hartsock's 'rather bleak view of women's unpaid domestic labour', she offered an 'empirical' objection, to the effect that women's activity is 'not so uniform as standpoint theory requires'.[49] Women do much apart from domestic labour, Fricker urged, and anyway, men are helping more with domestic labour than used to be the case: 'shared domestic labour between men and women has

45 For the Marxist roots of standpoint theory, see the discussion of the 'standpoint of the proletariat' in Georg Lukács, *History and Class Consciousness: Studies in Marxist Dialectics*, pp. 149–209.

46 Nancy C. M. Hartsock, 'The Feminist Standpoint: Developing the Ground for a Specifically Feminist Historical Materialism', p. 284.

47 Miranda Fricker, *Epistemic Injustice: Power and the Ethics of Knowing*, p. 147.

48 Miranda Fricker, 'Epistemic Oppression and Epistemic Privilege', p. 192.

49 Ibid., p. 195.

increased'.[50] The most striking part of Fricker's paper is a section entitled, with some irony in light of the nature of her modification of Hartsock away from Marxism in the direction of liberalism, 'A Radical Re-think'. Fricker here offered to 'substitute talk of women's "social experience" for the vocabulary of women's "labour"'.[51] The class category crucial to Hartsock's argument could now be got rid of, to be replaced by an amorphous 'social world' inhabited by an undefined 'we', loosely derived from Wittgenstein's 'forms of life'. Epistemic oppression was now no longer, as for the Marxists, a matter of one group suffering at the hands of another, and so being motivated to counter this oppression in its own class interests. Instead, Fricker wrote, 'epistemic oppression arises from a situation in which the social experiences of the powerless are not properly integrated into collective understandings of the social world'.[52] The concerns of women as a class are dissipated into the 'collective understandings' of the amorphous societal 'we'. Concomitantly, the realities of material life can find no place, and give way to a completely intellectualist understanding of how epistemic oppression is to be countered. Fricker finds herself puzzled by Dorothy Smith's injunction, characteristic of standpoint theory, to 'start thought from marginalized lives' (a turn of phrase given wide currency by the work of Sandra Harding). In grappling with what Smith could possibly have meant, Fricker is unable to offer anything but: 'starting thought from marginalized lives is something we may be able to do, and something we should do as lovers of truth and understanding'.[53]

Others, outside analytic philosophy, such as the American sociology professor Patricia Hill Collins, have discussed the phenomena of epistemic oppression with deft and detailed attention to concrete social reality.[54] The contrast with Fricker's handling of the same phenomena is instructive. By recasting the issues in terms of standard liberal philosophy, and offering them up for consumption within a sphere in which the assumptions of liberalism do not so much as show up as challengeable, Fricker limits the power of her ideas as tools of social understanding. While she uses such examples of testimonial injustice as Black people being disbelieved by the police, the idea of challenging the police as an institution is never presented as a possibility. She even

50 Ibid., p. 199.
51 Ibid., p. 201.
52 Ibid., p. 208.
53 Ibid., p. 209.
54 See Patricia Hill Collins, *Black Feminist Thought.*

writes that her work identifying the virtues of epistemic justice helps to 'lay a foundation for a conception of correlative institutional virtues – virtues possessed, for instance, by the judiciary, the police, local government, and employers'.[55] The institutions of the liberal order are not only assumed as given, but are even treated as coming with their own 'virtues' attached.

Although Fricker's overtly liberal feminism is highly distinct from Haslanger's ameliorative social ontology in the guise of a version of critical theory, as also from Langton's Austinian critique of pornography, here too it is assumed that the aim is, as Judith Butler has put it in discussing MacKinnon and Langton, to 'devise a communicative speech situation in which speech acts are grounded in consensus where no speech act is permissible that performatively refutes another's ability to consent through speech'.[56] Analytic feminism is united in serving the Habermasian project of devising the perfect conditions for the operation of a liberal communicative marketplace.[57] The flipside of this concern with the liberal communicative marketplace is its inability to get a grip on social reality. Sometimes it is necessary, in dealing with social reality, to grapple with the material lived experience of actual individuals. An indicator of this is what happens when analytic philosophers attempt to deal with the complexities of trans identity. Haslanger has felt the need to issue the following retraction of her earlier handling of the terms 'man' and 'woman':

> For example, by appropriating the terms 'woman' and 'man', I problematically excluded some women from being counted as women and some men from being counted as men. Although my view does *not* require that one have male genitalia to be a man or female genitalia to be a woman, it does require being subject to subordination/privilege that is linked by ideology to the local bodily markers of reproductive role. This is a mistake: some women are prevented from presenting as women, and some men are prevented from presenting as men, and so do not meet the conditions I proposed.[58]

55 Fricker, *Epistemic Injustice*, p. 176.

56 Judith Butler, *Excitable Speech: A Politics of the Performative*, p. 86.

57 Butler goes on to say that 'neither Langton nor MacKinnon consults Habermas' (ibid.). Langton actually does consult Habermas: see her 'Speech Acts and Unspeakable Acts', p. 315*n*44.

58 Sally Haslanger, 'Going On, Not in the Same Way', p. 236.

The underlying problem with this is that analytic philosophy struggles to treat the people being discussed here, and their lived experience, as something other than counters in a game. Schematic formulae purporting to define 'man' and 'woman' in terms of necessary and sufficient conditions will not provide the requisite illumination.

Analytic Philosophy of Race: Appiah's Framework

Haslanger has argued that the schematic approach she applies to gender can, *pari passu*, be transferred to the case of race. She provides parallel definitions for the social constructs 'woman' and 'racialized group', as follows:

> *S is a woman* iff_{df} S is systematically subordinated along some dimension (economic, political, legal, social, etc.), and S is 'marked' as a target for this treatment by observed or imagined bodily features presumed to be evidence of a female's biological role in reproduction.

> A group is *racialized* iff_{df} its members are socially positioned as subordinate or privileged along some dimension (economic, political, legal, social, etc.), and the group is 'marked' as a target for this treatment by observed or imagined bodily features presumed to be evidence of ancestral links to a certain geographical region.[59]

Such a schematism of oppression leaves out of account the actual social texture of how either misogyny or racialization work. In Haslanger's work, there is no actual philosophy of race to speak of, if that is thought to involve discussion of the history and reproduction of racialization in concrete terms.

Insofar as there is a distinctively analytic philosophy of race, the terms for its principal debate were, like those of analytic feminism, set in the early 1990s. As the writings of Langton and Haslanger set the original framework for analytic feminism, so analytic philosophy of race takes as its point of departure the work of Kwame Anthony Appiah, in particular Appiah's book *In My Father's House* (1992). Appiah advanced the

59 Sally Haslanger, 'Gender and Race: (What) Are They? (What) Do We Want Them to Be?', in *Resisting Reality*, pp. 230, 236. The notation 'iff_{df}' indicates that what comes after it is a definition of what comes before it.

position that became known as 'eliminativism', which advocates the elimination of the category of race altogether.[60] In response to Appiah, analytic philosophers of race have spent a great deal of time debating whether races exist. Even if many have disagreed with Appiah's own view, it is within the framework of such questions that much of the analytic philosophy of race has been conducted.

Appiah was born in London, the son of Joe Appiah, a Ghanaian politician, and his wife Peggy Cripps, descended from an English dynasty of political landed gentry. His childhood was divided between Ghana and Bryanston School, a 'public school' (private boarding school) in the English countryside. There, as he recalled in his book, he 'learned that not everybody had family in Africa and in Europe; not everyone had a Lebanese uncle, American and French and Kenyan and Thai cousins'.[61]

Appiah was, he wrote, taught by his father 'to be as completely untempted by racism as he was'.[62] For him, as for his father, racism was simply something to be rejected. In his book, he accordingly criticized the works of the African American anti-racism campaigners Alexander Crummell and W. E. B. Du Bois. Against their invocation of the idea of an African race, he urged his readers instead to 'reject the rhetoric of descent'.[63] African self-consciousness about race imported experiences of racism from America, where they were genuine enough; it had not similarly emerged on African soil. White Europeans had, it was true, colonized Africa, but Africans had only experienced 'an essentially shallow penetration by the coloniser'.[64] Crummell, far from connecting with an indigenous African tradition, was, Appiah wrote, 'one of the first people to speak *as* a Negro in Africa: and his writings effectively inaugurated the discourse of Pan-Africanism'.[65] Du Bois, like Crummell, erroneously spoke of races as if they were real. But, according to Appiah, 'the truth is that there are no races: there is nothing in the world that can do all we ask race to do for us'. It was not only biological conceptions of race that were to be rejected; even what Crummell and

60 Appiah's position has changed in various ways over time. My focus here is on the version of his view that helped to set the terms of the debate, and has been the most influential.

61 Kwame Anthony Appiah, *In My Father's House*, p. ix.

62 Ibid., p. xi.

63 'Rejecting the rhetoric of descent requires a rethinking of Pan-Africanist politics' (ibid., p. xiv).

64 Ibid., p. 8.

65 Ibid., p. 5.

Du Bois talked about under the heading of race 'refers to nothing in the world at all'. It was not, it turned out, race that was the problem, but merely the *concept* of race: 'The evil that is done is done by the concept, and by easy – yet impossible – assumptions as to its application.'[66] As for Fricker, for Appiah oppression and what to do about it seemed to be a curiously intellectual matter.

Appiah has been widely criticized for painting a 'Eurocentric history of colonialism' through which he 'would like his reader to believe that colonialism was a civilizing mission'.[67] For our purposes here, however, the most significant feature of his contribution is the way it spawned a literature focused on the use of the term 'race' itself. As Quayshawn Spencer, a professor of philosophy at the University of Pennsylvania, has put it, 'What is race? Is race real? Is it biologically real? Is it a real social construct? Is it both? Is it real in a different way? Is race not real at all? These are the main questions that metaphysicians of race have addressed since the 1990s.'[68] In 2019, Spencer, together with Sally Haslanger and fellow American philosophers Joshua Glasgow and Chike Jeffers, published a book setting out their respective positions on the philosophy of race.[69] Spencer presented himself as a 'naturalist' about race, for whom there really are biological races, without this justifying any 'social hierarchy among the races'. For Jeffers and Haslanger, by contrast, races are merely 'socially constructed groups'; where, for Jeffers, these groups are cultural, for Haslanger they are sociopolitical. According to Glasgow, 'the concept of race includes, as a necessary condition, that there be a set of visible features that are disproportionately held by each race'.[70]

What these authors hold in common is, first of all, a concern with what races are (if anything) – a question they largely examine by asking how 'competent users of English' use the word 'race'. In addition, they are all concerned with what Glasgow calls 'the Normative Question' – whether to 'keep or abandon racial discourse'.[71] Such debates, in which race is made the topic of abstract philosophical theorizing, have not

---

66 Ibid., p. 72.

67 Victor O. Okafor, 'An Afrocentric Critique of Appiah's *In My Father's House*', p. 202.

68 Quayshawn Spencer, 'A More Radical Solution to the Race Problem'.

69 Joshua Glasgow, Sally Haslanger, Chike Jeffers and Quayshawn Spencer, *What is Race? Four Philosophical Views*.

70 Ibid., p. 2.

71 Joshua Glasgow, *A Theory of Race*, p. 3.

been without salutary effect. For one thing, they have created a presence for the topic of race in analytic philosophy, with symposia held at the discipline's flagship annual conferences (such as the American Philosophical Association's Eastern Division meeting, or, in Britain, the Joint Session of the Mind Association and Aristotelian Society) routinely being devoted to the topic. But they are severely limiting. It does not require special philosophical tools to discover that race is a social construct and that race is real. Activist work has always been well ahead of such evident truths, while analytic philosophers remain, at best, caught up in their careful recalibration; at worst, they threaten a regress into the conceptual space of Appiah's father's house.

Critical Race Theory for Liberals

Much of the analytic philosophy of race that flowed from Appiah's focus on the existence or otherwise of races operated in splendid isolation from the burgeoning movement of critical race theory, whose key founding figure was the lawyer, legal scholar and activist Derrick Bell.[72] Critical race theory emerged in the 1970s, out of a frustration with ways in which the achievements of the Civil Rights movement of the 1960s had stagnated, or were even being subverted. It had in common with such diverse approaches to feminism as MacKinnon's and Hartsock's an origin in basically Marxist forms of social analysis, seeking to understand and counteract the material bases of historically produced forms of oppression. As Richard Delgado and Jean Stefancic put it, 'critical race theory questions the very foundations of the liberal order, including equality theory, legal reasoning, Enlightenment rationalism, and neutral principles of constitutional law'.[73] It considers race to be socially constructed, racism to be the norm rather than the exception, and racialization to be differential. Analogous to the 'feminist standpoint' advocated by Hartsock and others is the important role within it of the 'legal storytelling' movement, which seeks to give due credence to the narratives of the racialized.

The tendency for analytic philosophy to remain insulated from critical race theory has been, to a significant extent, mitigated by the work

72 For an excellent primer, see Richard Delgado and Jean Stefancic, *Critical Race Theory: An Introduction.*

73 Ibid., p. 3.

of Charles Mills, a philosopher with strong analytic sympathies who has in turn been well received within analytic philosophy. Mills, who had grown up in Jamaica and studied physics at the University of the West Indies, wrote his PhD dissertation at the University of Toronto on 'The Concept of Ideology in the Thought of Marx and Engels'. His supervisor, Danny Goldstick, who had done his own doctoral work under the supervision of A. J. Ayer at Oxford, combined analytic philosophy with activism in the Communist Party of Canada. Mills, himself certainly a Marxist sympathizer, was at the same time influenced by analytic philosophy, characterizing his work as explicitly a 'dissertation in philosophy' that 'approached the subject matter with an eye to such traditional concerns as the meaning of the term ("ideology")'.[74]

Mills made his mark with *The Racial Contract*, published in 1997, a book which he himself said 'could be seen as an example' of critical race theory.[75] Modelled on the British feminist scholar Carole Pateman's *The Sexual Contract* (1988), it differed in significant ways from standard analytic philosophy of race in its historical treatment of its subject matter. Mills sought not only to criticize the 'racial contract' under which racialized people have to live, as a present reality, but to understand it in terms of its historical emergence. The social contract as presented in the theories of Hobbes, Locke and Rousseau, Mills argued, far from being the fair contract between all free people that they presented it as, was a contract between whites (who substituted themselves for universal humanity). Contrary to appearances, only whites were signatories to the contract; non-whites were 'the objects rather than the subjects of the agreement'.[76]

Mills's historical argument struck at the core of the liberal project – to that extent, Mills seemed aligned with the fundamentally anti-liberal stance of critical race theory. He excoriated the tendency of whites to conflate themselves with universal humanity, as when he wrote, with biting irony, of 'persons, whites'.[77] Nevertheless, and for all the fault Mills found with the Rawlsian project, he was amenable to a reconstruction of liberalism. By contrast with Pateman, who subjected contractual thinking itself to critique, Mills was happy with a contract, so long as it was fair. Even in the face of the deep defects of Rawls's

---

74 Charles W. Mills, 'The Concept of Ideology in the Thought of Marx and Engels', p. iv.

75 Charles W. Mills, *The Racial Contract*, p. 126.

76 Ibid., p. 12.

77 Ibid., p. 17.

liberal project, including its structural blindness to race, Mills tirelessly sought to find means to rebuild such a project so as to overcome these defects, instead of regarding it as irremediably a principal source of the problem.[78] In effect, then, the most powerful advocate of critical race theory known to analytic philosophers led his followers back into the ideology of liberalism, not away from it.

The Logic of Colonization

Analytic philosophy simply cannot help thinking of itself as just philosophy as such – not unlike the way in which, as Charles Mills underlined, whites simply cannot help thinking of themselves as just humanity as such. There is, analytic philosophers like to say, only 'good' and 'bad' philosophy – one is left to draw the inference by oneself that the 'good' philosophy is the kind that analytic philosophers approve of. 'Bad' philosophy can become 'good' if it meets the bar of assimilation into the analytic mode. Thus, even Heidegger and Derrida can turn out to be producers of 'good' philosophy. Analytic philosophy professors can write about them and teach them to their students, with the 'continental' literature on them eventually to be displaced by analytically orientated secondary literature.

This phenomenon is at its most insidious, and even perverse, where what analytic philosophy has set about colonizing are the oppositional, anti-oppressive discourses of feminism and critical race theory: it colonizes even the anti-colonial. Furthermore, it exercises its colonial effect even on the drive to decolonize the curriculum. Efforts to reform the philosophy curriculum in universities go back to the 1960s.[79] In the late 2010s, a new wave of such efforts gathered pace under the banner of 'decolonizing the curriculum', against the background of the Black Lives Matter movement that had begun in 2013 in protest at the acquittal for second-degree murder of a man who had shot dead the seventeen-year-old Trayvon Martin in Sanford, Florida, and was further fuelled by the deaths the following year of Michael Brown in Ferguson, Missouri, and Eric Garner in New York City. A spike in public awareness of the movement after

78 See Charles W. Mills, *Black Rights/White Wrongs: The Critique of Racial Liberalism.*

79 See Chapter 6, above.

the murder of George Floyd in Minneapolis in 2020 led to further protests.

In 2014, University College London produced an online video entitled 'Why Is My Curriculum White?', featuring students and academics.[80] In 2015, students at the University of Cape Town initiated the 'Rhodes Must Fall' campaign. Such efforts brought about a higher level of consciousness about the 'whiteness' of the curriculum in philosophy, as in other disciplines. A leading issue was the contrast between the whiteness of what was being taught and the diversity of the student body – a disconnection that was thought to make the curriculum alienating and 'irrelevant'. Another was the question of the replication of colonial discourses itself.

Philosophy here found itself in a peculiar position. It is a characteristic of analytic philosophers, as this book has explored, that they lack consciousness of their own status as the upholders of a hegemonic version of their discipline. They are just philosophers. They are what it is to be a philosopher; the question of what else it might be to be a philosopher does not so much as come up, since it is written into analytic philosophy's self-conception that it leaves no stone unturned. As a result of this (lack of) self-conception, analytic philosophy importantly lacks a notion of the difference between itself and 'Western philosophy'. If analytic philosophers were to reflect on the question of their relationship to Western philosophy as a whole, they would find a highly specific, repeated pattern. The pattern is that practitioners of analytic philosophy, in its leading, Anglophone domains, have always widely promoted the scholarly study of Plato, and more narrowly the scholarly study of Aristotle. When it comes to later periods, there has been selective study of Descartes, Leibniz, Hume and Kant, but in a less scholarly and more anachronistic vein. (The difference in levels of scholarship, and the tendency to greater anachronism in the study of 'modern', that is, post-1492, philosophy, owes much to the traditional Oxford training in 'Greats', which cultivates high levels of proficiency in ancient Greek, but not in modern languages.) Analytic philosophers, however, tend not to question their relationship to Western philosophy as a whole. Worse, when it comes to the decolonization of the curriculum, they tend to make an entirely uncritical use of the concept 'Western philosophy' as a contrast class to what it is felt needs to be promoted in order to counteract the coloniality of the curriculum – 'non-Western philosophy'.

80 'Why Is My Curriculum White?' (UCL), at youtube.com.

The very notion that decolonization should take the form of the supplementation of 'Western philosophy' with 'non-Western philosophy' is, however, highly dubious. 'The West' is – although analytic philosophers, due to their high levels of studied historical ignorance, tend not to realize this – a political term. Their obliviousness to this is signalled by the frequency with which discussions among them of what is 'Western' or 'non-Western' in philosophy begin from geographical considerations. It ought to be obvious that 'the West' is not a geographical designation, but the name of a political project. The concept of 'the West' which this project underwrites is of much more recent origin than is often thought, gaining currency only in the closing decades of the nineteenth century. Its function was to legitimate the imperialist intensification of the project of global domination through capital, by which whites had gained political and economic ascendancy over the entire globe, begun in the wake of Columbus's 'discovery' of the Caribbean in 1492. The idea of the 'West' implies an 'other': as the Jamaican-born cultural theorist Stuart Hall put it, 'the Rest'.[81]

The South African philosopher Lucy Allais has pointed out the risk, attending efforts to expand the canon, of replicating the logic of colonialism.[82] One risk is the replication of the West/Rest structure. The West gets to 'own' notions such as rationality and objectivity, to which it has laid claim; in light of these proprietary claims, those belonging to the 'Rest' then either have to come up with revised notions of rationality and objectivity of their own, or to reject those notions in favour of something else. The opportunity to question the West's 'ownership' in the first place has then already been foregone.

The manner in which analytic philosophers wield the pair of concepts 'Western philosophy' and 'non-Western philosophy' brings further risks. When it comes to decolonizing the curriculum, analytic philosophers suddenly become oblivious to the difference between Western philosophy, as a tradition, and itself: analytic philosophy. Analytic philosophy departments are to enrich themselves by incorporating into their curriculum 'other' traditions. This denies what analytic philosophy elsewhere asserts: that it is not one tradition – a 'Western' tradition, to be contrasted with other, 'non-Western' traditions – but itself living, breathing philosophy as such, transcending tradition. Thinking of itself

81 Stuart Hall, 'The West and the Rest: Discourse and Power'.

82 Lucy Allais, 'Problematising Western Philosophy as One Part of Africanising the Curriculum'.

as such, it is in fact unable to see itself as the local, ideologically specific tradition that it is: philosophically, an outgrowth of Hume that has bypassed everything in European philosophy since Kant; ideologically, the perpetuation of eighteenth-century liberalism.

The set of alternative traditions – Africana philosophy, Chinese philosophy, indigenous 'American' philosophies, and so on – are cast into a role that is to be expected, given the general way in which analytic philosophy, as the hegemonic form of philosophy in the service of liberal-colonial capital, operates. We saw that analytic philosophers would have feminists enter the liberal marketplace of ideas, neutralizing the 'feminist standpoint' by absorbing it into an amorphous Wittgensteinian 'we', and place critical race theorists back under a 'veil of ignorance', but now factoring historical wrongs into the calculations taken care of under that veil. Similarly, the possibility of decolonial forms of philosophy challenging hegemonic philosophy at its core is circumvented by a pre-emptive colonial stance. 'Non-Western philosophy' can figure as a set of alternatives to the hegemon, now disingenuously refigured as 'Western philosophy'. Connections can be sought between various traditions. But the liberal nucleus is steadfastly preserved intact. Its tremendous fragility must not be challenged, lest its pretensions to inclusivity be unmasked. The tradition of empiricism-liberalism represented by Hume, continued by analytic philosophy in spite of its ignorant self-image as just philosophy as such, rightly trembles at the wrath that might be unleashed by the powerful critical forces that its hegemony helps to keep suppressed.

Bibliography

Adams, Pauline, *Somerville for Women: An Oxford College 1879–1993*, Oxford: Oxford University Press, 1996.

Adorno, Theodor W., and Max Horkheimer, *Briefwechsel*, vol. 1, Frankfurt: Suhrkamp, 1994.

Akehurst, Thomas L., 'The Nazi Tradition: The Analytic Critique of Continental Philosophy in Mid-Century Britain', *History of European Ideas* 34 (2008): 548–57.

——'British Analytic Philosophy: The Politics of an Apolitical Culture', *History of Political Thought* 30 (2009): 678–92.

——*The Cultural Politics of Analytic Philosophy: Britishness and the Spectre of Europe*. London/New York: Continuum, 2010.

Allais, Lucy, 'Problematising Western Philosophy as One Part of Africanising the Curriculum', *South African Journal of Philosophy* 35 (2016): 537–45.

Amadae, S. M., *Rationalizing Capitalist Democracy: The Cold War Origins of Rational Choice Liberalism*, Chicago, IL: University of Chicago Press, 2003.

Anderson, Perry, 'The Minstrels of MI5', *The Isis*, 6 November 1957.

——*Considerations on Western Marxism*, London: NLB, 1976.

Andow, James, 'How "Intuition" Exploded', *Metaphilosophy* 46 (2015): 189–212.

Anellis, Irving H., 'Parry, William Tuthill (1908–88)', in John R. Shook, ed., *Dictionary of Modern American Philosophers*, Bristol: Thoemmes Continuum, 2005.

Anon., 'Aristotelian', *The Athenaeum*, 4570 (29 May 1915): 487.

Anon., 'Mr H. W. B. Joseph', *Manchester Guardian*, 16 November 1943.

Anscombe, G. E. M., *An Introduction to Wittgenstein's* Tractatus, 2nd edn, London: Hutchinson, 1971.

——*Ethics, Religion and Politics*, Oxford: Blackwell, 1981.

——*Human Life, Action and Ethics*, ed. Mary Geach and Luke Gormally, Exeter: Imprint Academic, 2005.

Appiah, Kwame Anthony, *In My Father's House*, London: Methuen, 1992.

Aptheker, Bettina, *The Morning Breaks: The Trial of Angela Davis*, New York: International, 1975.

Arrow, Kenneth J., *Social Choice and Individual Values*, New York: Wiley, 1951.

——'Decision Theory and Operations Research', *Operations Research* 5 (1957): 765–74.

Astroh, Michael, Ivor Grattan-Guinness and Stephen Read, 'A Survey of the Life of Hugh MacColl (1837–1909)', *History and Philosophy of Logic* 22 (2001): 81–98.

Ayer, A. J., *Language, Truth and Logic*, Harmondsworth: Pelican, 1971 [1936].

——'Some Aspects of Existentialism', *Rationalist Annual* (1948): 5–13.

——'The Claims of Philosophy', in *Reflections on Our Age: Lectures Delivered at the Opening Session of UNESCO at the Sorbonne University Paris*, London: Allan Wingate, 1949.

——*Part of My Life*, London: Collins, 1977.

Bacharach, Michael, *Economics and the Theory of Games*, London: Macmillan, 1976.

Bahr, Hermann, *Bilderbuch*, Vienna/Leipzig: Wila, 1921.

Baldwin, Thomas, *G. E. Moore*, London: Routledge, 1990.

Banfield, Ann, *The Phantom Table: Woolf, Fry, Russell and the Epistemology of Modernism*, Cambridge: Cambridge University Press, 2000.

——'Cambridge Bloomsbury', in Victoria Rosner, ed., *The Cambridge Companion to the Bloomsbury Group*, Cambridge: Cambridge University Press, 2014.

Barcan, Ruth C., 'A Functional Calculus of First Order Based on Strict Implication', *Journal of Symbolic Logic* 11 (1946): 1–16.

Barton, Stephen E., 'The Success and Failure of Strong Rent Control in the City of Berkeley, 1978 to 1995', in W. Dennis Keating, Michael B. Teitz and Andrejs Skaburskis, eds, *Rent Control: Regulation and the Rental Housing Market*, Abingdon/New York: Routledge, 1998.

Baz, Avner, *The Crisis of Method in Contemporary Analytic Philosophy*, Oxford: Oxford University Press, 2017.

Beck, L. J., ed., *La philosophie analytique*, Paris: Minuit, 1962.

Bentham, Jeremy, *An Introduction to the Principles of Morals and Legislation*, London: Payne, 1789.

Bergmann, Gustav, 'Two Types of Linguistic Philosophy', *Review of Metaphysics* 5 (1952): 417–38.

——'Logical Positivism, Language and the Reconstruction of Metaphysics', *Rivista Critica di Storia della Filosofia* 8 (1953): 453–81.

——*The Metaphysics of Logical Positivism*. New York: Longmans, Green and Co., 1954.

——'Strawson's Ontology', *The Journal of Philosophy* 57 (1960): 601–22.

Berlin, Isaiah, 'Austin and the Early Beginnings of Oxford Philosophy', in Isaiah Berlin et al., *Essays on J. L. Austin*, Oxford: Clarendon, 1973.

Bernhard, Peter, 'Carnap und das Bauhaus', in Christian Damböck and Gereon Wolters, eds, *Der junge Carnap in historischem Kontext: 1918–1935*, Cham: Springer, 2021.

Beyer, Hans, *Die Revolution in Bayern 1918/1919*, Berlin: Deutscher Verlag der Wissenschaften, 1982.

Blackmore, John T., *Ernst Mach: His Work, Life, and Influence*, Berkeley: University of California Press, 1972.

Block, Ned, 'Troubles with Functionalism', *Minnesota Studies in the Philosophy of Science* 9 (1978): 261–325.

Bloom, Allan, *The Closing of the American Mind*, New York: Simon & Schuster, 1987.

Bloor, David, *Knowledge and Social Imagery*, 2nd edn, Chicago, IL: University of Chicago Press, 1991.

Blumberg, Albert E., and Herbert Feigl, 'Logical Positivism: A New Movement in European Philosophy', *The Journal of Philosophy* 28 (1931): 281–96.

Bonino, Guido, Paolo Maffezioli and Paolo Tripodi, 'Logic in Analytic Philosophy: A Quantitative Analysis', *Synthese* 198 (2021): 10,991–11,028.

Boole, George, *An Investigation of the Laws of Thought, on Which Are Founded the Mathematical Theories of Logic and Probabilities*, London: Walton & Maberly, 1854.

Bourdieu, Pierre, *The Political Ontology of Martin Heidegger*, trans. Peter Collier, Cambridge: Polity, 1991.

Broda, Engelbert, *Ludwig Boltzmann: Mensch, Physiker, Philosoph*, Berlin: VEB, 1957.

Brooke, Christopher N. L., *A History of the University of Cambridge, Volume IV: 1870–1990*, Cambridge: Cambridge University Press, 1993.

Buonomo, Valerio, and Eugenio Petrovich, 'Reconstructing Late Analytic Philosophy: A Quantitative Approach', *philinq* 6 (2018): 149–80.

Butler, Judith, *Excitable Speech: A Politics of the Performative*. London/New York: Routledge, 1997.

Cahoone, Lawrence, 'The Pluralist Revolt: Forty Years Later', *Philosophy Today* 65 (2021): 747–65.

Cappelen, Herman, *Philosophy without Intuitions*, Oxford: Oxford University Press, 2012.

Carnap, Rudolf, *The Logical Structure of the World, and Pseudoproblems of Philosophy*, trans. Rolf A. George, Chicago/La Salle, IL: Open Court, 2003.

———*The Unity of Science*, trans. Max Black, Bristol: Thoemmes, 1995.

———*The Logical Syntax of Language*, trans. Amethé Smeaton (Countess von Zeppelin), London: Kegan Paul, Trench, Trubner, 1937.

———'Intellectual Autobiography', in Paul Arthur Schilpp, ed., *The Philosophy of Rudolf Carnap*, La Salle, IL: Open Court, 1963.

Cartwright, Nancy, Jordi Cat, Lola Fleck and Thomas E. Uebel, *Otto Neurath: Philosophy between Science and Politics*, Cambridge: Cambridge University Press, 1996.

Carus, A. W., *Carnap and Twentieth-Century Thought: Explication as Enlightenment*, Cambridge: Cambridge University Press, 2007.

Case, Thomas, *Physical Realism*, London: Longman, 1888.

Caute, David, *The Great Fear: The Anti-Communist Purge Under Truman and Eisenhower*, London: Secker & Warburg, 1978.

Chapman, Siobhan, *Susan Stebbing and the Language of Common Sense*, Basingstoke: Palgrave, 2013.

Cohen, G. A., *Marx's Theory of History: A Defence*, expanded edn, Oxford: Clarendon, 2000.

Coleman, James S., *The Mathematics of Collective Action*, London: Heinemann, 1973.

Collingwood, R. G., *An Essay on Philosophical Method*, rev. edn, ed. James Connelly and Giuseppina d'Oro, Oxford: Clarendon, 2005 [1933].

———*An Autobiography*, Oxford: Clarendon, 1939.

———*An Essay on Metaphysics*, Oxford: Clarendon, 1940.

Collins, Patricia Hill, *Black Feminist Thought*, New York: Routledge, 1999.

Collins, Randall, *The Sociology of Philosophies*, Cambridge, MA: Harvard University Press, 1998.

Conradi, Peter J., *Iris Murdoch: A Life*, London: HarperCollins, 2001.

Cook, Roy, 'Frege's Logic', *Stanford Encyclopedia of Philosophy* (first published 7 February 2023), at plato.stanford.edu.

Cook Wilson, John, *Statement and Inference: With Other Philosophical Papers*, Oxford: Clarendon, 1926.

Copleston, Frederick C., '*Philosophic Thought in France and the United States*, edited by Marvin Farber' (book review), *Philosophy* 28 (1953): 362–63.

Cornell, Drucilla, *Beyond Accommodation: Ethical Feminism, Deconstruction, and the Law*, new edn, Lanham, MD: Rowman & Littlefield, 1999.

Cornforth, Maurice, 'Is Analysis a Useful Method in Philosophy?', *Proceedings of the Aristotelian Society*, Supplementary Volume 13 (1934): 90–118.

——*In Defence of Philosophy: Against Positivism and Pragmatism*, London: Lawrence & Wishart, 1950.

——*Marxism and the Linguistic Philosophy*, London: Lawrence & Wishart, 1965.

Couturat, Louis, *La Logique de Leibniz, d'après des documents inédits*, Paris: Alcan, 1901.

Dahms, Hans-Joachim, *Positivismusstreit*, Frankfurt: Suhrkamp, 1994.

Damböck, Christian, Günther Sandner and Meike G. Werner, eds, *Logischer Empirismus, Lebensreform und die deutsche Jugendbewegung*, Cham: Springer, 2022.

Davidson, Donald, *Inquiries into Truth and Interpretation*, Oxford: Clarendon, 1984.

——'Intellectual Autobiography', in Lewis Edwin Hahn, ed., *The Philosophy of Donald Davidson*, Chicago, IL: Open Court, 1999.

——*The Structure of Truth: The 1970 John Locke Lectures*, Oxford: Oxford University Press, 2020.

Davidson, Donald, J. C. C. McKinsey and Patrick Suppes, 'Outlines of a Formal Theory of Value, I', *Philosophy of Science* 22 (1955): 140–60.

Davis, Angela Y., *An Autobiography*, New York: Random House, 1974.

Dawkins, Richard, *The Selfish Gene*, Oxford: Oxford University Press, 1976.

Delgado, Richard, and Jean Stefancic, *Critical Race Theory: An Introduction*, New York: New York University Press, 2001.

Dell, William, 'St Dominic's: An Ethnographic Note on a Cambridge College', *Actes de la recherche en sciences sociales* 70 (1987): 74–8.

Della Rocca, Michael, *The Parmenidean Ascent*, New York: Oxford University Press, 2020.

Dennett, Daniel C., *Elbow Room: The Varieties of Free Will Worth Wanting*, Oxford: Oxford University Press, 1984.

Derrida, Jacques, *Marges de la philosophie*, Paris: Minuit, 1972.

——*The Post Card: From Socrates to Freud and Beyond*, trans. Alan Bass, Chicago, IL: University of Chicago Press, 1987.

——*Limited Inc*, trans. Samuel Weber and Jeffrey Mehlman, Evanston IL: Northwestern University Press, 1988.

——*Without Alibi*, ed. and trans. Peggy Kamuf, Stanford: Stanford University Press, 2002.

Descartes, René, *The Philosophical Writings of Descartes*, vol. 2, trans. John Cottingham, Robert Stoothoff and Dugald Murdoch, Cambridge: Cambridge University Press, 1984.

Diamond, Cora, *The Realistic Spirit: Wittgenstein, Philosophy, and the Mind*, Cambridge, MA: MIT Press, 1991.

——'What If x Isn't the Number of Sheep? Wittgenstein and Thought-Experiments in Ethics', *Philosophical Papers* 31 (2002): 227–50.

Dotson, Kristie, 'Concrete Flowers: Contemplating the Profession of Philosophy', *Hypatia* 26: 2 (Spring 2011): 403–9.

——'How Is This Paper Philosophy?' *Comparative Philosophy* 3: 1 (2012): 3–29.

Dummett, Michael, 'What Is a Theory of Meaning?', in Samuel Guttenplan, ed., *Mind and Language: Wolfson College Lectures 1974*, Oxford: Clarendon, 1975.

——*Truth and Other Enigmas*, London: Duckworth, 1978.

——*Frege: Philosophy of Language*, 2nd edn, London: Duckworth, 1981.

——*Frege: Philosophy of Mathematics*, London: Duckworth, 1991.

——*Origins of Analytical Philosophy*, London: Duckworth, 1993.

——'Intellectual Autobiography', in Randall E. Auxier and Lewis Edwin Hahn, eds, *The Philosophy of Michael Dummett*, Chicago, IL: Open Court, 2007.

——*On Immigration and Refugees*, London: Routledge, 2001.

——'Elizabeth Anscombe', *Tablet*, 13 January 2001.

Duncan-Jones, A. E., 'Does Philosophy Analyse Common Sense?', *Proceedings of the Aristotelian Society*, Supplementary Volume 16 (1937): 139–61.

Einstein, Albert, *Relativity: The Special and the General Theory*, trans. Robert W. Lawson, Harmondsworth: Penguin, 2006 [1920].

Elster, Jon, *Making Sense of Marx*, Cambridge: Cambridge University Press, 1985.

Erickson, Paul, *The World the Game Theorists Made*, Chicago, IL: University of Chicago Press, 2015.

Evans, Gareth, and McDowell, John, eds, *Truth and Meaning: Essays in Semantics*, Oxford: Clarendon, 1976.

Farnell, Vera, *A Somervillian Looks Back*, Oxford: Oxford University Press, 1948.

Farquharson, A. S. L., 'Memoir', in John Cook Wilson, *Statement and Inference*.

Feferman, Anita Burdman, and Solomon Feferman, *Alfred Tarski: Life and Logic*, Cambridge: Cambridge University Press, 2004.

Feigl, Herbert, and Wilfrid Sellars, ed., *Readings in Philosophical Analysis*, New York: Appleton-Century-Crofts, 1949.

Finlayson, Lorna, 'How to Screw Things with Words', *Hypatia* 29 (2014): 774–89.

Fisette, Denis, 'The Reception of Ernst Mach in the School of Brentano', *Hungarian Philosophical Review* 69 (2018): 34–49.

Foot, Philippa, 'Goods and Practices', *Times Literary Supplement*, 25 September 1981: 1,097.

——*Virtues and Vices*, Oxford: Clarendon, 2002.

——*Moral Dilemmas*, Oxford: Clarendon, 2002.

Foucault, Michel, *The Order of Things*, London: Tavistock, 1970.

Frank, Philipp, *Modern Science and Its Philosophy*, Cambridge, MA: Harvard University Press, 1949.

Frankfurt, Harry G., 'Alternate Possibilities and Moral Responsibility', *The Journal of Philosophy* 66 (1969): 829–39.

Franklin, James, *Corrupting the Youth: A History of Philosophy in Australia*, Sydney: Macleay, 2003.

Frege, Gottlob, *Translations from the Philosophical Writings of Gottlob Frege*, ed. Peter Geach and Max Black, Oxford: Blackwell, 1966.

——*Conceptual Notation and Related Articles*, ed. Terrell Ward Bynum, Oxford: Clarendon, 1972.

——*The Frege Reader*, ed. Michael Beaney, Malden, MA: Blackwell, 1997.

Fremlin, Celia, 'Dialectical Grammar', *Analysis* 6 (1938): 10–15.

——*The Seven Chars of Chelsea*, London: Methuen, 1940.

Fricker, Miranda, 'Epistemic Oppression and Epistemic Privilege', *Canadian Journal of Philosophy*, Supplementary Volume 25 (1999): 191–210.

——*Epistemic Injustice: Power and the Ethics of Knowing*. Oxford: Oxford University Press, 2007.

Frost-Arnold, Greg, 'The Rise of "Analytic Philosophy": When and How Did People Begin Calling Themselves "Analytic Philosophers"?', in Sandra Lapointe and Christopher Pincock, eds, *Innovations in the History of Analytical Philosophy*, London: Palgrave Macmillan, 2017.

Galilei, Galileo, *Dialogue Concerning the Two World Systems – Ptolemaic and Copernican*, trans. Stillman Drake, 2nd edn, Berkeley: University of California Press, 1967.

Gališanka, Andrius, 'Just Society as a Fair Game: John Rawls and Game Theory in the 1950s', *Journal of the History of Ideas* 78 (2017): 299–308.

——*Rawls: The Path to a Theory of Justice*, Cambridge, MA: Harvard University Press, 2019.

Galison, Peter, 'Aufbau/Bauhaus: Logical Positivism and Architectural Modernism', *Critical Inquiry* 16 (1990): 709–52.

Garrett, Don, *Hume*, Abingdon/New York: Routledge, 2015.

Gellner, Ernest, 'Use and Meaning', *Cambridge Journal* 4 (1951): 753–61.

——'Knowing How and Validity', *Analysis* 12 (1951): 25–35.

——'Maxims', *Mind* 60 (1951): 383–93.

——'Analysis and Ontology', *Philosophical Quarterly* 1 (1951): 408–15.

——'Determinism and Validity', *Rationalist Annual* (1957): 69–79.

——'Logical Positivism and After, or the Spurious Fox', *Universities Quarterly* 11 (1957): 348–64.

——'Reflections on Linguistic Philosophy', *The Listener* 58 (1957): 205–7, 237–41.

——*Words and Things*, London: Gollancz, 1959.

Gettier, Edmund, 'Is Justified True Belief Knowledge?', *Analysis* 23 (1963): 121–3.

Gibbs, Benjamin, 'Academic Philosophy and Radical Philosophy', *Radical Philosophy* 1 (Spring 1972): 5.

Gilligan, Carol, *In a Different Voice: Psychological Theory and Women's Development*, Cambridge, MA: Harvard University Press, 1982.

Glasgow, Joshua, *A Theory of Race*, Abingdon/New York: Routledge, 2009.

Glasgow, Joshua, Sally Haslanger, Chike Jeffers and Quayshawn Spencer, *What Is Race? Four Philosophical Views*, Oxford: Oxford University Press, 2019.

Glendinning, Simon, ed., *Arguing with Derrida*, Oxford: Blackwell, 2001.

Glock, Hans-Johann, *What Is Analytic Philosophy?*, Cambridge: Cambridge University Press, 2008.

Goldman, Alvin I., 'Philosophical Intuitions', *Grazer Philosophische Studien* 74 (2007): 1–26.

Gopnik, Alison, 'Could David Hume Have Known about Buddhism? Charles François Dolu, the Royal College of La Flèche, and the Global Jesuit Network', *Hume Studies* 35 (2009): 5–28.

Gramsci, Antonio, *Selections from the Prison Notebooks*, ed. and trans. Quintin Hoare and Geoffrey Nowell Smith, London: Lawrence & Wishart, 1971.

Grattan-Guinness, I., ed., *Dear Russell – Dear Jourdain: A Commentary on Russell's Logic, Based on His Correspondence with Philip Jourdain*, London: Duckworth, 1977.

Griffin, Nicholas, 'Joachim's Early Advice to Russell on Studying Philosophy', *Russell: The Journal of the Bertrand Russell Archives*, New Series 7 (1987–88): 119–23.

——— *Russell's Idealist Apprenticeship*, Oxford: Clarendon, 1991.

Gross, Neil, *Richard Rorty: The Making of an American Philosopher*, Chicago, IL: University of Chicago Press, 2008.

Gutting, Gary, '"Rethinking Intuition": A Historical and Metaphilosophical Introduction', in Michael R. DePaul and William Ramsey, eds, *Rethinking Intuition: The Psychology of Intuition and Its Role in Philosophical Inquiry*, Lanham, MD: Rowman & Littlefield, 1998.

Habermas, Jürgen, 'Hermeneutic and Analytic Philosophy: Two Complementary Versions of the Linguistic Turn?', *Royal Institute of Philosophy* Supplement 44 (1999): 413–41.

Hacker, P. M. S., 'The Linguistic Turn in Analytic Philosophy', in Michael Beaney, ed., *The Oxford Handbook of the History of Analytic Philosophy*, Oxford: Oxford University Press, 2013.

Hacohen, Malachi Haim, 'The Culture of Viennese Science and the Riddle of Austrian Liberalism', *Modern Intellectual History* 6 (2009): 369–96.

Hall, John A., *Ernest Gellner: An Intellectual Biography*, London: Verso, 2010.

Hall, Stuart, 'The West and the Rest: Discourse and Power', in Stuart Hall and Bram Gieben, eds, *Formations of Modernity*, Cambridge: Polity, 1992.

Harding, Sandra, and Merrill B. Hintikka, eds, *Discovering Reality: Feminist Perspectives on Epistemology, Metaphysics, Methodology, and Philosophy of Science*, Dordrecht: Kluwer, 1983.

Hare, Peter H., 'William Tuthill Parry 1908–1988', *Proceedings and Addresses of the American Philosophical Association* 62 (1988): 314–15.

Hare, R. M., 'A School for Philosophers', in *Essays on Philosophical Method*, London: Macmillan, 1971 [1960].

Harris, Daniel W., and Elmar Unnsteinsson, 'Wittgenstein's Influence on Austin's Philosophy of Language', *British Journal for the History of Philosophy* 26 (2018): 371–95.

Harris, James A., 'Hume and the Common Sense Philosophers', in C. P. Bow, ed., *Common Sense in the Scottish Enlightenment*, Oxford: Oxford University Press, 2018.

Harris, Roy, *Language, Saussure and Wittgenstein: How to Play Games with Words*, London: Routledge, 1988.

Harrod, Roy, *The Life of John Maynard Keynes*, London: Macmillan, 1951.

Hartsock, Nancy C. M., 'The Feminist Standpoint: Developing the Ground for a Specifically Feminist Historical Materialism', in Harding and Hintikka, *Discovering Reality*.

Haslanger, Sally, 'Changing the Ideology and Culture of Philosophy: Not by Reason (Alone)', *Hypatia* 23 (2008): 210–23.

——*Resisting Reality: Social Construction and Social Critique*, New York: Oxford University Press, 2012.

——'Going On, Not in the Same Way', in Alexis Burgess, Herman Cappelen and David Plunkett, eds, *Conceptual Engineering and Conceptual Ethics*, Oxford: Oxford University Press, 2020.

Heijenoort, Jean van, ed., *From Frege to Gödel: A Source Book in Mathematical Logic, 1879–1931*, Cambridge, MA: Harvard University Press, 1967.

Herok, Tomasz, 'Intuitions Are Never Used as Evidence in Ethics', *Synthese* (2023).

Hook, Sidney, 'The Institute for Social Research – Addendum', *Survey* (Summer 1980): 177–8.

Horkheimer, Max, *Gesammelte Schriften*, Frankfurt: Fischer, 1985–.

———*Critical Theory: Selected Essays*, trans. Matthew J. O'Connell, New York: Herder & Herder, 1972.

——*A Life in Letters: Selected Correspondence*, ed. and trans. Manfred R. Jacobson and Evelyn M. Jacobson, Lincoln, NE: University of Nebraska Press, 2007.

Horwich, Paul, *Meaning*, Oxford: Clarendon, 1998.

Howard, Don, 'Two Left Turns Make a Right: On the Curious Political Career of North American Philosophy of Science at Midcentury', in Gary L. Hardcastle and Alan W. Richardson, eds, *Logical Empiricism in North America*, Minneapolis: University of Minnesota Press, 2003.

Huddleston, T. F. C., *University Expenses and Non-Collegiate Students*, Cambridge: Deighton, Bell, 1892.

Hume, David, *A Treatise of Human Nature*, ed. L. A. Selby-Bigge and P. H. Nidditch, Oxford: Clarendon, 1978.

——*Enquiries Concerning Human Understanding and Concerning the Principles of Morals*, ed. L. A. Selby-Bigge and P. H. Nidditch, Oxford: Clarendon, 1975.

Humphreys, Paul W., and James H. Fetzer, eds, *The New Theory of Reference: Kripke, Marcus, and Its Origins*, Dordrecht: Kluwer, 1998.

Hurka, Thomas, 'Moore in the Middle', *Ethics* 113 (2003): 599–628.

Hutcheson, Francis, *An Inquiry into the Original of our Ideas of Beauty and Virtue*, 2nd edn, London: Dary, 1726.

Hutchison, Katrina, and Fiona Jenkins, eds, *Women in Philosophy: What Needs to Change?* Oxford: Oxford University Press, 2013.

Hylton, Peter, *Russell, Idealism, and the Emergence of Analytic Philosophy*, Oxford: Clarendon, 1990.

Iversen, Robert W., *The Communists and the Schools*, New York: Harcourt, Brace, 1959.

Jackson, Annabel Huth, *A Victorian Childhood*, London: Methuen, 1932.

Jackson, Frank, *From Metaphysics to Ethics: A Defence of Conceptual Analysis*, Oxford: Clarendon, 1998.

Jaggar, Alison M., *Feminist Politics and Human Nature*, Totowa, NJ: Rowman & Allanheld, 1983.

Jakobsen, David, 'In What Sense Is J. N. Findlay the Founding Father of Tense-Logic?', *History and Philosophy of Logic* 42 (2021): 180–8.

Janik, Allan, and Stephen Toulmin, *Wittgenstein's Vienna*, New York: Simon & Schuster, 1973.

Janssen-Lauret, Frederique, 'The Quinean Roots of Lewis's Humeanism', *The Monist* 100 (2017): 249–65.

Jay, Martin, *The Dialectical Imagination: A History of the Frankfurt School and the Institute of Social Research 1923–1950*, London: Heinemann, 1973.

Johnson, Gordon, *University Politics: F. M. Cornford's Cambridge and His Advice to the Young Academic Politician*, 2nd edn, New York: Cambridge University Press, 2008.

Jordan, Z. A., *Philosophy and Ideology: The Development of Philosophy and Marxism–Leninism in Poland Since the Second World War*, Dordrecht: Reidel, 1963.

Kalish, Donald, and David Kaplan, 'A Statement of Facts Concerning the Appointment and Threatened Dismissal of Professor Angela Davis, Provided by the UCLA Department of Philosophy, September 29, 1969', Online Archive of California, at oac.cdlib.org.

Katzav, Joel, and Krist Vaesen, 'On the Emergence of American Analytic Philosophy', *British Journal for the History of Philosophy* 25 (2017): 772–98.

Katzav, Joel, 'Analytic Philosophy 1925–69: Emergence, Management, and Nature', *British Journal for the History of Philosophy* 26 (2018): 1,197–221.

Kauppinen, Antti, 'The Rise and Fall of Experimental Philosophy', *Philosophical Explorations* 10 (2007): 95–118.

Kenny, Anthony, 'Arthur Norman Prior, 1914–1969', *Proceedings of the British Academy* 57 (1971): 320–49.

Keynes, John Maynard, *Two Memoirs*, London: Rupert Hart-Davis, 1949.

Kim, Jaegwon, 'Concepts of Supervenience', *Philosophy and Phenomenological Research* 45 (1984): 153–76.

Kim, Minsun, and Yuan Yuan, 'No Cross-Cultural Differences in the Gettier Car Case Intuition: A Replication Study of Weinberg et al. 2001', *Episteme* 12 (2015): 355–61.

Kleinerüschkamp, Werner, ed., *hannes meyer 1889–1954: architekt urbanist lehrer*, Berlin: Ernst, 1989.

Kluge, Ulrich, *Die deutsche Revolution 1918–1919: Staat, Politik und Gesellschaft zwischen Weltkrieg und Kapp-Putsch*, Frankfurt: Suhrkamp, 1985.

Kneale, William, and Martha Kneale, *The Development of Logic*, Oxford: Clarendon, 1962.

Knobe, Joshua, 'Intentional Action and Side Effects in Ordinary Language', *Analysis* 63 (2003): 190–4.

——'Intuitions in the Test-Tube', *Philosophers' Magazine* 28: 4 (2004): 37–9.

Knobe, Joshua, and Shaun Nichols, eds, *Oxford Studies in Experimental Philosophy*, vol. 5, Oxford: Oxford University Press, forthcoming 2024.

Kramer, Andreas, and Evelyn Wilcock, '"A Preserve for Professional Philosophers": Adornos Husserl-Dissertation 1934–37 und ihr Oxforder Kontext', *Deutsche Vierteljahrsschrift für Literaturwissenschaft und Geistesgeschichte* 73 (1999): 115–61.

Kremer, Michael, 'Margaret MacDonald and Gilbert Ryle: A Philosophical Friendship', *British Journal for the History of Philosophy* 30 (2022): 288–311.

Krentel, W. D., J. C. C. McKinsey and W. V. Quine, 'A Simplification of Games in Extensive Form', *Duke Mathematical Journal* 18 (1951): 885–900.

Kripke, Saul A., 'A Completeness Theorem in Modal Logic', *The Journal of Symbolic Logic* 24 (1959): 1–14.

——*Naming and Necessity*, Oxford: Blackwell, 1980.

Krishnan, Nikhil, *A Terribly Serious Adventure: Philosophy at Oxford 1900–60*, London: Profile, 2023.

Kuklick, Bruce, 'Philosophy at Yale in the Century after Darwin', *History of Philosophy Quarterly* 21 (2004): 313–36.

——*A History of Philosophy in America 1720–2000*, Oxford: Clarendon, 2001.

Kurtz, Paul W., 'International Congresses and International Tensions', *The Journal of Philosophy* 55 (1958): 1,132–41.

Kusch, Martin, *Psychologism: A Case Study in the Sociology of Philosophical Knowledge*, London: Routledge, 1995.

Ladyman, James, Don Ross, David Spurrett and John Collier, *Every Thing Must Go: Metaphysics Naturalized*, Oxford: Oxford University Press, 2007.

Langton, Rae, 'Whose Right? Ronald Dworkin, Women, and Pornographers', *Philosophy and Public Affairs* 19 (1990): 311–59.

——'Speech Acts and Unspeakable Acts', *Philosophy and Public Affairs* 22 (1993): 293–330.

Leavis, F. R., *The Common Pursuit*, London: Chatto & Windus, 1952.

Lenin, V. I., *Materialism and Empirio-Criticism: Critical Notes Concerning a Reactionary Philosophy*, London: Lawrence, 1927.

Levy, Paul, *Moore: G. E. Moore and the Cambridge Apostles*, London: Weidenfeld & Nicolson, 1979.

Lewis, C. I., 'Implication and the Algebra of Logic', *Mind* 21 (1912): 522–31.

——'Interesting Theorems in Symbolic Logic', *The Journal of Philosophy, Psychology and Scientific Methods* 10 (1913): 239–42.

——*A Survey of Symbolic Logic*, Berkeley: University of California Press, 1918.

——'Logic and Pragmatism', in George P. Adams and William Pepperell Montague, eds, *Contemporary American Philosophy: Personal Statements*, vol. 2. London: Allen & Unwin/New York: Macmillan, 1930.

——'Autobiography', in Paul Arthur Schilpp, ed., *The Philosophy of C. I. Lewis*, La Salle, IL: Open Court, 1968.

Lewis, C. I., and C. H. Langford, *Symbolic Logic*, New York: Century, 1932.

Lewis, David, *Counterfactuals*, Oxford: Blackwell, 1973.

——*Philosophical Papers*, vol. 1, New York: Oxford University Press, 1983.

——*Philosophical Papers*, vol. 2, New York: Oxford University Press, 1986.

——*On the Plurality of Worlds*. Oxford: Blackwell, 1986.

——*Papers in Metaphysics and Epistemology*, Cambridge: Cambridge University Press, 1999.

Lewis, Stephanie R., 'Intellectual Biography of David Lewis (1941–2001): Early Influences', in Barry Loewer and Jonathan Schaffer, eds, *A Companion to David Lewis*, Malden, MA: Wiley, 2015.

Lloyd, Genevieve, *The Man of Reason: 'Male' and 'Female' in Western Philosophy*, London: Methuen, 1984.

Locke, John, *An Essay Concerning Human Understanding*, ed. P. H. Nidditch, Oxford: Clarendon, 1975.

Lowe, Victor, 'A Resurgence of "Vicious Intellectualism"', *The Journal of Philosophy* 48 (1951): 435–47.

Lukács, Georg, *History and Class Consciousness: Studies in Marxist Dialectics*, trans. Rodney Livingstone, London: Merlin, 1971.

Luxemburg, Rosa, *The Accumulation of Capital*, trans. Agnes Schwarzschild, London/New York: Routledge, 2003.

Mabbott, J. D., *Oxford Memories*, Oxford: Thornton's, 1986.

——'Gilbert Ryle: A Tribute', in Gilbert Ryle, *Aspects of Mind*, Oxford: Blackwell, 1993.

McClendon, John H., III, and Stephen C. Ferguson II, *African American Philosophers and Philosophy: An Introduction to the History, Concepts, and Contemporary Issues*, London: Bloomsbury, 2019.

MacColl, Hugh, 'Symbolical Reasoning', *Mind* 5 (1880): 45–60.

——'Symbolic Reasoning (II)', *Mind*, New Series 6 (1897): 493–510.

——'Symbolic Reasoning (III)', *Mind*, New Series 9 (1900): 75–84.

——'Symbolic Reasoning (V)', *Mind*, New Series 12 (1903): 355–64.

——*Symbolic Logic and Its Applications*, London: Longman, Green, 1906.

——'"If" and "Imply"', *Mind* 17 (1908): 453–5.

McCumber, John, *Time in the Ditch: American Philosophy and the McCarthy Era*, Evanston, IL: Northwestern University Press, 2001.

——*The Philosophy Scare: The Politics of Reason in the Early Cold War*, Chicago, IL: University of Chicago Press, 2016.

Mac Cumhaill, Clare, and Rachael Wiseman, *Metaphysical Animals: How Four Women Brought Philosophy Back to Life*, London: Chatto & Windus, 2022.

——'Interrupting the Conversation: Donald MacKinnon, Wartime Tutor of Anscombe, Midgley, Murdoch and Foot', *Journal of the Philosophy of Education* 56 (2022): 838–50.

MacDonald, Margaret, ed., *Philosophy and Analysis: A Selection of Articles Published in* Analysis *Between 1933–40 and 1947–53*, Oxford: Blackwell, 1954.

Mach, Ernst, *Contributions to the Analysis of Sensations*, trans. C. M. Williams, Chicago, IL: Open Court, 1897.

——*The Science of Mechanics*, trans. T. J. McCormack, 4th edn, Chicago, IL: Open Court, 1919.

——'On Thought Experiments', trans. W. O. Price and Sheldon Krimsky, *Philosophical Forum* 4 (1973): 446–57.

Machery, Edouard, *Philosophy Within Its Proper Bounds*, New York: Oxford University Press, 2017.

MacIntyre, Alasdair, 'The Hunt Is Up!', *New Statesman*, 31 October 1959: 597–8.

MacKinnon, Catharine A., *Feminism Unmodified: Discourses on Life and Law*, Cambridge, MA: Harvard University Press, 1987.

——*Toward a Feminist Theory of the State*, Cambridge, MA: Harvard University Press, 1989.

MacKinnon, Donald M., 'Philosophers in Exile', *Oxford Magazine*, Eighth Week, Michaelmas Term, 1992: 15–16.

Maclaurin, James, and Heather Dyke, 'What Is Analytic Metaphysics For?', *Australasian Journal of Philosophy* 90 (2012): 291–306.

Malle, Bertram F., and Joshua Knobe, 'The Folk Concept of Intentionality', *Journal of Experimental Social Psychology* 33 (1997): 101–21.

Manne, Kate, *Down Girl: The Logic of Misogyny*, Harmondsworth: Penguin, 2019.

Marcus, Ruth Barcan, 'A Philosopher's Calling', in Michael Frauchiger, ed., *Modalities, Identity, Belief, and Moral Dilemmas: Themes from Barcan Marcus*, Berlin: de Gruyter, 2015.

Marion, Mathieu, 'Was Royaumont Merely a *Dialogue de Sourds*? An Introduction to the *Discussion Générale*', *Philosophical Inquiries* 6 (2018): 197–214.

McDowell, John, *Meaning, Knowledge, and Reality*, Cambridge, MA: Harvard University Press, 1998.

McGuinness, Brian, *Young Ludwig: Wittgenstein's Life, 1889–1921*, Oxford: Clarendon, 2005.

McKay, Floyd J., 'After Cool Deliberation: Reed College, Oregon Editors, and the Red Scare of 1954', *Pacific Northwest Quarterly* 89 (1997/1998): 12–20.

Mehta, Ved, *Fly and the Fly-Bottle: Encounters with British Intellectuals*, London: Weidenfeld & Nicolson, 1963.

Meyer, Hannes, 'Building', in Ulrich Conrads, ed., *Programs and Manifestoes on 20th-Century Architecture*, trans. Michael Bullock, Cambridge, MA: MIT Press, 1970.

Midgley, Mary, *The Owl of Minerva: A Memoir*, London: Routledge, 2005.

——'The Golden Age of Female Philosophy', *The Guardian*, 28 November 2013.

Mill, John Stuart, *On Liberty*, London: Parker, 1859.

——*Dissertations and Discussions*, 3rd edn, London: Longman, Green, Reader & Dyer, 1875.

Mills, Charles W., 'The Concept of Ideology in the Thought of Marx and Engels', PhD dissertation, University of Toronto, 1985.

——*The Racial Contract*, Ithaca, NY: Cornell University Press, 1997.

——*Black Rights/White Wrongs: The Critique of Racial Liberalism*, Oxford: Oxford University Press, 2017.

Mitchell, Allan, *Revolution in Bavaria, 1918–1919: The Eisner Regime and the Soviet Republic*, Princeton, NJ: Princeton University Press, 1965.

Mitchell, Basil, *Looking Back: On Faith, Philosophy and Friends in Oxford*, Durham: Memoir Club, 2009.

Monk, Ray, *Wittgenstein: The Duty of Genius*, London: Vintage, 1991.

——*Bertrand Russell: The Spirit of Solitude, 1872–1921*, London: Vintage, 1997.

——'He Was the Most Revered Philosopher of His Era. So Why Did G. E. Moore Disappear From History?' *Prospect*, 3 April 2020.

Montague, William Pepperell, 'Philosophy as Vision', *International Journal of Ethics* 44 (1933): 1–22.

Moore, A. W., *The Evolution of Modern Metaphysics*, Cambridge: Cambridge University Press, 2012.

Moore, G. E., *Early Philosophical Writings*, ed. Thomas Baldwin and Consuelo Preti, Cambridge: Cambridge University Press, 2011.

——'The Nature of Judgment', *Mind*, New Series 8 (1899): 176–93.

——*Principia Ethica*, ed. Thomas Baldwin, Cambridge: Cambridge University Press, 1993 [1903].

——*Philosophical Papers*, London: Allen & Unwin, 1959.

——'An Autobiography', in Paul Arthur Schilpp, ed., *The Philosophy of G. E. Moore*, 2nd edn, New York: Tudor, 1952.

Mühsam, Erich, *Von Eisner bis Leviné: Die Entstehung und Niederlage der Bayerischen Räterepublik*, Hamburg: MaD-Verlag Schulenburg, 1976.

Munk, Michael, 'Oregon Tests Academic Freedom in (Cold) Wartime: The Reed College Trustees Versus Stanley Moore', *Oregon Historical Quarterly* 97 (1996): 262–354.

Murdoch, Iris, 'Metaphysics and Ethics', in D. F. Pears, ed., *The Nature of Metaphysics*, London: Macmillan, 1957.

——'Mr Gellner's Game', *Observer*, 29 November 1959.

——*Living on Paper: Letters from Iris Murdoch 1934–1995*, London: Chatto & Windus, 2015.

Mure, G. R. G., *Retreat from Truth*, Oxford: Blackwell, 1958.

Murphey, Murray G., *C. I. Lewis: The Last Great Pragmatist*, Albany, NY: SUNY Press, 2005.

Myhill, John, 'Berkeley's "De Motu": An Anticipation of Mach', *University of California Publications in Philosophy* 29 (1957): 141–57.

Nagel, Ernest, 'Impressions and Appraisals of Analytic Philosophy in Europe', *The Journal of Philosophy* 33 (1936): 5–24, 29–53.

——'*Wahrscheinlichkeitslehre*, by Hans Reichenbach' (critical notice), *Mind* 45 (1936): 501–14.

Neale, Stephen, 'No Plagiarism Here', *Times Literary Supplement*, 9 February 2001: 12–13.

Neurath, Otto, *Economic Writings: Selections 1904–1945*, ed. Thomas E. Uebel and Robert S. Cohen, Dordrecht: Kluwer, 2004.

——*Philosophical Papers 1913–1946*, ed. and trans. Robert S. Cohen and Marie Neurath, Dordrecht: Reidel, 1983.

——'Das neue Bauhaus in Dessau' (1926), in *Gesammelte Schriften*, Band 8, Ergänzungsband: *Varia*, ed. Ulf Höfer, Christopher Burke and Günther Sandner, Münster: LIT, 2022.

——et al., 'Wissenschaftliche Weltauffassung: Der Wiener Kreis [The Scientific Conception of the World: The Vienna Circle]' (1929), in Otto Neurath, *Empiricism and Sociology*, ed. Marie Neurath and Robert S. Cohen, Dordrecht: Reidel, 1973.

——'Unity of Science and Logical Empiricism: A Reply' (1937), in John Symons, Olga Pombo and Juan Manuel Torres, eds, *Otto Neurath and the Unity of Science*, Dordrecht: Springer, 2011.

Ney, Alyssa, *Metaphysics: An Introduction*, 2nd edn, London/New York: Routledge, 2023.

Nyíri, J. C., 'Beim Sternenlicht der Nichtexistierenden: Zur ideologiekritischen Interpretation des platonisierenden Antipsychologismus', *Inquiry* 17 (1974): 399–443.

Offer, Avner, and Gabriel Söderberg, *The Nobel Factor: The Prize in Economics, Social Democracy, and the Market Turn*, Princeton, NJ: Princeton University Press, 2016.

Okafor, Victor O., 'An Afrocentric Critique of Appiah's *In My Father's House*', *Journal of Black Studies* 24: 2 (1993): 196–212.

Olsen, Stein Haugom, 'Why Hugh MacColl Is Not, and Will Never Be, Part of Any Literary Canon', in Willie van Peer, ed., *The Quality of Literature: Linguistic Studies in Literary Evaluation*, Amsterdam/Philadelphia, PA: John Benjamins, 2008.

O'Neill, John and Thomas Uebel, 'Horkheimer and Neurath: Restarting a Disrupted Debate', *European Journal of Philosophy* 12 (2004): 75–105.

Pap, Arthur, *Elements of Analytic Philosophy*, New York: Macmillan, 1949.

Parfit, Derek, *Reasons and Persons*, Oxford: Oxford University Press, 1984.

——*On What Matters*, 3 vols., Oxford: Oxford University Press, 2013–16.

Parsons, Howard L., 'The Philosophy of Barrows Dunham: The Progress of an American Radical', *Transactions of the Charles S. Peirce Society* 33 (1997): 410–44.

Passmore, John, *A Hundred Years of Philosophy*, Harmondsworth: Penguin, 1968.

Pateman, Carole, *The Sexual Contract*, Cambridge: Polity, 1988.

Paton, H. J., 'Fifty Years of Philosophy', in H. D. Lewis, ed., *Contemporary British Philosophy*, Third Series, London: Allen & Unwin, 1956.

Plato, *Collected Works*, ed. John M. Cooper, Indianapolis: Hackett, 1997.

Pogge, Thomas, *Rawls: His Life and Theory of Justice*, Oxford: Oxford University Press, 2007.

Popper, Karl R., 'A Note on Berkeley as Precursor of Mach', *British Journal for the Philosophy of Science* 4: 13 (1953): 26–36.

Potter, Michael, *Wittgenstein's Notes on Logic*, Oxford: Oxford University Press, 2008.

——*The Rise of Analytic Philosophy: From Frege to Ramsey*. London: Routledge, 2019.

Potochnik, Angela, and Audrey Yap, 'Revisiting Galison's "Aufbau/Bauhaus" in Light of Neurath's Philosophical Projects', *Studies in History and Philosophy of Science* 37 (2006): 469–88.

Preston, Aaron, *Analytic Philosophy: The History of an Illusion*, London/New York: Continuum, 2007.

Preston, John, 'Phenomenalism, or Neutral Monism, in Mach's *Analysis of Sensations*?', in John Preston, ed., *Interpreting Mach: Critical Essays*, Cambridge: Cambridge University Press, 2021.

Price, H. H., *Perception*, London: Methuen, 1932.

——'The Permanent Significance of Hume's Philosophy', *Philosophy* 15 (1940): 7–37.

——'Harold Arthur Prichard', *Proceedings of the British Academy* (1947): 330–50.

Prichard, 'H. W. B. Joseph, 1867–1943', *Mind* 53 (1944): 189–91.

Putnam, Hilary, 'Meaning and Reference', *The Journal of Philosophy* 70 (1973): 699–711.

Quine, W. V., 'The Problem of Interpreting Modal Logic', *Journal of Symbolic Logic* 12: 2 (1947): 43–8.

——*From a Logical Point of View: Nine Logico-Philosophical Essays*, Cambridge, MA: Harvard University Press, 1953.

——*The Time of My Life*, Cambridge, MA: MIT Press, 1985.

——'Autobiography', in Lewis Edwin Hahn and Paul Arthur Schilpp, eds, *The Philosophy of W. V. Quine*, 2nd edn, Chicago/La Salle IL: Open Court, 1998.

——*Confessions of a Confirmed Extensionalist and Other Essays*, ed. Dagfinn Føllesdal and Douglas B. Quine, Cambridge, MA: Harvard University Press, 2008.

——*Word and Object*, new edn, Cambridge, MA: MIT Press, 2013.

Quine, W. V. and Rudolf Carnap, *Dear Carnap, Dear Van: The Quine–Carnap Correspondence and Related Work*, ed. Richard Creath, Berkeley, CA: University of California Press, 1991.

Rader, Melvin, *False Witness*, Seattle/London: University of Washington Press, 1969.

Rajchman, John, and Cornel West, eds, *Post-Analytic Philosophy*, New York: Columbia University Press, 1985.

Ramsey, F. P., *Philosophical Papers*, ed. D. H. Mellor, Cambridge: Cambridge University Press, 1990.

Rawls, John, 'Justice as Fairness', *The Philosophical Review* 67 (1958): 164–94.

——*A Theory of Justice*, Cambridge, MA: Harvard University Press, 1971.

Rée, Jonathan, 'Professional Philosophers', *Radical Philosophy* 1 (Spring 1972): 2–4.

——'English Philosophy in the Fifties', *Radical Philosophy* 65 (Autumn 1993): 3–21.

Reichenbach, Hans, *Selected Writings 1909–1953*, ed. Robert S. Cohen and Maria Reichenbach, Dordrecht: Reidel, 1978.

——*The Rise of Scientific Philosophy*, third printing, Berkeley/Los Angeles, CA: University of California Press, 1958 [1951].

Reinhoudt, Jurgen, and Serge Audier, *The Walter Lippmann Colloquium: The Birth of Neo-Liberalism*, Basingstoke: Palgrave Macmillan, 2017.

Reisch, George A., *How the Cold War Transformed Philosophy of Science: To the Icy Slopes of Logic*, New York: Cambridge University Press, 2005.

Rescher, Nicholas, *Instructive Journey: An Essay in Autobiography*, Lanham, MD: University Press of America, 1997.

Rieser, Max, 'Remarks on the Eleventh International Congress of Philosophy', *The Journal of Philosophy* 51 (1954): 99–105.

Roemer, John E., *A General Theory of Exploitation and Class*, Cambridge, MA: Harvard University Press, 1982.

Romizi, Donata, 'The Vienna Circle's "Scientific World-Conception": Philosophy of Science in a Political Arena', *HOPOS* 2 (2012): 205–42.

Rorty, Richard, ed., *The Linguistic Turn: Essays in Philosophical Method, With Two Retrospective Essays*, Chicago: University of Chicago Press, 1992 [1967].

——*Philosophy and the Mirror of Nature*, Princeton, NJ: Princeton University Press, 1979.

——'Kripke Versus Kant' (review of Saul Kripke, *Naming and Necessity*), *London Review of Books*, 4 September 1980.

——'Philosophy in America Today', in *Consequences of Pragmatism*, Minneapolis, MN: University of Minnesota Press, 1982.

Rowe, M. W., *J. L. Austin: Philosopher and D-Day Intelligence Officer*, Oxford: Oxford University Press, 2023.

Rumfitt, Ian, '*The Structure of Truth: The 1970 John Locke Lectures*, by Donald Davidson' (book review), *Mind* 131 (2022): 1,027–38.

Russell, Bertrand, *The Collected Papers of Bertrand Russell*, London/Boston, MA: G. Allen & Unwin, 1983.

——*German Social Democracy: Six Lectures*, London: Longman, Green, 1896.

——*An Essay on the Foundations of Geometry*, Cambridge: Cambridge University Press, 1897.

——*The Principles of Mathematics*, Cambridge: Cambridge University Press, 1903.

——*Our Knowledge of the External World as a Field for Scientific Method in Philosophy*, London: George Allen & Unwin, 1914.

——'My Mental Development', in Paul Arthur Schilpp, ed., *The Philosophy of Bertrand Russell*, Evanston/Chicago, IL: Northwestern University Press, 1944.

——*A History of Western Philosophy and Its Connection with Political and Social Circumstances from the Earliest Times to the Present Day*, New York: Simon & Schuster, 1945.

——*Portraits from Memory and Other Essays*, London: Allen & Unwin, 1956.

——'Philosophy and Politics', in *Unpopular Essays*, London: Allen & Unwin, 1950.

——*My Philosophical Development*, London: Allen & Unwin, 1959.

——*Autobiography*, London/New York: Routledge, 2010.

Russell, Frank, *My Life and Adventures*, London: Cassell, 1923.

Ryle, Gilbert, *Collected Papers*, London: Routledge, 2009.

——'*Sein und Zeit*, by Martin Heidegger' (critical notice), *Mind* 38 (1929): 355–70.

——'Autobiographical', in Oscar P. Wood and George Pitcher, eds, *Ryle*, London: Macmillan, 1970.

——'G. E. Moore's "The Nature of Judgment"', in Alice Ambrose and Morris Lazerowitz, eds, *G. E. Moore: Essays in Retrospect*, London: Allen & Unwin, 1970.

Sayers, Sean, *The Making of a Marxist Philosopher*, London: Routledge, 2024.

Schaar, Maria van der, *G. F. Stout and the Psychological Origins of Analytic Philosophy*, Basingstoke: Palgrave Macmillan, 2013.

Schaffer, Jonathan, 'On What Grounds What', in David J. Chalmers, David Manley and Ryan Wasserman, eds, *Metametaphysics: New Essays on the Foundations of Ontology*, Oxford: Clarendon, 2009.

Schorske, Carl E., *Fin-de-Siècle Vienna: Politics and Culture*, London: Weidenfeld & Nicolson, 1980.

Schrecker, Ellen W., *No Ivory Tower: McCarthyism and the Universities*, New York: Oxford University Press, 1986.

Schulz-Forberg, Hagen, 'Embedded Early Neoliberalism: Transnational Origins of the Agenda of Liberalism Reconsidered', in Dieter Plehwe, Quinn Slobodian and Philip Mirowski, eds, *Nine Lives of Neoliberalism*, London: Verso, 2020.

Searle, John R., *Speech Acts: An Essay in the Philosophy of Language*, Cambridge: Cambridge University Press, 1969.

——*The Campus War: A Sympathetic Look at the University in Agony*, Harmondsworth: Pelican, 1972.

——'Reiterating the Differences: A Reply to Derrida', *Glyph* 2 (1977): 198–208.

——'Minds, Brains, and Programs', *Behavioral and Brain Sciences* 3 (1980): 417–57.

——'J. L. Austin (1911–1960)', in A. P. Martinich and David Sosa, eds, *A Companion to Analytic Philosophy*, Malden, MA: Blackwell, 2001.

——'Contemporary Philosophy in the United States', in N. Bunnin and E. P. Tsui-James, eds, *The Blackwell Companion to Philosophy*, Oxford: Blackwell, 1996.

Sellars, Wilfrid, 'Empiricism and the Philosophy of Mind', in Herbert Feigl and Michael Scriven, eds, *Minnesota Studies in the Philosophy of Science*, vol. 1, Minneapolis, MN: University of Minnesota Press, 1956.

Shapin, Steven, and Simon Schaffer, *Leviathan and the Air-Pump*, with a new introduction, Princeton, NJ: Princeton University Press, 2011.

Sider, Theodore, *Four-Dimensionalism: An Ontology of Persistence and Time*, Oxford: Clarendon, 2001.

Sigmund, Karl, *Exact Thinking in Demented Times: The Vienna Circle and the Epic Quest for the Foundations of Science*, New York: Basic, 2017.

Singer, Marcus G., 'Memoir', in Arthur E. Murphy, *Reason, Reality, and Speculative Philosophy*, Madison: University of Wisconsin Press, 1996.

Singer, Peter, 'Famine, Affluence, and Morality', *Philosophy and Public Affairs* 1 (1972): 229–43.

Skyrms, Brian, 'Possible Worlds, Physics and Metaphysics', *Philosophical Studies* 30 (1976): 323–32.

Slobodian, Quinn, *Globalists: The End of Empire and the Birth of Neoliberalism*, Cambridge, MA: Harvard University Press, 2018.

Sluga, Hans D., *Gottlob Frege*, London: Routledge & Kegan Paul, 1980.

Smith, Quentin, 'Marcus, Kripke, and the Origin of the New Theory of Reference', in Humphreys and Fetzer, *New Theory of Reference*.

Smith, Sophie, 'Historicizing Rawls', *Modern Intellectual History* 18 (2021): 906–39.

Soames, Scott, 'Revisionism about Reference: A Reply to Smith', in Humphreys and Fetzer, *New Theory of Reference*.

Sorensen, Roy A., *Thought Experiments*, New York: Oxford University Press, 1992.

Spencer, Quayshawn, 'A More Radical Solution to the Race Problem', *Aristotelian Society Supplementary Volume* XCIII (2019): 25–48.

Srinivasan, Amia, 'Stop the Robot Apocalypse' (review of William MacAskill, *Doing Good Better*), *London Review of Books*, 24 September 2015.

Stadler, Friedrich, *The Vienna Circle: Studies in the Origins, Development, and Influence of Logical Empiricism*, rev. edn, Cham: Springer, 2015.

Stebbing, L. Susan, 'Logical Positivism and Analysis', Annual Philosophical Lecture, Henriette Hertz Trust, London: British Academy, 1933.

Strassfeld, Jonathan, *Inventing Philosophy's Other*, Chicago, IL: University of Chicago Press, 2022.

Strawson, P. F., 'On Referring', *Mind* 59 (1950): 320–44.

——*Individuals: An Essay in Descriptive Metaphysics*, London: Methuen, 1959.

——'Analysis, Science, and Metaphysics', in Rorty, *Linguistic Turn*.

——'Intellectual Autobiography', in Lewis Edwin Hahn, ed., *The Philosophy of P. F. Strawson*. Chicago, IL: Open Court, 1998.

——*Philosophical Writings*, Oxford: Oxford University Press, 2011.

Struik, Dirk, 'Howard Selsam 1903–1970', *Proceedings and Addresses of the American Philosophical Association* 45 (1971–72): 225.

Suppes, Patrick, 'The Pre-History of Kenneth Arrow's Social Choice and Individual Values', *Social Choice and Welfare* 25 (2005): 319–26.

Tanner, J. R., ed., *The Historical Register of the University of Cambridge, Being a Supplement to the Calendar with a Record of University Offices Honours and Distinctions to the Year 1910*, Cambridge: Cambridge University Press, 1917.

Tarski, Alfred, 'The Concept of Truth in Formalized Languages', in Tarski, *Logic, Semantics, Metamathematics: Papers from 1923 to 1938*, trans. J. H. Woodger, Oxford: Clarendon, 1956.

Taylor, Charles, 'Can Political Philosophy Be Neutral?', *Universities and Left Review* 1 (Spring 1957): 68–70.

——'*La Philosophie Analytique*' (book review), *The Philosophical Review* 73 (1964): 132–5.

——*Hegel*, Cambridge: Cambridge University Press, 1975.

——'Dwellers in Egocentric Space' (review of Gareth Evans, *The Varieties of Reference*), *Times Literary Supplement*, 11 March 1983.

——*Human Agency and Language: Philosophical Papers 1*, Cambridge: Cambridge University Press, 1985.

Thomson, Judith Jarvis, 'Killing, Letting Die, and the Trolley Problem', *The Monist* 59 (1976): 204–17.

——'How It Was', *Proceedings and Addresses of the American Philosophical Association* 87 (2013): 109–21.

Todd, Olivier, *Un fils rebelle*, Paris: Grasset, 1981.

Tuboly, Ádám Tamás, 'The Early Formation of Modal Logic and Its Significance: A Historical Note on Quine, Carnap, and a Bit of Church', *History and Philosophy of Logic* 39 (2018): 289–304.

Tversky, Amos, and Daniel Kahneman, 'Rational Choice and the Framing of Decisions', *Journal of Business* 59 (1986): S251–S278.

Unger, Peter K., *Living High and Letting Die: Our Illusion of Innocence*, New York: Oxford University Press, 1996.

Verhaegh, Sander, 'Coming to America: Carnap, Reichenbach, and the Great Intellectual Migration', *Journal for the History of Analytical Philosophy* 8: 11 (2020): 1–47.

Villemaire, Diane Davis, *E. A. Burtt, Historian and Philosopher*, Dordrecht: Kluwer, 2002.

Vrahimis, Andreas, *Encounters Between Analytic and Continental Philosophy*, Basingstoke: Palgrave Macmillan, 2013.

——'Sense Data and Logical Relations: Karin Costelloe-Stephen and Russell's Critique of Bergson', *British Journal for the History of Philosophy* 28 (2020): 819–44.

——*Bergsonism and the History of Analytic Philosophy*, Cham: Palgrave Macmillan, 2022.

Wahl, Jean, *Les philosophics pluralistes d'Angleterre et d'Amérique*, Paris: Alcan, 1920.

——*Vers le concret. Études d'histoire de la philosophie contemporaine. William James, Whitehead, Gabriel Marcel*, Paris: Vrin, 1932.

Wale, Fred G., 'Chosen for Ability', *Atlantic Monthly*, July 1947: 81–5.

Warnock, G. J., *English Philosophy Since 1900*, London: Oxford University Press, 1958.

——'John Langshaw Austin, a Biographical Sketch', in K. T. Fann, ed., *Symposium on J. L. Austin*, London: Routledge & Kegan Paul, 1969.

——'Gilbert Ryle's Editorship', *Mind* 85 (1976): 47–56.

Wasserman, Janek, *Black Vienna: The Radical Right in the Red City, 1918–1938*, Ithaca, NY: Cornell University Press, 2014.

Watson, John B., *Behaviorism*, Abingdon: Routledge, 2017.

Weinberg, Jonathan M., Shaun Nichols and Stephen Stich, 'Normativity and Epistemic Intuitions', *Philosophical Topics* 29: 1–2 (2001): 429–60.

Weiner, Joan, 'Frege and the Linguistic Turn', *Philosophical Topics* 25 (1997): 265–88.

Whitley, Edward, *The Graduates*, London: Hamilton, 1986.

Williams, Bernard, 'The Hatred of Philosophy', *The Isis*, 4 December 1957 (with a reply by Perry Anderson).

——'*English Philosophy since 1900*, by G. J. Warnock' (book review), *Philosophy* 34 (1959): 168–70.

——*Philosophy as a Humanistic Discipline*, Princeton, NJ: Princeton University Press, 2006.

Williamson, Colwyn, 'Searle's Idea of a University', *Radical Philosophy* 5 (1973): 17–22.

Williamson, Timothy, 'Laudatio: Ruth Barcan Marcus (1921–2012)', in Michael Frauchiger, ed., *Modalities, Identity, Belief, and Moral Dilemmas: Themes from Barcan Marcus*, Berlin: de Gruyter, 2015.

——*The Philosophy of Philosophy*, 2nd edn, Malden, MA: Wiley Blackwell, 2022.

Wilshire, Bruce, *Fashionable Nihilism: A Critique of Analytic Philosophy*, Albany, NY: State University of New York Press, 2002.

Wilson, Duncan, *The Making of British Bioethics*, Manchester: Manchester University Press, 2014.

Winstanley, D. A., *Later Victorian Cambridge*, Cambridge: Cambridge University Press, 1947.

Wisdom, John, *Interpretation and Analysis, in Relation to Bentham's Theory of Definition*, London: Kegan Paul, 1931.

Wittgenstein, Ludwig, *Tractatus Logico-Philosophicus*, trans. C. K. Ogden, London: Routledge & Kegan Paul, 1922.

——*Philosophical Investigations*, trans. G. E. M. Anscombe, 2nd edn, Oxford: Blackwell, 1958.

——*The Blue and Brown Books*, Oxford: Blackwell, 1958.

——*Cambridge Letters: Correspondence with Russell, Keynes, Moore, Ramsey and Sraffa*, ed. Brian McGuinness and G. H. von Wright, Oxford: Blackwell, 1995.

Wood, Ellen Meiksins, *Citizens to Lords: A Social History of Western Political Thought from Antiquity to the Middle Ages*, London: Verso, 2008.

——'Happy Campers' (review of G. A. Cohen, *Why Not Socialism?*), *London Review of Books*, 28 January 2010.

Woolf, Leonard, *Beginning Again: An Autobiography of the Years 1911–1918*, London: Hogarth, 1964.

Yablo, Stephen, *Aboutness*, Princeton, NJ: Princeton University Press, 2014.

Zimring, Fred, 'Academic Freedom and the Cold War: The Dismissal of Barrows Dunham from Temple University, a Case Study', EdD dissertation, Columbia University Teachers College, 1981.

Index